Modernization as Ideology

The New Cold War History

John Lewis Gaddis, editor

MICHAEL E. LATHAM

Modernization

American **as Ideology**

Social

Science

and

"Nation

Building"

in the

Kennedy

Era

The

University

of North

Carolina

Press

Chapel Hill

and London

© 2000 The University of North Carolina Press
All rights reserved

Designed by April Leidig-Higgins
Set in Minion by Keystone Typesetting, Inc.
Manufactured in the United States of America

The paper in this book meets the guidelines for
permanence and durability of the Committee on
Production Guidelines for Book Longevity of the
Council on Library Resources.

Library of Congress Cataloging-in-Publication Data
Latham, Michael E.   Modernization as ideology:
American social science and "nation building" in the
Kennedy era / Michael E. Latham.
    p.   cm.—(New Cold War history)
Includes bibliographical references and index.
ISBN 0-8078-2533-6 (cloth: alk. paper)
ISBN 0-8078-4844-1 (pbk.: alk. paper)
1. United States—Foreign relations—1961–1963.
2. Social sciences— Political aspects—United
States—History—20th century.   3. Nationalism
—United States—History—20th century.
4. Economic development—Developing countries
—History—20th century.   5. Social change—
Developing countries— History—20th century.
6. Alliance for Progress.   7. Peace Corps (U.S.)
8. Economic development projects—Vietnam—
History—20th century.   I. Title.   II. Series.
E841.L34 2000   327.73—dc21   99-35517 CIP

04 03 02 01 00   5 4 3 2 1

For Peter Richard Latham
and Nancy Wagner Latham

CONTENTS

Ideologies make it easier than it might otherwise be to cope with reality. They provide simple models of complex phenomena. They suggest directions in which history is moving. They generate rhetorical justifications for action. And because ideologies perform these tasks, they tempt the leaders of states into relying upon them as guides to action.

Historians of the Cold War have been reassessing the role of ideology in the former Soviet Union, its Eastern European satellites, and the People's Republic of China. New archival sources suggest that within these states ideology played all of these roles: that Marxism-Leninism frequently determined foreign policy priorities.

But what about the United States? Was there a comparable American ideology during the Cold War? Michael Latham's careful study of three Kennedy administration initiatives—the Alliance for Progress, the Peace Corps, and the Strategic Hamlet Program in Vietnam—shows that theories of modernization indeed became an ideology during the early 1960s. Based upon a remarkable injection of social science into the realm of policy, these ideas claimed to provide an objective basis for diagnosing and acting to alleviate conditions that might make for Communist revolutions in the Third World. They became, for a time, extraordinarily influential.

Latham also demonstrates, though, that what purported to be a new and dispassionate analytical instrument in fact reflected an old and passionately held set of cultural assumptions, extending all the way back to the days of Manifest Destiny. The resulting confusion of science with a sense of national mission made it difficult for American officials to distinguish successes from failures, for if ideology facilitates action, it can also cloak the effects of one's actions. It obscures reality's irritating tendency not to fit models constructed for it.

Most historians now acknowledge that the Soviet Union's collapse resulted in large part from the gap between its ideological aspirations and the realities it confronted. Latham's contribution is to show that the United

States also suffered from ideological illusions in the years leading up to its greatest foreign policy failure: the Vietnam War. The consequences were not as devastating as they were for the USSR and its allies; but they were bad enough. This important new study provides the clearest explanation yet of how Americans fell victim to them.

Modernization as Ideology reveals, as few other books have, the power of ideas in international history. It is a most welcome addition to the New Cold War History series.

JOHN LEWIS GADDIS

ACKNOWLEDGMENTS

Research and writing demand solitary labor, but I could never have completed this book alone. Throughout the project, many individuals and institutions provided essential support. Grants from the John F. Kennedy Library, the Lyndon B. Johnson Foundation, and the Ames Fund of Fordham University's Graduate School of Arts and Sciences provided the financial assistance I needed to travel to archival collections. Michael Parrish at the Johnson Library and Maura Porter at the Kennedy Library stand out among the many archivists who helped refine my research strategies and pointed me toward sources of which I was not previously aware. Leonard Binder, Carl Kaysen, Lucian Pye, and Walt Rostow set their present work aside and consented to interviews with a historian asking critical questions about the past. A fellowship from the University of California's Institute on Global Conflict and Cooperation (IGCC) allowed me to write up my findings during a year away from other academic commitments, and a Mellon Foundation stipend funded two intellectual history seminars in which I began to think more seriously about ideology. Part of the third chapter of this book first appeared as an article in *Diplomatic History* 22 (Spring 1998), and I appreciate the journal's permission to include the material here.

I would also like to express my sincere thanks to several colleagues. I am particularly indebted to Michael Salman, my adviser while I was a doctoral student at UCLA, for pushing me to develop more challenging and productive lines of inquiry. Always ready to hear my ideas, he helped identify conceptual problems, encouraged creative solutions, and supported this project from the start. Joyce Appleby, James Drake, Frank Ninkovich, Theodore Porter, Dorothy Ross, Anders Stephanson, and Mariko Tamanoi also provided valuable comments and insightful criticism of my thinking about modernization. I am grateful to them all. John Lewis Gaddis, the series editor, carefully evaluated the manuscript, made several perceptive suggestions to improve its clarity, and helped me produce a stronger book. Lewis Bateman, executive editor at the University of North Carolina Press, skillfully managed the production process and guided me through the revisions with patience and humor. Grace Buonocore, the copy editor, and Pamela Upton, the project editor, brought their expertise to the final stages. I also thank my colleagues at Fordham University's Department of History for their congenial advice on the challenges of balancing teaching and research. Richard Harrison, a great friend and former teacher of mine, did not live to see this book's completion. But his inspiration and steadfast commitment to my efforts made an immeasurable difference.

Finally, my greatest thanks go to my family. My wife, Jennifer Briggs Latham, constantly supported my work, celebrated the turning points with me, and reminded me that there are other things in life. Nancy and Peter Latham, my parents, were also my first teachers. This book is dedicated to them.

Modernization as Ideology

CHAPTER 1

Modernization as Ideology

Approaching the Problem

In June 1961, as colleges and universities across the United States conferred degrees and charged their graduates to go out and improve the world they lived in, Walt Whitman Rostow delivered his own unique commencement address. The ceremony, held at Fort Bragg, North Carolina, must have looked very different from the ones the economist had participated in back at the Massachusetts Institute of Technology. Staring out at the crowd assembled before him, the newly appointed White House deputy national security adviser did not see students, faculty, administrators, and trustees dressed in academic regalia. In their place were eighty military officers wearing the uniforms of twenty different national armed forces, all of them graduates of the U.S. Army Special Warfare Center course in counterguerrilla strategy.

As different as the setting may have been, however, Rostow probably found himself at home. His social scientific model, he believed, had even more relevance for this audience than the ones he had taught at MIT. Dispensing with the usual greetings and congratulations, Rostow cut right to the point. The world, he warned, had become a most dangerous place. In Cuba, the Congo, Laos, and Vietnam, the Kennedy administration faced crises. Each of them "represented a successful Communist breaching—over previous years—of the Cold War truce lines which had emerged from the Second World War and its aftermath. In different ways each had arisen from the efforts of the international Communist movement to exploit the inherent instabilities of the underdeveloped areas." The United States and its allies now had to meet that challenge in ways that went well beyond the limited foreign aid programs and military assistance of the past. They had to find the means to win a battle "fought not merely with weapons but fought in the minds of the men who live in the villages and the hills; fought by the spirit and policy of those who run the local government." They had to intervene directly and engage themselves actively in "the whole creative process of modernization."[1]

For Rostow, his intellectual cohort, and the policymakers they advised, the concept of modernization was much more than an academic model. It was also a means of understanding the process of global change and identifying ways the United States could accelerate, channel, and direct it. The unprecedented power America had enjoyed at the end of World War II, they feared, had eroded. The collapse of European empire and the formation of "new states" posed dire challenges for a nation determined to contain the spread of Soviet communism. Within five years after the Second World War, India, Pakistan, Ceylon, Burma, the Philippines, Indonesia, Jordan, Syria, Lebanon, and Israel all gained independence. Following the Geneva Accords of 1954, Cambodia, Laos, and Vietnam left France's empire. Within a few more years, Malaya, Libya, Sudan, Morocco, and Tunisia gained official freedom from imperial control, and Ghana, Togoland, the Cameroons, and Guinea soon followed. By 1960, there were approximately forty newly independent states with a population of about 800 million.[2] As these "emerging" countries combined with older nations of Latin America, Africa, and Asia to call for international assistance in meeting their economic and social needs, the Cold War became a global confrontation. Unstable regimes and impoverished, discontented populations, many American policymakers argued, could only provide fertile ground for Marxist revolutionaries. As Truman administration strategist Paul Nitze and his associates put it in the striking document known as NSC-68, "the defeat of Germany and Japan and the decline of the British and French Empires" had led to a dangerous contest between the United States and a relentless Soviet adversary determined "to impose its absolute authority over the rest of the world." Amid the instability produced by decolonization, the potential for revolutionary advance only seemed to grow.[3]

Though most American strategists did not believe that the Soviets would risk a direct military confrontation during the 1950s, they were certain that the Kremlin was determined to chip away at the "underdeveloped periphery," destroy America's international credibility, and steadily undermine the system of political and economic alliances the United States had attempted to construct. In the aftermath of the Soviet Union's successful detonation of an atomic bomb, the stunning Communist revolution in China, and the shock and sacrifice of the Korean War, American officials became increasingly concerned with the course of global social change. In the Philippines and South Vietnam, the United States intervened in attempts to defeat armed challenges to its allies. In Guatemala and Iran, the Eisenhower administration used covert operations to support coups against left-leaning governments and tried to do so in Indonesia. Troubled by Middle Eastern instability and worried about Russian links to Egypt and Syria, Eisenhower also deployed the U.S. Marines to defend a pro-American elite in Lebanon. Around the world, the United States channeled large quantities of military aid to foreign leaders promising an unyielding anti-Communist stance.

Committed to halting what they perceived as Soviet-promoted aggression, determined to display resolution and determination, and worried that revolutionaries might capture the force of nationalist aspirations, Kennedy planners inherited the containment framework and searched for more effective ways to implement it. The Cuban revolution, Ngo Dinh Diem's increasingly fragile regime in South Vietnam, and an escalating civil war in the newly independent Congo only intensified their concerns. When Soviet premier Nikita Khrushchev used a January 1961 speech to pledge support for the "sacred" struggles of colonial peoples and promised to defend "wars of national liberation," the new administration's worst fears seemed confirmed. From the Senate floor, Kennedy himself had previously warned of the vulnerability of the developing countries. Now, as he moved into the Oval Office, he urged his advisers to study Khrushchev's address and mark his words. "You've got to understand it," he told them; "this is our clue to the Soviet Union."[4]

In that context of heightened anxiety, theories of "modernization" proved particularly appealing to policymakers hoping to contain revolutionary expansion.[5] Products of the early Cold War, they were built on a set of fundamental assumptions about the nature of global change and America's relationship to it. By the time the Kennedy administration came to power, a broad range of scholars working across disciplines at many different academic centers had started to translate their ideas into policy recommendations. Armed with the tools of social science and confident in their rational, analytical powers, representative thinkers such as Rostow, Lucian Pye, Daniel Lerner, Gabriel Almond, and James Coleman called for a comparative evaluation of the differences between what they termed "traditional" and "modern" societies and made use of a dramatic increase in federal government funding to define the requirements for movement from one condition to another.[6] In their emerging synthesis, "modernization" involved a series of integrally related changes in economic organization, political structures, and systems of social values. The research problem at hand was nothing less than creating a set of universal, empirical benchmarks to describe the overall patterns of global transformation. As Princeton University's C. E. Black broadly defined it, "modernization" was the "process by which historically evolved institutions are adapted to the rapidly changing functions that reflect the unprecedented increase in man's knowledge, permitting control over his environment."[7]

By the early 1960s, studies of the modernization process had come to dominate scholarship on the problem of international social change. As intellectuals debated, refined, and applied their ideas to a complex array of regions and societies, their definitions and models often varied. Beneath the dense academic jargon, however, the concepts at the core of modernization theory centered on several overlapping assumptions: (1) "traditional" and "modern" societies are separated by a sharp dichotomy; (2) economic, political, and social changes are integrated and interdependent; (3) development tends to proceed toward the modern state along a common, linear path; and (4) the progress of developing societies can be dramatically accelerated through contact with developed ones.[8] Theorists placed Western, industrial, capitalist democracies, and the United States in particular, at the apex of their historical scale and then set about marking off the distance of less modern societies from that point. Convinced that the lessons of America's past demonstrated the route to genuine modernity, they stressed the ways the United States could drive "stagnant" societies through the transitional process.

By the late 1960s, arguments over the validity of the modernization model had started to generate their own massive literature. Scholars attacked the idea of an identifiable, sharp break between "traditional" and "modern" conditions by noting that older types of social organization were not always swept away by the modernization process. "New forms," a critic argued, "may only increase the range of alternatives. Both magic and medicine can exist side by side, used alternatively by the same people."[9] Dissenters also challenged the idea of an integrated process of change. Case studies demonstrated that social structures often remained unaffected by changes of national government and that, rather than stable democracies, increases in political participation produced volatile situations that frequently ended in military regimes, oligarchies, ethnic conflict, or civil war. When the Vietnam War brought a renewed focus to the problem of imperialism, critics questioned the idea that contact with Western institutions and culture could accelerate movement through the "transitional stages." Rejecting the ethnocentric assumption that those living in "traditional" societies could only absorb techniques and not innovate on their own, dissenters argued that, far from producing a beneficial "demonstration effect," contact with the industrialized world often left a legacy of destruction and violence.[10]

Before long, systematic challenges emerged from both ends of the political spectrum. On the left, dependency theorists drew on Marxist thought to argue that the past of today's industrial countries did not at all resemble the present of nations such as those in Latin America. Western Europe and the United States, they claimed, might once have been "undeveloped," but not as the result of impoverishing relationships with other parts of the world. Directly challenging claims to a universal path of progress, world systems theorists stressed the long, historical course by which transnational economic relations had enriched industrial metropoles and kept peripheral satellites locked in subservience to an exploitative, global capitalism. From the opposite side of the spectrum, conservative thinkers of the mid-1970s mounted a "counterrevolution" by rejecting evidence of a widening per capita income gap between poor and rich nations and insisting that foreign aid, like domestic forms of welfare assistance, only hindered local entrepreneurial incentive. Most recently, modernization has even been resurrected in post–Cold War analyses celebrating the collapse of state socialism and the transformative power of capitalist markets.[11]

As an explanatory schema, modernization theory has clearly had a volatile career. Beyond the long-running debate over the concept's intellectual validity, however, stands another set of important and largely ignored questions about its historical context, political function, and cultural meaning. By returning to the era in which modernization dominated the field of inquiry and examining its relationship to the conduct of American foreign relations, I have sought to show that it was not merely a social scientific formulation. Modernization, I argue, was also an ideology, a conceptual framework that articulated a common collection of assumptions about the nature of American society and its ability to transform a world perceived as both materially and culturally deficient. Such an interpretation raises serious questions about the intellectual worth of the modernization model. It also illuminates the profound role of social science in the exercise of American power and the definition of a national sense of self at the height of the Cold War.[12]

Focusing on the Kennedy period, I have investigated the way modernization functioned as an ideology by addressing three fundamental, overlapping questions. First, I have considered how a community of social scientists established the political relevance of the knowledge it produced. Second, I have analyzed the relationship between social scientific theory and foreign policy through a study of three specific cases: the Alliance for Progress, the Peace Corps, and the Strategic Hamlet Program during the Vietnam War. Finally, I have investigated the way Cold War claims that the projection of American resources would modernize economically and culturally impoverished areas reformulated much older constructions of American national identity. As practiced in the early 1960s, modernization resonated strongly with earlier ideologies of Manifest Destiny and imperialism.

In exploring the first of these issues, the rise of modernization theory in American social science, I have found that many scholars closely identified their research with an effort to serve the state. Much like the Gilded Age social scientists analyzed by Dorothy Ross, modernization theorists of the 1950s and 1960s were deeply concerned with finding the means to ensure the health of their society. They, too, sought to chart "the fate of the American Republic in time."[13] But, in contrast to that earlier cohort, their overwhelming sense of national power and cultural superiority did not lead them to identify the problems they faced as coming from such internal factors as labor unrest, economic depression, or social radicalism. For a United States that had risen to become the world's greatest economic and military force, the most severe threats now appeared to arise from a hostile, subversive, and alien ideology. As historians such as Elaine Tyler May have shown, Mc-Carthyist arguments of the early and mid-1950s reflected the degree to which a perceived foreign danger had blurred the boundaries between America's domestic culture and its external role.[14] The central challenge of the post–World War II era, according to many modernization theorists, was to find ways to rejuvenate and project abroad America's liberal social values, capitalist economic organizations, and democratic political structures. Victory, they claimed, would depend on defeating the forces of monolithic communism by accelerating the natural process through which "traditional" societies would move toward the enlightened "modernity" most clearly represented by America itself.

In this Cold War context, "truth," as one historian has observed, was far more than a desired intellectual product. It was also understood as "our weapon."[15] In the years following World War II, academic research was increasingly shaped by federal funding. Scholarly inquiry also became more policy-oriented as the wartime partnership between government and university scientists was extended and the state supported research projects specifically intended to produce knowledge useful for solving military and strategic problems. Though the bulk of this funding went into developing defense technology, by the early 1950s private organizations such as the Carnegie Corporation and the Ford Foundation were also supporting research in international relations. Following the launch of *Sputnik*, the National Defense Education Act of 1958 also poured vast federal resources into area studies programs, language training, and international relations institutes.[16] National security, American officials argued, demanded that academia deliver politically relevant knowledge about the world and the ways in which the United States could directly promote and manage social change within it.

During the late 1950s and early 1960s, many modernization theorists endeavored to produce the kind of scholarship the U.S. government would find most useful. Meeting the Soviet challenge, they claimed, would require just the type of rigorous social research that they could undertake. Systematic inquiry, they promised, could identify the advantages that enabled America to emerge as the world's most modern nation, explain the deficiencies that caused other societies to lag behind, and detail the conditions in which Marxist-led social revolutions might arise. Even more important, they argued, it could identify the essential levers of social change. The United States did not have to wait for "less advanced" peoples to emulate the nation's achievements. Objective analysis and scientific research would show policymakers how to provide the material resources and moral tutelage needed to assist those struggling in the American wake. Building infrastructure, furnishing technology, providing training, and even demonstrating the virtues of efficiency, long-term planning, pluralist politics, and personal discipline would promote "progress" in a world imperiled by Communist insurgencies. Modernization, they explained, would enhance America's ability to win the Cold War—a war waged to capture the "hearts and minds" of peoples desperate to share in the economic growth, political democracy, and achievement-oriented social ethos that an enlightened and benevolent West had attained long before.

The modernization model fit especially well with the Kennedy administration's concerns, and many theorists rushed to join the "best and the brightest."[17] Rostow, for example, left MIT's Center for International Studies to become a White House national security adviser and later chairman of the State Department's Policy Planning Council. Harvard University economist Lincoln Gordon joined Kennedy's Latin American Task Force and became the U.S. ambassador to Brazil. MIT political scientist Lucian Pye taught courses in counterinsurgency theory for the State Department and advised the new U.S. Agency for International Development. Stanford Research

Institute economist Eugene Staley accepted Kennedy's request to head a development mission in Vietnam. Drawing on networks of personal ties, making use of federal funds, and actively seeking positions in the policy-making arena, many social scientists claimed their expertise was essential to contain communism in a world made vulnerable by the perils of poverty and the decline of Western empire.

As important as those personal networks and connections were, however, an exploration of the second problem that I have raised, the relationship between social science and political action, reveals that modernization functioned in ways that did not always reflect the intentions of specific theorists and policymakers. As an ideology, modernization crystallized a deeper, much older set of cultural assumptions already shared by intellectuals, officials, and broad segments of the American public. The rhetoric the social scientists used, the conceptual framework they presented, and the claims they made were also manifestations of a larger, liberal internationalist understanding of the very nature of American society and the sweeping, global transformations that a projection of American power could bring about. Modernization theory, I must emphasize, was not the sole or wholly determinative cause behind any of the policies this book analyzes. Each of them, as subsequent chapters explain, was the product of a wide range of concerns, events, and historical forces. As an ideology, however, modernization did reflect a worldview through which America's strategic needs and political options were articulated, evaluated, and understood.

By using the concept of ideology to analyze modernization theory and its relationship to Kennedy-era development policy, I have also sought to show how intellectual and cultural analyses can broaden the historiography of American foreign relations. Critical scholarship on the three programs I have analyzed generally rejects the arguments made by former government officials and Kennedy loyalists. Some historians have stressed the fallacies of an irrationally rigid anticommunism and lamented the way an obsession with Soviet power led policymakers to miscalculate America's essential strategic objectives. Other scholars have raised provocative questions about the way material and economic forces shaped Kennedy administration foreign policy. A determination to expand the capitalist world order, they claim, drove the United States to challenge any threats to its economic dominance. A larger, more deliberate analysis of ideology and identity, I believe, can open new areas for inquiry by introducing a less reductive analysis of the "interests" that critics have typically discerned behind official discourse. Rather than dismissing ideological formulations as propaganda employed to legitimate and rationalize genuine intentions, I propose to investigate the ways in which conceptions of national security and economic needs were integrally connected to understandings of America's historical position and modernizing potential.

Often uncritical of their sources, many early accounts of Kennedy administration policymaking accepted the official representation of U.S. development initiatives as altruistic, visionary attempts to create societies in which everyone, except those bent on violence or repression, would clearly benefit. Many scholars, often former policymakers or advisers themselves, have also written about Kennedy-era foreign relations from within the modernization paradigm. In the case of the Peace Corps, their interpretations generally praise the organization's leaders and volunteers as agents spreading freedom around the globe. Emphasizing the wisdom, determination, and courage of Kennedy and the Peace Corps's founders, such works generally describe an organization sending out Americans to revolutionize the world by their shared sacrifices. A few of Kennedy's admirers cite bureaucratic obstacles and administrative failures that made the agency an "unmet hope," but all generally agree that the Peace Corps was a remarkably enlightened, free-thinking response to the Cold War. As Robert Carey's early narrative suggested, "the Corps has a litany to be sure, but it is the litany of the explorer and the frontiersman." Though Kennedy sold the Peace Corps idea in anti-Communist terms, such accounts maintain, the agency was most successful because it resonated with America's creative, humanitarian ideals.[18]

While at times pessimistic in assessing long-term results, favorable interpretations of the Alliance for Progress between the United States and Latin America also reiterated government explanations of the program's goals. Here as well, the Kennedy administration was praised for a bold step forward. Although most of these accounts acknowledged that massive transfusions of economic aid, technical advice, and comprehensive development planning did not always produce high regional growth rates, social advances, and democracy, they still described a progressive program with genuinely transformative potential. Convinced that the alliance could have engineered the "peaceful revolution" necessary to combat entrenched destitution and dictatorship, scholars such as Arthur M. Schlesinger Jr. typically wrote in tragic tones. In an analysis that stressed organizational weakness and cumbersome bureaucracies, a betrayal of Kennedy's attempt to promote genuine democracy by Lyndon Johnson's emphasis on private investment, and the failure of Latin American oligarchs to spread the alliance vision of a better life to indigenous peoples, Jerome Levinson and Juan de Onís argued that a promising, even revolutionary, project "lost its way" and came to a premature, unfortunate end.[19]

Laudatory histories of Kennedy administration counterinsurgency planning in Vietnam, especially those written by former officials, also read like postmortems of an effort that, if it had only been given a fair chance, would have succeeded. Though striking in the degree to which his memoirs serve as an apology for the Saigon regime's violent repression, former ambassador Frederick Nolting's argument that the United States tried to defend "the right of the South Vietnamese people to determine their own future without coercion, force, or terror" is a common theme. Roger Hilsman, the primary U.S. official advocating the resettlement of Vietnamese peasants into strategic hamlets, wrote a history defending the potential of that practice years later. Providing the government services and political socialization necessary to cut off the Vietcong from their bases of local support, he maintained, just might have succeeded in creating a new, nationalistic loyalty to Ngo Dinh Diem's South Vietnamese state. As he placed the blame for eventual failure on short-sighted American military leaders and corrupt Vietnamese officials, Hilsman lamented that the administration "had developed a strategic concept for fighting guerrilla warfare, an idea for a political program into which military measures were meshed," but could not "convince the Diem regime or even the top levels of the Pentagon to give it a fair trial." American intentions, these writers argued, were reformist and progressive. Given the right conditions, they claimed, counterinsurgency based on modernization would have worked.[20]

Subsequent scholarship has gone a long way toward providing a more sophisticated and critical interpretation of the Kennedy administration's goals and policies. Accounts citing the distorting effects of Cold War concerns have placed the Kennedy programs in the context of a "flexible response to communism." According to Julius Amin, the Peace Corps reflected some authentic idealism on the part of its creators but was primarily an attempt to improve relations with "Third World" leaders in areas vulnerable to subversion. Where formal military or economic aid might not have been politically possible, the agency was used as a gesture of American support.[21] Those identifying strategic concerns as the ruling interest of the Alliance for Progress have made similar arguments. Emphasizing the degree to which anti-Communist determination warped political decision making, William Walker, Joseph Tulchin, Stephen Rabe, and Howard Wiarda have argued that the alliance, for Kennedy as well as Johnson, had at least as much to do with Castro and counterinsurgency as it did with democracy and development. Confronted with a seriously limited capacity to produce major improvements in living standards or promote democratic gains, policymakers remained obsessed with the dangers of subversion. They also trained right-wing military forces entirely uncommitted to liberal government and popular welfare. As officials in Washington became alienated by political instability and recurrent radicalism, Latin Americans increasingly identified the United States with reaction instead of reform.[22] Careful archival research on the Vietnam War by George Herring, Robert Schulzinger, and George McT. Kahin has also identified the degree to which the Kennedy administration understood South Vietnam as central to a strategy in which the overriding goal of containment, if not enough to produce a total commitment to the war, precluded far wiser courses of negotiated settlement or withdrawal. Obsessed with the problem of credibility, Kennedy planners pushed the United States deeper into a quagmire.[23]

By linking America's expansionist goals with a continual search for markets and a drive for economic hegemony, historians stressing material interests have analyzed Kennedy-era development and counterinsurgency policies through a different interpretive frame. Though the Peace Corps did not suffer nearly the degree of criticism directed at the Alliance for Progress and U.S. counterinsurgency efforts, at least one account argued that the agency sought to "deflate revolutionary pressures" and lent "the appearance of virtue" to a government engaged in policies of deliberate economic exploitation.[24] For Paul J. Dosal and other historians working within dependency and world systems frameworks, the Alliance for Progress only accelerated a pattern by which U.S. investors and Latin American elites enriched themselves at the expense of impoverished peasantries. Lamenting a "new era of dollar diplomacy" in which public resources were used to control unrest and prop up a dictatorial status quo, Walter LaFeber and Simon G. Hanson have focused on the way class interests functioned across national borders. The real "alliance," in their view, emerged between foreign business and local bourgeoisie as the program solidified the repressive institutions it was called to restructure.[25] Criticism along these lines by Noam Chomsky and Patrick Hearden has also identified American involvement in Vietnam with an attempt to defeat social revolutions that, by threatening to nationalize industry and redistribute income, challenged the structures assuring international capitalist control at the expense of local welfare.[26]

Though writing from different analytical perspectives, scholars stressing strategic preoccupation as well as those focusing on economic relationships have succeeded in finding interests hidden behind the rhetoric of idealism and benevolence—interests grounded either in terms of Cold War security goals or, alternatively, global capitalist demands. While many of their arguments have great merit, they have also suffered from a common tendency to marginalize the significance of ideas and culture in shaping the objectives of national policy. As Michael H. Hunt has argued, historians ranging from George F. Kennan and Hans Morgenthau in the 1950s through John Lewis Gaddis in the early 1980s focused on the "state as a central actor" in the "pursuit and exercise of power." In analyses "marked by references to such self-evident concepts as 'national interests,' 'vital interests,' " and " 'international realities,' " critics of American Cold War strategy have evaluated the success or failure of policymakers in protecting the nation from supposedly clear, external threats.[27] As Anders Stephanson has pointed out, by invoking "national security" as an "apparently neutral explanatory device," they have also tended to write in ways that eliminated questions of ideology from the history of policymaking.[28] Scholarship focused on the international "capitalist system" has also given short shrift to the relationship between ideas and the formation of national goals and programs. Gabriel Kolko's disregard for "declarations of belief" as "all too often scarcely more than public-relations exercises" and his insistence that America's policy toward the "Third World" must be evaluated in terms of "the overwhelming pursuit of its national interests, economic above all," reveal a common tendency to describe the search for markets and the logic of international trade as self-evident, unproblematic, and unquestioned motivating forces.[29]

Through their tightly constructed narratives of executive decisions and political strategy, many historians of American foreign relations from across the interpretive spectrum have continued to treat ideas and rhetoric separately from interests—as if national needs and priorities stood entirely apart from the concepts, values, and language through which they were apprehended, articulated, and presented to a wider public. Neglecting the role played by cultural understandings of America's identity and history, they have foreshortened their analyses of what Frank Ninkovich has called "the specific issue of how interests are defined."[30] In the case of Kennedy administration development policy, that problem is particularly important. If modernization was at times a strategic tool or an instrument for preserving an international capitalist order, it was also a broader worldview, a constellation of mutually reinforcing ideas that often framed policy goals through a definition of the nation's ideals, history, and mission. Much of modernization's political power did derive from expectations that it would help the United States combat Soviet geopolitical ambitions and preserve opportunities for America's economic expansion. But modernization also became influential at the height of the Cold War because it resonated with assumptions deeply embedded in American culture.

I have written about modernization here as an ideology that functioned in diverse contexts. In one sense, it certainly did serve as a political instrument. It was, in some cases, an analytical model deliberately used in private, institutional settings to evaluate options and generate effective policies. At other times, it was a rhetorical tool employed to justify particular actions. On a different and much more powerful level, however, modernization was also a cognitive framework that, often unconsciously, was closely linked to what historian Eric Foner has described as the "system of beliefs, values, fears, prejudices, reflexes, and commitments—in sum, the social consciousness—of a social group."[31] Much like the early-twentieth-century "liberal-developmentalism" that Emily Rosenberg has analyzed, the ideology of modernization functioned as far more than a narrow "political weapon."[32] Understood in Karl Mannheim's terms, it was also a perceptual framework through which much broader, widespread understandings of America's national identity, mission, and world role were apprehended.[33]

Modernization, in this more far reaching sense, was thus an element of American culture, an ideology shared by many different officials, theorists, and media sources about the nation, its historical "development," and its ability and duty to transform the "less developed" around it. In using modernization to link culture and identity with foreign policy programs, my thinking, like that of many other historians, has been influenced by the work of anthropologist Clifford Geertz. By treating ideologies as "cultural systems" and "a public possession, a social fact, rather than a set of disconnected, unrealized private emotions," Geertz emphasized their function to "render otherwise incomprehensible social situations meaningful, to so construe them as to make it possible to act purposefully within them."[34] Ideologies, in these terms, make sense out of apparent chaos and rapid change, order complex information and events into meaningful, intelligible relationships, and prove valuable in planning future courses of action amid uncertainty. As helpful as that formulation has been, however, I have also attempted to avoid the problems of embarking on a "thick description" in which, as Aletta Biersack insightfully put it, "meaning is described, never derived." "Geertz," she explained, "asserts that 'man is an animal suspended in webs of significance that he himself has spun.' The webs, not the spinning; the culture, not the history; the text, not the textualizing—these attract Geertz's attention."[35] Historians attempting to emulate Geertz, another critic observed, tend to describe reality "as a drama in which the focus is upon symbolic exchanges, not social consequences. Words like 'class,' 'exploitation,' and—most important—'power' recede, drop out of the analysis."[36] Defining modernization simply as culture, in Geertz's terms alone, risks ignoring vitally important historical questions about how, why, in what conditions, and to what effect the ideological "web" has been spun over time.

Thinking along these critical lines has led me to explore additional questions about national identity and the potential resonance between modernization and much older ideologies of Manifest Destiny and imperialism. If not an entirely original model, how might modernization have recast previous visions of Western superiority and articulated them as American power continued to expand in changing historical circumstances? In the historiography of American foreign relations, my consideration of this problem has been influenced by the work of William Appleman Williams and Walter LaFeber. Although both scholars were labeled economic determinists by their critics, each of them worked to reconstruct the ideological worldview of those in power and argued that the guiding perceptions were firmly grounded in a deeply historical construction of the nation's identity. The "Open Door" of Williams's *Tragedy of American Diplomacy* and the imperial vision of LaFeber's *The New Empire* were both rooted in the belief, derived from a broadly accepted cultural understanding of the Turnerian frontier, that America's domestic vitality would depend on continued expansion through either commercial or colonial means.[37] As Williams argued in explaining the dominant weltanschauung, those in power reached back as far as the westward movement of the early nineteenth century to argue that America was the "world's best hope" and "deduced from that axiom the conclusion that American expansion naturally and automatically 'extended the area of freedom.'"[38] According to Williams and LaFeber, early-twentieth-century proposals to reshape the world in America's image effectively refashioned a sense of Manifest Destiny and contributed to the growth of the United States as an imperial power.

Examining similar issues in the Cold War era, I argue that the social scientific theories and policies of modernization, despite the claims of their proponents, were neither decisive intellectual breakthroughs nor completely new political initiatives. In terms that echoed Enlightenment explanations of Western superiority and imperial justifications of the need for an altruistic, benevolent West to provide both material assistance and moral tutelage to direct the course of the less "advanced," American modernizers drew on elements of an earlier worldview to articulate one suited to their times. Although not a mere appropriation, the ideology of modernization, in both its intellectual and institutional forms, incorporated and revised much older perceptual frameworks. In changed historical conditions and amid different cultural understandings of race, religion, and national duty, modernizers had to compose an ideology and language of their own. But in asserting the historical validity of a single path to modernity and laying claim to a superior understanding of it, they played the notes of a very familiar song.

In my approach to this problem of ideological and historical resonance, I have also found the questions raised by thinkers such as Michel Foucault and Edward Said particularly suggestive. The development of a position of power, Foucault argued, requires the "correlative constitution of a field of knowledge." Like the nineteenth-century social reformers he describes, the proponents of modernization theory and policy constructed a taxonomic categorization in which "all offences must be defined; they must be classified into species from which none can escape." As they identified the "deficiencies" of the "developing" world, theorists and officials echoed much older representations of Western power and used political, administrative, and economic controls to define a particular trajectory, a "social time of a serial, orientated, cumulative type: the discovery of an evolution in terms of 'progress.'" Like their Enlightenment predecessors, the modernizers of the Cold War also marshaled what Foucault referred to as an "'evolutive historicity' . . . bound up with a mode of functioning of power." "No doubt," Foucault argued in explaining the Enlightenment impact, "the 'history-remembering' of the chronicles, genealogies, exploits, reigns and deeds had long been linked to a modality of power. With the new techniques of subjection, the 'dynamics' of continuous evolutions tends to replace the 'dynastics' of solemn events."[39] Armed with a model they claimed was based on empirical and historical evidence of an organic, natural order, twentieth-century American social scientists and policymakers recast much older representations to define "modernization" as a unitary variable of global change and claim authority over its management. American power, exercised through the practices of modernization, also found new channels into the foreign world—it became more highly institutionalized and pervasive.[40]

By placing their own society at the endpoint of a social scientific, linear scale, American modernizers also defined their nation in terms of its relationship to the cultures they perceived as struggling to emulate U.S. achievements. As Edward Said has argued regarding the "Orientalist" patterns of Western scholarship about the Middle East, the construction of identity stands at the very center of the intersection between knowledge and its political application. "Indeed," Said emphasized, "my real argument is that Orientalism is—and does not simply represent—a considerable dimension of modern political-intellectual culture, and as such has less to do with the Orient than it does with 'our' world." Like the Orientalists Said has analyzed, modernization theorists, policymakers, and the nation's media also went about framing an identity for the United States based on a "positional superiority." They emphatically characterized their society as uniquely advanced "in comparison with all the non-European peoples and cultures."[41] While holding that all societies passed through the same, universal stages of development, theorists and policymakers also drew sharp distinctions between the West they belonged to and the world they classified. Rooting the difference neither in geography and natural resources nor in the legacies of imperial exploitation, they instead focused on the West's "rational," "activist," "achievement-oriented" social values and explained the apparent stagnation and unfulfilled potential of the "less developed" world in ways that reinforced a sense of their own nation's intrinsic cultural vitality and dynamism.

In the Cold War context, the scientism of modernization theory also allowed for a necessary and politically desirable reformulation of the older ideologies on which it was based. As they described America's world role in terms of an objectively determined, scientifically verified process of universal development, theorists and officials used the ideology of modernization to project an appealing image of expanding power during a period of decolonization. Modernization, Rostow explained to another Kennedy adviser, would replace colonialism. It would create "a new post-colonial relationship between the northern and southern halves of the Free World. . . . As the colonial ties are liquidated, new and most constructive relationships can be built . . . a new partnership among free men—rich and poor alike."[42] Articulated in this way, modernization was a means for the continued assertion of the privileges and rights of a dominant power during an era in which the nations of Africa, Asia, Latin America, and the Middle East increasingly demanded independence. By describing modernization as a benevolent, universally valid, scientifically and historically documented process, social scientists, policymakers, and the nation's media also elided America's own imperial past.[43] Rather than the nation that expanded across the continent, waged imperial war in 1898, fought for possession of the Philippines, and remained ambivalent on the subject of European empire after World War II, the United States was presented as a force capable of guiding a destitute world along the transformative path it once traveled. The American Revolution and New Deal, in this sense, became historical blueprints for the kind of anticolonial, democratic progress and reform that struggling states might emulate. Modernizers invoked older conceptions of America's destined role as world leader and redefined them through a supposedly objective developmental schema. They did so, moreover, at a moment when the forces of nationalism and Marxist social revolution called American assertions sharply into question.

Having explained what I aim to demonstrate through an ideological analysis, I would also like to clarify some additional issues regarding the scope of this book and its argument. The reader should recognize, first, that I am not seeking to produce a comprehensive or exhaustive account of either the history of development theory or each of the three Kennedy programs in which I argue it became institutionalized. As mentioned previously, other scholars have undertaken those specific and separate tasks in far greater detail than space will permit me to here. My goal, in this work, is to open new areas for inquiry by illustrating the power of relationships cutting across social science, national identity, and Cold War foreign relations. I also disavow any claim that concepts of modernization were solely responsible for the Kennedy-era initiatives. As later chapters show, modernization certainly did play a major role. But it did so in the midst of an interaction of personalities, historical forces, human experiences, and even haphazard, contingent occurrences. Modernization theory alone was incapable of "causing" anything. As an ideology in specific institutional settings, however, it was one of the significant factors that gave meaning to complex events and shaped thinking in consequential ways. I would like to point out as well that this ideological analysis, critical as it is, does not necessarily depend on an accusation of conspiracy, deception, or "bad faith" on the part of Kennedy policymakers and the intellectuals who advised them. They were convinced that modernization would benefit both the "developing" world and the industrialized West, and few of them perceived much conflict between the American objectives they defined and what they understood as a kind of internationalist idealism and altruism. By the end of the 1960s, however, their largely unquestioned assumptions and supreme self-confidence would be much harder to maintain.

One should also bear in mind that those on the "receiving end" of modernization responded in diverse ways to Western efforts to transform them in cultural and political terms. The chapters on the Alliance for Progress and the Strategic Hamlet Program, in particular, reveal that responses to modernization came from different political perspectives and varied widely. Although liberal Latin Americans were among the strongest advocates of the Alliance for Progress and supported its efforts, Castro's Cuba rejected its goals and ideology directly. In South Vietnam, Ngo Dinh Diem sought to use American aid to bolster his repressive regime while the National Liberation Front mobilized in revolutionary opposition to the U.S. nation-building campaign. The analyses produced by scholars such as Albert Memmi, Eduardo Galeano, Walter Rodney, and, more recently, Gyan Prakash and Arjun Appadurai also reveal that the ideology of modernization has certainly not escaped critical examination by those it proposed to reform and enlighten. Far from breaking down "traditional" cultures and producing a convergence of uniformly "modern" ones, contemporary forces of mass communication and human migration have fostered the formation of diverse, unpredictable, and overlapping religious, ethnic, and group identities in transnational settings.[44] Modernization, in practice, rarely produced the kind of effects its advocates anticipated on paper.

Finally, it is important to acknowledge that, even in the late 1950s and early 1960s, not all Americans shared the vision of their nation presented by modernization in scholarly work and public policy. Although I do maintain that most of the limited criticism of Kennedy "development" policies did not challenge the dominant assumptions, it is certainly true that radicals such as C. Wright Mills, Paul Goodman, and William Appleman Williams produced early and thoroughgoing attacks on the idea of a modern and modernizing America. Many returning Peace Corps volunteers, especially African American ones, also came to reject Washington's description of their ability to produce dramatic, sweeping, and transformative progress abroad.[45] In time, broad-based social movements challenged the way "modernization" was articulated in the domestic context of the "Great Society" and criticized the definition of a "culture of poverty" to be redeemed by federal programs. Later in the decade, a more radical civil rights movement and the rise of the New Left gave such comprehensive dissent a more forceful, public voice. During the early 1960s, however, those arguments remained comparatively rare in an America that had not yet begun to ask the fundamental questions that the Vietnam War would eventually push to the center of national debate.

During the Kennedy era, the promotion of liberal democracy and the acceleration of economic development were mutually reinforcing parts of an ideology that contributed to the definition of strategic goals and projected a national identity suited to the Cold War context. In the midst of a collapsing European colonial order, the Kennedy administration conceived of modernization as part of a comprehensive response to a dangerous Communist threat. As they identified the United States as an altruistic, benevolent nation positioned at the apex of a modernity defined by democratic politics, high living standards, and individual freedom, theorists and officials also reconstructed much older, imperial visions of America's global power. Modernization theory alone did not cause the Peace Corps, the Alliance for Progress, or the Strategic Hamlet Program. It did, however, function as a conceptual framework through which the assumptions of social scientists and policymakers about America's character and international role became embedded in both foreign policy and public, cultural representation. Rather than substituting an ideological determinism for that of "national security" or "capitalist demands," my goal for this analysis is to complement the best of previous historical interpretations. Instead of replacing "power" and "interests" with "culture," I explore the ways in which they are integrally related. American empire, as William Appleman Williams argued, certainly was about political containment and market dominance. But it was also a "way of life."[46]

CHAPTER 2

American Social Science, Modernization Theory, and the Cold War

McGeorge Bundy, who moved from serving as dean of Harvard University's faculty of arts and sciences to the position of national security adviser under Presidents Kennedy and Johnson, believed that American academics should do more than produce new scholarship for review by their intellectual peers. They were also expected to serve the state in the midst of a Cold War that demanded nothing less than a full mobilization of the nation's reservoir of intelligence. As Bundy argued in 1964: "In the life of our universities there is much room for men writing the kind of history which is possible only when there is a deep engagement of sympathy to the battlefield of politics and to the way the men on that battlefield conceive of their war." Both the academy and the country as a whole would benefit when scholars worked from the "same center of concern as that of the man who is himself committed to an active part in government . . . the taking and use of power itself."[1] In the decades following the close of World War II, many American social scientists agreed with that formulation. They perceived little tension between their intellectual endeavors and the creation of knowledge intended to solve strategic problems. Accepting the Cold War construction of international economics and politics, they believed that, with the state's support, they could determine the fundamental forces of universal change and identify the levers needed to manipulate them. The search to infuse their disciplines with a more rigorous, scientific status could proceed hand in hand with an attempt to contain the Communist threat that challenged America in both geopolitical and moral terms. As Walt Rostow put it in the concluding sentence of his most famous book, the stakes involved nothing less than the ultimate survival of the nation and its fundamental, defining values. "There may not be much civilization left to save," he warned, "unless we of the democratic north face and deal with the challenge implicit in the stages-of-growth, as they now stand in the world, at the full stretch of our moral commitment, our energy, and our resources."[2]

For many American social scientists the Cold War became what political scientist Ira Katznelson has called a "mobilizer of purpose," a force that shaped their sense of themselves as "producers of knowledge and as part of the guardian class for liberal democracy."[3] Identifying with the "vital center" defined by such Cold War intellectuals as Arthur M. Schlesinger Jr., Rostow and his scholarly cohort argued that extremism of the left or the right would lead the "peripheral" world down a false path. Instability, they believed, provided openings for social revolution to take hold. The history of their own nation, understood along the lines of a deep consensus grounded in the sweeping acceptance of liberal values, capitalist forms, and pluralist institutions, became the benchmark for a scheme of linear stages into which all societies could be ordered, regardless of ethnic, cultural, or geographic variation.

Decolonization in the "underdeveloped" world, modernization theorists believed, presented a new and potentially dangerous force to be channeled and controlled. It also demanded rigorous social analysis. A comparative method, backed by carefully directed, often quantitative data, theorists maintained, would make the problem of understanding global development less a matter of abstract speculation than a task involving the evaluation of solid, objective facts. Armed with their analytical tools, many American social scientists endeavored to meet the challenges that Bundy and Rostow identified. Although not all of those working within the modernization framework endeavored to produce policy-relevant conclusions, a wide range of scholars drew a strong correlation between the production of knowledge and the demands of a struggle fought on multiple and shifting fronts. Cold War intellectuals, historian Ellen Herman explains, forged links "between professional responsibility and patriotic service to the state; between scientific advance, national security, and domestic tranquillity."[4]

This chapter investigates the rise of modernization in American social science by focusing on the theory's political context and intellectual roots. First, it explores the way American officials became interested in the "development" process during the Cold War. Concerned with the rapid erosion of European empire and the rise of revolutionary movements, policymakers increasingly sought to use American power to direct the course of change in the "emerging" world. The second and third parts of this chapter examine modernization as a response to that problem. In the fields of sociology, political science, and development economics, modernization was conceived of as a grand theory, a common framework capable of uniting diverse forms of social analysis. Though the model was certainly influential in other disciplines, such as anthropology, a brief intellectual history set in each of these three areas provides especially clear examples of how theorists across different disciplines converged on a common model of social change. Scholars from different fields also invoked modernization to integrate their research, claim a new level of scientific rigor, and serve the state by participating in the Cold War struggle. When social scientists began to address modernization as a central strategic problem, they found a very receptive audience in Washington. Finally, this chapter investigates important questions about the way in which modernization drew on and refashioned Enlightenment models and imperial ideals. Much like their intellectual predecessors, American theorists analyzed a foreign world in ways that stressed their own nation's historical virtue, continuing superiority, and right of benevolent intervention. As subsequent chapters demonstrate, ideas about modernization moved well beyond the realm of academic and intellectual debate. Part of a larger ideology about the nature of American society and what its power could achieve, they played significant roles in broader Cold War constructions of national interest, foreign relations, and cultural identity.

The Cold War Context

Shaped by state support and oriented toward the problems of policymakers, the rise of modernization theory proceeded in tandem with growing official interest in the nature of development and its strategic significance. During the 1940s and 1950s, the United States increasingly sought ways to use its economic resources and planning expertise to engineer social change in both Europe and the "emerging areas." Though some efforts were certainly more successful than others, the American experience during those decades added to the later conviction of Kennedy policymakers that modernization would prove an effective response to an aggressive and opportunistic adversary in a decolonizing world. By 1961, the contours of the Cold War and the determination of a new presidential administration would give modernizers a high level of institutional influence as officials sought more innovative, effective ways of meeting the Soviet challenge. The programs that resulted, of course, were not the result of a simple, hermetic translation of intellectual theory into foreign policy. In each case, the ideology of modernization became influential in a specific historical context, and policies often had multiple sources. But by outlining the way Americans might fight and even win a dangerous struggle in which image and identity became inseparable from definitions of security and strategy, modernization became an important component of American Cold War planning.

The Kennedy administration's development initiatives followed a long series of attempts to marshal America's economic power for diplomatic purposes. Since the 1944 Bretton Woods meeting in the mountains of New Hampshire, the United States had worked with its allies to ensure that a strong, liberal, international economic order would be put in place for the postwar era. The International Monetary Fund and the International Bank for Reconstruction and Development (later known as the World Bank), planners hoped, would provide a multilateral framework to address balance-of-payments problems, stabilize currency, secure loans for Europe's recovery, and provide aid to the "emerging" countries. Far more concerned with promoting an overall increase in production and trade than redistributing existing wealth, the new order reflected the dominance of the United States, a nation that held a clear majority of the world's gold reserves and insisted on a system linked to its own dollar. The "overwhelming economic strength of the United States," historian Diane Kunz has explained, "allowed it to determine the shape of the international organizations then on the drawing board. American goals became international reality; multilateralism often became unilateralism in disguise."[5]

Although the Soviet Union soon made it clear that the American aspiration to create a market-based postwar structure would not go unchallenged, U.S. planners found new ways to use their economic might. As Stalin expanded Soviet political and military control across Eastern Europe, he also rejected participation in the Bretton Woods system and began to seek economic autarky through a new five-year plan. Rather than join an American-led order, the Soviets aimed to rebuild their own industry, military, and self-sufficiency. U.S. hopes to bring the Soviet Union into an open, free-trading system failed, but American strategists moved quickly to reconstruct Western Europe along liberal lines by launching the Marshall Plan in 1947. Concerned about Communist political gains in countries such as Italy, France, and Austria, Truman administration policymakers hoped that a return to prosperity would undercut leftist appeals and reduce the danger that European populations, impoverished in war's aftermath, might turn toward Marxist solutions.

The Marshall Plan, like later attempts at modernization, was also based on a close relationship between economic expertise and assumptions that America's own historical experience might be replicated abroad. As Michael J. Hogan has argued, the Marshall Plan was bolstered by the claims of American economic experts who "tried to transform political problems into technical ones that were solvable, they said, when old European ways of doing business and old habits of class conflict gave way to American methods of scientific management and corporative collaboration."[6] Expert economic planning, Marshall Plan enthusiasts argued, would do more than deliver aid to meet immediate crises. It would also bring to Europe the kind of institutions that Americans had created in the New Deal's Tennessee Valley Authority and Rural Electrification Administration. It would restore prosperity, rebuild industry, and drive European economies forward to the point that they would become self-sufficient once more. No longer dependent on American aid, they would again serve as valuable U.S. trading partners.[7] The program, moreover, was a stunning accomplishment. By mid-1951, the United States channeled more than $12 billion into European industry and agriculture. With infrastructure, government institutions, and skilled labor in place, U.S. aid had a major impact as Western Europe's aggregate gross national product increased by 32 percent.[8] Truman and his advisers reveled in the results. Communism remained a serious threat, but America's effort, Truman proclaimed, "brought new hope to all mankind. We have beaten back despair and defeatism. We have saved a number of countries from losing their liberty."[9]

In his inaugural address of January 1949, Truman also advocated an initiative to meet urgent crises in the countries of Asia, Africa, the Middle East, and Latin America. The United States, he promised, would launch "a bold new program for making the benefits of our scientific advances and industrial progress available for the improvement and growth of the underdeveloped areas."[10] Scientific training and technical assistance, Truman and others hoped, would promote higher living standards and help limit Communist expansion. In May 1950, Congress passed the Act for International Development, and in October of that year, the State Department created the Technical Cooperation Administration to implement the new policies.[11] Though hardly a program on the scale of the Marshall Plan, "Point Four," as it came to be called, marked the start of a prolonged American attempt to direct change in the "emerging" areas, an attempt that would reach its highest point in the 1960s. "Development itself," Melvyn Leffler explains, "was becoming increasingly intertwined with U.S. national security thinking."[12]

New challenges during the 1950s amplified American interest in the development process. By the time Mao's Communist forces claimed victory in China, American planners were certain that they were engaged in a struggle of truly global dimensions and stunningly high, almost limitless stakes. As the strategic blueprint known as NSC-68 stated in 1950, "The assault on free institutions is world-wide now, and in the context of the present polarization of power a defeat of free institutions anywhere is a defeat everywhere."[13] Following the Korean War, the United States continued to shift away from what, at times, had been an almost wholly European focus and gave increased attention to the problem of directly influencing developments in Asian, Latin American, Middle Eastern, and African states. As colonial empires crumbled and new countries "emerged," American officials concluded that strategically important territory and valuable natural resources were at risk in a dangerous contest between two opposing world systems. U.S. policymakers also struggled to balance European ties with policies designed to respond to the new threat. "The collapse of colonialism," John Lewis Gaddis recently explained, "was creating new opportunities for Soviet and now Chinese expansionism; but propping up colonialism risked accelerating that tendency. Western authority seemed to be fragmenting even as the 'Sino-Soviet bloc' was consolidating."[14]

The fear of losing "credibility" before both international allies and domestic audiences, moreover, drove the Eisenhower administration to challenge movements, including nationalist ones, in which they discerned the possibility for an expansion of Communist strength. After France met defeat in Vietnam at the battle of Dienbienphu, the United States willfully violated the Geneva peace agreements by bolstering the new South Vietnamese regime with military aid and covert operations. In 1953, the Eisenhower administration helped overthrow a government in Iran to block the nationalization of oil reserves and, a year later, orchestrated a coup in Guatemala to prevent Jacobo Arbenz, a left-leaning nationalist, from maintaining power. In 1956, Eisenhower opposed an invasion of Egypt by Britain, France, and Israel when Gamal Abdel Nasser nationalized the British-run Suez Canal. But, two years later, the United States landed troops in Lebanon to shore up that country's conservative regime, confront a pro-Nasser government in Iraq, and proclaim America's determination to oppose "communism."

In the struggle between "freedom" and "totalitarianism," American authorities also saw little acceptable middle ground. In 1955, at Bandung, Indonesia, India's Jawaharlal Nehru and Indonesia's Achmed Sukarno convened a meeting of countries seeking to form a "nonaligned movement." When the group rejected the U.S. system of military alliances and pledged itself to the maintenance of independent, national sovereignty, American policymakers were less than sympathetic. Secretary of State John Foster Dulles worried that countries such as Indonesia would play the United States and the Soviet Union off against each other, a risky game that kept the door open for revolutionary gains. After Sukarno obtained a $100 million credit from Khrushchev, increased his own executive power by converting Indonesia's existing parliamentary system into a what he called a "guided democracy," and laid claim to Dutch territory on New Guinea, American frustrations at Soviet competition continued to grow.[15]

Perceiving decolonization, nationalism, and the erosion of Western empire as dangerous forces besieging America on all fronts, strategists sought to do more than react to changes on the "periphery." They also searched for ways to manage the forces that produced them. Interested in using foreign aid to shape the course of economic growth, the Eisenhower administration established the International Cooperation Administration (ICA) in 1955 as an organization that would oversee the provision of development loans and the export of American crop surpluses. Foreign investment, Eisenhower believed, was the engine of economic progress, and firm capitalist ties were an essential bulwark against Marxist inroads. Productivity, he argued, "relieves pressures in the world that are favorable to Communism."[16] In time, Eisenhower also acknowledged that incentives for private investment would have to be matched by more direct government commitments. In 1957, his administration introduced legislation for the Mutual Security Program to establish a large Development Loan Fund providing $2 billion for soft loans. Even in the midst of the Cold War, however, pushing for a more dedicated approach to development was a difficult political task. Because they lacked a natural domestic constituency, Eisenhower's foreign aid initiatives were unpopular with Congress, and his efforts were sharply curtailed. Unwilling to provide a multiyear authorization in the first place, Congress cut the first year's appropriation from $500 million to $350 million.[17]

But American concern regarding Communist actions in the "underdeveloped world" continued to escalate. By the late 1950s, Soviet leaders claimed that their nation's rapid, impressive rate of growth made it an ideal model for the world's "new states." As China began its first five-year plan in 1957 and Khrushchev sought to compete with a rival for leadership in the "developing" world, the Soviets stepped up their appeals. Soviet officials toured Egypt, Indonesia, and India promising lavish amounts of economic aid. In Latin America, they increased trade ties and launched their own program of technical assistance. When Fidel Castro took power in early 1959, called for revolutions in other Western Hemisphere countries, and negotiated a trade treaty with the USSR, American anxiety only deepened. If the United States intended to compete with the Soviets on the "periphery," many American strategists argued, it would have to take a more assertive, innovative stance. With programs involving foreign aid, scientific advising, trained personnel, and a combination of agricultural and industrial planning, America would have to demonstrate to the "emerging countries" that development along liberal, capitalist lines could alleviate poverty and raise living standards at least as fast as revolutionary and Marxist alternatives.[18]

As John F. Kennedy campaigned for the presidency, he constantly emphasized that theme. While a member of the Senate Committee on Foreign Relations, he was a persistent critic of the Eisenhower administration's reliance on nuclear deterrence and mutual assured destruction. Though he advocated an increase in the national defense budget and lamented a strategic "missile gap" later found to be nonexistent, Kennedy also insisted that Eisenhower's nuclear emphasis had cost the United States crucial ground in the struggle over "world development." In a 1957 speech, Kennedy decried the French use of U.S. arms in Algeria and charged that persistent European colonialism, unchecked by the United States, was driving embittered nationalists into the Communist camp. Though there was little concrete difference between his views on foreign policy and those of Richard Nixon, his Republican opponent in the 1960 election, Kennedy constantly argued that America had lost ground to the Soviets in education, technology, and prestige among the "new nations." Only a week before the election, Kennedy declared that the Republican administration and the State Department were ill prepared to meet the challenges they faced. Ambassadors were poorly trained, diplomats lacked language skills, and policymakers had little sensitivity to the goals of a decolonizing, nationalist-minded world. Taking the Eisenhower administration to task for failing to stop the tide that swept over Cuba, Kennedy also warned that the situation could only get worse. While Americans wasted time, "out of Moscow and Peiping and Czechoslovakia and Eastern Germany are hundreds of men and women, scientists, physicists, teachers, engineers, doctors, nurses . . . prepared to spend their lives abroad in the service of world communism."[19]

Part of a generation that came of political age during World War II and the early years of the Cold War, Kennedy and his advisers were also, as historian Thomas G. Paterson reflected, "captives of an influential past." Kennedy had entered Congress just a few months prior to the Truman

Doctrine, and his experiences, along with those of his staff, were profoundly shaped by the central tenets of the Cold War. Witnesses to the Marshall Plan's success, the formation of NATO, the "loss" of China, and the Korean War, they accepted the domino theory and believed that the security of the United States demanded a willingness to confront an aggressively expansionist Soviet Union around the world. Like their predecessors, they were also strongly averse to revolution. While differing in degree from the Eisenhower administration in their sensitivity to the forces of nationalism, they continued to perceive the prospect of revolution as a dangerous threat that opened doors for Communist gains.[20]

When, therefore, Nikita Khrushchev declared that Asia, Africa, and Latin America were "the most important centers of revolutionary struggle against imperialism" and promised to support "wars of national liberation," Kennedy and his associates responded with alarm. Though the Soviet leader's January 1961 message was probably directed more toward competition with China, Kennedy's inaugural pledge to "pay any price" and "bear any burden . . . to assure the survival and success of liberty" reflected his administration's determination to meet what it perceived as a formidable challenge. "To those new states whom we welcome to the ranks of the free," Kennedy declared, "we pledge our word that one form of colonial control shall not have passed away merely to be replaced by a far more iron tyranny. . . . To those peoples in the huts and villages of half the globe struggling to break the bonds of mass misery, we pledge our best efforts to help them help themselves, for whatever period is required."[21] Just as Truman had done in the Marshall Plan, Kennedy set forth a sweeping American commitment to produce economic progress. This time, however, the expanded arena of contest centered directly on the problems of decolonization, development, and the dynamics of global social change.

The United States, moreover, seemed to face a multitude of "Third World" crises by the start of the 1960s. In Southeast Asia, Laos raised the most pressing initial concern, and the departing Eisenhower warned his younger successor that Communist forces were on the verge of dominating that country. Supplies airlifted by the Soviets and training provided by the North Vietnamese had strengthened the Pathet Lao guerrillas to the point that a negotiated political settlement would prove difficult and dangerous. Premier Ngo Dinh Diem's fragile and repressive South Vietnamese regime also appeared unable to curb the expanding strength of the National Liberation Front and its revolutionary insurgency. How would the new administration handle its troubled inheritance there? Civil war in the Congo and Belgian support for the secession of the mineral-rich province of Katanga forced the administration to choose between backing a European ally and the possibility that the Soviets might exploit nationalist outrage in Africa. Kwame Nkrumah's determination to chart an independent course for Ghana and seek contacts with both the United States and the USSR also aroused anxiety. Cuba's revolutionary state stood out as an alternative model for Latin American development, and with each passing day, Fidel Castro moved closer to the Soviet line. In the Middle East, Nasser's attempt to support a revolutionary regime in Yemen aroused fears that Egypt would radicalize much of the Arab world and threaten more conservative governments such as those in Jordan and Saudi Arabia. The administration also worried what impact economic and military aid to neutralist India would have on U.S. relations with Pakistan and wrestled with fears that a border conflict between China and India might escalate. Everywhere the president and his advisers turned, the tightly related questions of development, anticommunism, and revolution seemed to come to the fore. For Kennedy administration strategists, modernization became the answer to an urgent policy problem.[22]

A Grand Theory

By the time Kennedy moved into the White House, theories of modernization were starting to shape American foreign policy in significant ways. But they also possessed deep intellectual roots and powerful cultural appeal. As a grand theory, modernization promised to unite different branches of social analysis and order the evidence derived from a complex, foreign world. For professional scholars concerned with the rapid pace of international change, it also seemed to provide a universal framework that would place their research on a more rigorous, empirical plane. In the midst of an escalating Cold War, American social scientists believed that modernization theory would define their nation's historic accomplishments, identify the deficiencies of an "emerging world," and allow them to respond to the needs of the state in a time of crisis.

The scientific claims of post–World War II modernization theory first appeared in the field of sociology, and they were, from the start, an American creation. European scholarship had dominated previous theoretical work in the field, but the first half of the twentieth century had taken a heavy toll. Older universities committed to classical scholarship and humanities refused to recognize the value of the upstart discipline, many of its leading students died in the First World War, and the optimistic hopes of European sociologists that "reasonable solutions could be found for the problems of secular industrial society" seemed destroyed by the rise of fascism and the devastation that followed in a second, cataclysmic global conflict. Across the Atlantic, on the other hand, a thriving economy and a growing number of well-funded, less intellectually rigid institutions made conditions ripe for a scholarly revival. As sociologist Jeffrey Alexander has pointed out, "In the post–World War II period, theory underwent a sea change. It moved decisively toward America."[23]

Created in the midst of that shift, modernization emerged in the United States as part of a determined, deliberate drive toward a comprehensive theory of society. Surveying the field in 1948, the University of Chicago's Edward Shils observed that his intellectual predecessors had left a mixed legacy. Robert E. Park, William I. Thomas, C. H. Cooley, and Edward Ross, he argued, "stood midway between the sociology of the library and learned meditation on the one hand and the increasingly circumspect research techniques of the present day on the other." Their influence was certainly profound, but the hypotheses and problems they explored often remained implicit. Because such scholars failed to pursue the theoretical questions behind their work, their "Chicago School" students had embarked on a vast range of empirical studies of discrete communities and urban environments without working toward a larger, cohesive system to guide their analyses. Surveys of class stratification, ethnic identity, the family, religion, public opinion, and small groups produced valuable data and might help solve specific local problems, but their proliferation had left the field in a condition of "vast disorder." Because it lacked a theory integrating the discipline and giving it a central focus, Shils lamented that American sociology had not yet "ascended to the heights of science—it [was] still in the foothills."[24]

Shils expected, however, that American sociology would soon pass out of its "recent atheoretical prehistory into a more sophisticated stage,"[25] and developments at Harvard seemed to confirm his hopes. Talcott Parsons, the field's rising star, had taken an important step in his 1937 work *The Structure of Social Action*. Concerned with the individual's role in the social environment, Parsons had produced a work of challenging abstraction. Tempering what he considered the naive assumptions of nineteenth-century liberalism, he sought to balance his respect for the power of independent human agency against a recognition of the powerfully constraining elements inherent in any social structure. The actions individuals took, Parsons emphasized, were mediated by the set of regulating values transmitted through the institutions that ensured social order and equilibrium. In isolated or more "primitive" societies, family and community sanctions played the most decisive roles. In those in which capitalist markets had expanded and industry appeared, the regulations of a formal legal system and the nation-state had the greatest impact. Classical economic theory, Parsons believed, gave excessive weight to the individual drive for utility maximization. The Marxist alternative, however, was not much better, for long-term social cohesion often belied claims of dialectical conflict. The "base" of the economic relations of production did not simply determine the "superstructure" of human consciousness. As he articulated his own sense of society, Parsons instead emphasized the power of cultural values in shaping the patterns of an integrated, stable social order.[26] It was just the kind of broad social theory for which Shils was searching.

Although Parsons's arguments received relatively little attention when first published, his optimistic conclusions about the potential for liberal values to ensure cohesive, healthy democracy contributed to his rapid professional success. In a nation enjoying a postwar position of unequaled economic and political strength, his approach seemed to make perfect sense. Appointed chair of Harvard's new Department of Social Relations in 1946, Parsons took the reins of an ambitious project designed to combine the insights of sociology, social and cultural anthropology, and social and clinical psychology. With a new institutional platform and new professional legitimacy, he also turned his attention from the problem of understanding human action to mapping the essential structures necessary for social integration. Like Edward Shils, Parsons believed that the key to a rigorous new science would not be found in radical empiricism, and he soon invited his colleague from Chicago to participate in a new attempt to give sociology what they both believed it needed—analytic power.[27]

The results of their collaboration, largely driven by Parsons's penchant for theorizing, proved decisive both for the future of sociology in general and for what soon came to be known as modernization theory. Basing their scheme on a "functioning system," Parsons and Shils argued that the range of roles found in each individual's personality could be correlated with the different structures of society. When the structures of the social system met the varied needs of individuals and complemented the ideals of the culture, the system would be at perfect, consensual equilibrium. The allocation of resources and roles would be matched by the integrating potential of common values, just as they seemed to be in the United States at the time. If these forces were thrown out of balance, however, as they had been in interwar Germany, then disjunction and disorder would produce unrest, violence, repression, and increased social control. In Germany, Parsons argued, the harsh economic consequences of the peace of Versailles and subsequent turmoil brought about by rapid shifts in industry, technology, urbanization, and occupational mobility had destabilized integrative institutions and unleashed "drastic extremes of attitudes." The phenomenon of National Socialism could be linked to the weakness of the German Parliament, the lack of an independent legal system, and even a pattern of gender relations that desexed women and promoted an idealization of militant, closed groups of young men, "sometimes with at least an undercurrent of homosexuality." Cast adrift from the essential moorings of social stability, the "extremely deep-seated romantic tendencies of German society" were pressed into the service of a "violently aggressive political movement, incorporating a 'fundamentalist' revolt against the whole tendency of rationalization in the Western world, and at the same time against its deepest institutionalized foundations."[28] The United States and its democratic allies, fortunately, had escaped such turmoil. The dangers of a loss of social balance, however, were clear.

Though consistently more concerned with the "effects rather than the origins of culture patterns,"[29] Parsons and Shils soon attempted to link their sweeping, structural analysis with a more dynamic component. Influenced by his reading of Max Weber, Parsons was particularly concerned with finding a way to describe how the point of social equilibrium might shift over time. Parsons and Shils's proposed solution was a set of "pattern variables," an expanded list of binary oppositions to refine the dichotomy between "traditional" and "modern" conditions. With this tool, they suggested, complex social relationships could be placed along a progressive index. Culture, personality, and society could be evaluated on the basis of whether they emphasized universalism or particularism, achievement or ascription, orientation toward self or the collective, role specificity or diffuseness, and affective or nonaffective relationships.[30] The bounded system of variables, simply amplifying the original separation posited between "tradition" and "modernity," did not directly address the causes of change that might drive a society from one pole to another. Parsons did, however, suggest that forces such as population growth and technological advance might place new demands on a social order and, in turn, require a change in the structures necessary to maintain a stable equilibrium. Following Weber, he also argued that the nature of a society's values would have a profound impact on the direction that change would take.[31]

Based on a linkage between the specific structures of society and the performance of necessary functions, this theoretical model, soon known as "structural-functionalism," had three especially significant ramifications. First, it established the importance of viewing societies as integrated systems in which political, social, and economic sectors were interrelated. A change in one area would necessitate changes and adjustments in the others. As one sympathetic critic of Parsons explained, this argument resulted in a sense of "the interdependence of parts, forming a whole, bound together in such a way that change and movement cannot occur in a disorderly or accidental manner, but are the outcome of a complex interaction resulting in structures or processes."[32] Second, the model appeared to allow for a universal and comparative analysis. Because all human beings were assumed to have a similar set of basic needs that social structures must function to fulfill, systems could be compared on this basis, regardless of historical or environmental variation. Diverse, "empirical" studies, many advocates believed, could finally be correlated with one another in the hope of producing a larger synthetic and scientific view. No area of the world, no matter how culturally distinct or geographically remote, would remain outside the realm of comparative analysis. Finally, the "pattern variables," while essentially descriptive "snapshots" of a static social order, appeared to provide a means of indexing social change. Using the set of dichotomies to form a complex matrix, theorists from several different disciplines grasped structural-functionalism as a way to order societies on a historical, linear, and sequential scale of "development," a crucial component for studies of modernization as a comprehensive process. As he sought to transform his static scheme into a dynamic model, Parsons himself came to argue that terms such as "primitive" and "modern" were not merely descriptive. They were instead points on an evolutionary line marked by increases in "adaptive capacity." "Modern" societies could maintain social order despite changes of technology, population, or environment because they created more highly specialized institutions, made greater use of natural resources, developed a more inclusive polity, and formalized their essential value system in legal codes that could be deliberately and progressively modified.[33]

Because he used few concrete examples, selected arbitrary dichotomies, and privileged liberal, consensual harmony in ways that tended to understate continuing institutional repression, Parsons drew fire from a number of frustrated critics. A Parsonian analysis, C. Wright Mills commented, "delivers the sociologist from any concern with power."[34] Another dismayed reader observed, "When Parsons announces a 'breakthrough' or an 'advance' in sociological theory—something he does all too often—it means not that he has discovered something new about society or social relations or even social action. It only means that he has noticed a symmetry or parallelism among the concepts of his own conceptual scheme."[35] Though arguably the most powerful American social scientist of the Cold War era, Parsons did not enjoy universal acclaim.

For those seeking to understand the sweeping international changes after the Second World War, however, his elevated abstractions seemed to offer just the right set of flexible, analytical tools. Marion J. Levy's *The Family Revolution in Modern China* (1949) provides a particularly striking example of this "Parsonian revolution" in American social theory. Originally a doctoral dissertation supervised by Parsons himself, Levy's book proposed to study kinship relations in both "traditional" and "transitional" China. Arguing that the family performed the necessary functions of "(1) role differentiation, (2) the allocation of solidarity, (3) economic allocation, (4) political allocation, and (5) the allocation of integration and expression," Levy took the vague, cumbersome Parsonian categories and used them as the framework for his study of a specific, "modernizing" society. In an analysis based on sources written in both English and Chinese as well as contact with informants in China during World War II, Levy argued that the arrival of Western industry would irrevocably shift the emphasis in Chinese social relations toward universalist criteria and necessarily change the family structures that functioned to fulfill society's essential requirements. Because modern industry "is not concerned with who a person is" and focuses merely on "whether or not he can perform certain specific technical functions with a particular level of skill," its influx from the West would necessarily erode the traditional power of filial piety as an organizing principle for interpersonal relationships. Mass communications, the presence of a growing Western community, and the expansion of a foreign market economy would all contribute to the proliferation of new ideals stressing political freedom, individualism, functional specificity, and self-reliance. Some "traditional patterns" might persist in the short run. But if the growth of Western industry continued, it would ultimately undermine them and fundamentally alter the structures used to produce social equilibrium. Using the family as his index of change, Levy determined that China would, in effect, become modernized.[36]

In his foreword to Levy's book, Parsons hailed it as the "first major work by a new type of scholar in the comparative study of social institutions."[37] Although the Chinese revolution soon invalidated Levy's predictions of movement toward a new, capitalist social order, many other researchers followed his example, and what came to be called "modernization theory" dominated sociological analyses of historical change. Scholars praised modernization as a means for studying emerging "new states" in a rigorous, scientific way. They tried to identify the values necessary for modernization to proceed, speculated about Weber's emphasis on the importance of Protestantism in the Western past, and explored the interaction of modernizing forces with non-Western religious and ethical systems. As they branched out toward psychology, sociologists also turned their attention to defining the qualities of a "modern" personality and elaborated on the contrast between an active, "future-oriented" individual willing to manipulate his environment and the more passive, change-fearing personalities they found in "traditional" peoples.[38] Over the next two decades, modernization became the central organizing principle of inquiry throughout the field.

Perhaps no work reveals the universal and broadly transformative power that sociologists ascribed to the modernization process more clearly than Daniel Lerner's hugely popular account titled *The Passing of Traditional Society*. Claiming to use concrete analysis to penetrate the mysteries of foreign cultures, religions, and societies, the MIT professor analyzed aggregate economic and social data from a broad range of nations and interpreted the results of sixteen hundred interviews conducted by the United States Information Service in Turkey, Lebanon, Egypt, Syria, Jordan, and Iran. Lerner was unconcerned with any questions that collaboration with the federal government might raise concerning the objective quality of his evidence, and he boldly argued that "the same basic model reappears in virtually all modernizing societies on all continents of the world, regardless of variations in race, color, or creed." Driven by contact with the West, the modernization of the Middle East would penetrate all sectors of society and fundamentally change their structures. Commercial and, later, industrial relations would contribute to the rise of a "mobile personality" and encourage an individual to make "a personal choice to seek elsewhere his own version of a better life." As rural populations moved toward cities, urbanization would expand, literacy would increase, and people would come into contact with the power of mass media and global communications. These integrated, "historical phases," in turn, would cause migrants to become aware of themselves as part of a larger, interdependent polity and lead them to feel a sense of "empathy" for their compatriots. In contrast with the isolated traditional society of the agricultural village, this new culture would carry within it a growing participatory ethos on which the foundations for political democracy could be built. Modernization, Lerner also proclaimed, was irresistible. Even in the tradition-bound Middle East it represented "the infusion of 'a rationalist and positivistic spirit' against which, scholars seem agreed, 'Islam is absolutely defenseless.' "[39]

Presented with a striking level of confidence, Lerner's universal, sequential stages implied that all societies would inexorably move toward the common endpoint of the "modern" West. His indexes of urbanization, literacy, media, and political participation, he insisted, "provided suitable terms for describing the degree of modernization present in a given society at a given time." Lerner maintained that the progress of all countries toward the Western apex could be carefully measured. Equally important, he also held that the entire process could be accelerated through Western action. The key to motivating "the isolated and illiterate tribesmen who compose the bulk of the [Middle Eastern] population" rested on the pressing need to "provide them with clues as to what the better things in life might be."[40]

For sociology, therefore, the concept of modernization presented an analytical structure through which an entire process of social change, encompassing both the past of the West and the future of the "developing" world, might be understood. It provided a template into which concrete, empirical data seemed to fit, and it organized the tasks for continuing study by drawing diverse branches of the field toward a common, overarching research agenda. With its focus on an integrated process of change and its emphasis on a universal set of social structures and functions, modernization theory also promised to provide for a new type of temporal, comparative analysis. At its high point, modernization appeared to be a pivotal breakthrough, a "unified field theory" for the social sciences.

As a "grand theory," modernization made a similar impact on the study of global "development" in American political science. Although the field had previously been divided among experts on different countries, cultures, and regions, the rapid rate of international political change following the end of the war seemed to demand a broader framework. Amid the dissolution of empire and the rise of the "new states," the Social Science Research Council (SSRC) established the Comparative Politics Committee in December 1953. Because of its central role in articulating an agenda for the field, its influence over the distribution of resources, and its high level of professional prestige, this body provides a particularly good case for analysis. Since the SSRC's creation in 1923, its leadership had constantly emphasized the application of social scientific expertise to practical problems. The first national social science institution in the world, it was premised on the idea that scholarly objectivity and public advocacy could be made mutually reinforcing.[41] The new SSRC committee, many hoped, would also further the institution's mission to promote interdisciplinary inquiry and cooperation. Modernization, it turned out, fit the bill perfectly.

In a paper that first set forth the Comparative Politics Committee's agenda, George Kahin, Guy Pauker, and Lucian Pye noted that "profound social and cultural changes are taking place as traditional societies have been exposed to the ideas and ways of the West." Conditions for analyzing that trend also seemed promising. As the authors commented, "non-Western political systems have many features in common," and "the pace of change in these countries during the last decade has been such as to make these questions matters for empirical investigation." At this point, however, the group stopped short of formulating a general theoretical framework. Aware of what they described as common patterns, they also acknowledged the complex realities of the varied regions and societies they wished to study and reflected that "change has thus far been a far from uniform process." Political scientists, they warned, needed to be "sensitive to the differences among cultural heritages" and recognize the resilience of many different "traditional" political forms. Although they believed that all new political systems had to overcome similar obstacles, the authors concluded that the committee should approach the problem of change with caution and warned the field's researchers to avoid the temptation to "arrange social and political systems in an evolutionary sequence."[42]

As political scientists turned toward sociological models, however, those theoretical reservations rapidly dissolved. At a 1956 planning seminar, Gabriel Almond and Myron Weiner, both from Princeton, delivered a paper they hoped would "codify the views of the committee on research strategy." Almond, a political scientist without a particular area of geographic expertise, explained his view in a separate report to the SSRC. "The present state of the field did not justify a global comparative effort," he argued, because "no common body of scholarship deals with comparative politics." Instead of a unified discipline, the profession "was divided into specialists on Europe, Africa, the Middle East, South Asia, Southeast Asia, and East Asia." Selecting "15 research sites in the roughly 100 independent countries in the world today" and trying to draw conclusions from the results simply would not solve the problem.[43]

There was, however, a way out. According to Almond, researchers working on the same region could select common problems to study, report their research results on an "inter-area basis, and stimulate comparative theoretical efforts to synthesize the findings of these studies." Inspired by the recent emphasis in sociology, Almond also argued that fieldwork could "stress *function* and the interrelationships between political, cultural, and social processes." "Talcott Parsons' concept of 'pattern variables,'" he also noted, "appeared to be applicable in distinguishing the cultures and ideologies of different political systems."[44] Persuaded by those arguments, the group commissioned a number of theoretical studies, built on its earlier impression that contact with the West was often the stimulus for change, and sought to transcend its previous reservations about the particularities of cultural difference and the persistence of distinct "traditional" forms. As they formulated a new strategy for comparative analysis, the committee members also suggested that researchers should consider social change as a common, integrated process and moved closer to a view that, even across regions, the nature of "political development" could be placed in a common, historical framework.[45]

Those shifts in American thinking were also propagated by a series of international conferences. The Congress for Cultural Freedom, an organization with a membership dominated by intellectuals determined to challenge Communist appeals, proved particularly instrumental. Supported in part by the Central Intelligence Agency, the group sponsored several meetings focusing on problems of "Third World" political development. At Rhodes and in Ibadan, Nigeria, in 1958 and 1959, interdisciplinary seminars organized by Shils discussed issues of "representative government" and "political democracy" in the "new states" of Asia and Africa. Sessions centered on the theme "Tradition and Change—Problems of Progress" and gave Western scholars a chance to exchange ideas with academics from a wide range of countries. Meetings with African and Asian politicians, intellectuals, lawyers, and journalists aroused intense debate and diverse, opposing views on how political change should proceed. But, among American academics, the encounters did little to shake confidence in a larger, integrative scheme. In fact, they may have actually accelerated the quest for a global theory of managed social change. Placing their focus on nation building, state institutions, leadership, and the dangers of extremism, American political scientists continued to push forward in the integrative direction that Almond and his colleagues advocated.[46]

Within a few years, "political modernization" came to dominate the work of the SSRC committee and defined the basic problem of research for the field as a whole. Eager to embark on the quest for "a more dynamic approach to comparative politics," Lucian Pye moved beyond the cautious formulation he had previously contributed to explain that structural-functionalism was the answer. In his report on a June 1959 meeting of the SSRC group at Dobbs Ferry, New York, he heralded the theoretical breakthrough and argued that it marked "a new stage in the intellectual history of the committee." As he explained it: "We had begun by rejecting the comparative analysis of structures or institutions in favor of seeking ways of comparing total processes; this had led to the analysis of 'actors' in the process—political groups; but to achieve order and a basis for comparison it was necessary to posit certain universal functions of all political processes, some of which must be performed by one structure or another." Once they accepted the idea of common political functions across all societies, investigators came to understand corresponding political structures in a new light. By comparing structures on the basis of the common roles they played, the overall political development of different nations and societies could be made part of a larger, integrated, conceptual scheme. Once ordered in a linear, temporal sequence, the range from traditional to modern structures could be used to chart the relative progress of societies along the developmental path. Convinced that the method would prove "particularly useful in studying the transitional systems of newly emerging countries, and also in comparing the political systems of traditional societies and even of primitive societies with those of advanced industrial countries," the committee went on to plan an ambitious program of research.[47]

The result was a sudden flood of literature seeking to articulate the new theory and apply it to a variety of geographic regions. In addition to offering research grants and using Ford Foundation funding to continue ongoing seminars, the committee members arranged with Princeton University Press to publish the collected papers of their meetings in a multivolume series entitled "Studies in Political Development." With introductory and concluding chapters dedicated to theoretical overviews, the work shaped the course of research, defined the modernization model, and planted it firmly on the leading edge of the field's agenda. Gabriel Almond boldly declared in the opening essay of the inaugural volume that "this book is the first effort to compare the political systems of the 'developing' areas, and to compare them systematically according to a common set of categories." The "new conceptual unity," he continued, was not to be mistaken for "an *ad hoc* matter." It represented nothing less than an analytical revolution, the "intimation of a major step forward in the nature of political science as science."[48] As they mapped out the process of political modernization in universal, comparative terms, scholars sought to refine the theory and guide the field's research efforts within its framework.[49]

Political scientists also tried to carry the new model into their monographic studies of specific countries. Lucian Pye's *Politics, Personality, and Nation Building* (1962) provides an especially striking example of the degree to which modernization theory came to shape political analysis. Interested in the quest for political "modernity" in Burma, Pye conducted interviews with local respondents in the hope of learning how "those who would build democratic institutions in transitional societies arrived at their commitments" and how "their experiences affected their capacities to build such institutions." Yet, as he did so, Pye determined that even his initial observations about individual psychology would have to be pursued in conjunction with an analysis of larger global trends. As he put it, "There was much more to the story than mere alien domination followed by a search for sovereignty. For colonialism and nationalism are only partial aspects of a far more profound historical process—the process of change, of acculturation and transformation in which both whole societies and individual personalities are forced to take new forms." Just as Daniel Lerner had done, Pye also placed his study of specific cultural processes in the context of a universal pattern. His impressions of the durability of provincial and traditional attitudes made him significantly less optimistic about the facility of a transformation in traditional worldviews, but, like his MIT colleague, Pye also leaped toward a broad set of conclusions. Relating socialization, family structures, occupational roles, and political aspirations to economic growth, he argued that the Burmese case was not an anomaly: "There may be differences as to the degree and the form of reactions, depending upon the circumstances of acculturation and the nature of the traditional culture. These differences, however, can only occur within the limits imposed by the inherent and universal character of the human personality."[50] As it had in sociology, modernization theory promised to provide political science with a way of understanding societies in terms of integrated systems. It would allow for a dynamic perspective and outline a sweeping process common to all societies.

Development economics, the final field in which this chapter explores modernization as a "grand theory," presents a somewhat different case. Where sociologists and political scientists had found themselves searching for a larger, integrative model of change, most economists believed that they already had one. As Albert O. Hirschman has pointed out, the majority were certain their discipline rested on "a number of simple, yet 'powerful' theorems of universal validity: there is only one economics ('just as there is only one physics')."[51] Development economists, therefore, had to prove that problems in the "emerging" countries were sufficiently different and that their theoretical solution demanded a new set of approaches. The range of positions taken on this matter, moreover, paralleled a long-running debate over the degree to which poorer nations could actually achieve substantial gains by following the example of the "advanced," industrialized ones. Theorists such as W. Arthur Lewis, for example, remained deeply skeptical that economic growth and development could proceed along the same lines that they had in the West and raised serious questions about the impact of unrestricted international trade on impoverished societies.[52] More optimistic formulations, however, received a much larger share of public acclaim and, as later sections of this chapter illustrate, political support. Perhaps because of these intellectual schisms, the subfield's practitioners also tended to enjoy less academic prestige than those working in other areas of the discipline. In this field as well, however, the concept of modernization proved influential in transforming the categories of analysis and the way they were understood.

As World War II drew to a close, an increasing number of economists turned their attention to the tools that the Western industrialized powers could use to expand markets and increase production in Asia, Latin America, and Africa. Because they defined "development" largely in terms of raising the overall level of economic equilibrium between supply and demand, the primary matter appeared to be one of simply finding the proper fiscal instruments and putting them to work. For these problems, many economists found a slightly modified version of Keynesian theory entirely appropriate. Balancing investment across several industries, raising the overall level of savings, and striving to increase the amount of output per unit of capital invested were all seen as ways that Keynes's short-run employment theory might be translated into a viable approach to overall, long-run growth.[53] Influenced by their own personal experiences in dealing with the depression, coordinating wartime planning, and working toward European reconstruction, many American theorists initially conceived of "development" as a problem of simply increasing aggregate economic performance. "Keynes," one scholar recalled, "was the hero of the new revolution. He demonstrated that there could be equilibrium at levels lower than full employment—indeed at any level of output and employment." With gross national product as the "key variable" for theory to explain, the analytical issue was reduced to one of determining the proper ratios of investment and savings to produce the desired growth levels.[54]

Projected improvements failed to materialize by the early 1950s, however, leading many economists to the conclusion that, because the problems of

"emerging" economies were significantly different from those currently confronting the already industrialized West, the same remedies simply would
not work. Initially growing out of the arguments presented by Argentinean
Raúl Prebisch and the United Nations Economic Commission for Latin
America, based in Santiago, Chile, "structuralist" theories presented a direct
challenge to those advocating purely Keynesian solutions. Where Keynesians
might point to an unbalanced equilibrium as the reason for a problem such
as chronic inflation, structuralists insisted that the real obstacles to development lay in the particular barriers to production and consumption that
made the difficulties of poorer, agricultural countries distinct from those
encountered by the industrialized West. Structuralists, one economist has
explained, viewed these countries as inflexible: "Change is inhibited by obstacles, bottlenecks and constraints. People find it hard to move or adapt,
and resources tend to be stuck."[55] Lack of infrastructure and communications made it difficult to move goods rapidly, population growth frequently
outran capital investments, and peasants, living in "traditional" social systems, did not always behave as "rational" or "profit-maximizing" economic
actors. As a result, the price mechanism did not function smoothly, and the
market failed to provide a self-correcting mechanism.

As structuralism came to shape analyses of economic development in the
1950s, it generated a range of different perspectives. In some circles, it lent
support to ideas that, reformulated in later decades, eventually formed the
core of dependency theories. For scholars such as Prebisch, the lack of
infrastructure, communications, financial resources, and capital necessary
to compete in the realm of manufactures resulted from a specific cause. The
terms of trade for agricultural nations, he insisted, had consistently eroded
since the late nineteenth century. As export crop prices failed to keep pace
with increases in the price of finished goods, many Latin American nationalists came to argue that economic liberalism, unchecked investment, and
capital flight had prevented the savings necessary for consistent economic
and institutional growth. Latin America's lack of development, in this conceptual frame, was due to an interaction between powerful economic centers
and exploited peripheries. With the heart of the global capitalist economy
moving from Britain to the United States, Latin America's crisis could only
accelerate.[56]

Structuralist thinking, however, also contributed to a theoretical viewpoint in which apparent economic "stagnation" was explained not through a
critical analysis of trade relations but was instead attributed to closely related
deficiencies in social values and political leadership. Like sociologists and

political scientists, many development economists began to describe the transformations they studied in terms of an entire system made up of inter-dependent, functional sectors. The thinking of Paul N. Rosenstein-Rodan, a British citizen who taught at MIT, reflected this perspective. If attempts at development were to be successful, Rosenstein-Rodan argued, they would have to be comprehensive and decisive. The state would have to take a larger role in promoting the production of consumer goods to expand the func-tioning of the market, and it would need to make a concentrated effort to build transportation networks, establish public utilities, and encourage the application of new technology. Because structural and psychological obsta-cles were tenacious, they would have to be attacked all at once through a "big push" involving massive foreign investment, education, and comprehensive social engineering.[57] Swedish Nobel laureate Gunnar Myrdal, a most influen-tial figure in the field, also advocated this type of overall central planning. His language, moreover, reveals the degree to which many development econo-mists, like sociologists and political scientists, came to consider economic change as part of a larger, socially integrated problem: "A whole cumulative expansion process has to be blueprinted in real terms of the concrete invest-ment projects[:] their effects on the volume of production in various lines and on consumption, on employment of workers and natural resources, the induced changes in health education and productiveness of labour, et cetera, in various sectors and different years, with main attention focussed on the circular causal interactions between all the factors in the system."[58] As they joined other fields in considering social change as part of a larger, holistic process, many development economists agreed that the complex problem was not merely one of "growth." It was one of "modernization."

No one gave more sweeping or more popular expression to that way of thinking than MIT economics professor Walt Whitman Rostow. Originally written as a series of lectures at Cambridge University, *The Stages of Eco-nomic Growth: A Non-Communist Manifesto* both built on and transformed previous definitions of economic development. Rostow continued to discuss the problem of how macroeconomic theory might direct investment to increase per capita income, but he also proposed to answer more profound questions about "the broader problem of relating economic to social and political forces, in the workings of whole societies." Invoking the historical record to delineate a series of specific positions for nations on a line running from a "traditional society" to a final "age of high mass consumption," he promised nothing less than an explanation of how certain parts of the West had become advanced while other areas of the world had not.[59]

Part of the answer, Rostow argued, could be found within the transitional process itself. Citing Louis Hartz's *The Liberal Tradition in America*, he placed the United States in the company of a "small group of nations that were, in a sense, 'born free'" and "already far along in the transitional process" at the time of their founding. Americans, along with those from other countries "created mainly out of Britain," possessed a set of ideas about individualism, democracy, and economic opportunity that facilitated a "natural" and rapid climb toward "modern" social organization and living standards. Although less fortunate societies would have a more difficult time of it, there was still hope for them. If they could fulfill certain "preconditions," they, too, could overcome the "pre-Newtonian science" and "long-run fatalism" that left them mired in "traditional" folkways and superstitions. This would require significant changes in attitudes as well as an increase in savings and investment, but if these goals were achieved, the entire society could experience a rapid "take-off" during which "old blocks and resistances to steady growth are finally overcome." If a national state was put in place, infrastructure built, agricultural productivity increased, and banks and investment institutions established and if a new elite came to view economic growth as desirable, then the entire system could be transformed. Starting with "limited bursts and enclaves," the modernizing society would suddenly accelerate through the historical watershed of self-sustaining economic growth and finally approach the level that the advanced nations had achieved long before.[60]

The Stages of Economic Growth made an immensely complex process suddenly simple. All nations passed through the same fundamental set of stages regardless of their historical, cultural, or geographic particulars. Some would advance more rapidly than others, and the process would often be destabilizing. But the basic direction of change, and the means to accelerate it, were clear. According to the *New York Times*, Rostow's analysis was nothing less than "a shaft of lightning through the murky mass of events which is the stuff of history."[61] Though similar in its use of stages and its broad, universal claims, Rostow's "non-Communist manifesto" of consensual, linear progression was heralded as the definitive response to Marx's dialectic. Liberal culture and compound interest, not class conflict, were the real engines of history. Modernization, Rostow argued, was best generated through planned capitalism and foreign aid, not social revolution.

As a "grand theory," modernization did seem to illuminate a complex and shifting intellectual landscape. A model of comprehensive change, it integrated social, political, and economic factors. Because it correlated specific structures with necessary functions, it promised social scientists the ability to compare different societies across the boundaries of time and space. As a universal process, it also made the complex variations of particular cultures appear far less important than the common factors believed to unite them. The decolonizing world had been fundamentally transformed after 1945, but, equipped with their new set of theoretical tools, American social scientists believed that they had the power to define the global pattern of change, explain its sources, and shape the world's future.

Scientism and the State

As modernization grew in popularity as an intellectual model, its authors also rode a powerful wave generated by heightened expectations of what science could provide in service to American society. By the time modernization theorists made specific policy recommendations to Kennedy planners, they had found positions in a strong network between professional scholarship and government patronage. In a 1925 speech on behalf of the National Research Council (NRC), Herbert Hoover had lamented the fact that American scientists depended on a paltry ten million dollars a year, funding that came largely from private foundations. Under Woodrow Wilson, the NRC had become the official government adviser on scientific preparedness. During World War I, it had also brought scientific expertise into military agencies and corporate laboratories to produce major advances in radio signals technology, submarine detection, artillery range finding, and even chemical weaponry. Yet, less than a decade later, the nation's scientific budget had been dramatically cut. As he called for a larger national commitment, Hoover reminded his audience that "a host of men, great equipment, [and] long patient scientific experiment to build up the structure of knowledge" were the essential sources of "invention and industry."[62]

Hoover's personal appeal had little immediate impact. But, in a second global conflict, the U.S. government took steps that must have gone well beyond his wildest imaginings. The connections established between the war effort, academic talent, and vast amounts of federal funding irrevocably changed the relationship between science and the state. As Stuart Leslie has argued, both the scale of mobilization for World War II and the practice of funneling huge amounts of funding directly to universities put government-supported science on an entirely new plane. Massive war contracts poured $117 million into MIT alone. California Institute of Technology received $80 million, and Harvard and Columbia went to work with $30 million each.

Vannevar Bush, a former MIT vice president and head of the Carnegie Institution, lobbied hard for those increases. Convinced that the United States was not ready for the war's scientific challenges, Bush pressed Franklin Delano Roosevelt to establish the Office of Scientific Research and Development (OSRD). As head of the OSRD, Bush presided over the spending of $450 million on weapons research and development by 1945. The concrete return on that investment in American science, moreover, was quick and highly impressive. Radar, solid fuel rockets, and the atomic bomb were the "wonder weapons of the war."[63]

The Manhattan Project and MIT's Radiation Laboratory, in particular, set important precedents for federally funded physical science. Success in the desert of Los Alamos, New Mexico, and the halls of Cambridge, Massachusetts, stimulated government efforts to support a cooperative, institutional framework that would endure into peacetime. The lessons of the wartime accomplishments were clear, and a new pattern of knowledge production emerged involving "large, multidisciplinary teams of researchers, coordinated assaults on complex problems, increasingly sophisticated and complex instruments—in short, Big Science."[64] Funding, moreover, did not taper off as it had after the First World War. Stalin's coercive actions in Eastern Europe, the Chinese Communist revolution, and the Soviet development of an atomic bomb all perpetuated the sense of emergency and kept federal commitments high. By the start of the Korean War, annual research and development appropriations had reached approximately $1.3 billion.[65] American physical scientists and engineers, from World War II onward, enjoyed major increases in resources and professional prestige. As research and development contracts flowed into American universities, science and engineering faculties reaped the benefits of public investment and set out to produce knowledge that the United States needed to meet a dangerous threat.

Though their efforts are certainly less well known, professional social scientists also took up the wartime struggle against Nazi Germany and imperial Japan. The "displaced faculty seminar" that made up the Research and Analysis Branch of the Office of Strategic Services, including historian Arthur M. Schlesinger Jr., sociologists Edward Shils and Alex Inkeles, and economists Edward S. Mason and Walt Rostow, marshaled their own analytical tools for the nation's defense. Ordered to map enemy supply systems, chart the organization of munitions firms, and identify the locations of oil and other industrial resources, members of the group analyzed prospective bombing targets and studied the ratio of damage inflicted per unit cost.[66]

By combining economics and management accounting with mathematical modeling, such work later contributed to the rising field of "operations research," a major influence on Cold War weapons design and global military strategy.[67] Other social scientists, especially psychologists, studied the effects of bombing on enemy morale, analyzed enemy and allied public opinion, prepared standardized aptitude and mental health tests for military personnel, and attempted to develop principles of community management for application in Japanese American internment camps.[68]

At war's end, however, the more modest contributions of social science seemed to pale in comparison with the work done on the physical end of the spectrum. Many officials also argued that social science did not merit the same kind of future support. Where the physicists produced radar technology and atomic fission that directly shaped the course of the war and the peace that followed, the social scientists appeared to have much less to their credit. The initial bill passed by the U.S. Senate in 1946 to authorize the National Science Foundation (NSF) reflected that divide and revealed widespread doubts about the very nature of social scientific inquiry. Thomas C. Hart, the measure's sponsor, argued that federal funding was undeserved because "no agreement has been reached with reference to what social science really means." Because some definitions might include such amorphous or even subversive topics as "philosophy, anthropology, all the racial questions, all kinds of economics, including political economics, literature, perhaps religion, and various kinds of ideology," Hart insisted that there was "no connection between the social sciences, a very abstract field, and the concrete field which constitutes the other subjects to be dealt with by the proposed science foundation."[69] The empirical work of physicists, senators agreed, produced tangible, dramatic, and cumulative advances in human understanding of the universe. Social scientists, however, living in a world clouded by values and biases, could do no more than generate normative judgments. In any event, how would the "success" of government-funded social research be evaluated? On what standard would new "discoveries" be registered? How would the expected payoff on public investment be verified?[70]

In responding to such skepticism, social scientists relied on two related strategies. First, they insisted that their work was rigorous, objective, and every bit as "scientific" as the research conducted by those studying the natural world. "Value-free" social science, they claimed, could discern universal laws and apply them to produce knowledge independent of the viewpoint of the scientist. Second, they argued that the validity and "concreteness" of their research would produce authentic, practical contributions. Rigor, they declared, would yield results. In a paper prepared for the SSRC, Talcott Parsons himself hammered away at those two themes. Objective social analysis, he argued, could provide the fundamental tools necessary for shaping the world's future: "Do we have or can we develop a knowledge of human social relations that can serve as the basis of rational, 'engineering' control? . . . The evidence we have reviewed indicates that the answer is unequivocally affirmative. Social science is a going concern; the problem is not one of creating it, but rather of using and developing it. Those who still argue whether the scientific study of social life is possible are far behind the times. It is here, and that fact ends the argument."[71] Social scientists, Parsons confidently declared, were much like physicians engaged in biological research on human affliction. Through the rigorous, objective study of a range of cases, they would build up a reservoir of knowledge valuable for treating all kinds of pathology.[72]

The lessons of events such as the NSF debate were clear to many prominent social scientists. Since the bulk of federal research funding was flowing into the physical sciences, and since universities increasingly rewarded faculty securing institutional support, it would behoove social researchers to emulate the "hard" science model. Many social thinkers, of course, were attracted to more "scientific" rhetoric and design out of their own personal sense of what their disciplines required to deliver concrete advances in knowledge. The institutional context, however, certainly contributed to those trends. From the late 1940s onward, social scientists aiming for funding, professional stature, and inclusion in the network created by Cold War concerns turned toward a rhetoric that combined claims of public relevance with assertions of rigorous objectivity.

In the McCarthy era, moreover, such an approach had additional advantages. Social science that was deemed too critical of the nation's domestic life came under fire as being unpatriotic, and conservatives were quick to denounce such research as a facade for subversive, left-wing "ideology." To protect themselves from those attacks, Harry Alpert, a sociologist hired by the NSF, recommended that his colleagues "eschew identification with social reform movements and welfare activities, and especially, the unfortunate phonetic relationship to socialism."[73] Claims of rigorous objectivity would serve to avoid any charges of subversive content and promote a sense of intellectual progress. Social scientists would make it clear that they were on the right side of the Cold War struggle and that they could help secure an American victory.

Modernization theorists benefited directly from the alliances that formed between the national security state, philanthropic foundations, federal funding, and social scientific research. Confident that they could deliver just the sort of "rational 'engineering' control" that Parsons had promised, they also followed his lead by insisting that their work was genuinely "scientific" and making their expertise available to policymakers. Objective analysis, they argued, would take social theory out of the realm of speculation. It would convince a vulnerable, impressionable "developing" world that liberal, capitalist democracy was the true and only path to political freedom and high living standards. Actively seeking involvement in what David Hollinger has referred to as a "system of capital-intensive research funded by a government responsive to popular political pressures and preoccupied with military priorities,"[74] theorists combined their claims of investigative rigor with statements of policy relevance. The defense of the "free world," as that group of intellectuals understood it, demanded a scientific enterprise. In language that obscured the inherent problem of political judgment, they endeavored to make "ideology" disappear beneath the force of their methods. As they attempted to harmonize scientific integrity with the production of intellectual weaponry, theorists insisted and often believed that their relationship to the state had no effect on the "truth" they produced. Modernity and modernization, they argued before both foreign and domestic audiences, were not political constructions. They were objective phenomena revealed by social scientific inquiry. They were facts.

Convinced of modernization's value as a developmental model for the "emerging" countries, theorists helped policymakers challenge Marxist analyses of an alternative route to progress by defining an impartially derived, scientifically proven phenomenon. In books and articles bolstered by quantification, multiple indexes, and the use of standardized practices and methods, they employed techniques of argument that sought to erase evidence of bias.[75] Rostow's five stages created a set of categories into which "developing" nations could be classified, but other theorists did an even more thorough job of making the emerging world an object for analysis. In his *Dynamics of Modernization*, C. E. Black gave the vagaries of social theory what appeared to be a concrete, empirical turn. The holistic process of modernization, he implied, could be best understood through a design that identified five major qualitative themes, four different temporal phases, and five variations on those phases based on the timing of power transfer, the source of the impetus for change, size of territory, population, the presence or absence of colonial experience, and the adaptability of the institutional structure to forces of change. Black's analysis finally emerged with a matrix of seven different patterns of modernization and a five-page table purporting to classify 148 different countries.[76] The subjectivity of Black's approach got lost under the weight of his standard categories and indexes. Urbanization, activist behavior, expectations of change in social status, psychological attitudes toward Western values, and the malleability of organizations appeared less as abstract, arbitrarily constructed social terms or theoretical ideas and more as self-evident pieces of data used in objective representation and analysis.

Scholars such as Daniel Lerner produced similar effects by quantifying the process that Black had categorized. Lerner's *Passing of Traditional Society* argued that modernization depended on the rise of a "mobile personality" among the citizens of a "developing" nation. Where a sense of human interdependence and an activist social ethic were high, the foundations would be set for modern, capitalist, economic life and democratic political institutions. Like Black, Lerner argued that his conclusions were not subjective products. After demonstrating multiple correlations to prove that "urbanization, industrialization, secularization, democratization, education, [and] media participation" were all part of a common process, he attempted to relate these sociological factors to the psychological quality of human empathy, the "key variable" and "unifying factor of response made by people living in a modernizing environment." Though he based his analysis on answers culled from hundreds of interviews conducted by the U.S. Information Service, Lerner took great pains to avoid any appearance of less than perfect scholarly independence. Employing a "Latent Structure Analysis," he attempted to prove that the individual, empathetic component of modernization correlated with what he held to be its social, institutional manifestations. Based on the assignment of positive or negative values to individuals on the basis of urbanism, literacy, status of occupation, exposure to mass media, and, finally, empathy, Lerner's scheme produced thirty-two possible combinations of the five variables.

Because high percentages of the individuals surveyed clustered around particular response patterns, Lerner determined that his assumptions about the relationship between psychological and sociological variables were correct. Though he admitted that his dichotomous scoring was somewhat arbitrary, his five-column, thirty-two-row table set forth sixteen "modern," five "transitional," and eleven "traditional" "item patterns" and lent itself to the identification of "high," "middle," and "low" transitional subclasses. With these "reassuringly empirical" results, Lerner claimed to have placed social research on a new plane. In his model, the subjective elements of measuring modernization and quantifying the shadowy quality of "empathy" seemed to vanish amid the standardized, statistical correlations.[77] Modernity, contrary to the assumptions of Marxist theorists, hardly eroded the quality of human relationships. Rather than impoverished, isolated, and alienated individuals, "modern" citizens were decidedly empathetic, attuned to the needs of their fellow citizens, and ready for democratic life.

Striking as the work of Black and Lerner appears, the most elaborate attempt to prove the empirical validity of modernization was produced by Alex Inkeles and David H. Smith in *Becoming Modern: Individual Change in Six Developing Countries*. Social psychology, the two reasoned, would illuminate the transitional passage. Inkeles, Smith, and their research assistants questioned nearly six thousand men between the ages of eighteen and thirty-two in Argentina, Chile, India, Israel, Nigeria, and East Pakistan (later Bangladesh). Classifying as modern "those personal qualities which are likely to be inculcated by participation in large-scale productive enterprises such as the factory," the authors combed their interview results for evidence of attributes such as "openness to new experience," "readiness for social change," "growth of opinion," the effective use of time, a willingness to trust others, personal aspirations, and respect for the dignity of others. They then combined these qualities with a series of topical observations including kinship structure, attitudes toward women's rights, religion, commitment to work, and social stratification. The results of these two selections were finally added to a third set of behavioral measures based on voting, attendance at religious services, reading the paper, listening to the radio, and discussing political issues.[78]

In addition to the standardized tools of multiple regression, correlation, and variance testing, the group also employed the benefits of computer analysis. When the machines stopped humming and the data tapes and thousands of IBM cards were finally sorted, the result was the "Overall Modernity Scale," a composite index used to compare cultivators in "traditional villages" with those who had moved to the city and spent three or more years in industrial work. With a scheme that mapped out twenty-four major themes of modernity and scored individuals from a level of zero to one hundred, the authors correlated their scale against the degree of exposure that an individual had to "modern" institutions such as schools and factories. Placing the score on the Overall Modernity Scale on the vertical axis and the degree of contact with "modern life" on the horizontal, the team then plotted points for the individuals they surveyed and found that, for each of the different countries, the graphs were basically the same.

Modernization, they claimed, was indeed a universal, general syndrome that changed the lives of people in the same way in all regions of the globe. In each case, newly modern citizens became "informed participants," "independent and autonomous" and "open-minded and cognitively flexible." Of men "fully exposed" to the factory labor and school instruction their theory deemed modernizing, the authors found that a convincing 76 percent of them scored as "modern." As Inkeles and Smith proudly stated, "the multiple correlation between our small set of basic explanatory variables and individual modernity scores went as high as .79." The circular logic of a study that found "modern" qualities among people working in what the researchers themselves labeled "modern" institutions seemed to fade away. Through empirical analysis, Inkeles and Smith had overcome "the sense of despair our profession frequently feels because our statements must so often be hedged about with so many reservations as to make sociology less a basic science and more a clinical discipline limited to diagnostics." An objective, scientific method, they claimed, had proved that liberal, capitalist modernization was neither a mere taxonomic category nor a destructive or damaging force. It was instead a universal process with a decidedly beneficial impact on the individual and society.[79]

In the Cold War context, the federal government as well as private, philanthropic foundations backed social research that promised to define the modernization process and identify the means by which it might be accelerated. To control Communist expansion, theorists argued, the United States would have to do more than invest in new military technology. It would also require a science of society to produce knowledge about the structures of political authority, economic organization, and human relations in the Soviet Union as well as the "peripheral" areas. The conviction that the USSR had launched a program of "political, economic and psychological warfare" designed to weaken the "relative world position of the United States" stimulated a new level of interest in American social analysis.[80] In 1948, the Carnegie Corporation and the Central Intelligence Agency collaborated with Harvard University to start the Russian Research Center, an institution that sent analyses of the Soviet social system to the federal government well before they appeared in published form.[81] Two years later, the Ford Foundation announced a new program of support for research on human behavior and launched projects designed to answer questions of how the United States could promote peace, foster democracy, and improve the stability of the world economy. Especially committed to supporting sociology, social anthropology, and social psychology, Ford spent $54 million on international programs between 1951 and 1954.[82] Following the Soviet launch of *Sputnik* in 1957, the National Defense Education Act also provided major federal government support for college student loans, graduate fellowships, and extensive language and area studies programs.[83]

Modernization theorists seeking financial support, personal prestige, and an opportunity to contribute to their nation's fight against the Communist specter found an eager audience for their work among the architects of U.S. foreign policy. The creation and career of the Center for International Studies at the Massachusetts Institute of Technology provide a striking example of this attempt to couple objective theories of modernization with the Cold War struggle. In 1950, the State Department approached MIT for assistance with "Project TROY," an effort to combat the USSR's effective jamming of Voice of America broadcasts into Soviet territory. A group of social scientists and engineers led by John E. Burchard, MIT's dean of humanities and social sciences, took on the project and proposed to complement their investigation of the technical components of the problem with an examination of the larger benefits to be achieved by communicating with Soviet citizens. Under the direction of economist Max Millikan, a former assistant director for the Central Intelligence Agency, the MIT Center for International Studies was established in 1952 with funding from the Ford Foundation and the CIA. Its mission, as team member Walt Rostow put it, was "to bring to bear academic research on issues of public policy."[84] "The Korean War," he later recalled, "convinced some of us that the struggle to deter and contain the thrust for expanded communist power would be long and that new concepts would be required to underpin U.S. foreign policy in the generation ahead."[85]

Made up of a collection of sociologists, political scientists, and economists that included modernization theorists Daniel Lerner, Lucian Pye, and Paul Rosenstein-Rodan, the center set about producing two related types of reports. Analyses of the modernization process in the "Third World" were paid for by the Ford and Rockefeller foundations. Studies of modernization (or its reported absence) in Communist societies, however, continued to receive CIA backing.[86] Within four years, the center also employed over seventy people and supported a "revolving research contingent" of postdoctoral scholars, visiting professors, and foreign experts.[87] Constantly approaching the process of "development" through the modernization framework, the MIT group explained that its collective works were "an exercise in interdisciplinary analysis." In place of the separate studies produced by economists, political scientists, and sociologists, they decided to "try to weave the various insights from this research into a reasonably integrated account of the transition through which the emerging nations are passing." The group also suggested that the United States could fend off Communist subversion of the "transitional" process. By promoting modernization through foreign investment and development planning, the United States could "help these societies move in directions compatible both with their long-run interests and with our own."[88]

Despite undertaking state-initiated projects, depending on federal support, and treating modernization as an explicit policy goal, the MIT center consistently claimed that its analyses were the product of independent, objective scholarship. The fact that they tailored their research to address the specific variables available for manipulation by policymakers generated little concern for a group pledged to academic social research. Promising to link modernization, the alleviation of poverty, and the promotion of democracy with national strategy, MIT's analysts claimed that no tension existed between scholarly pursuits and Cold War commitments. According to Rostow, the Center for International Studies never failed to meet MIT provost Julius Stratton's demand that it "maintain rigorous intellectual standards and, of course, complete intellectual independence from the government." As long as "high standards of academic professionalism and integrity were sustained, work on contemporary and foreseeable problems of the active world could add to the body of scientific knowledge." Even as it continued to fund the center, Rostow claimed that the CIA never "tried to influence our analysis or conclusions."[89] Although the MIT group explicitly mixed its goals of producing policy-relevant knowledge with those of fundamental scientific advance, its members perceived no conflict between the two.

While making those claims, moreover, Rostow and his associates actively pursued a partnership with Washington's foreign policy makers. As early as 1954, Millikan and Rostow had emphasized modernization's strategic significance to senior officials. In a memo to CIA director Allen Dulles, the two explained, "Where men's energies can be turned constructively and with some prospect of success to the problems of expanding standards of living in a democratic framework we believe the attractions of totalitarian forms of government will be much reduced. In the short run communism must be contained militarily. In the long run we must rely on development, in partnership with others, of an environment in which societies which directly or indirectly menace ours will not evolve." The economists did acknowledge that "each society must find that form of growth appropriate to its own traditions, values, and aspirations." But their advice betrayed little doubt about what the proper direction was or what the benefits of increased American engagement would be. "Free world success in seeing the underdeveloped countries through their difficult transition to self-sustaining growth," they emphasized, "would deny to Moscow and Peking the dangerous mystique that only Communism can transform underdeveloped societies."[90]

In 1957, Rostow and Millikan also published a declassified version of their argument in *A Proposal: Key to an Effective Foreign Policy*. Widely discussed in Washington's political circles, the book called for new programs to "promote the evolution of a world in which threats to our security and, more broadly, to our way of life are less likely to arise." The "bulk of the world's population has been politically inert," the two explained, but now the United States could begin "steering the world's newly aroused human energies in constructive rather than destructive directions." A long-term capital fund of $10–12 billion, national development plans, and assistance geared to each recipient nation's "stage of development" would fulfill America's "mission to see the principles of national independence and human liberty extended on the world scene." The "transition" toward modernity was inevitably destabilizing. Confronted with modern technology and values, older forms of social organization would erode, leaving societies vulnerable to "foreign" appeals for Marxist social revolution. But if the United States guided the developing nations through that dangerous window of uncertainty, a more liberal, democratic world would result. The key, thinkers such as Rostow and Millikan argued, was to accelerate the modernization process.[91]

Impressed by that thinking, Kennedy, as a senator from Massachusetts, approached the MIT center in 1957 for advice in formulating policy proposals on South Asian development. Kennedy expected that the Republican administration's failure to manage continual uprisings in the "periphery" would make a valuable campaign issue, and he sent aide Fred Holborn to meet with economists Paul Rosenstein-Rodan, Bill Malenbaum, and Rostow. After inviting Rostow to testify before the Senate Foreign Relations Committee, Kennedy and Senator John Cooper successfully passed a resolution calling on the Eisenhower administration to study South Asian development issues, a move that led to a formal World Bank mission.[92] The MIT group, glad to be of further use, also furnished Kennedy and Cooper with speech drafts, reports, and data on Indian development from its research center in New Delhi.[93] As Kennedy moved toward the Oval Office and his convictions about the problem of decolonization deepened, the relationship became even tighter. In February 1959, Millikan personally presented his ideas to the senator and emphasized his conviction that "an American initiative which goes well beyond the [Eisenhower] Administration's present position is exceedingly critical this year."[94] Kennedy brought members of the MIT group directly into White House planning after the election. Rostow and Millikan served on the Kennedy transition task force on foreign economic policy, and the two lobbied for a new initiative to project a much "clearer and more constructive image of our purpose and interest in nation-building."[95]

The Kennedy administration took that advice. Confident in the ability of American economic power, expertise, and comprehensive planning to make rapid international gains, policymakers shared a conviction that the United States could channel nationalist forces and developing economies in liberal, democratic directions. In a March 1961 speech before Congress, Kennedy boldly articulated his approach. Emphasizing the gravity of the development process, the president argued, "We live in a very special moment of history. The whole southern half of the world—Latin America, Africa, the Middle East and Asia are caught up in the adventures of asserting their independence and modernizing their old ways of life." Communist pressure, Kennedy warned, threatened to subvert progressive efforts, but American aid would repel Marxist advances and make a "historical demonstration that in the twentieth century, as in the nineteenth—in the southern half of the globe as in the north—economic growth and political democracy can develop hand in hand." Long-term lending authority, financial contributions from other "free industrialized nations," and special attention to the countries most ready to drive toward the "stage of self-sustaining growth," the president maintained, were all necessary in a time of crisis. To coordinate the effort, Kennedy established the Agency for International Development (AID) and gave it authority over technical aid, lending programs, development projects, and military assistance. Kennedy also outlined a broader mission for American foreign aid than any presented before. Funding for infrastructure, scientific technology, and civil service training programs, as well as comprehensive development planning, would all form integral parts of a sweeping "Decade of Development." Where the Marshall Plan had successfully rebuilt Western European economies and Truman's "Point Four" had offered technical assistance to poor countries, Kennedy and his advisers set out to build entirely new nations.[96]

The involvement of social scientists in Kennedy planning was extensive. In addition to Rostow and Millikan, many other scholarly experts were commissioned to help manage modernization. Harvard economists Edward S. Mason, David Bell, Lincoln Gordon, and John Kenneth Galbraith, all of whom had argued that macroeconomic policy could produce dramatic gains in foreign development, also went to work for the new government.[97] Concerned with security issues but also convinced that the interests of the United States and the "emerging" world were mutually reinforcing, these social scientists enjoyed a high degree of access to policymakers and shared a sense that their research could foster nation building for both strategic needs and humanitarian goals. As Rostow later recalled, "I was, simply, an early member of what was to become in 1959–1960 a large group of academics interested in public policy who were purposefully recruited by Kennedy. We were about the same age. Our outlook on affairs was similar. . . . We were greatly concerned with the dangers to both America and the wider cause of stable peace on the world scene."[98]

Those activist social scientists, many of whom had spent their careers shuttling between government and academia, were also accustomed to pushing theoretical ideas through bureaucratic channels. Confident liberal internationalists, they took important positions in the new administration and helped provide its intellectual foundation. Rostow became a deputy national security adviser and later served as chairman of the State Department's Policy Planning Council. Galbraith worked on the administration's foreign economic policy task force and became the U.S. ambassador to India. Gordon joined Kennedy's Latin American task force and was appointed the U.S. ambassador to Brazil. Bell moved from the Bureau of the Budget to become the administrator of AID, and Mason was appointed chairman of an AID advisory committee that included Millikan and Lucian Pye.[99] Stanford University development expert Eugene Staley became a consultant on Vietnam policy, and University of Michigan professor Samuel P. Hayes played an influential role in planning for a United States Peace Corps.

The personal connections, however, are only part of the story. Modernization also became engaged in the Cold War battle because it specified the universal requirements for change and provided Americans with what appeared to be a new and powerful set of analytical tools. Like the older, imperial ideology that preceded it, it linked the study of a "backward," external, foreign world with the characterization of an "advanced," internal, domestic identity. Concepts of modernization, in academia and government, lent social scientific credence to underlying cultural assumptions. Basing their knowledge claims on a supposedly impartial, objective "view from nowhere," modernizers also considered the world from what they defined as the summit of modernity itself.[100] And here their confidence was particularly stunning. As Arthur Schlesinger Jr. later reflected, "Euphoria reigned; we thought for a moment that the world was plastic and the future unlimited."[101] From that perspective, modernization was not merely a model of social change for academic debate and discussion. It was also a vision of the United States and the nation's mission to transform a world eager to learn the lessons only America could teach.

In the context of the Cold War, these qualities made modernization a theoretical source for Kennedy administration policy design. They also made it an ideology that reflected a new sense of Manifest Destiny and a refashioned imperial ideal in which the strategic and material goals of the United States appeared to mesh seamlessly with the nation's idealistic, moral mission to promote democracy, alleviate poverty, and "develop" a benighted world. Modernization theory reiterated a much older linkage between social inquiry and the expansion of political power. Colonization, earlier European and American social scientists had hoped, would provide a new laboratory for social research and a vehicle for patriotic service to the state. The rhetoric of modernization eschewed colonial claims, but the assumption that expanded American power would promote scientific knowledge and opportunities for its strategic application remained.[102] During the Cold War, as the United States sought to increase its influence in a region altered by the collapse of European empire, those themes would reappear with striking clarity. Modernizers would also rely on concepts with a deep, imperial past.

Intellectual Antecedents and Ideology of Empire

As one historian has recently pointed out, "modernization theorists usually denied any connections with earlier philosophies of history" and, instead, presented their work as "modern and scientific, implicitly exemplifying the best of the rationalization process."[103] Despite these claims, their thinking bears a strong resemblance to much older European social theory. In the use of stages, the definition of change as an integrated process, and the emphasis on the ability of "developed" societies to push more "primitive" ones toward the endpoint of modernity, Parsons, Rostow, and their colleagues employed a logic strikingly similar to that driving Enlightenment and evolutionary models of social change. Asking how it was that the West had advanced while the rest of the world stagnated, Cold War social scientists also returned to a question firmly rooted in an imperial history. Even as the world became formally decolonized, modernizers continued to define the virtues of the "advanced" nations in opposition to the intrinsic "deficiencies" of the poorer ones, argued that contact with the West could only produce a beneficial, catalytic effect on "backward" societies, and asserted that promoting global "development" involved finding the right lessons in America's own historic past. Modernization theory resonated with previous combinations of missionary vision and imperial control.

Reflections on the causes of apparent Western superiority were not new in the years following the Second World War. As George Stocking describes it, within the great "Crystal Palace" of the 1851 London International Exhibition, the wonders of Britain's industrial revolution were displayed alongside artifacts from Africa, Asia, and the Middle East. Machines with interchangeable parts, requiring dozens of laborers and serving a multitude of urban consumers, were juxtaposed with objects such as pandanus mats from tropical climates and the strange vestments worn by the mysterious leaders of "savage" or "despotic" nations. The exhibits were arranged to reflect a linear, temporal order, and for the English public attending they presented an "obvious lesson." All peoples, it was understood, were expected to employ their God-given reason to discern the laws of the universe and manipulate the natural world to their advantage. It was clear, however, "that in pursuing their general mission, not all men had advanced at the same pace, or arrived in the same point."[104] According to Timothy Mitchell, the London Exhibition's 6 million visitors encountered the "mark of a great historical confidence. The spectacles set up in such places of modern entertainment reflected the political certainty of a new age. . . . Exhibitions, museums, and other spectacles were not just reflections of this certainty, however, but the means of its production, by their technique of rendering history, progress, culture and empire in 'objective' form."[105]

Several scholars have shown that the message presented at such Victorian exhibits was similar to the one reflected in social theories proposing to explain a distinctly "European miracle."[106] Though modernization theorists put postwar America atop the list of those countries that had "arrived," a common question links them with their intellectual predecessors. Adam Smith, Condorcet, and Max Weber, among others, all believed they could explain Europe's uniquely advanced status, even if their answers were not always the same. Smith, in *The Wealth of Nations*, turned to political economy and the division of labor to account for how the living standard of an "industrious and frugal" European peasant might so greatly exceed that of "many an African king, the absolute master of the lives and liberties of ten thousand naked savages."[107] In his *Sketch for a Historical Picture of the Human Mind*, Condorcet argued that the matter of Europe's superior status lay in a different rate of advancement in the faculty of human experience. Just as individuals developed their own cognitive powers at different speeds, societies, as collections of individuals, did the same. Europeans, turning toward systematic agriculture, the institution of private property, and written language long before other peoples, had reached a degree of civilization that contrasted sharply with that of the "savage" tribes. Weber's *Protestant Ethic and the Spirit of Capitalism* provided yet another interpretation. Noting that "in Western civilization, and in Western civilization only, cultural phenomena have appeared which (as we like to think) lie in a line of development having *universal* significance and value," Weber analyzed the moral dictates of a religious system to explain the rise of a particularly Western form of capitalist rationality.[108] Ascetic values and the anxiety generated by the Calvinist pursuit of a divine calling had given secular business and investment practices a meaning and sense of exigency that drove capitalism far ahead in Western Europe's Protestant countries.

Not all these thinkers produced unqualified celebrations of their own culture's advanced position. Weber's famous closing reflections on the "iron cage" of modern capitalist society, for example, reveal a particularly dark pessimism. Fearing what he described as "mechanized petrification, embellished with a sort of convulsive self-importance," Weber warned of a hollow world in which "the idea of duty in one's calling prowls about in our lives like the ghost of dead religious beliefs."[109] Ferdinand Tönnies, also writing in the late nineteenth century, lamented the transition from rural, communal gemeinschaft to cosmopolitan, contractual gesellschaft as the loss of genuine, affectionate relations and the rise of a society composed of atomized, antagonistic competitors.[110] Adam Smith, too, tempered his analysis with the stoic observations found in his *Theory of Moral Sentiments*. Although "power and riches" could give those who possessed them many advantages in life, their demanding pursuit left an individual "as much, and sometimes more exposed than before, to anxiety, to fear and sorrow; to diseases, to danger and to death."[111] Each of these thinkers, however, sought to explain Europe's prodigious development by citing the vital role of innovations, intellectual qualities, or spiritual values unique to that region of the world. Because these essential factors were absent in other areas, comparable "progress" had yet to appear there.

Modernization theorists in the Cold War United States also constructed a sharp cultural disjunction between the "advanced" nations and the developing world they sought to analyze. Almost always held to exemplify the qualities of modernity itself, the United States and Western Europe enjoyed a special status. In his analysis of Western scholarship about the Middle East, Edward Said has argued that "European culture gained in strength and identity by setting itself off against the Orient as a sort of surrogate or even underground self."[112] A similar dynamic can be found within modernization theory. Theorists such as Rostow, Parsons, and even S. N. Eisenstadt, an early and significant critic of some of modernization's core assumptions, all expressed the special qualities of American and Western European societies in opposition to the deficiencies they discerned in a world continuing to struggle in the Western wake. Rostow's identification of the United States, Australia, New Zealand, and Canada as a "special case" made up of nations that "never became so caught up in the structures, politics and values of traditional society" reflects a division paralleled by Parsons. According to his *Structure and Process in Modern Societies*, Western, Judeo-Christian ideals stood as "highly activistic in relation to the external environment" in contrast to "the great civilizations of the Orient, namely China and India," which had "quite a different character." Eisenstadt also followed suit with his definition of a select group of societies including those of "Western Europe, England, the Netherlands, the Scandinavian countries, the United States" in which modernization proceeded "more or less simultaneously both at the center and from within the broader strata." Echoing Weber, he explained that, owing to middle-class, Protestant entrepreneurial values, these areas became "to a very great extent open to modernizing influences" while other regions did not.[113] Like their intellectual predecessors, these theorists explained the success stories of development by arguing that the required transformations resonated with the unique practices and values found in a "modern," "Western" culture. As they defined these assets in opposition to the deficiencies that kept the "traditional" world shackled in its backward ways, they also made it clear that, at bottom, the advantage described was not due to natural resources, military conquest, or the spoils of imperialism and capitalist exploitation. The decisive factor remained rooted within the inherent values of the Western heritage itself.

In explaining this fundamental dichotomy, American social scientists framed the process of modernization through a model that mirrored evolution in the natural world. Like nineteenth-century thinkers before them, many twentieth-century theorists argued that the history of nations was analogous to the growth of organisms. Such themes played a large role in the thinking of those who, like Herbert Spencer, endeavored to produce an integrated, general theory of universal history and social evolution. Because societies were integrated wholes and "progress" could be correlated with an increase in structural "order," Spencer maintained that differences in relative advance could be discerned by the degree to which social organization became increasingly clear, codified, and specific. Much like the modernization theorists who followed him, Spencer interpreted variations in static, structural portraits as evidence of differential rates of temporal movement toward a more concrete, "determinate" arrangement. As he put it, "a wandering tribe of savages, being fixed neither in its locality nor in its internal distribution, is far less definite in the relative positions of its parts than a nation. In such a tribe, the social relations are similarly confused and unsettled. Political authority is neither well established nor precise. Distinctions of rank are neither clearly marked nor impassable. And save in the different occupations of men and women, there are no complete industrial divisions. . . . Any one of those primitive societies that evolves, however, becomes step by step more specific." "Sharpness of definition," Spencer maintained, grew "both greater and more variously exemplified as societies advance[d] to maturity."[114]

Because the laws of change and nature operated uniformly across time and space, all societies traveled the same path. Different societies, therefore, represented earlier stages in the history of the most developed people, or, more broadly, in the history of all society or culture.[115] Movement toward the Western endpoint not only was beneficial but was the result of a natural, evolutionary process through which different societies passed at different speeds. Such assumptions, George Stocking has demonstrated, filled the travel literature of European expansion. Claims that the "tribal societies of antipodal man" showed "striking similarity to those of ancestral Europe" appeared to make perfect sense. As Europeans' minds and cultures evolved, their ways of life were expected to progress well beyond those of other peoples. "So long as sociomental evolution was viewed in the framework of the comparative method," Western scholars concluded that "it was not simply our Neanderthal or Pithecanthropic ancestors, but living groups of 'savage' men who were regarded as beings of a lower mental order."[116]

Although they usually replaced explicit appeals to biological determinism with an increased emphasis on advantages rooted in cultural values, American modernization theorists also naturalized the inequalities of wealth and power that they identified. Parsons's emphasis on the importance of "an explicit and well-analyzed evolutionary dimension" and Rostow's references to the "essentially biological field of economic growth" reflect their understanding of social change as an organic, integrated process.[117] By setting off the United States as the ultimate example of modernization, theorists simply measured other nations by their distance from that point of intrinsic, evolutionary supremacy and promoted a construction of superiority that appealed to both policymakers and public audiences alike. This classification of the "developing" solely in terms of its relation to the "developed," Dean Tipps has pointed out, "provided the modernization theorist with a cognitive map consisting of familiar, stable categories drawn from his immediate experience as a citizen of 'modern' society, according to which data derived from 'relatively non-modernized societies could be gathered, sorted and interpreted."[118] Like their predecessors, many Cold War theorists invoked a set of teleological, natural laws that allowed them to evade the responsibility of studying the specific historical and cultural characteristics of any particular "emerging" nation. Because foreign societies were treated as integrated, organic systems and placed on a common continuum, evaluating them required only fixed indexes drawn from the pedestals of Western or American self-identities. The world represented a "record of temporal succession," and the less advanced peoples populating it were "contemporary ancestors" or, conversely, "primitive contemporaries."[119]

Because America had already reached the peak of modernity and the less advanced societies were bound to travel the same road, the national past also became eminently useful. Mining the historical record for "lessons" that the rest of the world could follow, theorists infused it with a nostalgic, harmonious glow that made America's present institutions the fulfillment of pristine origins and aspirations. As a model for nations struggling in the present, the American Revolution seemed a particularly appropriate historical case. Although he did not go so far as to claim that it was a design that others might replicate exactly, political scientist William Nisbet Chambers argued that America's political development during the revolutionary period demonstrated to the world the "value of moderate and pragmatic approaches," the importance of "broad as well as specialized education for promoting and training leaders," the worth of a "responsible opposition," and the function of parties to "contain the forces of pluralism and bring coherence to public policy." Run through the sieve of modernization theory, the ideological conflict, interclass tension, and real violence of the American Revolution disappeared. All that remained were vague, sweeping generalizations about how an "emerging" society needed to arrive at a liberal, consensual equilibrium in order to "develop."[120]

Sociologist Seymour Martin Lipset carried the point even further. New nations, he argued, would learn a great deal if they sought to acquire the same "key values" of equality and achievement that "stem from our revolutionary origins." As the "first major colony successfully to revolt against colonial rule," the United States had dramatically broken with "traditional sources of legitimacy" and distinguished between "the source of sovereignty and the agents of authority" in a democratic polity. Lipset admitted that these transformations were not always easy ones but optimistically concluded that "the entire Western world has been moving in the American direction . . . and . . . America, which was democratic and equalitarian before industrialization, has merely led the way in these patterns."[121] As far as modernization theorists were concerned, the American past proved that the path through the transitional process was liberal and consensual, not radical or divisive. Theorists enjoyed a "utopia apprehended" in the idealistic images they created of their own societies. As presented through demonstration, the modern society became the flawless result of a natural, perfect process.[122]

American modernization theorists, moreover, went beyond analyzing the process of change and the essential differences between "the West" and "the rest." Like their intellectual predecessors, they also investigated the effects of interaction between the "advanced" and the "emerging" regions of the world. A number of scholars have convincingly illustrated the ways in which social scientific inquiry, by providing knowledge about the economy, political structure, and religious beliefs of African and Asian societies, facilitated the establishment and expansion of European colonial enterprise.[123] Yet imperial social science did more than provide data useful for policymakers. It also contributed to what Nicholas Dirks and others have referred to as a "cultural project," the reflection of a "subtle relationship between power and knowledge, between culture and control."[124] As they produced analyses that reiterated older assumptions rooted in the justification of colonial expansion, American modernization theorists argued that contact with the United States could serve as a great catalyst for change in "stagnant" societies and that a demonstration of Western ways could accelerate a slow development process. Even as they sincerely applauded the end of official, legal colonialism, liberal modernization theorists, in the name of scientific and social progress, drew on the ideology that had justified it. Colonial powers, Rostow acknowledged, "did not always optimize the development of the preconditions for take-off," but "they could not avoid bringing about transformations in thought, knowledge, [and] institutions . . . which moved the colonial society along the transitional path."[125] Contact with the West, as he explained it, often produced a "demonstration effect" through which external values and methods transformed stagnant, indigenous institutions and drove traditional cultures toward progress. According to a lecture broadcast internationally on the Voice of America, developing countries could look west to "foresee the course of modernization." All that "nations on their way up" had to do was "investigate the conditions of life in today's so-called 'advanced' societies and then project an immediate future."[126] As one perceptive scholar commented some years later, theorists believed that "human progress was possible because the more backward of the races at least had the ability to imitate."[127] Mimicry, they maintained, would promote modernity.

Yet many theorists believed that America did not have to wait for expected emulation. A "modern" society could actively create institutions affecting the social life of an "emerging" country. In addition to providing external investment, the "advanced" state could furnish scientific technology and training, provide instruction in the virtues of democratic systems, help produce more efficient forms of business organization, and even instill a new spirit of rationality. Countries on the receiving end, moreover, had little choice in the matter. Scholars such as Daniel Lerner believed that "traditional" forms and religions were "defenseless" against Western contact, but Rostow took that argument another step forward. Indigenous protest and resistance to intrusion, he insisted, could actually promote modernization. A "reactive nationalism," after all, had been a "most important and powerful motive force in the transition. . . . Men holding effective authority or influence have been willing to uproot traditional societies not, primarily, to make more money but because the traditional society failed—or threatened to fail—to protect them from humiliation by foreigners."[128] Modernization was thus more than a way of looking at the world. A force with the power of history on its side, it was also the most important stimulant of change for "stagnant" societies. Because the real impetus came from the West, "Third World" nationalism could never be wholly indigenous or authentic. The "traditionals" could protest against modernity, but they could not reject it. They could imitate but not create, react but not act. The world, it appeared, was bound to move toward the universal endpoint represented by a West that had already arrived there.

Like the social theorists before them, Cold War modernizers believed that there was only one true route to successful development, the one they articulated from the heights of their own sense of national and cultural supremacy. The essential qualities found only within Western civilizations had led to their prodigious advancement, but other societies could still look to that history for lessons to follow. Because deviations from the charted path would only delay a necessary and vital transformation, nationalistic resistance on the part of the developing society was xenophobic and irrational. The process was universal, but the catalysts of change were Western, and the West had the power to accelerate a desirable and ultimately inevitable process. As modernization theorists presented them, moreover, these conclusions were not the result of abstract speculation or library erudition. They were instead held to be the product of objective, scientific analysis coupled with the fulfillment of disciplinary purpose, national mission, and patriotic, ethical duty.

It was that ideological fusion, the combination of objectivist analysis and national identification, that gave modernization much of its power in shaping both Kennedy administration foreign development policy and Cold War constructions of America's national identity. With claims of methodological rigor and scientific integrity, theorists naturalized one particular pattern of social change and depoliticized the external means they suggested to accelerate it. Emphasizing their country's power, they also framed an appealing identity for America as a progressive nation assisting others in their fight against poverty, oppression, and debilitating fatalism. Americans, as Lucian Pye put it, were called to "associate ourselves for better or worse in assisting and strengthening those transitional peoples who would build democratic societies." "By communicating our genuine concern and respect for them and their problems," he explained, "we can produce a quality of relationship which will make it possible for us to confront together fundamental issues."[129] In articulating this sort of missionary impulse, modernizers spoke of a collective "we" in two different senses. In the first case, they defined their American audience as a specific and distinct nation, a superior community of modern citizens that, they hoped, would be united by its dedication to improving the world. In the second, they spoke of the universal concerns and processes that their modernity allowed them to perceive, comprehend, and face together with the societies they sought to assist.[130]

During the early 1960s, modernization reinforced the connections between U.S. strategic concerns and assumptions about America's role as a moral, benevolent world leader. To ask whether modernizers were motivated by genuine altruism or the pursuit of national interest is to pose a false dichotomy. One need not search for signs of conspiracy or deceit to find evidence of the ideology of modernization at work. Optimistic about the potential for American-sponsored nation building to combat poverty, contribute to the formation of democratic governments, improve global living standards, and allow for the protection of individual freedoms, most theorists sincerely believed that preventing "wars of liberation" and promoting "development" went hand in hand.

It is certainly true, of course, that not all theorists sought to influence U.S. government policy. Some individuals did have a specific impact on the conduct of U.S. foreign relations. Others remained in academic settings and did not achieve or even pursue access to the policymaking arena. As an analysis of the Alliance for Progress, the Peace Corps, and the Strategic Hamlet Program in Vietnam illustrates, however, the ideas and assumptions of modernization played a large role. The theory's rhetoric and its primary assumptions were firmly rooted in American Cold War culture. Both in institutional, policymaking settings and in public discourse, the ideology of modernization reframed imperial ideals, told Americans who they were, and defined what a projection of their nation's power could achieve.

CHAPTER 3

Modernity, Anticommunism, and the Alliance for Progress

On March 2, 1961, Walt Whitman Rostow sent President John F. Kennedy a memorandum. Endorsing a proposal made by Kennedy's Latin American task force, the modernization theorist and deputy national security adviser told the president that the time was right for launching a new "Economic Development Decade." As he put it, "Barring a catastrophe, it is likely that a good many of the countries in the underdeveloped world will, during the 1960s, either complete the take-off process or be very far advanced in it. When take-off is complete a nation may be poor but it is normally in a position to draw its external capital from private commercial sources." Argentina, Brazil, Colombia, and Venezuela, Rostow argued, could all be weaned off what he called the "international dole." Through a massive transfusion of foreign aid, the United States could drive more than 80 percent of Latin America's "underdeveloped" population into "self-sustained growth." Such a program, he added, would do more than reduce the poverty that led to social unrest and political instability. It would also have "enormous power in catching the public imagination in all countries" and keep the "underdeveloped" areas "off our necks as we try to clean up the spots of bad trouble."[1]

Started by the Kennedy administration in March 1961, the Alliance for Progress was an urgent and comprehensive attempt to reverse increasingly widespread Latin American poverty and political oppression. A program that included growth-rate targets and advocated a host of reforms in education, health care, and housing, the alliance also called for industrialization, land reform, and income redistribution. Comprehensive planning and support for democratic institutions, Kennedy advisers promised, would provide Latin America with a peaceful revolution of unprecedented magnitude. Assisted by social scientists from the United States, Latin American nations were expected to submit detailed national development plans and projects for review. When approved, funding was to flow directly from U.S. government sources as well as international lending institutions such as the Inter-American Development Bank and the International Monetary Fund. Latin Americans were also expected to promote policies that would result in increased private investment in national economies. The long list of overall goals, expressed in a formal charter ratified by the Organization of American States, included overall economic growth for each country; a "more equitable distribution of national income"; diversification of exports; accelerated industrialization; higher agricultural productivity; agrarian reform; a life expectancy increase; low-cost housing; regional economic integration; and the elimination of adult illiteracy. These ambitious objectives, moreover, were to be pursued by governments committed to promoting "the framework of personal dignity and political liberty."[2]

One of the most dramatic and widely discussed of the Kennedy administration's development initiatives, the Alliance for Progress provides a striking example of the way modernization functioned in the context of a particular institutional site and policy problem. In many instances, theorists used their official positions as consultants, advisers, or policymakers to influence the definition of program objectives and the means for achieving them. As a set of principles about the ways in which the development process could be accelerated, modernization theory suggested specific policy options to give alliance efforts maximum impact in moving societies along the "transitional path" toward liberal, capitalist modernity. Beyond such direct connections between social scientific argument and policy design, however, modernization also functioned powerfully as a perceptual and cognitive framework. In that sense, modernization was often far more than a set of analytical, instrumental tools used to produce a given outcome. It was also an ideology that established the connections between mutually reinforcing ideas. Through its claims to objective, scientific knowledge, modernization gave forceful expression to deeply rooted cultural assumptions about America's ability to project a nation-building power. In addition to satisfying strategic demands by alleviating the poverty and repression believed to foster social revolutions, modernization promised to fulfill a benevolent national mission. The promotion of a liberal, democratic vision of development in opposition to Marxist doctrine and Soviet support, many believed, went hand in hand with the nation's historical destiny. In private, official sources as well as public representations made by government and media, the alliance reflected an identity for the United States that was well suited to a Cold War contest in the "developing world." Amid heated competition with the model promoted by the USSR and Cuba, the alliance presented the United States as an advanced and deeply altruistic nation, a country that regenerated its greatest strengths by assisting a region desperate to emulate its exemplary innovations and past accomplishments.

The relationships between theory, policy, and identity, of course, cannot explain or account for the entire history of the Alliance for Progress. As an extensive body of literature has shown, the program was the product of a broad range of factors including Latin American demands, strategic anxieties, previous development experience, worries about the repercussions of military action, and efforts to shape hemispheric economic ties.[3] By tracing the vision of modernization through the program's formation, major practices, and public presentations, however, this chapter demonstrates the functioning of a political and cultural ideology within that historical context. First, considering the role of modernization theory in shaping alliance objectives, this interpretation analyzes a conceptual framework through which "development" became integrally involved in the definition of threats to national security produced by the Cuban revolution. In their effort to accelerate Latin America's passage through the dangerous "transitional period," modernizers proposed specific practices and techniques to guide the region's countries from "tradition" into "modernity" before social revolution might interrupt that idealized process. Carrying that theme into public representations, this chapter also investigates the way modernization, in both official and media sources, gave expression to national identities for both the donor and recipients of material aid and activist values. Anticommunism, as the Alliance for Progress reveals, was a cultural battleground as well as a strategic and economic one.

Finally, this interpretation of the Alliance for Progress explores the way an ideology of modernization constrained dissent and criticism even as the program proved incapable of achieving its declared goals. An ideology that linked a particular policy with an underlying national sense of self, modernization actually diminished the ability of leading officials and advisers to recognize and respond to the clear evidence of policy failure. While many lamented a particular administrative problem, blamed Latin Americans for the program's apparent lack of success, or called for greater attention to private investment, very few questioned the fundamental assumption that a projection of "modern" values, resources, and tutelage could engineer the dramatic transformation of an "underdeveloped" region. In the case of the Alliance for Progress, the ideology of modernization shaped and legitimated an ambitious, highly publicized effort to combine the promotion of Latin American development with the containment of communism. It also forced analyses of social change into a particularly rigid template, presented sweeping economic and political reform as matters of simple volition, and reiterated a profound sense of historical destiny for the United States, a nation claiming the power, knowledge, and right to transform a struggling world. As it proposed to "replace" the older legacy of Iberian colonialism and promised to challenge Castro's more recent revolutionary overtures, the United States fashioned an imperial ideal of its own.

Several scholars have pointed out that the first postwar calls for a hemispheric development program came from within Latin America itself. Between the early 1930s and the early 1950s, the health of the region's economies fluctuated widely. During the depression, markets for Latin American exports in the United States and Europe dried out, and widespread poverty curtailed internal demand as well. World War II stimulated a renewed pursuit of the raw materials that Latin American nations could provide, and nonmilitary agencies of the U.S. government purchased almost $2.4 billion in Latin American commodities out of a global total of almost $4.4 billion. Precious metals, oil, and meat made Latin America what historian Stephen G. Rabe has called "an arsenal for the United States and the United Nations."[4] By the late 1940s, however, the boom faded, and the region's foreign exchange earnings in key commodities such as wheat, coffee, tin, and copper again fell behind the cost of imported manufactured goods. New advances in public health reduced death rates, but, as overall population growth increased, unemployment climbed with it. Latin American nations possessed little internal savings for investment purposes, and orthodox demands that they make use of their "comparative advantage" through trade often led to increased poverty and the promotion of elite-controlled export sectors that did little to alleviate popular destitution. Strategies of import-substituting industrialization also raised difficult problems as capital-intensive manufacturing, usually funded by foreign investment, failed to provide the jobs and popular income necessary to create a substantial domestic market for expensive goods. Not all Latin American nations were affected equally by these trends, but living standards and education levels in most countries remained painfully low.[5]

Prospects for the future were not much brighter. Established in 1948 as a regional agency of the United Nations, the Economic Commission for Latin America (ECLA) conducted quantitative studies demonstrating that, since the late 1880s, global trade relations had worked to the systematic disadvantage of countries exporting primary products. The "terms of trade," Argentine economist Raúl Prebisch warned, were also deteriorating at an even faster rate than before. The combined price index for principal agricultural and mineral products was tumbling relative to that for finished goods, and as Latin American nations fell deeper into debt trying to import manufactures, their export income would not close the gap. Because of the "unequal exchange" between "center" and "periphery," Prebisch and his associates argued, Latin America's already pervasive poverty would only increase. This was grim news for a region in which the per capita income of the early 1950s averaged less than $250 per year and life expectancy was only forty-three years, fully twenty-five years less than it was in the United States at the time. To be sure, much of the problem was also linked to internal dynamics. In many Latin American countries, a tiny oligarchy controlled massive amounts of land and wealth. In Peru, 1.1 percent of the population owned 82 percent of the nation's soil. In Brazil, the top 1 percent of the nation's rich collected a full 19 percent of all income. It became clear to many economists and officials, however, that no progress at all would be made without drastic action.[6]

The depth of the region's poverty and predictions such as those made by the ECLA stimulated a wave of Latin American appeals for economic assistance from the United States and other industrialized nations. For some time, however, their requests were pushed into the background by U.S. administrations that kept military priorities firmly in mind. At an international conference in Chapultepec, Mexico, in early 1945, Latin American leaders pledged their solidarity with the United States by agreeing to a public declaration that an attack on any American nation would be considered an attack on all of them and that, in the event of aggression, they would mutually consult to determine an appropriate response. Amid heightened Cold War tensions, the Latin American states also addressed U.S. security concerns by confirming that agreement in a formal treaty at Rio de Janeiro in August 1947. Only a few months after issuing his famous doctrine dividing the world into two ideological camps and "alternative ways of life," President Harry S. Truman traveled to Rio for the Latin American meeting. After arriving in grand style on the battleship *Missouri*, site of the Japanese surrender in World War II, he proudly celebrated "a New World pact of peace which possesses teeth." "We have translated Pan-American solidarity from an ideal into a reality," he proclaimed. "This is sunlight in a dark world."[7] Created a year later at Bogotá, Colombia, the Organization of American States (OAS) also solidified a united stand against Communist subversion by creating a formal legal framework for inter-American cooperation. Though the Truman administration agreed to a requirement that the hemisphere's nations refrain from intervening in one another's internal affairs, the United States did not hesitate to sign bilateral mutual defense pacts with ten Latin American countries over the next few years. In exchange for the delivery of military equipment and services, Latin American nations agreed to expand their defense capabilities, send strategic materials directly to the United States, and restrict their trade with the Soviet bloc.[8]

Such developments reflect the degree to which, by the early 1950s, a deep chasm had opened between the social and economic concerns of Latin American officials and the U.S. focus on security needs. From the time of the Chapultepec meeting, Arturo Escobar has argued, Latin American leaders "made clear the importance of industrialization in the consolidation of democracy and asked the United States to help with a program of economic transition."[9] U.S. policymakers, however, typically ignored such requests or replied with lectures stressing the need for continued vigilance against communism. When Latin Americans raised the aid issue again at the 1948 conference in Bogotá, U.S. secretary of state George Marshall simply informed them that European security needs took precedence. Because the United States was already committed to the reconstruction of Western Europe, Marshall insisted that Latin Americans would have to wait. While the Truman administration poured $19 billion into Western Europe between 1945 and 1950, frustrated Latin American leaders received little more than vague promises of future consideration. According to Gaddis Smith, "the pervading sense of worldwide danger made the highest officials in the American government think about Latin America in terms of global strategy, not in terms of the problems within individual countries or the region or even in terms of the perennial issues between the other American republics and the United States."[10]

That perspective was compounded by the prevailing attitudes among prominent American strategists. Few of Truman's advisers had spent time in Latin America, and many of them looked on the peoples of the region as emotional, irrational, and unworthy of serious U.S. consideration. On a tour through Central and South America in 1950, George F. Kennan, then head of the State Department's Policy Planning Council, visited Mexico City, Caracas, Rio, São Paulo, Montevideo, Buenos Aires, and Panama City.

Struck by the contrast between the extremes of wealth and poverty, disturbed by left-wing attacks on his character, and troubled by what he perceived as uninspired and self-aggrandizing leadership, Kennan concluded that the dangers of Communist infiltration and subversion were quite real. Latin Americans, however, appeared to him beyond redemption. They were, he believed, unprepared for democracy and intrinsically incapable of real economic advance. As he recorded in his memoirs, the region's failings were "written in human blood and in the tracings of geography; and in neither case are they readily susceptible of obliteration. . . . The answers people have suggested to them thus far have been feeble and unpromising."[11] The United States, many senior analysts believed, could not afford to ignore Latin American security problems. But an effort to promote sweeping political or socioeconomic progress there would end in futility.

In late 1954, at a meeting of the Inter-American Economic and Social Council of the OAS, Latin Americans petitioned once more for U.S. aid. This time, moreover, they proposed a comprehensive, long-term program for economic development. Guided by the work of Prebisch and the ECLA, Chilean president Eduardo Frei argued that Latin American economic development required foreign assistance to stabilize commodity prices, promote new industries, assist with regional economic integration, and raise general living standards. In their request for the establishment of an inter-American bank, a group of Latin American economists also estimated that, over the next decade, the region would require at least $1 billion of foreign assistance each year, the majority of which would have to come from public funds. To increase growth and diversify regional economies, they argued, domestic savings would have to be augmented by the infusion of a massive amount of capital. The United States, moreover, would need to provide most of the aid.[12]

Fiscally conservative, narrowly focused on anticommunism, and infused with many of the same prejudices as its predecessors, the Eisenhower administration rejected that plan outright. Economic growth, Eisenhower and his advisers maintained, would have to be achieved through the workings of free market capitalism and private enterprise. State-run programs, they argued, would only create a vast aid bureaucracy and harm business interests. Far more concerned with preserving stability than promoting progressive reform, Eisenhower also saw little need to introduce social and economic Programs that might undermine the Latin American dictators his government supported. Never pressing Latin American leaders on issues of human or civil rights, the Eisenhower administration awarded the prestigious Legion of Merit medal to Manuel Odría of Peru and Marcos Pérez Jiménez of Venezuela. U.S. ambassadors also praised the brutal regimes of Rafael Trujillo in the Dominican Republic and Fulgencio Batista in Cuba as stalwart allies of the United States and defenders of freedom. Where it seemed necessary, moreover, the Eisenhower administration did not hesitate to use covert force to preserve its dominance in the region. In 1954, only months before Frei and his associates appealed for U.S. aid, Eisenhower's CIA had orchestrated a coup against Guatemalan nationalist Jacobo Arbenz, a constitutionally elected leader who refused to expel Communists from his government and instituted a progressive land reform measure expropriating some holdings of the U.S.-owned United Fruit Company. In conjunction with the Eisenhower administration's flat refusal of Latin America's development proposals, that use of force to stifle the challenge of an independent course of economic organization and political assertion sent a strong message to the hemisphere that the status quo was much preferred to socioeconomic radicalism. As Eisenhower's actions made clear, the United States would not support proposals for sweeping change. Countries that went too far from the established order, moreover, did so at their peril.[13]

Several events in the late 1950s, however, eventually provoked a partial shift in United States policy. On a Latin American "goodwill tour" in 1958, Vice President Nixon was confronted by angry student demonstrators at San Marcos University in Lima, and a rock-throwing crowd of protesters nearly succeeded in overturning his car as he attempted to travel into Caracas. Those incidents reflected a growing wave of Latin American resentment of U.S. policy, but the real shocks came during 1958 and 1959 as Castro's guerrilla force emerged from the Sierra Madre, defeated the Batista government, and marched victoriously through the streets of Havana. As the new Cuban government began to support further revolutionary efforts and aligned itself with the Soviet Union, the worst of American nightmares came true. Revolutionary nationalism, Eisenhower administration strategists worried, would quickly spread from Cuba to other impoverished, alienated populations throughout the hemisphere. If Fulgencio Batista had proved vulnerable, they wondered, what might happen to regimes like that of Trujillo in the Dominican Republic or the Somoza family in Nicaragua? Members of the powerful Senate Foreign Relations Committee, including Mike Mansfield, Hubert Humphrey, Wayne Morse, Frank Church, J. William Fulbright, and a politically ambitious John F. Kennedy, began to ask similar questions and subjected administration policy to prolonged, public criticism. Support for dictatorship also generated resentment among Latin American liberals such as Rómulo Betancourt of Colombia and Costa Rican president José Figueres. Pressed by intense criticism at home and abroad, the Eisenhower administration watched in frustration as its efforts to support an anti-Castro "third force" in Cuba crumbled. It also began a reappraisal of policy that, for the first time, put Latin American issues in the spotlight and gave serious consideration to socioeconomic forces and needs.[14]

In that context, Brazilian president Juscelino Kubitschek's 1958 proposal for a large-scale, government-funded economic development program, "Operation Pan-America," enjoyed a strikingly different reception among U.S. strategic planners.[15] Holding that the source of the revolutionary uprisings was not Communist conspiracy but instead popular misery and desperation, Kubitschek's analysis received unprecedented attention in Washington's political circles. In September 1960, in Bogotá, the Eisenhower administration finally agreed to establish the $500 million Social Progress Trust Fund to promote agricultural reforms, construct housing, and improve public health and education. As the United States approved the measure, Treasury Secretary C. Douglas Dillon and other administration strategists coupled social reform with the fulfillment of common strategic objectives. Anti-Communist success remained an essential goal. Now, however, the United States added economic growth and the reduction of popular misery as significant ways of achieving it. Reformist, development-oriented Latin American leaders, historian Lars Schoultz points out, had finally prodded the United States into recognizing that communism, although a dangerous "intervening force," was not the sole "root of the problem."[16] By the fall of 1960, the Eisenhower administration began to accept aid as a weapon against the threat presented by Castro's revolutionary regime.

U.S. officials, one should also note, never abandoned strategies based on force and coercion. When the Castro government negotiated an agreement to receive Soviet oil and nationalized American firms that refused to refine it, the U.S. government responded by cutting the Cuban sugar quota and starting a trade embargo. By March 1960, the CIA also began to plan the ill-fated Bay of Pigs invasion. Confident that force had worked in Guatemala in 1954, strategists displayed no hesitation to use it again. Latin American policy from that point on, however, moved along two frequently intersecting tracks. In addition to military measures and counterinsurgency, foreign aid and development became central parts of U.S. strategic thinking in the region.

By the time Kennedy took office in January 1961, therefore, Latin America had become a major arena of ideological struggle in the Cold War. A group of activists convinced that Eisenhower's rigidity had ceded major gains to the Communists, Kennedy's advisers were also determined to engineer a regional transformation in which there would be no second Cuba. As they built on the Act of Bogotá, they also radically expanded the scale and purpose of U.S. foreign assistance. It was not enough to patch up the worst instances of poverty-driven unrest. Communist inroads could only be contained with a program that would fundamentally alter the region's developmental course. Where the Eisenhower administration envisioned a limited program of economic advance and public welfare, Kennedy and his intellectual counselors would launch a massive, decade-long initiative combining objectives for political reform, economic prosperity, and even the creation of new cultural values. Where Eisenhower and his associates had finally and reluctantly turned toward "growth," the Kennedy team would speak with supreme confidence of "modernization."

In planning a Latin American initiative, the new administration thought big from the start. Ordered to make recommendations for action, a Latin American task force including Harvard economist Lincoln Gordon, New Deal veteran Adolf Berle, Rutgers economist Robert Alexander, University of Pennsylvania historian Arthur Whitaker, and Puerto Rican development experts Teodoro Moscoso and Arturo Morales Carrión declared that, during the 1950s, the United States had "claimed that private enterprise and a good climate for it and for American investment would accomplish all necessary social and economic development." Now, however, the region's chronic unrest had proved those assumptions wrong. Convinced that they confronted serious dangers of "extra-continental interference," the group reasoned that the "present ferment in Latin America, which facilitates Communist penetration, is the outward sign of a tide of social and political change the United States cannot and should not check." The key to preventing revolution, they claimed, would be a systematic, long-range plan to direct those forces "into channels that are or ought to be, acceptable as well as beneficial to the peoples involved."[17]

According to the Kennedy administration planners, that problem demanded a comprehensive approach. Where earlier Latin American proposals had focused on the details of trade and industry and the Act of Bogotá had emphasized the need for specific social development projects, Kennedy's advisers now sought a more integrated platform in which economic, social, and political change could be addressed simultaneously. The Soviet Union and China, they noted, both had well-publicized, persuasive revolutionary doctrines and could invoke Marxist principles to appeal to Latin Americans searching for ways to alleviate poverty, achieve social justice, and end political repression. "On its side," the task force lamented, "the United States has stated no clear philosophy of its own, and has no effective machinery to disseminate such a philosophy."[18] Channeling the aspirations of Latin Americans and directing the region's future, they argued, would require a new policy design and, more important, a new, appealing ideology to go with it.

Through the Alliance for Progress, modernization theory was applied to fulfill both of those needs. Theoretical, social scientific arguments about the transition toward modernity, the interdependence of social, economic, and political change, the linear path to progress, and the potential for modernization to be accelerated by American knowledge, values, and investment were all incorporated into the design of the new program. Identifying the methods for the effective infusion of capital and the promotion of new values, the alliance proposed to move "traditional" societies toward "modernity" through the simultaneous promotion of social programs, economic growth, and political reform. A concerted, large-scale effort, Kennedy planners believed, would drive Latin America out of the unstable, destitute condition in which communism appealed to desperate peoples. The "transitional period" necessarily eroded older values as populations drifted away from traditional beliefs. Through modernization, however, an "advanced" society such as the United States might supply a new system of meaning and accelerate a nation's progress down the road toward "take-off" before the Communists could disrupt that "natural" chain of events.

Accelerating the modernization process, moreover, would promote the interests of both the Latin American countries and the United States. As Harvard economist and task force member Lincoln Gordon later recalled, "Thinking in both academic and official circles had been deeply influenced by Walt Rostow's *Stages of Economic Growth*, with its conceptions of 'preconditions' and 'take-off into sustained growth.' The underlying thought . . . was the conviction that American values of freedom, responsible government, and equality of opportunity, together with American economic prosperity, would be more likely to flourish at home if they were widely shared abroad. We had benefited from the revival of Europe and Japan, and would benefit similarly from the modernization of the underdeveloped world."[19] Having helped formulate the Marshall Plan, advisers such as Gordon and Rostow now dreamed of even more dramatic accomplishments. If the United States had rebuilt the economy of Western Europe, they reasoned, why couldn't it now fundamentally transform the politics, economy, and social life of the rest of its own hemisphere? In many respects, the Marshall Plan was a poor analogy. In that case, Diane Kunz has observed, success derived from the fact that strategists "had aimed their economic weapons at economic problems that were susceptible to an economic solution. . . . Western Europe provided the ideal setting for the American approach. The governing structure, infrastructure, and labor power availability previously existed."[20] The proposed task in Latin America was a far more complex one. Kennedy planners, however, remained undaunted. Modernization, in their view, was not a matter of divisive political choices and competing agendas. It was instead part of the natural extension of an American mission to shape a world in which the ideals of liberal, democratic capitalism would serve the reciprocally reinforcing interests of all.

Latin America, moreover, appeared to be most suited to the project, and many Kennedy advisers were convinced that there were "special opportunities for accelerating development in this hemisphere." As Gordon put it, "We believed that most of the region, especially the larger countries of South America and Mexico, were on the threshold of a Rostovian take-off." There were, of course, "institutional and social obstacles, but not cultural ones such as Oriental fatalism, sacred cows, or caste systems." Much of Latin America, with growing middle classes, an industrial base, and democratic aspirations, appeared to have fulfilled many of the necessary requirements for advancement and had reached a point of historic possibilities. "All of this was in sharp contrast to most of Africa, which still lacked the preconditions for take-off, and South and Southeast Asia, which would have to overcome ancient cultural obstacles." More familiar with Latin America than previous policymakers, many Kennedy advisers were also more optimistic about the region's potential. Perceived by them as closer to the United States geographically, economically, and socially, Latin America seemed "ripe for a big push."[21]

Arthur Schlesinger Jr., Harvard historian and White House adviser, concurred with those observations. As he reported to Kennedy after a trip through the region, "Latin America is irrevocably committed to the quest for modernization." To be successful, the United States would have to assist in the "drastic revision of the semi-feudal agrarian structure of society which still prevails" and challenge both a landed oligarchy and Castro-backed revolutionaries. Though not to be taken lightly, these obstacles could be overcome. Through investment in industry, stabilization agreements for crop production, support for land reform, funding for social programs, and consistent opposition to dictatorship, the United States could win the battle. With a commitment to fight on several fronts, the Kennedy administration could engineer a "middle class revolution where the processes of economic modernization carry the new urban middle class into power and produce, along with it, such necessities of modern technical society as constitutional government, honest public administration, a responsible party system, a rational land system, an efficient system of taxation."[22] Echoing the qualities that social theorist Max Weber had emphasized as essential to capitalism, Schlesinger argued that the challenge was great but a fundamental transformation linking economic, political, and social spheres was indeed possible.

As advisers such as Rostow, Schlesinger, and Gordon all insisted that the United States could "demonstrate in this Hemisphere that economic growth, social equity, and the democratic development of societies can proceed hand-in-hand," Kennedy prepared a public statement to express his administration's position.[23] On March 13, 1961, in soaring rhetoric, the U.S. president told the assembled Latin American diplomatic corps that the Alliance for Progress would be "a vast cooperative effort, unparalleled in magnitude and nobility of purpose." By the close of the decade, Kennedy predicted, "the living standards of every American family will be on the rise, basic education will be available to all, hunger will be a forgotten experience, the need for massive outside help will have passed, most nations will have entered a period of self-sustaining growth, and, although there will be still much to do, every American Republic will be the master of its own revolution and its own hope and progress."[24] Modernization, Kennedy promised, would make the miraculous transformation a reality.

Failure at the Bay of Pigs, moreover, gave the Alliance for Progress an additional push. Only a month after Kennedy announced the alliance, anti-Castro exiles trained by the CIA at camps in Miami, New Orleans, Nicaragua, and Guatemala landed on Cuban beaches in the hope of catalyzing a nationwide movement to derail the revolution. The invasion, launched on April 17, 1961, was an unmitigated disaster. CIA pilots destroyed part of Castro's small air force prior to the landing, but Cuban planes managed to sink ships ferrying vital communications equipment and ammunition. Some of the fifteen hundred commandos became stranded when their small boats ran aground on coral reefs offshore. Others reached the beaches only to find that expected U.S. air support never came. It probably would have made little difference. The exiles quickly ran out of ammunition, never established a defensible beachhead, and suffered heavy losses fighting the overwhelmingly superior Cuban militia forces. The surviving invaders hoped to escape through surrounding swamps and flee into the mountains to continue a protracted struggle, but most of them were quickly captured. Having failed dismally in an effort to dislodge Castro with an invasion force, the Kennedy administration turned toward secret attempts to sabotage the Cuban economy and assassinate the revolutionary leader. The United States also gravitated even more strongly toward a prolonged, public effort to curtail the Cuban revolution's appeal throughout the rest of Latin America. The alliance, many strategists hoped, would deflect the humiliation suffered at Castro's hands and convince Latin Americans that genuine development could be achieved through U.S. assistance instead of revolutionary action.[25]

In the months between the announcement of the program and its formal presentation to the representatives of the Latin American nations in August 1961, Kennedy planners sought to frame a charter that would give the Alliance for Progress a resonating, ideological appeal. To hold off protest stemming from the Cuban debacle and offer a progressive alternative to the Communist revolutions it feared, the Kennedy administration attempted to craft a document that would turn Latin American aspirations in liberal, capitalist directions. During the summer of 1961, Rostow, Schlesinger, White House aide Richard Goodwin and Puerto Rican policy adviser Arturo Morales Carrión all collaborated on the draft. Putting his imprint on the document, Rostow argued that the charter should emphasize the alliance commitment to "enlist the full energies of the peoples and governments of the American Republics in the task of modernizing their social and economic life along lines of their own choice. This requires that comprehensive and well-conceived national programs for economic and social development be carried out, formulated in accordance with democratic principles."[26] Schlesinger proposed similar language. In words that assumed the right to speak for Latin Americans, he wrote that all peoples of the hemisphere needed to pledge to work "within the framework of civic freedom and representative institutions" and should "declare that, for rapid and effective benefits, sharp and profound changes must be made in the structure of our societies, changes to facilitate the process of modernization."[27]

The final version of the charter, completed at Punta del Este, Uruguay, in 1961, did not preserve the exact phrasing that Rostow and Schlesinger suggested. It did, however, make modernization its foremost goal by setting forth the fundamental objective of "accelerat[ing] the economic and social development of the participating countries of Latin America, so that they may achieve maximum levels of well-being, with equal opportunities for all, in democratic societies adapted to their own needs and desires." Impressed by a U.S. pledge to contribute no less than $1 billion in public funds during the first year and to secure $20 billion in aid from a combination of private investment and international lending over the course of the decade, representatives from all the OAS member nations except Cuba signed the agreement. The charter set a minimum target growth rate for Latin American countries at 2.5 percent per capita per year and encouraged each nation to define goals for industrialization and popular welfare "in the light of its stage of social and economic evolution." A document that firmly linked the social and economic spheres with the goals of political development, the agreement also stated that reforms had to be made through comprehensive national plans under "democratic principles."[28]

Committed to support the modernization process, the United States matched its allocation of capital with the provision of social scientific skill. To facilitate comprehensive planning, the Kennedy administration supplied "experts contracted in agreement with governments to work under their direction" to prepare investment projects, field investigations, and programs in "agrarian reform and rural development, health, cooperatives, housing, education and professional training and taxation."[29] Agents for fundamental change, American advisers were expected to analyze an entire society as an integrated unit and identify the necessary preconditions for rapid advancement. After proposals for development projects were submitted to the Agency for International Development mission in the applicant country, U.S. analysts reviewed them to determine their likely impact and relation to the nation's overall development plan. Regional "project officers" assessed financial requirements, and specialists in industry, agriculture, education, and other fields examined a proposal's specific provisions. If AID's financial and monetary committees in Washington approved, loan agreements were then concluded.[30]

While at work for the Colombian government during the mid-1950s, economist Albert O. Hirschman got a sense of just what social planners were expected to accomplish in that brave new world. As he recalled some years later, he had gone to South America interested in trying to solve concrete policy problems in local situations. His assignment, however, proved to be a different one.

> Word soon came from World Bank headquarters that I was principally expected to take, as soon as possible, the initiative in formulating some ambitious economic development plan that would spell out investment, domestic savings, growth, and foreign aid targets for the Colombian

economy for the next few years. All of this was alleged to be quite simple for experts mastering the new programming technique: apparently there now existed adequate knowledge, even without close study of local surroundings, of the likely ranges of savings and capital-output ratios, and those estimates, joined to the country's latest national income and balance of payments accounts, would yield all the key figures needed.[31]

Working for the alliance, development experts were also expected to find the key ingredients for social transformation and direct capital and technology toward them. As Alliance for Progress coordinator Teodoro Moscoso told the Senate Appropriations Committee, the new focus on "institution building" demanded far more than the mere transmission of specific technical skills. In areas such as agriculture, for example, the alliance program required "a complete reorganization of U.S. AID Missions in the field." In place of "equipment specialists, agronomists, livestock specialists and agriculture extension technicians," AID programmed "rural development officers, cooperatives advisors, chief engineers . . . economic advisors, planning officers, and program support officers."[32] As technical specialists were replaced by social science generalists, positions became more vague and aspirations for comprehensive, integrated social engineering more exalted.

Social scientific knowledge was also expected to help the United States tailor its assistance to the particular stage of development of a given recipient nation. Because not all societies had made the same amount of progress toward modernity, they would not be able to use the same types and quantities of aid. Charting their degree of advancement and determining where to spend U.S. tax dollars, however, were not presented as subjective matters. A few months prior to the start of the alliance, Kennedy's task force on foreign economic policy recommended "a forthcoming paper by Paul Rosenstein-Rodan [that] contain[ed] new estimates of total aid requirements, country by country."[33] A member of MIT's Center for International Studies and later an appointee to a panel of nine alliance experts charged with reviewing national development plans, Rosenstein-Rodan sent his article, "International Aid for Underdeveloped Countries," to the Kennedy White House several months before it was formally published. In his view, outside aid was important not to "directly raise standards of living in the recipient countries but to permit them to make the transition from economic stagnation to self-sustaining economic growth." Citizens of recipient countries would ultimately have to carry that process through, but aid could provide "a positive incentive for maximum national effort." The idea was to direct it for the "maximum catalytic effect." Foreign aid, in other words, had to be transmitted in such a way as to "increase the rate of domestic capital formation" and bring a nation toward the takeoff point.[34]

The amount of aid a country should receive, Rosenstein-Rodan explained, could be calculated on the basis of "absorptive capacity." Foreign capital and "know-how" allowed a country to increase its production and opened the way for a greater rate of savings than was previously possible. Because marginal rates of saving could be raised above average rates, more resources could be made available for investment purposes, and development could be accelerated. The problem, therefore, became one of determining the ability of a given nation to use foreign capital to generate increases in production and investment. Because "the capacity to absorb more capital is more limited on a low level of development, where a higher proportion of technical assistance must precede a large capital inflow," Rosenstein-Rodan argued that donor nations needed to categorize aid recipients on the basis of their overall position on the developmental ladder. The success of foreign assistance initiatives, he claimed, depended on evaluating comprehensive national development plans and determining which societies were ready for the push toward "take-off" and which still needed to fulfill the "preconditions" to it. "The various projects comprising a development program are interrelated and reinforce each other," Rosenstein-Rodan explained, and some nations were more acceptable targets for high levels of assistance than others. Even for those on the lower rungs of the socioeconomic ladder, however, "education in the long run and revolution of habits in the short run" could "widen the scope."[35]

Equipped with this framework, Rosenstein-Rodan claimed that the United States could estimate a recipient's absorptive capacity through three different indexes: the rate of investment increase; the deviation between average and marginal savings rates; and the recipient's "over-all administrative and developmental organization." Noting that the first two of these were "verifiable facts," Rosenstein-Rodan suggested that the third, while relying on "rough common sense rules of thumb," was by no means as " 'arbitrary' as it might seem." "Modern" observers, he implied, could easily form a reasonable opinion about the probable success of those nations still struggling to develop. There was, after all, very little disagreement "among businessmen, economists, or even average tourists" when it came to evaluating the "potential" of different nations and placing them in "a ranking order of magnitudes." To make the planning task easier, Rosenstein-Rodan included a set of tables classifying eighty-six of the world's countries on the basis of stationary, low-, or high-growth projections for the next fifteen years. Objective social science, he argued, could prove the validity of American common sense. In countries ripe for "take-off," capital-intensive foreign aid could catalyze the critical push toward self-sustaining growth. In those still inching through the lower stages, technical aid would allow recipients at least to "imitate and absorb other countries' methods of production."[36]

Administration planners took such arguments to heart. Hollis Chenery, an economist working as AID's assistant administrator for programming between appointments at Stanford and Harvard, agreed that foreign assistance could create a "community of free nations cooperating on matters of mutual concern, basing their political systems on consent and progressing in economic welfare and social justice." As aid recipients benefited from their contact with more advanced societies and attained the "sense of prestige and progress that characterize the Atlantic community," they would be able to overcome the "traditional values and lines of authority" that "often block effective use of existing resources and skills." Echoing Rosenstein-Rodan's perspective, Chenery argued that AID could key its efforts to the "current stage of development" of each recipient. In early stages, technical assistance and training personnel would be most important in developing administrative programs, providing education, and setting up credit and trade associations. As nations moved toward fulfilling the "preconditions" and gained the ability to use available resources, more infrastructure could be put in place, and AID would concentrate on "institution building" to increase domestic savings and break "bottle necks."[37]

Because U.S. foreign assistance would facilitate the passage of "traditional" societies toward the "modern" forms most clearly reflected in the West, many Kennedy planners fully expected the alliance to guide a "revolution of rising expectations" into liberal, democratic, and capitalist directions. The problem, however, was that the United States did not possess a monopoly on transformative power. As Rostow and other strategists argued, one of the fundamental dangers in the world was the possibility that, in conjunction with trade, aid, and guerrilla warfare, the Soviets would succeed in "projecting an image of Communism as the most efficient method for modernizing the underdeveloped regions and as a system closing rapidly on the sluggish American front runner." Because those nations farther down the developmental ladder were given to imitating the more advanced countries, a modern society such as the United States could produce dramatic transformations. That same factor, unfortunately, also kept the field open for the Communists, aggressors that Rostow labeled "scavengers of the modernization process."[38] American efforts, Rostow explained in a 1960 speech at Dartmouth College, would depend on whether developing countries "can successfully modernize under auspices which leave open the possibility of a democratic evolution, in association with the United States and the West or whether, in frustration and desperation, they turn to the Communist alternative which is steadily being held out to them."[39] For those looking at the world through the lens of modernization, the Cold War certainly did become a struggle for the hearts and minds of the developing world. Those hearts and minds, moreover, appeared both promisingly and threateningly malleable.

Modernization, therefore, became a battle of image and identity as much as it was one of program and policy. The stakes in Latin America, moreover, appeared particularly high. As Adolf Berle argued in a letter sent to his fellow task force members, "While the great Cold War could not be decisively won in the Latin American theatre, it obviously could be lost there, and that situation seemed to me and to most of the Committee very dangerous."[40] Cuba presented just the sort of ideological competitor that Rostow and his associates were most concerned about, and the observations made by analysts such as Richard Gardner, a Columbia University law professor and economist, profoundly shaped the framework through which the Kennedy administration interpreted the significance of Castro's triumph. The Soviets, it appeared, had managed to transform their country from a "backward peasant society into the world's second industrial power" in the space of only forty years. Growing twice as fast as the U.S. gross national product, the booming Soviet economy had progressed to the point that the "American production lead over the Soviet Union was reduced to its lowest point in history in both absolute and relative terms." Because the Soviets diverted resources away from consumer goods, lacked a substantial popular market, and emphasized noncommercial sectors that could produce only limited returns, Gardner strongly doubted that the USSR's drive would last. In the short run, however, the international damage could be substantial. The "greater rate of Soviet growth," he explained, "has tremendous psychological significance. Its effect is felt by our own people, by the Soviet people and, perhaps most important, by the vast numbers of people in the underdeveloped countries of the world."[41] For U.S. strategic planners, Castro's Cuba was more than a base for guerrilla warfare and subversion. A Soviet-supported Marxist state in the Western Hemisphere, it also presented a decidedly revolutionary approach to the problems of poverty and oppression. Considered a dangerously seductive and deviant example, Cuba threatened to lead Latin American nations away from the task of modernization, a process that, by definition, could be genuinely pursued only along liberal, nonrevolutionary lines.

In responding to what they perceived as Castro's challenge, American policymakers promoted the alliance in two related ways. The first of these involved eliminating Cuba's position in inter-American decision-making bodies and gaining a public, Latin American renunciation of the Cuban model. Returning again to Punta del Este in January 1962, a U.S. delegation made up of Secretary of State Dean Rusk, White House aide Richard Goodwin, Rostow, and Schlesinger worked to secure passage of a series of OAS resolutions. With Cuba consistently opposed, twenty of the twenty-one member nations voted in favor of a resolution declaring the Cuban government inconsistent with the "inter-American system," nineteen agreed to study Castro's subversive efforts, seventeen promised not to trade arms with Cuba, and fourteen voted to expel the country from the OAS. Although successful in gaining the necessary majorities, the United States failed to secure collective agreement on actual sanctions against the Castro government and was confronted with the fact that, on the vote for expulsion, Argentina, Brazil, Chile, Mexico, Bolivia, and Ecuador all abstained.[42] Even with alliance aid on the table, it was clear that not all of Latin America was willing to follow the U.S. lead against what Rusk called "a powerful adversary who seeks to destroy the framework of freedom we are laboriously constructing."[43] Trying to salvage a victory, however, the State Department announced that the conference "made clear beyond doubt Cuba's political, social and economic isolation from the inter-American system" and gave the alliance "even greater recognition as [the] best means [to] achieve economic and social progress essential to strengthening representative democracy in this hemisphere."[44]

A second and much more sweeping approach to the prevention of "another Cuba" involved presenting the alliance to Latin Americans as the embodiment of essential, transformative ideals necessary for all societies to advance up the developmental ladder. As National Security Council strategists warned in 1961, "The revolutionary currents prevalent throughout Latin America are quickening . . . and no man nor government is likely long to contain them. Those who would survive and guide them into constructive channels must be prepared to work with the tide rather than try to stand against it." In order to identify its program with the "adventure of creating in this Hemisphere modern societies," the United States would need to present communism as an "alien ideology," a foreign system imposed only through force and subversion. The United States would also have to portray the Alliance for Progress as rooted in "the earliest and most fundamental commitments of our national life and political system" and derived from universal, "basic truths" that were "not limited to any single nation or group of men."[45] In the eyes of Kennedy administration planners, Latin American societies, seething with revolutionary energy, were dangerously unpredictable. By emphasizing the universal validity of the modernization model and supplying "traditional" nations with a set of ideals, goals, and aspirations, however, U.S. policymakers believed that they might overcome the Cuban challenge.

Just as modernization theorists claimed they could, the Kennedy administration set out to "demonstrate" the historically verified, "modern" values that would give transitional societies a push forward. As one State Department official explained, simple anticommunism would not be enough; the United States needed to present a captivating ideology of its own. To win the struggle, the United States would have to "assur[e] the Latin American masses that they are the active participants in a genuine, democratic, effective process of development."[46] The transitional period, Rostow had argued, involved the erosion of "traditional" values of "passivity" and "long-run fatalism." Stepping in to fill the ideological vacuum, the alliance was to become the fountainhead for a new set of cultural objectives. Designed to draw the region's peoples into the active, participatory ethos that theorists associated with the modern quality of "empathy," the program was to ensure that Latin Americans accepted a body of common goals—goals most fully realized in the history, institutions, and society of the United States.

For the Kennedy administration, engineering an ideologically powerful response among the Latin American public remained a central concern. In the middle of 1963, the U.S. Information Agency (USIA) triumphantly reported that a study of seven Latin American countries proved that the "much discussed revolution of rising expectations" had been matched by a high degree of awareness about the alliance and its objectives. Substantial proportions of urban populations knew about the program, and the "overwhelming majority" of those familiar with the alliance approved of it. Most of those interviewed, moreover, expected it to achieve "a great deal of progress in the future" and believed that it would "benefit the average person." Perhaps most heartening for the alliance planners, a majority of respondents even agreed that "if the program fails in its aim to improve the standard of living, it will be their own governments, rather than the U.S., who will be primarily to blame."[47]

Those results certainly encouraged U.S. policymakers, but many of them believed that modernization would require more than Latin American approval. For the alliance to serve as a powerful catalyst, it would have to become "fused with the national ideals of each country." According to Puerto Rican governor Luis Muñoz Marín, the Alliance for Progress faced the complex task of "rousing constructively a continent, much of which has slumbered in semi-feudalism for 400 years," and "telescop[ing] the French and American Revolutions, the Industrial Revolution, and the 20th century's social revolutions into one." To meet this immense challenge, he insisted, the alliance could not be a simple "economic undertaking, a transfusion of capital and skills. To succeed, it must stir the hearts of men, it must inspire them to dream and hope . . . it must have strong ideological content." Rather than "something done for them in distant Washington," the Latin American peoples needed to believe that the alliance had been "evolved by themselves out of their own needs."[48]

Muñoz Marín's foreign affairs adviser and Kennedy Latin American task force member Arturo Morales Carrión concurred. The alliance could not be understood merely as a money-lending operation, "made in the USA" and presented in economic and technical language. It would have to be "wedded to Latin American nationalism," which "provides the emotions and slogans for political action." To ensure that the Latin Americans took the transformative, modern values embodied in the alliance as their own, the United States would have to harness a region's revolutionary potential and guide the critical transition. Because the forces of nationalism were perceived as malleable, the essential rationality of the alliance could be made the focus of Latin America's emotional aspirations. But if the Kennedy administration failed to link its modernizing agenda with Latin America's inchoate, unchanneled revolutionary fervor, Morales Carrión warned, it would be pouring its resources into a "psychological void."[49]

The administration tried to address that problem in different ways. Kennedy directed national security adviser McGeorge Bundy to organize bimonthly meetings on the Alliance for Progress and instructed him to make sure that Morales Carrión was included to emphasize "the intellectual and psychological effects" of the program.[50] T. Graydon Upton, vice president of the Inter-American Development Bank, also advised Kennedy that one of the most serious problems facing the alliance was the "mobilization of the Latin American civic spirit" and the infusion of the program with a "true national mystique." Praising the U.S. Information Agency's efforts in the bilateral field, Upton suggested that the United States fund OAS plans to form separate national committees and use Latin American media to publicize alliance accomplishments in each country.[51]

The transition to liberal, capitalist modernity was a difficult process, and, as the alliance charter stated, success would also require "self help" on the part of Latin Americans. Charged with preparing development plans, identifying projects for funding, and reforming land ownership, Latin Americans were expected to restructure their societies. Insisting that sweeping changes could be achieved within a decade and emphasizing the importance of transformations in consciousness, moreover, the Kennedy administration presented these issues less as problems grounded in the distribution of Latin American power than as matters of determination and will. Poverty, the administration implied, was not political; it was a state of mind. If the United States could find the right formula to express the alliance ideals, strategists believed it would be possible to motivate Latin America's impoverished masses and its entrenched oligarchy to pursue the collective measures necessary for their common, long-run benefit. The charter did stress the need to support democratic government, but modernization in Latin America, it suggested, was not a question of contested resources. It was instead a natural, evolutionary process that would fulfill U.S. security objectives and harmoniously serve the needs of all Latin Americans, regardless of class, ethnicity, race, or religion. As theorists and policymakers insisted, the central tasks were to keep the hemisphere free from Communist influence and find the proper means of demonstrating the value of genuinely modern institutions. The overwhelming momentum of the "take-off" would carry the process forward from there.

Yet the Alliance for Progress did more than incorporate the central ideas of modernization theory in its policy objectives and practices. It also projected an identity for the United States as an advanced nation that assisted societies striving to follow a trail blazed by its own experience. Like the older ideologies of imperialism and Manifest Destiny, modernization on the "New Frontier" defined the virtue of a benevolent United States in terms of its ability to assist peoples trapped in lower positions on a hierarchical, cultural, and developmental scale. Incorporating the ideology of modernization, the alliance emphasized America's transformative power, legitimated direct intervention in Latin American nations, and allowed policymakers and broader, public audiences to envision themselves as part of a profoundly altruistic, humanitarian, missionary effort. In the context of the Cold War, the alliance cast the United States as a nation possessing the toughness of will and depth of understanding necessary to drive a struggling region toward progress in its image.

From its first days, the Kennedy administration sought to explain publicly the relevance of its modernization efforts and continually argued that the alliance involved much more than a simple transfer of funds. As Rostow told the president, if foreign assistance was to catch the "public imagination," the United States would need to dramatize the results achieved by moving societies into the "take-off" phase.[52] Secretary of State Dean Rusk, a former Rockefeller Foundation president, agreed with that view. As he explained to the nation's press, although the new Latin American program would require "substantial amounts of what is commonly called 'aid,'" the State Department thought of the problem "less as one of aid than of accelerated development."[53] Emphasizing his administration's dedication to the idea, Kennedy himself described the initiative as an attempt to help Latin America fulfill its "drive toward modernization" through the creation of "new institutions" and "new plans." "Posed between order and chaos," societies that were passing through the "turbulent transition of new expectations" needed American help if they were going to prevail in their "long twilight struggle for freedom."[54] Foreign aid, a part of United States policy since the Truman era, was nothing new. Programs such as the Alliance for Progress, however, claimed to represent a much more ambitious agenda.

The New Frontiersmen also dedicated themselves to uncovering the valuable lessons Latin Americans could learn by analyzing the U.S. drive toward democracy, sustained development, and prosperity. Latin Americans would do well to study the strategies their northern neighbors had used to rise to the summit of modernity, Rostow told a Chamber of Commerce meeting in Mexico City. The "development of nations," he explained, "is a little like the development of human beings." Societies in the "childhood" of modernization could emulate the more advanced countries of the world. Just as it is "possible to specify in broad terms the kinds of problems which, inevitably, must be confronted by an infant of nine months; a child of five; an adolescent of fourteen; a young man of twenty-one," Rostow argued, "the study of economic development, to the extent that it can be called a science, consists primarily in identifying the sequence of problems to be overcome and the kinds of efforts to solve them which have succeeded or failed at different times in different nations."[55] Echoing earlier expressions of Manifest Destiny as well as the arguments of those favoring imperial expansion at the turn of the century, Rostow suggested that a mature, advanced society could take the hands of wayward, childlike ones and guide them into the adulthood of modernity.

Kennedy administration officials, moreover, repeatedly presented the United States as a nation that had been especially successful in meeting the universal challenges of development. Thomas Mann, U.S. ambassador to Mexico, conceded that "cultures, situations, and problems differ from country to country," but he maintained that a number of "broad economic principles, tested in practice for more than 200 years," could nevertheless be drawn from the U.S. experience. Citing a stellar record of unmatched, consistent long-term growth, increasing wages, and rising domestic purchasing power, Mann advised a Mexican audience to take note of the way the U.S. Declaration of Independence and Constitution "guaranteed" a market characterized by the "free movement of capital goods and labor." Throughout American history, Mann emphasized, private ownership, freedom for innovation, and a "competitive economy" all allowed for "individual incentive" to function as the "mainspring of progress."[56] If Latin American states were to achieve sustained growth, Mann advised, they would do well to design institutions harnessing those same forces.

Choosing a different historical point for pedagogical purposes, U.S. officials also found highly instructive lessons in the New Deal. As Lincoln Gordon argued, Roosevelt's efforts proved that economic expansion and growth could be most effectively pursued when national planning provided the safeguards necessary for free enterprise to function efficiently. By regulating the stock market, providing housing and farm insurance, instituting a system of social security, and putting vast numbers of unemployed to work on government projects, the New Deal had given the U.S. economy the structure it needed to recover from economic shocks and achieve more stable, sustained advances. As he praised a "passion to include fully in the national society certain formerly forgotten groups—the Negroes, the migratory farm workers, the marginal farmers of the South, and the urban workers not yet organized into trade unions," Gordon also declared that Roosevelt had proved that social justice and economic progress could be pursued in tandem. Less an experimental response to capitalist crisis than a bold, heroic innovation, the New Deal became an example for Latin Americans to follow in promoting their own socioeconomic reforms within a progressive, liberal framework.[57]

Above all, Gordon continued, the New Deal demonstrated that rigorous, scientifically planned social engineering could produce dramatic results. Many Latin Americans, he lamented, still considered national planning the province of "dilettantes," the sport of "part-time students of law and economics taught by part-time professors." Believing that "verbal expression" could serve as "an adequate substitute for respect for hard facts and for rigorously objective thinking," they childishly gloried in philosophical eloquence instead of systematic analysis. If Latin Americans became as realistic, rational, and tough about facing their problems as the North Americans had been, they would stop their "emotional outbursts against communist scapegoats such as foreign investors or greedy speculators."[58] The past of the world's most modern nation, Gordon and his colleagues argued, presented a model, a blueprint for hard-nosed, progressive innovation within the framework of modern, liberal capitalism. Left unsaid, but certainly implied, was Gordon's view that "development" was in many ways a problem of will. If Latin Americans would only control their "emotions," stop searching for "scapegoats," and follow the examples of their disciplined northern neighbors, he suggested, many of their problems could be overcome. All the Latin Americans had to do, he suggested, was recognize their cultural failings, embrace the tools of objective social scientific analysis, and turn to the task. Constructing an image of a Latin America impoverished culturally as well as materially, Gordon also depicted a United States that had climbed to the heights of modernity through nothing more than its own rational skill and determination.

Views such as Mann's and Gordon's echoed throughout the Kennedy administration's public statements about the alliance and the need for other societies to chart a course based on the lessons of American success. At a ceremony marking the start of a plan to provide areas of Nicaragua, Colombia, and Brazil with electrical power through rural cooperatives, Kennedy invoked the legacy of the Rural Electrification Administration and suggested that "one of the most significant contributions that we can make to the underdeveloped countries is to pass on to them the techniques which we in this country have developed and used successfully." Fowler Hamilton, AID's first administrator, agreed with the president and expected that once U.S. consultants "get this thing going in some of these countries . . . it will spread through the contagion of example, because what these gentlemen and ladies are going to take down to Latin America in their heads is going to be a lot more important than what bureaucrats carry in their pockets."[59] As he celebrated the Tennessee Valley Authority and the Civilian Conservation Corps, Dean Rusk also claimed that America's past was a vital source for "lessons of great value to the leaders of scores of nations striving to guide the economic growth of their peoples."[60] Although the transition to modernity was difficult, developing nations could look back at the historical record to imitate the successful programs great American innovators had conceived of decades before.

The Kennedy administration also emphasized the potential for the United

States to replace the "apathy" and paralyzing "fatalism" of "traditional" Latin American societies with a powerful, activist worldview. In language reminiscent of the social theory articulated by Talcott Parsons and Marion Levy, alliance coordinator Teodoro Moscoso argued that modernization would penetrate to the very core of daily social life. "The extended family," he argued, "cannot remain intact, in a single village, rural region or city neighborhood, under the pressures of a modern economy." Parents "will have a hard time retaining the respect of children who know the modern world better than they," and "men will not appreciate having their traditional authority challenged by women who earn nearly as much as they do." Larger percentages of the population, Moscoso commented, would also move into urban areas and reject traditional ways as they became "tired of waiting for that happy tomorrow, that timeless *mañana*," and demanded "a better life today."[61]

Contact with a "modern" society, as Lerner, Pye, Rostow, and other theorists argued, transformed "traditional" understandings of life as external values of discipline, respect for achieved status, social mobility, and even human empathy shook less advanced societies out of fatalistic stasis and drove them toward progress. Looking toward Latin America, Kennedy administration officials explained that the United States would have to supply more than planning techniques and material resources. As Assistant Secretary of State Edwin Martin told a University of Southern California conference, the alliance also needed to "open new vistas of opportunity to millions of people" and "prepare them to take advantage of all the new possibilities offered by modern science and technology." "Bricks and mortar and machinery are clearly only means," Martin continued; "the attitudes, values, and enthusiasm of the people are the essential substance of the program." To modernize the Latin Americans, the United States promised to bring about a radical change among peoples who remained trapped within deficient, passive, and stagnant cultures. Latin Americans, Martin argued, needed U.S. help to develop an entirely new way of looking at the world.

First of all it is necessary to accept change as a good thing, more likely to bring better things than worse. Quantitative precision, exactness in work and production schedules, careful calculation of cost advantages, all must become second nature to have a modern society. Scientific or rational habits of thought, as opposed to the traditional or emotional approach to problems is equally imperative, as are the somewhat anti-romantic virtues of neatness and cleanliness and order. . . . I am not issuing prescriptions for the good life. I am merely stating the minimum needs for a modern society with a 20th Century standard of material well-being, something all countries say they want.[62]

As Martin described it, the alliance program struck a chord close to the ones that Taylorist factories and Chicago settlement houses had sounded long before. Latin American peoples, he argued, continued to struggle within the confines of a fatalistic, "traditional" perspective. To survive in modern institutions and acquire modern living standards, they would have to adopt a system of modern values as well.

Kennedy's alliance planners believed that education and technical training would help produce a "rational" ethic, but they also emphasized the need to bring Latin Americans into direct contact with U.S. institutions. By sending Labor Secretary W. Willard Wirtz to a conference of Latin American labor leaders, the United States hoped to demonstrate the ways in which "free, democratic" unions could raise wages, increase economic growth, and give workers an active role in liberal politics.[63] Through a contract with the League of Women Voters, the administration also sought to provide Latin American women with "citizenship education." A greater appreciation of the alliance's political goals, Moscoso argued, was essential for the program to succeed. Personal contacts would emphasize the value of democratic institutions for solving socioeconomic problems.[64] The alliance also brought Latin Americans to the United States to demonstrate how local communities could promote industrial growth. As one AID publication explained, visiting businessmen from El Salvador were awed by the massive factories of Detroit and Pittsburgh but found their most applicable lessons in the homespun values of Marceline, Missouri. When they visited the small town's industrial corporation, the group was greatly impressed by the low average investment of only fifty dollars and the fact that hundreds of workers owned shares. Within thirty days of returning home, an AID magazine reported, the visitors imitated the North Americans and started their own local development company.[65]

Exposing Latin Americans to the culture of the United States, alliance promoters claimed, would help overcome "traditional" inertia and apathy. In the words of one sympathetic magazine editor, the United States could serve as the "catalytic agent which activates Latin America's enormous domestic resources, attracts private investment from abroad, [and] encourages the local governments to initiate and support sound, democratic, 'aided self-help' programs of development."[66] If the United States treated the alliance as more of a "crusade" and less of a foreign aid program, Moscoso explained to the national media, it could encourage Latin Americans to play active roles in their own societies and inspire them to push for reforms. Disseminating American values and "evangelizing" the southern continent, the United States could export the universally valid principles of its own revolution, motivate Latin Americans to protect the dignity of the individual, and set the hemisphere on the path to progress.[67]

Presented in these terms, the Alliance for Progress became a symbol of national mission, a program through which all U.S. citizens could make significant contributions to the Latin American struggle. In rhetoric that paralleled that of many administration officials, two analysts at the Stanford Research Institute argued that the people of the "underdeveloped world" needed more than American capital and expert advice. They also required "sympathetic understanding, and the opportunity for sustained contact with institutions in the advanced nations to which they [could] turn for help across the whole spectrum of development programs." By broadening the mechanism of development assistance to include state governments, local towns, and individual citizens, they insisted, America could expand its modernizing power. Built on simpler economies and smaller budgets, U.S. state governments could share their experiences in agriculture, education, and manufacturing with developing nations. Exchanges of personnel, increased media coverage, and new business agreements all promised to "involve people and institutions, on both sides, in a set of relationships that are tangible, meaningful, compelling."[68]

Determined to put such ideas into action, White House adviser Richard Goodwin told Kennedy that a cooperative program between individual U.S. states and Latin American countries could "substantially modify our entire approach to foreign aid."[69] Within several months, the United States proudly started a "Partners of the Alliance" program highlighted by agreements between California and Chile to work on agricultural problems, an exchange of experts between Oakland County, Michigan, and the Cauca Valley of Colombia, and a medical mission from Pensacola, Florida, to Chimbote, Peru. Moscoso's assistant Jim Boren declared that the "program promotes itself" and welcomed a "contagious enthusiasm" for it. U.S. citizens reached out to Latin Americans, he explained, because of "a feeling that 'this program touches the heart of what the Alliance is all about'—people trying to help one another, by government where necessary, but in person where possible."[70] As in the case of the Peace Corps, administration officials described the contributions of individual citizens as symbols of a larger sense of national mission.

In language that masked America's own imperial past, theorists and policymakers also invoked the alliance to present the United States as the world's most successful anticolonial nation. The alliance, Rostow explained, was one of the New Frontier programs that established an awareness "in the minds of citizens in both the north and the south who are gradually coming to perceive that, however painful the memories of the colonial past may be, major and abiding areas of common interest are emerging between nations at different stages of the growth process."[71] Bringing the best of modern values, technology, and institutions to Latin America, the United States pledged to engineer the transformations that a history of Iberian colonialism had failed to provide. As alliance coordinator Teodoro Moscoso explained to the House Committee on Foreign Affairs, Spanish and Portuguese colonizers had gone to Latin America to "conquer and exploit," but the United States had been settled by people who fled religious persecution and went to "live and to make a country, to build a nation."[72] With rhetoric that distanced America from its own colonial enterprises, Moscoso presented the United States as an exceptional nation willing to share both the capital and values necessary for its southern neighbors to negotiate the difficult course to long-term success. Five hundred years after Latin America fell under the Iberian colonial yoke, the United States, itself the product of an anticolonial revolution, would spread its nation-building spirit to help Latin Americans complete their own drive toward progress. Communist aggression remained a dire challenge, but the alliance would prove to the world that the United States was neither a fading front-runner nor a reactionary obstacle to the alleviation of poverty. Still a "City on a Hill," the nation would disseminate the lessons of its experience for the mutual benefit of all.

The U.S. media agreed that the program held enormous potential. Tapping the wellspring of America's ideals, allowing other societies to learn from the nation's past, and confirming a long-standing humanitarian ethos, the program promised to transform Latin America and bring out the best of the United States in the process. In a gushing report on Kennedy's March 1961 speech, *Time* called the alliance "a mission to be grasped, a dream to be realized," and celebrated the president's "high degree of sensitivity to the trends, pressures and demands of Latin America today." In the wake of the Punta del Este conference, the magazine called the quick release of $973 million in aid "convincing evidence that the U.S. intends to put its money where its sentiments are" and advised its readers that Treasury Secretary C. Douglas Dillon "himself checks to be sure that loan applications do not get lost in the bureaucratic potholes." When one U.S. official told Dillon that he was not ready to process a request, Dillon replied, "'Fine . . . 'I'll just sit down and wait for it.' The 'processing,' that is, approval, came through in about 60 seconds." Cutting red tape and hurdling organizational barriers, the New Frontier appeared equal to the immense challenges that Latin America presented. In its own welcome to the Kennedy initiative, *Newsweek* called the alliance "the most hopeful plan so far launched [by the United States] to rescue its southern neighbors from poverty and discontent."[73]

Other sources were even more effusive. In lavish coverage lasting several weeks, *Life* magazine declared that the alliance was "historic in scope" and "revolutionary in its agreed upon goals" for massive advances in education, health, agriculture, and housing. Not "just another bit of Cold War fence-mending," the program represented a depth of mutual commitment between Latin America and the United States that even Che Guevara, Cuba's romantic revolutionary hero, could not unsettle. At Punta del Este, *Life* reported, Secretary Dillon, the pinstriped millionaire businessman, "had to take vilification and sneers" from the beret-wearing Cuban, "but here too he received help—from the uncouth Che himself. At the end of a Dillon speech Che tried to stalk out. But he chose the wrong door and led his entire retinue of pistol-packing 'secretaries' into the ladies' room." Representing the Alliance for Progress as a combination of vigorous, masculine Wall Street wisdom and enlightened humanitarianism, the nation's media argued that the irrational Communists had little chance of standing in the way of U.S. achievements.[74]

Before long, however, the alliance lost its initial momentum as the promised miracles failed to appear. Only one year after Latin American leaders signed the charter, the senior editor of *Look* commented that "few great projects in recent memory have been so hopefully launched and so quickly scorned as the Alliance for Progress." *U.S. News and World Report* observed that although the program had channeled about $1 billion to nineteen different Latin American countries, "in many ways this important part of the world is worse off than it was a year ago." According to the magazine, U.S. businesses continued to perceive the region as a risky one for investment, Latin American oligarchies failed to take steps toward mandated tax and land reforms, and most Latin Americans were apathetic, skeptical, or completely unaware of the program at all. *Newsweek* reported that in the first year of the alliance no Latin American nation had achieved the target rate of

2.5 percent per capita growth. Four had managed only 2 percent, two could achieve only 1 percent, five stood "stock still," and seven more actually declined. Agricultural production failed to keep up with population, import costs continued to climb over export revenues, and the outlook for the future did not appear any brighter. Even *Life* editorialized that, one year and $1 billion after Kennedy's speech, the program was "already in deep trouble."[75]

Though slightly more optimistic, the Organization of American States also gave the alliance only mixed reviews. According to the official OAS report on the alliance's first year, more external funds were made available, central planning agencies were established, an international coffee agreement increased Latin American incomes, and the region took steps toward economic integration. At the same time, however, the OAS warned that Latin America's economic growth rate had "improved only modestly and [was] still below the long-term objectives of the Alliance." Tax and land reform measures remained inadequate, development plans lacked "a framework of realizable goals," and capital inflows were insufficient to "provide the vigorous impulse needed by the regional economies."[76] In its second-year evaluation, the OAS noted that ten nations had now achieved the charter's target growth rate. But the organization also commented, "One cannot but be concerned with the slowness with which many countries are overcoming obstacles to the profound changes in institutions, policies, and internal structures that will be necessary to make the Alliance a living reality."[77] Though capital assistance appeared to facilitate economic growth, more equitable distributions of wealth and political power still seemed distant.

Faced with mounting criticism, the alliance also became a source of growing concern for the Kennedy administration. By April 1962, Moscoso reported to Kennedy that Latin America's problems were so severe that of the $1 billion the United States provided during the first year, only $75 million went into development loans, and, of that, only $5 million went to industry. As a result of immediate economic and political crises and a lack of Latin American project proposals, the remainder had been used to fund commodity imports, provide balance-of-payments credits, and deliver agricultural surpluses, activities that did nothing to further long-run goals for the region.[78] In October 1963, Moscoso had more bad news. U.S. disbursements for the current fiscal year were only 70 percent of the previous year's level, and new U.S. private investment in the region had fallen from $428 million in 1961 to only $255 million in 1962.[79] As one internal White House memorandum explained to the president, "We have not been able to begin a real development effort in Latin America. Plans and programs have not been prepared. Our own action has been slow and cumbersome. We cannot spend the money we have and we will have a difficult time in justifying our appropriation request to Congress. And we are slowing down. . . . It can be accurately said that, as of today, not a single Latin American nation is embarked on a development program under the Alliance for Progress."[80] Plagued by low growth rates and unable to begin long-term programming, the "Decade of Development" was off to a painfully slow start.

Yet, if the alliance was in trouble, the ideology behind it was not. Even as both popular and internal sources pointed out the program's failure to meet its projected goals, dissension over the alliance and explanations for its shortcomings rarely touched the set of ideas that lay at its core. While various parties blamed the bureaucratic structure in Washington, cited the need for higher levels of foreign investment, or criticized Latin American resistance to social and political reforms, very few challenged the fundamental assumption that the United States could function as the catalyst for Latin American modernization. Rather than addressing fundamental purposes, criticism of the alliance, with a few significant exceptions, remained confined within the modernization framework and limited to issues of administration, techniques for delivering aid, or the degree to which Latin American nations were really prepared for the "take-off" they would inevitably have to achieve. Although specific means were challenged, general objectives usually were not, and, in the early 1960s, programs such as the alliance reflected the continuing power of a widespread belief that America was both called to and capable of remaking the rest of the world.

One frequently cited explanation for the alliance's lack of progress centered around the intricacies of the U.S. government's foreign aid apparatus and the weakness of its bureaucratic personnel. In a report on Moscoso's declaration that the program's first anniversary should be "marked" but not "celebrated," *Time* commented that Latin American aid requests were run through "an obstacle course of government agencies." Though in extreme poverty, a nation such as Honduras had yet to receive promised help from the United States because its applications were "gathering dust in Washington's pigeonholes."[81] The Kennedy administration also identified administrative problems. In March 1962, White House troubleshooter Bill Haddad told Kennedy that the program was "disorganized and fragmented. Pieces of the *Alianza* are in Agriculture, Treasury, several spots in State, several spots in AID, in the OAS, the [Export-Import] Bank, [International Development Bank], etc. The left hand doesn't know what the right hand is doing. The other side of the coin is the red tape and the procedures established through

[Development Loan Fund] and [International Cooperation Administration]. These are cumbersome and designed to protect anyone from sticking his neck out too far."[82] Moscoso pointed out similar problems a few months later, explaining that loan disbursements had been slowed by "AID administrative problems" and the long "lead time" in major construction projects.[83] A Bureau of the Budget study found that difficulties in Washington were duplicated in the field. Country teams were suddenly expected to "move overnight from the position of political observers—largely carrying out the reporting and representational functions of traditional diplomacy—to the role of active engagement with conflicting political and social forces." Slow to respond to the new program's demands, bureaucrats had difficulty making the "shift from the technical cooperation approach of carefully applied pilot projects and gingerly-handled advisory roles to activist administrative and judgmental activities" and were unprepared to take on a "role of hard bargaining in the most sensitive areas of national sovereignty—justice, land ownership and distribution, tax policy, military alignments and expenditures."[84]

Though flagging serious problems, each analysis presented the alliance as troubled by a discrete obstacle that, if remedied, would unlock the program's real modernizing potential. As Haddad told Kennedy, the president could "get any bureaucrat to do what [he wanted] by signing [his] name to it" and could give the alliance greater internal strength by allowing it to have a "separate image" outside the rest of the U.S. foreign aid program. Although it would take "some ramrods around Moscoso to follow through on this," Haddad remained convinced that "it can be done, can be done quickly."[85] In a similar fashion, Moscoso implied that the alliance had been hindered by working through AID in the first, "transitional year" of its creation and that the difficulties would soon pass.[86] Interpreting the problem as one of implementation rather than objectives, the Bureau of the Budget expressed a similar perspective. The central question regarding the radically altered function of the country teams was "not whether this is proper—but how well it is being done."[87]

Turning its focus toward personnel issues, the Kennedy administration only continued to analyze discrete problems in ways that precluded a reassessment of the alliance's ideological foundation. Adviser Richard Goodwin, in a memorandum written in September 1963, expressed his disappointment that "a program which is sound in conception and historically right is operating at about one-half effectiveness." Ironically condemning Washington's bureaucracy in the very terms U.S. officials used to describe Latin

American governments, Goodwin lamented a damaging "pattern of lack of imagination, daring, [and] administrative efficiency." The alliance, he argued, suffered from a "complete lack of a good recruiting effort, impossible personnel procedures, a structure which discourages individual initiative and responsibility, a careerist mentality," and an "inability to recognize mediocrity when it is seen." Because the reasons for the program's "stagnation" were perceived as administrative, setting the alliance straight did not seem to require an analysis of underlying objectives. Kennedy simply had to replace the individuals carrying it out. Admiring the Peace Corps's popular success and convinced that the alliance was "intrinsically more exciting, bigger and more glamorous" than that other New Frontier program, Goodwin insisted that Kennedy "tell [Sargent] Shriver he must run the Alianza for at least a year, get it on its feet and recruit a successor." If the Peace Corps's dynamic director was given the freedom to make "radical organizational and personnel changes," Goodwin was certain that the alliance could be redeemed.[88]

The problem of securing private investment for the alliance was also the subject of considerable public and official debate. Although they wanted foreign capital to promote economic growth, many Latin American governments were determined to avoid compromising their sovereignty by becoming dependent on multinational corporations run by U.S. businessmen. The alliance charter recommended that development plans promote foreign investment, but moves to open Latin America for U.S. business ventures were tempered by calls for social justice, land reform, and income redistribution. Determined to gain the allegiance of Latin America's reform-minded "democratic left" and anxious to avoid the resentment aroused by Eisenhower-era policies, the Kennedy administration did not provide the tax breaks or guarantees that, in Latin American eyes, might have transformed the alliance into the "entering wedge for a great new expansion of U.S. investment."[89] As Arthur Schlesinger Jr. put it in a 1962 memorandum, the Eisenhower policy "is wrong today as it was in the fifties—more so, because of the churning up of political sentiment in the intervening years. . . . If we return to the Eisenhower policy and make the creation of a 'proper' climate for investment our main objective in Latin America, we might as well kiss the Alliance—and the hemisphere—goodbye."[90]

Through the first two years of the alliance, the level of U.S. foreign investment in Latin America continued a decline that had started after the Cuban revolution. Even here, however, debates over the administration's failure to provide business incentives took place within the ideological framework used to justify the alliance itself. The United States, Chase Manhattan Bank president David Rockefeller admitted, could not force the Latin American nations to follow its lead. But "our example of a prosperous nation, operating under a system of free enterprise supplemented by government, can be an inspiration to peaceful revolution by less-favored peoples everywhere."[91] In a report echoing Rockefeller's emphasis on historical demonstration, the *Morgan Guaranty Survey* faulted Latin Americans for ignoring the merits of the U.S. example. The United States would have to take the lead in promoting the private sector because "among those [Latin Americans] doing the planning, there is little enthusiasm for free enterprise—a system they associate with its failures in their own region rather than with its successes in the U.S. . . . Traditionally in the history of economies, the rapid build-up of productive facilities has been based on uneven distribution of income, giving rise to high rates of saving."[92] Merck and Company president John T. Connor also attempted to link the promotion of the private sector with the values that Latin Americans lacked. As he put it, private investment was "the product of work and savings, it abhors irresponsibility, wastage and misuse. . . . In the midst of the current mess in Latin America, the U.S. corporation is about as comfortable as a bishop in a poker game."[93] According to these critics, successful modernization depended on vigorous private enterprise. If it was to become more than just another foreign aid program, the alliance would have to educate Latin Americans about the relevance of the U.S. example and make their traditional societies more attractive to rational, productive businesses. The question, it appeared, was not whether the United States could or should modernize Latin America. The issue was simply what the best strategy for going about it might be.

Additional attacks on the alliance and its apparent stagnation centered on the resistance of Latin American governments to calls for social, political, and economic restructuring. Writing in the *New Republic*, Alaska senator Ernest Gruening commented, "The noble concept of the *Alianza para el Progreso* is about to fail, because those in power in Latin America have not, in the great majority of cases, initiated or carried through the needed reforms."[94] Because oligarchies and fragile democracies did not fulfill their pledges to support public welfare programs and continued to stifle the forces of political opposition, many commentators argued that, instead of promoting social justice, alliance dollars were simply tightening the concentration of power within a long-standing elite. "The Alliance," *Time* reported, "runs only one way; in effect the U.S. foots the bill while Latinos drag their feet." During the program's first year the United States dispersed $1 billion, but only one-third of the Latin American nations "embarked on anything like the kind of painful land, tax and other reforms needed to reconstruct their societies." Some countries, it appeared, were "talking reform. But only a few are anywhere near the take-off point."[95]

In this case as well, both the Kennedy administration and the national media treated the problem as one of educating Latin Americans about the benefits that modernization would bring. Undersecretary of State Chester Bowles stressed the "depth and extent" of Latin American poverty and worried about the sense of "apathy" that might grow out of it unless the alliance could inspire a sense of hope.[96] *Newsweek* commented, "The sluggishness about reform and the lack of over-all planning suggest that many Latins simply don't understand what the Alliance is all about."[97] In a similar vein, *U.S. News and World Report* cited a U.S. official's argument that Guatemala failed to make reforms because its leaders did not have the "slightest idea" of what the alliance proposed: "What is wrong is that you are dealing with a society here that has a concept of mankind opposed to that of Western civilization. In Guatemala, the educated, the people of means and their children are interested only in amassing as much as they can for themselves and their families. They have no sense of obligation to the rest of society."[98]

The problems appeared serious, but, focused on cultural values rather than contested resources or class structure, U.S. planners simply attempted to instruct Latin Americans about the benefits that modernization would provide for all. Chester Bowles suggested that the matter might be remedied by making Colombia an alliance showcase. Under the democratic leadership of President Alberto Lleras Camargo, that nation seemed more advanced than most others in the region. If the United States provided enough resources to "assure" success there, it might be possible to "demonstrate to all of Latin America that a resolute, competent, reform-minded government with vigorous U.S. assistance [could] fulfill the hopes of the Alliance for Progress within a reasonably brief period."[99] Other advisers looked toward plans to "sell" the alliance in more direct ways. Transistor radios, one U.S. official explained, were common even in "the worst barriadas." "I have heard many Latin American announcers selling soap, and beer, and reporting soccer games; they do this with gusto and excitement. I think it was time the Alianza received this kind of treatment across the board."[100] A few observers advocated a tougher, more interventionist stance toward governments that failed to follow U.S. instructions. *Life* called on Kennedy to make it clear that "the reforms we have a right to insist on are essential to the progress we and the Latin Americans both desire. There is no progress without pain, but honest taxes, sound money and fair land distribution cause less pain (and more progress) than other kinds of revolution. If Kennedy is rigorous in enforcing sensible terms for his aid, the progressive businessmen, citizens and governments of both Americas can unite to make a real alliance and demonstrate that prosperity and democracy are interdependent."[101]

Other commentators agreed and suggested that the United States would have to try to increase the "political capacity" of Latin America's lethargic leadership. Yale economics professor Charles E. Lindblom explained that Latin American leaders governed with the "fundamental disability" of inadequate information regarding the state of their nations, lacked experience in dealing with competing demands, and dealt with masses that remained uncertain of their primary desires. By exploring "the problem of developing appropriate political skills in Latin America," he suggested, the United States could promote a "new style" and "inventiveness." "We might," Lindblom proposed, "try to adapt the idea—once novel, now ordinary—of the county agent to the budding young politicos in the Latin American countryside. . . . If a swarm of county agents in the United States can increase the yield of wheat, cannot a counterpart swarm, for politicians rather than farmers, raise the productivity of the Latin American grass-roots politician?" U.S. trainers could "enlarge opportunities for Latin American politicians to observe our kind of politician, to see in what respects he has attitudes, dispositions, and habits of action that they might themselves find useful."[102] The alliance concept, in these interpretations, was sound. Latin American oligarchs were not rejecting the values and objectives that the alliance presented; they were simply unaware of them, misunderstood their importance, or had not yet developed the skills to put them into practice. Because the problem was less a matter of power relations than one of education, the United States simply needed to train responsible, democratic leaders. The tightly integrated modernization process would take off from there.

There were, to be sure, instances in which domestic dissent struck at the heart of the alliance's central assumptions and liberal ideals. The *National Review* ridiculed the administration's expectation "that the problems of four hundred years in two dozen Latin American countries might be solved by the simple scheme of the Alliance for Progress." Coups in Peru, Ecuador, the Dominican Republic, Honduras, Guatemala, and Argentina only proved that "Washington's plan to socialize the region before Castro does" had led to increased instability instead of democratic development.[103] The *New Republic* criticized the alliance for trying to promote social engineering in ways that had nothing to do with meeting concrete, immediate needs. In Mexico, the editor pointed out, the United States refused to fund existing programs that provided low-cost clothing, medical care, social security, and rental housing and instead tried to "stimulate new institutions which the Mexicans have not thought of—or, to put it another way, to make the Mexicans do things they would not do unless the U.S. paid for them."[104]

Academic and intellectual voices also criticized the ideology of modernization and the way it was applied in the alliance. Challenging the idea that democracy and economic development could be promoted through the "transfers of money and services," University of Chicago foreign relations expert Hans Morgenthau argued that the United States was engaged in a "policy of make believe." Because the truly viable objectives of aid were to enhance prestige or to bribe recipients to take specific actions, the rhetoric of development only raised false expectations on the part of both donors and recipients.[105] From another perspective, economist Albert O. Hirschman wondered if there might not be "something distasteful to the Latin Americans" about U.S. claims of having produced social justice in the hemisphere. As he put it, "Receiving gifts always makes for emotional strains. But it is far less hurtful to pride and dignity to accept food and machines from the 'richest nation in the world' than to risk being beholden to it for such intangible and invaluable achievements as independence, or social progress, or cultural advance."[106]

To a large degree, however, the Alliance for Progress was bolstered by a powerful consensus that the United States could modernize a world hoping to advance in its image. Though a few insightful critics pointed out the tensions between containment and development or questioned the applicability of the U.S. experience to Latin America, most dissent was deflected by a deep popular conviction that, at the height of its geopolitical power, the United States was called to transform the "developing" world. Casting all forms of change as either advances toward or deviations from the natural, scientifically validated American trajectory, modernizers paid far less attention to concrete needs, local situations, and cultural context than what they interpreted as the crucial balance of U.S. and Soviet power. Holding up the American past as a universally valid model and dismissing alternatives that strayed too far as the product of subversion, the alliance also cast the entire problem of social change itself as a Manichaean contest between genuine, legitimate growth and hostile, foreign aggression. By the end of the 1960s, persistent violence in Latin America and disaster in Vietnam would make the limitations of that worldview clear. Early in the decade, however, few intellectuals and political advisers critically questioned claims that American nation building could define and direct the world's future.

Modernization theory alone did not "cause" the Alliance for Progress. It did, however, function as an ideology through which dangers were perceived, strategies legitimated, and national identities projected. Proclaimed as a new, enlightened attempt to secure the advances that European colonialism had failed to provide, the alliance cast the role of the United States through an imperial discourse of its own. Presenting the United States as a transformative catalyst, it reframed an ideology that resonated with the nation's previous Western expansion and overseas empire building. On the New Frontier, just as on the old, Americans emphasized their own historical road to progress and their power to define and promote movement along it. Where expansionists once claimed that Providence ordained a continental Manifest Destiny, policymakers now turned toward social science to articulate a global vision.

Promising to remake "stagnant" cultures and countries, the ideology behind the Alliance for Progress also shared strong similarities with the New Frontier's Peace Corps and the Kennedy administration's attempts to promote counterinsurgency through "development" in Vietnam. In each case, nation building under U.S. auspices linked strategic objectives, liberal capitalism, and humanitarian mission with a reconstruction of America's ability, right, and duty to chart the course of the world's "underdeveloped" regions. In the United States of the early 1960s, moreover, the arrogance of that ideology aroused little debate.

CHAPTER 4

Modernization for Peace

The Peace Corps, Community Development, and America's Mission

Perhaps no Kennedy administration program captured more intense attention and widespread, enduring enthusiasm than the United States Peace Corps. From the moment the idea of sending young Americans to serve abroad was first put forward, officials discovered that it evoked an amazing surge of undiluted fascination. In both private policymaking and public declarations, the Kennedy administration described the Peace Corps as a unique agency, a force that transcended political and strategic interests to embrace a passionate idealism deep within American culture. The volunteers, President Kennedy and Peace Corps officials explained, would live abroad for two years in conditions of hardship equal to those of the impoverished people they served. Drawn from every walk of American life, they would willingly sacrifice the comforts of their affluent society to assist countries that requested their help. They would provide necessary labor and technical skills and build bridges of friendship between Americans and the peoples of Africa, the Middle East, Latin America, and Asia. According to the minutes of one early Peace Corps meeting, the volunteers would not be "instruments or agents of the Cold War or American foreign policy" but instead "free men and women, the products of a free society sent abroad to serve and do their assigned work with such dedication that their hosts will, by this example, be brought to reflect on the nature of the society that produced them."[1] Where the Agency for International Development and the Alliance for Progress provided funding for large infrastructure projects or sent experts to evaluate development plans, Americans would now shoulder tools themselves and work alongside their hosts. Where U.S. military advisers trained foreign soldiers in the techniques needed to defeat communism by force, the volunteers were to exemplify the virtues of American society through their humanitarian deeds and democratic values. The Peace Corps, a recruiting brochure proclaimed, provided what William James once called "the moral equivalent of war." It offered an "opportunity for individual citizens to work directly with the people of other countries to provide economic, social, or educational assistance and to further the cause of peace through personal relationships and the development of mutual understanding."[2]

Popular media sources echoed those themes and treated the Peace Corps as an inspired, daring organization ready to assist societies that looked to the American past for guidance in charting their futures. Celebrating the volunteers' willingness to make personal, humanitarian efforts, the nation's media sources gave the organization effusive praise. In accounts that stressed the genuine idealism, toughness, and commitment of young Americans, they described the agency as an institution that revealed the deeply altruistic, fundamentally benevolent impulses of the United States. As the editors of the New York Times proclaimed, the Peace Corps was "surely one of the most remarkable projects ever undertaken by any nation."[3]

Some truth resides behind the heroic image. Within months of the first announcement of the Peace Corps, letters from more than twenty-five thousand prospective volunteers flooded the agency's Washington offices. Inspired by an eloquent, charismatic president who asked them "what they could do for their country," many individuals joined the Peace Corps to fulfill sincerely humanitarian aspirations in a concrete, personally meaningful way. Like many of his comrades, a volunteer sent to Ethiopia recalled that he was compelled to serve "by the enthusiastic . . . young man who had just become the leader of our country. . . . Not only did he seem to be telling the truth, but he seemed to be talking to me, and I wanted to answer."[4] The Peace Corps established programs in Ghana, Tanzania, Iran, Colombia, the Philippines, Cameroon, Bolivia, and several other countries in its first few years. The agency also sent thousands of surveyors, teachers, farmers, engineers, and nurses to fight against poverty. In some cases, moreover, the results were particularly dramatic. In Ghana, for example, between 1961 and 1991 the Peace Corps met a serious shortage of trained teachers. During that period volunteers educated approximately 675,000 people, nearly 5 percent of the national population, and decisively improved literacy rates.[5] In other cases, volunteers found their experiences deeply life enriching and returned to the

United States with a much better understanding of a foreign language and culture. "Volunteers who served in Cameroon and other African countries," historian Julius Amin explains, "helped explode some of the myths about the so-called dark continent. Increasingly, returned Peace Corps volunteers denounced the parody of African history offered by Hollywood filmmakers and missionary slide shows. They organized conferences, associations, and lectures through which they educated Americans about Africa."[6] In many countries, volunteers also established lasting friendships with the people they assisted.

Analyzing the Peace Corps at the ideological level, however, I am concerned with a fundamentally different set of issues. Rather than the motives, experiences, or contributions of the individual volunteers, I am most interested in the ideas that shaped the agency's intellectual foundation, sense of mission, and official purpose. In taking this approach, I do not mean to disparage those that served abroad, belittle their experiences, or challenge their idealism. Elizabeth Cobbs Hoffman's history of the organization quite rightly argues that the volunteers "surely were not all CIA agents or naive dupes."[7] One need not claim that they were, however, to find that the Peace Corps, at the level of its institutional foundation, was hardly a departure from other Kennedy-era development initiatives. Neither unique nor unprecedented, the Peace Corps's policy objectives and public rhetoric clearly resonated with programs such as the Alliance for Progress and the American counterinsurgency efforts deployed in Vietnam. Peace Corps director R. Sargent Shriver's argument that the volunteers were not called to "represent official American views" did not make their assignments or images any less valuable in the eyes of either strategists or journalists. Many of the volunteers undoubtedly did join the organization out of a sincere desire to help alleviate poverty, and some of them may have succeeded in that goal. Many volunteers also returned from their work abroad to participate in the civil rights movement and strongly dissented from America's intervention in the Vietnam War. But their motivations and activities were presented to the public through government and media sources in ways that they did not control and, in some cases, even came to resent. Rather than describing their experiences, a subject about which there is already an extensive literature,[8] this chapter addresses a different problem. Focusing on policy and public representations, it explores the way the Peace Corps reflected a cultural consensus that the United States was called to drive other societies toward a modernity most clearly embodied by America itself. Analyzed in these terms, the Peace Corps was hardly a striking anomaly or departure. It was grounded in a common conviction that American power could modernize a "developing" yet debilitated world.

Rather than attempting to illuminate a single, hidden reality concealed behind the official and popular discourse of the Peace Corps, this chapter treats cultural images and rhetoric themselves as worthy of serious study. Amid the strains and demands of the Cold War, a struggle in which ideology played an immense role, Kennedy's Peace Corps defined the United States as an exceptional nation, a country ready to help the "emerging" world overcome challenges that Americans had faced long before. The Peace Corps characterized the volunteers as embodiments of a national capacity to catalyze "development" efforts, and it encouraged Americans to imagine themselves as part of a uniquely empathetic, superior national community. The Peace Corps also claimed to reawaken the moral values of America's own national origins. Ministering to societies that lacked the cultural potential for nation building, officials suggested, would help America rediscover itself. The Peace Corps, like other elements of Kennedy foreign policy, defined a need and a method for the renewed projection of American power during an era of formal decolonization.

This chapter investigates the ideology of the Peace Corps in several ways. First, it evaluates the role that theories of modernization played in the design and practices of the agency. Just as they did in other Kennedy development programs, social scientists shaped definitions of the Peace Corps's purpose and potential. One of the most striking cases of the relationship between theory and policy, moreover, appeared in "community development," a particularly activist approach to reforming "traditional" societies. This interpretation also explores the ways in which the Peace Corps publicly represented America's relationship to the rest of the world and served as a cultural reference point. The volunteers, and the nature of their work, officials and media sources insisted, demonstrated a sense of national altruism mixed with hardened resolve. By modernizing the underdeveloped abroad, supporters maintained, the Peace Corps would also revitalize American society at home. Finally, this analysis places the Peace Corps firmly in the Cold War context. For the Kennedy administration, the agency provided an ideal means to defend the credibility of the United States amid challenges from Communist rivals. Like the Alliance for Progress in Latin America and the Strategic Hamlet Program in Vietnam, the Peace Corps promised to reject the legacy of imperialism. As in those other cases, moreover, the ideology of modernization reiterated some of its central values.

Kennedy's famous proposal for a federally sponsored, overseas volunteer corps drew on a concept already circulating through Washington's political corridors. In 1957, Wisconsin representative Henry S. Reuss returned from a visit to Southeast Asia concerned about America's image abroad. A volunteer corps, he suggested, would demonstrate American goodwill to postcolonial nations. It would also help repair the damage done by America's reluctance to support nationalist endeavors for fear of provoking tensions with European allies such as France, England, and the Netherlands. Part of a group in Congress that had become increasingly critical of Eisenhower's foreign policy, Reuss advocated a "Point Four Youth Corps" and secured passage of legislation to evaluate the program's feasibility. Congress allocated only ten thousand dollars for Colorado State University to draft a proposal, but Reuss's idea gained increasing publicity and credibility. Arguing that large-scale U.S. foreign aid programs often failed to improve the lives of common people, Reuss and Oregon senator Richard Neuberger also suggested that American youth would benefit from experience abroad.[9]

Hubert Humphrey, then a senator from Minnesota, also campaigned for an international service agency and introduced a bill for an "American Peace Corps," a project the liberal Democrat defined as "a genuine people to people program." "Talented and dedicated young American men," he explained, could alleviate poverty and promote peace by teaching "basic agricultural and industrial techniques, literacy, the English language . . . sanitation and health procedures in Asia, Africa, and Latin America." Like Reuss, Humphrey also distinguished between aid that went into massive infrastructure projects and the type of interpersonal assistance he believed most necessary to accelerate global "development" and demonstrate the depth of American altruism. In 1960, Humphrey made the Peace Corps idea part of his short-lived run for the presidency and, after withdrawing from the race in June, sent his files on the proposed agency to his fellow Democrat John F. Kennedy.[10]

Concerned with decolonization and the tepid American response to it, Kennedy found the Peace Corps idea an appealing one. In rhetoric that strongly emphasized American vulnerability, he had frequently lamented the U.S. failure to grasp the strategic importance of the "underdeveloped" nations. As he declared during a 1952 debate in the House, travel through Southeast Asia had opened his eyes to a dangerous threat. The region's population, its destitute conditions, and its growing political turmoil, he explained, led him to conclude that America had "concentrated its attention too much on Western Europe." "The Communists," he warned, "have a chance of seizing all of Asia in the next five or six years. What weapons do we have that will stop them?"[11] In a 1957 attack on Eisenhower's failure to criticize the French war in Algeria, Kennedy emphasized that the "challenge of imperialism" was a crucial Cold War problem. "On this test more than any other," he insisted, "this nation shall be critically judged by the uncommitted millions in Asia and Africa, and anxiously watched by the still-hopeful lovers of freedom behind the Iron Curtain. If we fail to meet the challenge of either Soviet or Western imperialism, then no amount of foreign aid, no aggrandizement of armaments, no new pacts or doctrines or high-level conferences, can prevent further setbacks to our course and our security."[12]

While campaigning for the White House, Kennedy also found the Peace Corps a useful way to combine his emphasis on anticommunism with an inspiring appeal to youthful idealism. On October 14, 1960, at two o'clock in the morning, the Democratic candidate arrived at the University of Michigan at Ann Arbor after his final televised debate with Richard Nixon. Met by ten thousand enthusiastic students, Kennedy emerged on the steps of the student union and challenged them to make direct, personal sacrifices in the Cold War struggle. "How many of you," he asked, "are willing to spend ten years in Africa or Latin America or Asia working for the United States and working for freedom? How many of you who are going to be doctors are willing to spend your days in Ghana; technicians or engineers, how many of you are willing to work in the foreign service and spend your lives traveling around the world? On your willingness to contribute part of your life to this country will depend the answer whether we as a free country can compete."[13] In a speech at the immense Cow Palace hall in San Francisco on November 2, 1960, Kennedy refined that appeal and linked it to an assault on the American diplomatic corps. Eisenhower's foreign service, he claimed, was riddled with poorly qualified ambassadors and pinstriped dilettantes. Condemning their ignorance of foreign languages and cultures, Kennedy declared that Republican appointees and State Department officials were losing ground to highly disciplined teams of Soviet technicians, doctors, and teachers "prepared to spend their lives abroad in the service of world communism." The United States, Kennedy argued, would have to match the Soviet drive with the skills, determination, and benevolence that characterized American citizens, with a "peace corps," largely made up of "talented young men and women" but open to all qualified "Americans, of whatever age, who wished to serve the great Republic and serve the cause of freedom."[14]

To define the Peace Corps and its mission, the Kennedy administration also sought the advice of several prominent social scientists and built on their proposals. In the annex to a 1951 report on ways to communicate with citizens behind the "iron curtain," faculty and administrators at MIT had recommended that the State Department start an international program of "face to face contact." Robert S. Morison, a Rockefeller Foundation executive who participated in the MIT study, advised "the recruiting of a group of American youth willing and able to spend two or four years of their lives in intimate personal contact with the village people of Asia." "If they were the right sort of representative Americans," he explained, "they would also make use of their position to transmit almost automatically American ideas of cooperation in the common job, respect for individual dignity, and the free play of individual initiative."[15] After his election, Kennedy himself consulted the leading experts. In a letter to Walt Rostow, he asked the economist to speak with his MIT colleague Max Millikan and requested that they "take on the responsibility of working up a Peace Corps idea into something I could implement in the winter of '61."[16] The Kennedy planning team also solicited a memorandum from Professor Samuel P. Hayes, a former Mutual Security Agency executive and director of the University of Michigan's Foundation for Research in Human Behavior, an institution that conducted social research for government operations.[17] With the funds secured by the earlier Reuss legislation, Maurice L. Albertson, Pauline E. Birky, and Andrew E. Rice of the Colorado State University Research Foundation also delivered a preliminary report on the possibility and potential contributions of a national Peace Corps.

Though differing over the operational details of the proposed agency and divided over whether the United States should coordinate its efforts with the United Nations, Millikan, Hayes, and the Albertson team all invoked theories of modernization to define the Peace Corps's central purposes. In each case, the social scientists emphasized the need to accelerate "development" and assist peoples trying to imitate America's historical accomplishments. Each of the various authors also identified the common, primary deficiencies that the Peace Corps would have to remedy in the "underdeveloped nations." The first of these problems, cited repeatedly, concerned the absence of technically skilled personnel. As Max Millikan argued, satisfying that need would have important strategic ramifications. "Many of the underdeveloped countries engaged in active programs of modernizing their political, social and economic life," he explained, "confront over the next two or three decades serious shortages of educated and trained people. . . . This gap in available skills could be at least partially filled and the modernization of these societies, so critical to their stability, accelerated if they could make use of substantial numbers of people from developed countries. . . . That this is a vital U.S. interest because of its contribution to a peaceful and orderly international community is a fundamental premise of current American foreign policy."[18] By providing technically trained workers, the United States could assist the "underdeveloped" nations through a crucial "bottleneck" to further growth and bring them one step closer to "take-off." If the Peace Corps could shorten the period of instability created by the erosion of "traditional" society, it would help deny the Communists an opportunity for subversion. Like other instruments of U.S. policy, the Peace Corps would help produce a world in which liberal democracies, able to serve popular needs and compatible with American strategic concerns, would emerge and be strengthened.

In a preliminary report that echoed Millikan's analysis, the Colorado State team also went beyond it. The volunteers could demonstrate the value of advanced techniques and labor patterns to enlighten their hosts. Like Millikan, Maurice Albertson and his coauthors emphasized that "the primary objective of the Youth Corps is to assist in accelerating the process of economic and social development in the less developed areas of the world." The authors added, moreover, that, "young American adults will transmit, through actual operational participation, technical information and skills from higher policy and technical levels."[19] As he considered the problem of agricultural production in *The Stages of Economic Growth*, Walt Rostow had suggested that advances in the "transitional nations" were limited "mainly [by] the size and competence of the pool of technicians willing and able to go into the countryside to demonstrate patiently the advantages of the newer methods."[20] The Peace Corps, the Colorado State group argued, would help solve that problem.

The lack of technical knowledge, moreover, was only one of the barriers to modernization that a Peace Corps could overcome. American volunteers, social scientists argued, could also transmit their personal knowledge of the modern world's challenges and pass on problem-solving experience to peoples who lacked it. As Samuel Hayes explained, many of the "social needs already facing our country are likely to face the underdeveloped nations as their own modernization, industrialization, and urbanization move forward. Already, in the great cities of Asia and Latin America, and to a lesser degree, in Africa, these needs are making themselves felt."[21] A strong advocate of an international youth service under United Nations auspices, Hayes recommended that the program send participants from all countries to work in both "developed" and "underdeveloped" areas. In his proposal, however, he implied that volunteers from "modern" societies would possess a degree of insight and relevant experience lacking in others.

The final version of the Colorado State report, though not completed until months later, insisted that American volunteers would have a particularly strong impact on the "less-developed areas of the world." In addition to transmitting production technologies, they would also "carry with them a typically American quality of knowing how to organize for effective action." Because the "emphasis on 'do-it-yourself'" was a "deep and lasting current in American life," the volunteers could remedy cultural deficiencies abroad. As Albertson and his associates explained, impoverished, fatalistic societies needed far more than instruction in specific industrial or agricultural skills:

> Our people have a tradition of being "self-starters," people who know how to size up a situation and organize effectively to handle it. We absorb this "organizational ability" in our school and community life and even young Americans normally have had experience in organizing to get a job done. Yet this quality is one which may often be lacking from peoples emerging from other culture patterns and paternalistic outside rule. The desire for the fruits of change is there but the ability to face a situation, analyze it, formulate a plan of action, and follow through is poorly developed. This ability constitutes much of the art of successful "institution building"— the creation of the governmental, educational and industrial institutions on which the continuing progress of the new society will depend.[22]

As they defined American society in opposition to the cultural shortcomings of the recipient nations, the administration's academic consultants reiterated the principal assumptions behind modernization theory. Not merely the beneficiaries of historical circumstance, America and the industrialized West enjoyed an advanced status and an inherent superiority. Through contact with a "modern" culture, those mired in stagnant societies might grow in the enlightened image of those who assisted them.

Shortly after entering the White House, Kennedy asked his brother-in-law, Sargent Shriver, to head a task force on the Peace Corps. A Yale graduate and World War II veteran, Shriver had built Joseph Kennedy Sr.'s Merchandise Mart from a small industry to a massive corporation, served as president of Chicago's board of education, and played an instrumental role in recruiting talent for the new administration. Kennedy also expected he would be an ideal Peace Corps director and sent his brother-in-law copies of the academic reports for use in planning the agency. Racing to get the Peace Corps under way, Shriver selected Harris Wofford, Kennedy's campaign adviser on civil rights, and Warren Wiggins and William Josephson, two officials working for the Far Eastern Bureau of the International Cooperation Administration, to assist him. Rather than starting with a small pilot operation, they decided the Peace Corps should aim for a large-scale impact. Wiggins had helped administer the Marshall Plan, and, along with Josephson, he was convinced that only a major volunteer initiative would capture public imagination at home and abroad. The Peace Corps, they agreed, should consider sending several thousand Americans overseas in its first twelve to eighteen months.[23]

As Shriver and his colleagues created the new agency, they framed a proposal that mirrored many of the previous scholarly assumptions. Like the social scientists, the New Frontiersmen shared the underlying belief that the Peace Corps could address both structural and cultural failings in the host nations. In addition to supplying "technical helpers" to meet the "shortage of skilled manpower," the volunteers would work in "personal partnership" with their hosts on projects to eradicate malaria, promote personal hygiene, improve irrigation, purify water supplies, and construct low-cost housing. They would also fill needs for schoolteachers and transmit vocational and engineering skills. Those contributions, however, would provide more than trained labor. As Shriver and his associates argued in one draft of their report to Kennedy, volunteers would also help build "viable nation-states." They would "stimulate dormant communities to undertake self-help programs," and "the psychological effect of having young Americans working in rural areas" would motivate urban elites to venture into the countryside and become involved as well. Engaged in a process that would transform indigenous worldviews, the volunteers would provide a renewed sense of purpose for nations in danger of straying from the correct developmental path. "With independence," Shriver and his colleagues insisted, "nationalism, which provided a unifying force, must be replaced with those efforts that will give it meaning—the creation of stable and self-reliant families . . . communities capable of withstanding the stresses of modern life . . . forward-looking and socially-conscious governments in modern democratic societies." In Latin America, the volunteers would supply "that intangible but essential element of participation in the present and hope for the future which is the keynote of political stability." In Asia, they would play a role in answering "the great question" of "whether through the democratic process the pace of development is adequate to satisfy the peoples' aspirations and bring nations fully within the twentieth century or whether these nations will turn to Draconian force as applied in China." By sharing practical knowledge and democratic ideals, Americans would supply the vision and experience that "lesser-developed nations" lacked. The volunteers, according to Shriver and his staff, would help countries modernize—they would combat a subversive ideology that foreclosed the possibility of genuine, liberal progress.[24]

On March 1, 1961, only a few days after Shriver delivered his recommendations, John F. Kennedy established the Peace Corps by executive order and supplied $1.5 million from his discretionary funds. The new organization, he declared, would draw on America's "immense reservoir of dedicated men and women willing to devote their energies and time and toil to the cause of world peace and human progress."[25] Applications for service quickly flooded the agency, and popular enthusiasm for it ran high. By March 6, the Peace Corps had received more than forty-five hundred letters of inquiry, and polls showed overwhelming public approval.[26] Shriver also made personal visits to Burma, Cameroon, Ghana, Guinea, India, Malaysia, Nigeria, Pakistan, and the Philippines promoting the Peace Corps and trying to line up agreements from foreign leaders to receive American volunteers. Along with his deputy Bill Moyers, he proved an equally determined lobbyist in Washington and met with nearly every member of Congress to secure approval for legislation establishing the Peace Corps on a permanent basis. By the end of August, the first party of American volunteers arrived in Ghana at the invitation of President Kwame Nkrumah. In mid-September, Congress formally approved the Peace Corps Act by a wide margin and appropriated $40 million to support it.[27]

From the start, the Peace Corps attempted to prepare its volunteers for a modernizing mission. By the middle of 1961, twelve thousand potential recruits had completed long questionnaires explaining their education, employment experience, and specific skills. Using an IBM mainframe computer, the Peace Corps staff sorted through 4.2 million different pieces of information about the growing applicant pool and put eight selection boards to work reviewing folders and checking five references for each eligible candidate.[28] Applicants also took a battery of standardized tests, were personally interviewed, and went to university campuses for two months of classes on the host country's language, culture, and the process of global "development." "Area Studies" courses, the Peace Corps Division of Training explained, were designed to provide the volunteer with "an empathy that is the prerequisite of continuing learning," and volunteers often completed a "World Affairs" unit emphasizing "the requirements of a viable political system" and the "aspirations of the new nations." Instructors also assigned works such as Stanford economist Eugene Staley's *The Future of Underdeveloped Countries*, Walt Rostow's *The Stages of Economic Growth*, and *The Emerging Nations*, a collection of essays published by MIT's Center for International Studies. Lest recruits misunderstand the gravity of their modernizing task, an amendment to the Peace Corps Act required the agency to teach them how to combat the "philosophy, strategy, tactics and menace of communism."[29]

At a government-sponsored conference titled "Peace Corps and the Behavioral Sciences," the agency also invited academic theorists to analyze volunteer training. Before an audience assembled in the State Department auditorium, A. A. Castagno of the City University of New York suggested that "political science can be utilized by those who, like the Peace Corps, are seeking to maximize their performance in developing societies." According to Castagno, recent intellectual efforts to "provide uniform theoretical categories for analyzing the dynamic political changes occurring in Africa, Asia, Latin America and the Middle East" made it possible to classify the political systems of the world. In "developing areas," he explained, "cultural fragmentation," "socialization to the particular," the "gap between constitutional intent and constitutional practice," and "the absence of a large middle class" presented serious problems for those concerned with "integrating the new nation along the pattern of Western states." But texts such as Gabriel Almond and James Coleman's *The Politics of Developing Areas* could enlighten the situation. Although volunteers would face challenging "psychological adjustments" in "societies very different than their own," the new "functional theory of politics" would provide "an objective framework" for understanding the host country and their role as "agents of change." Scientific analysis would enable volunteers to make sense of their personal and subjective encounters. It would also allow them to identify needs and remedies that the indigenous themselves failed to perceive.[30]

In a paper similar to Castagno's, James H. Stone of San Francisco State University pointed out that a scientific, comparative framework would encourage volunteers to move beyond "descriptive methods" that, "casually or traditionally employed, are at best accumulative, and at worst fragmentary." As Stone insisted, "the choice of behavioristic conceptual categories, instead of traditionally humanistic qualities, as ordering instruments derives from the nature of the Peace Corps mission." "Neutralized conceptual categories" drawn from comparative studies had been "technically refined by encounters with the difficulties arising when relatively exotic or primitive societies are scrutinized by sophisticated outsiders." Armed with a rigorous conceptual framework, the volunteers would be able "not only [to] compare an underdeveloped region with present-day America or Europe, but to compare it with another America—the underdeveloped, colonial or post-colonial America of the past."[31] The volunteers, according to Stone, came from a society that was unquestionably superior to the ones they were sent to assist. But modernization theory would allow the Americans to bridge the cultural gap. It would give them an objective, scientific way to understand the foreigners and their evolutionary distance from the United States. If they traded descriptive categories for analytical, functional ones, volunteers would begin to perceive the historically static, native society as one that might, with their assistance, begin the long journey toward the American apex.

Peace Corps training also defined the essential qualities of the country that the volunteers represented. The agency's guide for American studies courses encouraged instructors to consider "the major social problems confronting America" and suggested that trainees discuss "civil rights, school integration, [and] housing discrimination" along with "delinquency, family disintegration, mental health, slums and crime." Despite such problems, however, training manuals still presented the United States as a singularly successful nation. In contrast to the apathy, fatalism, dictatorship, and fragmentation repeatedly cited in descriptions of the "underdeveloped" nations, the "uniquely American qualities of character" included "the shared convictions of democracy, equality, freedom, pragmatism, localism, materialism, association, and individualism." The goal of the American studies unit, a Peace Corps training guide explained, was to give the volunteer "a rather clear conception of himself as a representative American." In the event that volunteers remained uncertain of the transformative values they possessed, the Peace Corps would clarify the matter for them. Service as a catalyst for modernization, the agency insisted, required nothing less than that kind of self-understanding.[32]

Peace Corps trainees received a wide variety of assignments. In its first four months, the agency announced projects that sent volunteer geologists, surveyors, and civil engineers to Tanzania to build roads, provided English teachers for public schools in the Philippines, placed high school science instructors in Ghana, and staffed health clinics on the West Indian island of St. Lucia. By 1964, the Peace Corps had trained almost seven thousand volunteers and sent them to forty-four different countries. Volunteer work included building schools, introducing new methods of livestock breeding, demonstrating higher-yield crop varieties, providing medical care, and instructing farmers in the use of machine tools.³³ Because the organization was engaged in such a wide range of tasks, Peace Corps practices resist easy generalization.

Of all the different Peace Corps assignments, however, "community development" provides the clearest example of the way the agency's leadership sought to produce dramatic, institutional change in host nations. Volunteers working in community development were expected to do more than meet an immediate, concrete need in an impoverished setting. Their assignments also required them to alter local social life and accelerate modernization at the town or village level. Community development projects, in this sense, were more ambitious than many other Peace Corps programs. They also provide an excellent opportunity to analyze the way the agency categorized deficiencies within the recipient cultures and authorized correctional interventions on the part of the United States.

Community development work was also a particularly useful assignment for the Peace Corps's programming division. Early declarations of the organization's purposes stressed the need for volunteers to fill a "middle-level manpower" gap in "developing countries." Volunteers would labor in skilled positions between the scientific expert and the unskilled native. Most countries requesting American volunteers also asked for trained specialists and professionals. Nigeria and India, for example, requested skilled, experienced workers in agriculture, medicine, and industry. Peace Corps officials tried to recruit candidates with experience in occupations such as nursing, farming, or engineering and placed advertisements in trade publications and farm journals. But their efforts generated little in the way of results. Even a fifteen-thousand-dollar contract between the Peace Corps and the United Auto Workers yielded only a half dozen volunteers. Older professionals in technical fields, the agency determined, often had dependent children or financial obligations that made service unfeasible. Younger applicants with some technical training, many of them right out of high school, lacked what Peace Corps officials considered a necessary maturity. The vast majority of the candidates approved for Peace Corps service, therefore, were what the agency referred to as "B.A. generalists," individuals who held a college degree but lacked the specific training or professional employment sought by the host nations. In the Kennedy era, B.A. generalists outnumbered other applicants by a wide margin, and by 1965 they made up more than 70 percent of the applicants invited to Peace Corps training.³⁴

Confronted with that situation, however, the Peace Corps never considered scaling back its size or its ambitions. As a senior staff member later recalled, the organization quickly became "firmly, though always unofficially, committed to a policy of building the overwhelming number of its programs around the liberal arts graduate."[35] While the majority of the generalists were assigned to teach English or other basic subjects, the Peace Corps channeled many of them into community development, an assignment that demanded "leadership abilities, practical experience, and a sensitivity to human values" but did not require a specific skill.[36] Interestingly enough, officials had especially high expectations of what generalists could achieve. As Kennedy declared, all volunteers were capable of giving the "underdeveloped" nations "a hand in building a society, and a glimpse of the best that is in our country."[37] Characterized as embodiments of America's participatory ethos and faith in the ability to improve one's environment, the generalists appeared perfectly suited to what the Peace Corps's *Second Annual Report* called the task of "awaken[ing] people to the possibilities for progress."[38] Generalists, simply by virtue of being Americans, could transform "traditional" worldviews.

Between 1961 and 1965, about 30 percent of all Peace Corps volunteers worked on community development assignments.[39] Though most heavily concentrated in Latin American countries, community development, often referred to as "CD," was promoted in several African and Middle Eastern nations as well. Definitions of the practice varied, but all centered on the common assumption that volunteers in rural and, occasionally, urban CD projects could stimulate a shift in indigenous worldviews. As one Peace Corps brochure explained, CD involved "teaching democracy on a community level; encouraging the people to work together—a new idea for most of them—to solve their own problems. . . . The results that show take the form of schools, roads, wells, gardens, aqueducts and latrines. But . . . the results that don't show are even more important—a community's realization that it can help itself."[40] According to the minutes from one of Sargent Shriver's early staff meetings, community development was more than a "baby public works program." It was "not merely the solving of one or a series of specific sanitation or agricultural problems but, more important, the awakening and continuing development of the community as a community and as an area of democratic cooperation."[41] Peace Corps trainers instructed community development volunteers to stimulate a new, participatory ethic, establish a sense of common needs, organize collective action, and assist the peasantry in carrying out a "self-help" plan. At the start, community development was expected to organize local initiatives using local resources. After volunteers trained the villagers, communities could petition public agencies for supplies and services.

As practiced in the Peace Corps, community development promoted a form of social engineering, a process necessary for nation building to proceed. Advancement toward liberal, democratic forms depended on the fulfillment of attitudinal, cultural "preconditions" as well as material ones. Like technical skills, moreover, the perceptual framework required for "underdeveloped societies" to develop could be passed on through the process of "demonstration." By promoting community development, the volunteers would stimulate isolated villagers to think of themselves as part of a larger, national entity. They would create and control a sense of progressive, activist nationalism and guide a desperate, drifting people through the turbulent period in which "traditional," essentially local cultures inevitably eroded. Richard W. Poston, "Coordinator for CD" at the Peace Corps Training Center at the University of New Mexico, explained that community development was "concerned with the task of molding a society in such a way that self-determination, the exercise of social and political responsibility, civic initiative, cooperation, and united community effort for problem-solving purposes can and will become established as prime values by which the patterns of behavior of the mass of the population will be shaped and directed." After progress was made at the local level, much larger purposes would also be pursued. In Poston's formulation, "Increased political stability and national unity are brought about by linking up this local development effort which is being made by the people in communities throughout the nation with the nationwide development plans of the national government."[42] By supplying a new set of values and giving the poor a sense of identification with larger political structures, the volunteers were expected to channel a "revolution of rising expectations" into participatory, nationalistic forms that, instead of lending themselves to totalitarian deviations, would contribute to the long-run goals of consensual democracy.

To define this attempt at cultural programming, the Peace Corps also constructed an image of the "traditional" peasant or lower-class urban worker that stressed both passivity and malleability. In a paper commissioned by the Peace Corps for training purposes, Harvard University business professor and former assistant secretary of state George C. Lodge argued that community development could remedy long-standing cultural impairments. Using Panama's Veraguas Province as a case study, Lodge did not locate the primary causes of the region's poverty in its exploitation by an elite, landed oligarchy or the impact of international, structural forces. The root of the problem, he argued, lay in the fact that "the mentality of the campesino presents many impediments to his development. His lack of skills, not only agricultural and technical, but also in decision-making, can be viewed in terms of the information he gathers, the conceptual system into which it is fitted, the skill with which he makes decisions, and the value systems by which options are chosen." Because the campesino believed that God directs "every aspect of existence while man only lives out his destiny," Lodge found him afflicted with an "all-pervasive apathy" and characterized him as a "hapless wanderer in a socio-political void." Like others applying modernization theory to define the mission of the Peace Corps, Lodge suggested an approach that made a careful, detailed examination of a region's politics, history, and economy appear unnecessary. Eschewing these contextual elements and employing the category of the generic "campesino," he simply measured the distance of his subject from an abstract set of "modern" ideals. Lost in the "void" that Lodge creates, the "campesino" has no real culture or society of his own. The Peace Corps, and the United States, must provide one.[43]

Other analyses of the Peace Corps's mission also constructed an image of the peasant or urban migrant based less on material poverty or the forces of systematic exploitation than on assumptions that the "campesino" was intellectually, ethically, and cognitively retarded. Frank Mankiewicz, a Peace Corps representative for Peru who later became director for Latin American programs, told a staff colloquium on community development that volunteers commonly worked in settlements in which "there is no one indigenous to the town who has anything to say about how his economic, political or social system is run." Such pervasive apathy, Mankiewicz continued, was deeply internalized: "Rorschach tests given to lower-class people in Latin America . . . show that the subjects see men without hands or feet, which psychologists say indicates that a man believes that he himself is powerless, and his neighbors are powerless, to do anything about their environment. People talk about themselves as *abandoned* or *forgotten*. . . . They have lost the belief that they can accomplish anything for themselves. They wait dully for someone to do something for them, for the abandoner, the one who 'forgot' them, to return, to remember. But alas, he never existed."[44] A California journalist with strong convictions about civil rights, Mankiewicz had helped organize farm workers, protested school segregation, and worked for the NAACP and the Anti-Defamation League before joining the Peace Corps.[45] Once engaged in the modernizing mission, however, he, too, accepted its assumptions and employed its pejorative rhetoric. Echoing Rostow's description of the "traditional" person as afflicted with "long-run fatalism," Mankiewicz invoked psychological analyses to characterize the recipients of Peace Corps assistance as intellectually paralyzed and hopelessly devoid of all initiative. Because they came from societies thought to have been static for centuries, members of the Latin American "lower class" were considered incapable of taking independent steps to improve the quality of their lives. Utterly helpless, the destitute individual Mankiewicz described only wallowed in self-deception and denied responsibility for his situation.

To prepare these "traditional" peoples for the challenge of modernization, Peace Corps officials argued that community development programs had to penetrate to the roots of the individual and community psyche. They had to find a remedy for what Kirby Jones, operations officer for the Peace Corps's Latin American division, called "the poverty in men's minds." Peace Corps volunteers, Jones and others believed, were excellent instruments for that task. Models for emulation, the volunteers represented a society that was radically different from the one they assisted. They also carried a culture that would "demonstrate" the power of purposeful, planned action. As Jones explained, "Just as Americans are conditioned to take the initiative, to respect the law, and to believe almost naively in man's limitless possibilities, Latin-Americans are conditioned to the opposite. They tend to be disrespectful of authority, fatalistic concerning their future, dubious of their ability to control their destinies, suspicious of neighbors, desirous of any power or status symbol of their own, reluctant to attempt anything new, and blindly hopeful that something or someone will pull them out of their situation." By organizing communities, the volunteers were not just fighting material destitution. They were also stimulating a "changing of attitudes," teaching a debilitated society "the skill of collective action," and empowering a people to meet its own "felt needs and wants."[46] Like Mankiewicz, Jones entered the Peace Corps committed to positive change. As a twenty-three-year-old volunteer, he had assisted physicians in the midst of the American invasion of the Dominican Republic. When U.S. involvement in the Vietnam War deepened, he also joined activist Allard Lowenstein's attempt to organize a letter-writing campaign against the war and presented a petition bearing the signatures of eight hundred former Peace Corps volunteers to Lyndon Johnson.[47] Even Jones, however, endorsed the demeaning vision of the "traditional" world presented by an ideology of modernization.

To establish a methodology for community development, the Peace Corps drew heavily on structural-functional analyses to identify cultural deficiencies and the levers for change. The agency also specified a step-by-step procedure for social engineering. First, volunteers were to survey the population, material assets, lines of authority, family structures, and economic relations in the community to which they were assigned. Basing its "holistic approach" on techniques developed by consultants from Michigan State University, the Peace Corps emphasized that volunteers should view the community less as a collection of individuals and more as "a system made up of interrelated components and functions which provide the means for procuring, preparing, allocating and utilizing resources." By analyzing local institutions, technology, attitudes, and natural resources, the volunteer was expected to map "linkages and flows of materials, energy, people and information." Peace Corps instructors advised trainees to consider the factors of kinship, education, economics, politics, religion, recreation, and health in a community census categorizing each individual and physical structure in the settlement. Though difficult at first, in time CD workers would learn effective sociological techniques to perceive "systems and their relationships."[48] B.A. generalists, after a few months of practice, were to marshal their social scientific training to develop a diagnostic view, an objective, comprehensive analysis of a community's subjects and social lives.

After evaluating and modeling the life of a settlement, the volunteer then intervened to remedy the "deficiencies" he or she identified. Like the task of conducting a survey and census, this next step also demanded an ordered, social scientific approach. The volunteer first demonstrated the effectiveness of a "democratic framework" by calling together the inhabitants of a community and encouraging them to discuss their needs and problems collectively. Because many villagers would be unfamiliar and uncomfortable with gatherings in which they were encouraged to speak freely, volunteers needed to be very careful at this stage to "determine whether a voiced desire is indeed a true need and want." The locals, Peace Corps officials warned, might simply offer answers they thought the Americans would want to hear. By correlating these expressions with the objective data derived from the earlier survey of the community, however, volunteers could help the group identify its authentic necessities.[49] James Moody, the Peace Corps operations officer for the Near East and South Asia, argued that it was at this stage of "implanting new ideas" that volunteers helped "awaken villagers to the possibilities of change." "Recognized as having valuable knowledge by virtue of having lived in an advanced, mechanized society," Americans could use the respect naturally accorded them to bring the community together as a whole and break through centuries of passivity and fragmentation.[50] Through this type of "agitation," as one adviser put it, the volunteer would make the campesino "clearly aware of a need which is more compelling than his fears, his doubts, his conditioned hopelessness and indifference."[51]

Once the group identified its genuine needs, the volunteer then promoted institutions to mobilize the "passive" population. In Colombia, for example, volunteers working with counterparts from that nation's development agencies were to "move into a *vereda*, or village, discuss problems with the people, suggest a meeting, and help organize a *junta* (civic group) to decide which problem—a road, a school, an aqueduct—is most urgent. . . . The next step is forming a central coordinating *junta* composed of representatives of each *junta* from the dozen or more villages of the municipality."[52] Instructed to teach democracy from the grass roots up, the volunteers instituted elections for community officers and tried to build "the right kind of organization and civic attitude."[53] As consultant George C. Lodge put it in a most curious choice of words, this type of organization transformed the campesino into "a useful receptacle for material and technical inputs" and fostered commitment to a new group identity.[54] According to the Peace Corps's leadership, the volunteers, representatives of the world's most democratic culture, could create new forms of social organization. They could promote nation building by encouraging provincial peoples to conceive of themselves as part of a larger national body, a society organized along the same lines as their village.

With a new structure of democratic, local authority in place, the volunteer finally brought the community in touch with "subject matter specialists" and started cooperative actions. By helping the newly established village government contact health workers, land surveyors, and agricultural assistants provided by either the Peace Corps, AID, or the host government, volunteers were to promote an entirely new way of looking at the world. In Colombia, a Peace Corps official explained, volunteers were "helping villagers carry out cooperative action to build school houses, raise chickens, spray orchards, dig new wells," and "construct village roads." Impressive as those results were, however, the most important gains were neither financial nor material. Where it did not exist before, Americans stimulated "hard work, initiative, and imagination."[55] Cultural catalysts, the volunteers were to confer the benefits of Western progress on peoples who lacked the values and attitudes to achieve those transformations themselves. Representatives of America, they were to accelerate the modernization process.

As some Peace Corps officials described it, moreover, the results were nothing short of miraculous. Jack Hood Vaughn, the agency's first regional director for Latin America and Shriver's eventual successor as head of the Peace Corps, told a most dramatic personal story. A self-described "Latin lover since 1938," Vaughn held degrees in Latin American studies from the University of Michigan and had worked for both the United States Information Service and the International Cooperation Administration. As Vaughn explained to a group of Peace Corps staff, he was stationed in Bolivia during the 1950s, and his most recent assignment in that country had ended in 1958. During his last six months there he had found himself "reluctant to go up on the high plains near Lake Titicaca to hunt and fish because of the menacing hostile attitude of the Indians. They were all armed, they seemed resentful, didn't speak Spanish, and didn't care." On a return trip to five villages in the same area in 1965, however, he was utterly amazed by what he encountered. "In all five," he marveled, "I was carried into town on the backs of the Indians who wanted to show me that they were in the human race. They had all built a new school, the first school in a thousand years. They had a clinic for child deliveries, the first clinic in a thousand years. They all had potable water piped in, and they had done it themselves. They had made more physical progress in a couple of years than they had made in the previous thousand. But more important was the attitude, the openness, the willingness to look you in the eye and tell you about who they were and what they had done, and the pride and self-respect of citizenship." The work of Peace Corps volunteers, Vaughn declared, had produced the stunning turn of events. "What the Spaniards and the Incas and the Western miners and the diplomats and the AID people couldn't do in a thousand years, the Peace Corps had helped to do in about three years. This is real revolution."[56] Once perceived as a foreign intruder, the American had become a triumphant hero.

Vaughn's claim to modernizing success was anecdotal, but social scientists argued that the impact of community development could also be objectively verified. Much the same way that sociologists Alex Inkeles and David Smith did in constructing an "overall modernity" scale, the Peace Corps used quantitative indexes to defend its claims of social engineering. As one brochure proclaimed, the agency's intuitive belief in the power of community development was "recently supported by science." Cornell University anthropologists, through a two-year study of Peruvian villages, had determined that "young Americans fresh out of college with only three months of training can have a significant and lasting impact on developing societies." Using a "development scale" that evaluated political and social services, forms of recreation, and commercial activity within a community, the anthropologists assigned the capital of Lima a "perfect" score of 100 points and measured the relative distance of rural communities from that mark. In an analysis that surveyed fifteen settlements with volunteers and five without, the study determined that the Peace Corps had transformed "traditional" worlds. Chijnaya, a village supposedly "founded in large part by a Volunteer" when repeated flooding forced peasants to flee their lakeside homes, started with a score of zero but ended with a total of 21. Such increases on the development scale were not seen in urban settlements, but even there "existing institutions were substantially reinforced by Volunteer efforts." "Excluding the cities," the Peace Corps claimed, "communities having Volunteers advanced 3.47 times as rapidly as villages not having them."[57] Disappearing beneath the quantitative analyses of change, the deeper questions of how ideas of "progress" and "modernity" were defined never came to the surface.

The Peace Corps also developed methods to evaluate the transformative impact of specific community development practices. Using "control groups" in which there was no volunteer contact, the agency suggested that factors such as the "relative efficiency of communication" between peasants before and after a Peace Corps project could be calculated through a quantitative ratio. If the Peace Corps volunteer wanted to assess the effect of starting a weekly town meeting, for example, she or he could multiply the number of persons informed of a given idea at a meeting by the number of individuals making comments about it later. A volunteer would then divide that figure by the product of two other factors: the number expected to know about an idea prior to a meeting and the number who made comments about it at that time. If significantly larger numbers knew of an idea and commented on it after a meeting than before it, the value of the ratio would be high, and the satisfied volunteer could rest assured that the efforts at community development were successful. Peace Corps training programs also suggested measures of a town meeting's impact on the percentage of a village "organized," the number of "emerged leaders," the number of "persons aware of community action," and the quantity of "different problems articulated by members of the community." Other "before and after" measures could be taken to suggest the relative distribution of income, levels of capital investment, gross economic product, mortality rates, infection rates, literacy rates, hours of instruction, amount of reading done, and attitudes expressed about the United States.[58]

By repeatedly calling attention to the "empirical" data used to evaluate the specific impact of community development programs, Peace Corps attempts to prove that "CD works" diverted questions about inherently subjective goals with the techniques of a purportedly objective, scientific method. Behind the indexes used and compared, the potential for Americans to transform a society and guide it down a liberal, transitional path to become more like the United States remained unquestioned and unevaluated, as did the more fundamental concept of modernization itself. Accepted without question as an inevitable, inherently appealing result for both the United States and the host nations, signs of success in producing "development" only confirmed popular expectations that a powerful, benevolent America could intervene directly in the cultural life of other societies for the mutual benefit of all.

As in the case of the Alliance for Progress, deeply rooted confidence in America's modernizing potential also blinded policy planners to signs of failure and evidence of serious problems. In many areas, volunteers found themselves frustrated by vague job descriptions and uncertain of just how to apply abstract community development theory to a specific situation and context. According to former Peace Corps deputy director Brent Ashabranner, volunteers instructed to engineer dramatic social transformations often fell into despair at their apparent inability to start worthwhile projects or provide any meaningful service at all. Peace Corps evaluators, moreover, estimated "CD job frustration in certain countries running as high as seventy-five percent." Some of these dismayed volunteers eventually chose to resign. As Ashabranner recalled, "Often a volunteer was simply dropped into a town, village, or urban slum and told that he was to be a catalyst for community cooperation and action. How he did it was up to him, though he did have his CD theory about how to motivate people into juntas, agree on their common needs, and band together to help themselves or pressure the government into giving them their fair share of goods and services. He had no clearly defined job that the people could understand and no technical skill to apply if he found one. . . . The casualty rate among these free lance volunteers was very high compared to the rest of the Peace Corps."[59] The problems were most commonly reported in Latin America, but evidence from other parts of the world was similar. In Cameroon, historian Julius Amin has concluded, community development "was a failure. . . . During the twelve-week training program volunteers took voluminous notes on development theories. Also, they were taught techniques in surveying and construction. But once in the field, they discovered that they were ill equipped and ill prepared for the task. They never fully understood the terrain and village conditions in Cameroon. They were neither trained surveyors nor draftsmen nor architects. The volunteers were B.A. generalists without any experience in community development, and in such work, they found themselves in limbo."[60]

Many volunteers eventually discovered that they could be effective only by rejecting the community development approach altogether. As Fritz Fischer's history of the Peace Corps reveals, B.A. generalists often entered settlements only to find that the locals already possessed many collective institutions and resisted attempts to reorganize their social practices. Though living alongside their hosts and making new friends, volunteers despaired of generating the "revolutionary" progress that official community development doctrine called for. Realizing that complex local cultures were neither easily understood nor readily malleable, many volunteers ultimately discarded grand social engineering in favor of specific work using whatever concrete, practical skills they could acquire. Instructed to awaken "fatalistic" traditionals to the power of modernity, they instead chose such tasks as teaching music or helping to plant crops. They also rejected the charge to reprogram societies in favor of efforts to learn what they could from those around them. In Fischer's terms, "The real development in community development became the development of the volunteer, rather than that of the host country."[61]

Despite such results, Peace Corps officials were slow to respond to the signs that community development often defied their expectations. Instead of reevaluating their assumptions, they held fast to their understanding of the volunteer as the purveyor of transformative American values and institutions. In Ashabranner's words, "The evidence was abundant that the Peace Corps's community development programs were in trouble. But the agency did not slow down to let its staff program assignments more carefully and to learn from what was happening. Instead, it hurled thousands of B.A. generalist volunteers, like infantrymen storming a beachhead, into its own murky and ill-defined version of CD."[62] To question the practice of community development, Peace Corps administrators would have had to face the possibility that inexperienced, unskilled Americans were not capable of suddenly altering other societies in profound and even revolutionary ways. They would also have had to question the validity of modernization itself. Like most Americans in the early 1960s, they failed to do that.

In the ideological contest of the Cold War, the Peace Corps effort was also believed to have serious strategic significance. Described as incarnations of the American character or embodiments of uniquely American qualities, the volunteers were expected to demonstrate the benevolent power of the United States to "developing nations," Cold War adversaries, and domestic audiences as well. Characterized as enduring hardship, making sacrifices, and applying the nation's founding values, the volunteers were also invoked to prove that, despite apparent foreign policy setbacks or social ills, the United States still remained an ideal model for the rest of the world. In both official and popular discourse, the Peace Corps put forward a vision of confidence, an American identity defined by strength, vigilance, and vitality.

Many senior U.S. officials looked at the Peace Corps as a valuable weapon in what Kennedy called a "long twilight struggle." The president himself told Secretary of State Dean Rusk that Guinea's Sekou Touré had given Sargent Shriver a "completely enthusiastic" reception. Encouraged by the fact that "Ghana has accepted 50 to 70 Peace Corps volunteers" and "Guinea is asking for 40 to 60 road builders and engineers," Kennedy went on to speculate, "If we can successfully crack Ghana and Guinea, Mali may even turn to the West. If so, this [sic] would be the first communist-oriented countries to turn from Moscow to us."[63] Shriver, though determined to send volunteers only where they were invited, understood the strategic relevance of the Peace Corps in similar terms. After meeting with volunteers assigned to community development work in Latin America, he informed his brother-in-law that "ten days ago the leading Commie in Colombia returned from Moscow accompanied by 280 Colombian students he had taken on [a three] months['] tour of Soviet Russia." "Therefore," Shriver argued, "to make a real dent in the Colombian situation we should plan on 500 [volunteers]."[64] On the Cold War battleground, the Peace Corps was expected to make powerful contributions of its own.

U.S. government rhetoric and popular literature also made the Peace Corps a national symbol by depicting the volunteers as individual reflections of a vital and superior society. In a May 1, 1961, speech before the Peace Corps's National Advisory Council, Kennedy pointed out that the eight thousand applications for service ranged "through the whole spectrum of our culture and our skill. Doctor, farmer, mechanic, typist, teacher, engineer, student—all have asked to work with their fellow men against poverty, disease and hardship." Writing to Congress in July 1963, the president invoked the same theme and explained that the volunteers "have been warmly received because they represent the best traditions of a free and democratic society—the kind of society the people of Africa, Asia and Latin America long for as the ultimate end of their own revolution."[65] Regardless of background or profession, the volunteers were assigned a common mission, to share the highest values of the culture they embodied with those desperate to emulate the United States.

The Peace Corps's own rhetoric also emphasized that the volunteers would reshape host societies simply by virtue of their experience as representative Americans. As the Peace Corps's *First Annual Report* declared, "The Volunteers came from the cross section of American life. They are of every race, creed and religion. . . . Before they joined the Peace Corps, they lived in every state of the Union and Puerto Rico. . . . They were truck drivers and college professors. . . . They are old and young." Peace Corps director Sargent Shriver made a similar point by explaining, "We come simply to contribute our skills. . . . And the fact that we do this tells us something about the United States. It gives us a clue to the basic characteristics of the American people."[66] For Shriver and many other Peace Corps administrators, those "characteristics" centered on an altruistic, energetic citizenry ready to share the benefits of American civilization. Volunteers would help poor nations find the keys to modernity and progress that the United States had discovered long ago.

Peace Corps advertisements also appealed to potential recruits by claiming that service abroad would give them a chance to demonstrate the attitudes and insight woven into their nation's fiber. As one early ad trumpeted, "You will help to build, to measure, to cure, to teach, to give the fruits of what you know. You will receive the friendship of your hosts and the enrichment that arises from intimacy with another culture. You will stand in the eyes of the world as examples of the moral purpose that established the United States and now guides its course in world affairs." The most significant contributions volunteers could make centered less on the transmission of technology than on the propagation of essentially American attitudes. Quoting an "Indian official's" assessment of what a volunteer might bring to his country, another pamphlet emphasized the importance of "ingenuity, initiative and dedication, not only because he would not have been a Volunteer had he not had these qualities in ample measure, but also because there is the underlying assumption that it is these qualities . . . that have contributed to the making of modern America."[67] Agents charged with leading the rest of the world to a future modeled on the American past, the volunteers could make the most of an inherent, intuitive grasp of their nation's transformative ideals.

Descriptions of America's superior values appeared throughout the media's coverage of the Peace Corps. The volunteers, a popular *Science Newslet-*

ter argued, were valuable to poor nations simply because of their experience with basic American institutions and culture: "The qualities needed cannot be taught in a few weeks. They must arise out of our parents, homes and schools throughout the land." Americans, it appeared, did not require technical training or advanced degrees to solve the problems of the "underdeveloped" world. They only needed to carry their outlook and way of life into the wild. Daniel Lerner's sociological definition of "empathy" as a most "modern" quality was clearly paralleled by Sargent Shriver's explanation that volunteers drew on their own culture to awaken "the deep chords of common hope and principle which belong to all men."[68]

Symbol of a society powerful enough to fulfill universal aspirations, the Peace Corps also perpetuated impressions of the distance between America and the nations still mired in the transition. Like many modernization theorists, Kennedy emphasized that the Western tradition reflected unique advantages. In addition to sending engineers and nurses abroad, the Peace Corps also sent English instructors, men and women teaching a language that "opens up all of the great cultural, historical [and] judicial areas which have become identified with the *Anglo-Saxon world* and which are so vital in these difficult days." In a similar fashion, Sargent Shriver quoted General George Marshall to describe a revolution of "the little people all over the world" who are "beginning to learn what there is in life, and to learn what they are missing." Those at the top of the development ladder, in terms of both economic and physical stature, would fulfill the duties of noblesse oblige and share the benefits of their culture with those clinging to the lower rungs.[69]

Those expressions also hardened a common understanding of cultural and racial differences popularized by works such as *The Ugly American*, a best-selling novel published in 1958. With a story set in the mythical Southeast Asian country of "Sarkhan," William J. Lederer, a naval officer, and Eugene Burdick, a political scientist at the University of California, Berkeley, described a pitched battle to win hearts and minds away from Soviet influence and propaganda. They also used a "factual epilogue" to launch an attack on the bloated, pinstripe diplomats of the cocktail set and called for a "small force of well-trained, well-chosen, hard-working and dedicated professionals." Popular enough to run through twenty printings, later paperback editions stated on the cover that "President Kennedy's Peace Corps is the answer to the problems raised in this book."[70] Homer Atkins, hero of the novel, uses a bicycle pump to build a mechanism for rice irrigation and, in a burst of down-home American ingenuity, solves a problem that had perplexed the Sarkhanese for centuries. Atkins's logical reasoning and problem solving contrast strikingly with the primitive culture of the natives. The savvy American colonel Edwin Hillandale, modeled after U.S. counterinsurgency expert and CIA agent Edward Lansdale, makes the difference explicit by explaining the peculiarity of the "Asian mind." "The key to Sarkhan and to several other nations in Southeast Asia," he declares, "is palmistry and astrology. All you have to do to learn this is walk along the streets and look at all the occult establishments. The men who operate them are called doctors and they're respected. There are chairs of palmistry and astrology in every Sarkhanese University and the Prime Minister himself has a Ph.D. in occult science."[71] American practicality, scientific reasoning, and know-how stand out strongly against the construction of Asian superstition and submission to forces beyond human control. Just as modernization theory did, official explanations and popular accounts of the early Peace Corps emphasized the rational and "modern" over the emotional, fatalistic, and "traditional." Because the cultural divisions were visible to all, Americans could easily discern their virtues in sharp contrast to the "underdeveloped world" that required their assistance.[72]

The image of the Peace Corps also helped counter domestic social criticism. Postwar affluence enabled the United States to achieve the world's highest living standards, but many commentators and intellectuals of the late fifties and early sixties pointed to the debilitating effects of bureaucratic organization and hedonistic consumption. In books that lamented an erosion of American independence and masculinity amid the numbing material comforts of corporate life, William H. Whyte and Paul Goodman argued that the nation's adolescents would grow up in a society that afforded them few opportunities for genuinely challenging, meaningful experiences. Written in a similar vein, sociologist David Riesman's *The Lonely Crowd* identified an emerging "abundance psychology capable of 'wasteful' luxury consumption of leisure and the surplus product" and criticized the rise of anxious, "other-directed" personalities that conformed to social standards out of an overwhelming psychological need for approval. John Kenneth Galbraith's *The Affluent Society* analyzed related problems in an economy that, amid increased advertising, surplus wealth, and artificial, created need, had shifted from producing "more food for the hungry, more clothing for the cold, and more houses for the homeless" to satisfying only the "craving for more elegant automobiles, more elaborate entertainment—indeed for the entire modern range of edifying and lethal desires." As Galbraith wryly observed, "Among the models of the good society no one has urged the squirrel wheel." Troubled by what they perceived as the decay of the Protestant ethic and a weakening of "rugged individualism," influential voices suggested that prosperity had done grave damage to the American character.[73]

Influenced by those works, as well as the writings of philosophers such as Albert Camus and Jean-Paul Sartre, many serious young Americans envisioned the Peace Corps as an alternative to the perceived hollowness of mainstream, middle-class, suburban life. Work abroad, many volunteers believed, might provide them with an independent, fulfilling challenge and a measure of existential validation. Seeking to aid a humanitarian cause, many recruits anticipated Peace Corps service as a personally meaningful action.[74] In the hands of the agency's officials and the nation's media, however, those issues took on another cast. By presenting an image of the volunteers as willing to live in relative poverty, empathize with the "primitive," and finally return home to rejuvenate the life of their own society, government and media interpretations moved far beyond the sense of individual, private commitment. In its place, they projected a larger image. Where many individuals hoped that Peace Corps service would allow them to define themselves, the U.S. government and media used the agency to define Cold War America as a whole.

Kennedy, Shriver, and the Peace Corps leadership emphasized volunteer sacrifice to cast the United States as a uniquely tough, hardy, and determined nation. On signing the executive order that created the agency, the president noted, "Life in the Peace Corps will not be easy. There will be no salary and allowances will be at a level sufficient only to maintain health and basic needs."[75] In an article for *National Geographic*, Shriver pushed that fact toward a larger conclusion. Like Kennedy, he praised the volunteers for having "given up all opportunities to live comfortably at home. They go into distant countries to work for mere subsistence pay under difficult, sometimes hazardous conditions. They have found more meaning in service than in the easy life." Their work, moreover, made a profound statement to the world about the United States: "Nothing is more astonishing to people abroad than to see young Americans choosing to leave America . . . to share their lives. . . . The first law of Volunteers seems to be: The rougher it is, the better we like it. Their chief complaint has a reverse twist: Things are 'too easy.' "[76] Saluted for exposing themselves to disease, living in poverty, and leaving comfortable homes and careers behind, the volunteers were invoked to define an America that survived threats, took worthwhile chances, and proved itself capable of meeting Cold War challenges. Quoting the words of a veteran British geologist, the *Peace Corps Volunteer* reported, "These youngsters are really showing Africans what Americans are really like. They have what we call 'guts.' They can take the bush, a harsh taskmaster."[77] In public discourse, the Peace Corps symbolized a determined nation tough enough to meet the Communist challenge throughout a dangerous, postcolonial world.

Popular expressions occasionally gave the martial fitness of the volunteers an even more elaborate, romanticized treatment. On November 28, 1963, only days after the assassination of President Kennedy, Sargent Shriver took to the field during halftime at a National Football League game in Detroit, Michigan. In a ceremony that substituted the rugged volunteers in place of the usual gridiron heroes, marching bands formed the words "Peace Corps" while "one hundred fifty selected coeds" presented the flags of the nations in which the volunteers served. Finally, the musicians played the "Peace Corps Song," a tune composed by Wayne State professor Graham T. Overgard in honor of "Stalwart men" who "serve and care, Building Peace for all to share."[78] In a report on the challenges endured at the Peace Corps training center in Puerto Rico, *Time* proclaimed that, "regardless of their age," the volunteers "slid down sheer slopes by rope, learned to stay afloat with their hands tied behind them, jogged on three-mile runs," and "bivouacked overnight in a rain forest." As one recruit related to the magazine, their preparation was no less rigorous than that of other cold warriors: "We had some Puerto Ricans convinced we were training for the next assault on Cuba." Volunteers, readers learned, walked eight miles from their homes to teach in backcountry schools, traveled eleven hours to cover eighteen miles of rough Ghanaian road, and took mineral surveys in a region where natives murdered a scientist for "conjuring up evil spirits." They bundled up at frigid Andean villages, carried kits "containing an antidote against the deadly bite of the *fer-de-lance* snake," and confirmed that they, and the nation they represented, were hardy enough to meet any Cold War challenge. Even in the "underdeveloped" world, the United States would not shrink from the contest.[79]

Expressions of gratitude on the part of those assisted reinforced the sense of America's modernizing mission. In Lederer and Burdick's *The Ugly American*, Emma Atkins, the hero's wife, uses her bedrock practicality to show the primitive Sarkhanese peasants how to prevent back pain by lengthening their broom handles with mountain reeds. Over the centuries, it seems, the natives never quite solved that problem, and, in a fawning letter, the village headman tells Emma, "You showed us a new way to sweep. It is a small thing, but it has changed the lives of our old people. . . . We have constructed a small shrine in your memory. . . . We thank you and we think of you."[80] Emma's insight does more than transform Sarkhanese life; it also makes her an object of worship.

Many Americans understood the Peace Corps in similar terms. In February 1962, Arthur M. Schlesinger Jr. informed John F. Kennedy that, on a visit to a village schoolhouse south of Madras, he had discovered a photo of the American president "enshrined underneath the Mahatma." "I do not think this was a phoney for the purpose of our visit," he explained; "the picture of you looked far too battered for that."[81] In a similar episode, Sargent Shriver wrote that, on his last day in office as Peace Corps director, he learned that "the citizens of Gonbad-e-Kabus, in far-off Iran, had built a monument to Barkley Moore, the Volunteer who brought the town its first public library. In five years, I have come to expect such things, and yet I still find it amazing—a monument to a Peace Corps Volunteer there in the heart of Asia, only 32 miles from the Soviet border."[82] Descriptions of a volunteer schoolteacher in rural India as "one of those decently motivated, young Americans who turn up so often in the Peace Corps and who make you feel that there has got after all to be something good about us" solidified the image of a profoundly benevolent society.[83] Offerings of thanks by the recipients of aid reinforced those impressions, and a worker from the Dominican Republic told Sargent Shriver and the American public exactly what they expected to hear when he stated, "I have learned more in ten months working with this Volunteer than I have learned in thirty years."[84] Those reaping the benefits of Peace Corps help, official and media accounts related, were justifiably and uniformly grateful for America's modernizing impact. As Senator Albert Gore told Sargent Shriver when the Peace Corps director appeared for confirmation before the Committee on Foreign Relations, "It seems to me that one of the great values of the response to the [Peace Corps] idea and ideal is that it demonstrates to ourselves once more and to the world once more that we are an altruistic people, that our people respond overwhelmingly to a good cause."[85]

The demonstration of American fortitude and empathy, moreover, was set firmly in the context of anti-Communist anxiety. During the Cold War, as Elaine Tyler May has pointed out, U.S. officials and media sources often cast the Soviet Union "as an abstract symbol of what Americans might become if they became 'soft.' Anti-Communist crusaders called on Americans to strengthen their moral fiber so that they might preserve their freedom and security." The speed with which the Soviets acquired atomic technology, the launching of *Sputnik*, the "loss" of China, and Castro's victory in nearby

Cuba all seemed to point to an American inability to confront the Soviet challenge. The setbacks to containment, politicians such as Joseph McCarthy insisted, had less to do with a lack of American military resources abroad than a waning of national resolution at home.[86]

Before domestic audiences, foreign allies, and Cold War opponents, the Kennedy administration responded to such concerns by repeatedly invoking the Peace Corps as part of a renewed American commitment. Sargent Shriver, speaking at the University of Notre Dame's commencement ceremony, directly linked the Peace Corps to the crucial issue of U.S. credibility: "The Communists say that America has gone soft. Only recently Khrushchev branded American young people as 'dissident good-for-nothings.' On my recent trip around the world, I encountered serious doubts about the ability of Americans to make the sacrifices essential for the Peace Corps or any other program of voluntary service abroad. The one big question seems to be is America qualified to lead the free world?"[87] Through their depictions of the Peace Corps volunteers and their modernizing power, Shriver and his staff responded with a resounding affirmative. Americans, they insisted, were indeed willing to "pay any price" and "bear any burden" to win the Cold War.

Rugged, determined volunteers were to match the relentless, ascetic drive of those bent on Communist expansion throughout the "Third World." As Shriver told the press after returning from a tour of South America, "A high-ranking Venezuelan summed up our problems. . . . He said of the Communists: 'We think they're sleeping, but they're not. We like to eat good dinners and drive Cadillacs, but they don't care about anything like that. They care only about working with the people. They know how to talk and act and they're effective . . . very effective. They're working all the time.' "[88] In response to that danger, the volunteers would promote democratic empowerment. They would, as Shriver's assistant Bill Moyers explained, "display a side of America which it is important that the developing nations see. They will bring with them the energy and enthusiasm which will give the lie to Khrushchev's charge that ours is a spent society. They will show by their work and their willingness to adapt their mode of living that ours is a nation whose material well-being has its well-spring in our spiritual fiber. The volunteer will exemplify our nature."[89]

The early Peace Corps enjoyed tremendous popularity. Shortly after its creation, organizations ranging from the AFL-CIO to the Veterans of Foreign Wars and the Methodist Board of Missions endorsed the agency. The Senate passed the original Peace Corps Act by a nearly two-to-one margin, and the

House followed with a bipartisan approval of 288 to 97. In 1962, the Senate doubled the Peace Corps appropriation without a single dissenting vote, and the House concurred with an overwhelming 316 to 70. Congressmen across the spectrum from Barry Goldwater to Hubert Humphrey threw their support behind it, and a 1962 Gallup poll reported that fully 74 percent of the nation's public approved of the Peace Corps's performance. As the organization's director of public information informed Sargent Shriver, "Publicity regarding all aspects of the Peace Corps activities has been lavish. . . . About 98% of the newspapers stories have been favorable."[90]

There were, of course, a few dissenting voices. The Daughters of the American Revolution, from its own unique perspective, fretted that "Peace Corps idealism" might "lead to disaster" by separating "inexperienced youth" from the "moral and disciplinary influences of their homeland." A few critics argued that the Peace Corps was approved without a serious assessment of its effectiveness, that it ignored the need for private enterprise in the "underdeveloped nations," or that it sent volunteers overseas without sufficient training.[91] Volunteers themselves, challenging the agency's leadership as well as the tenets of modernization, pointed out the failings of the Peace Corps. Criticizing poorly defined job assignments, their lack of specialized skills, and the exaggerated claims of "hardship" and "sacrifice," they also rejected the image that the agency created for them. As an editorial in a volunteer newsletter in Borneo put it, "The Peace Corps we saw lavishly portrayed in slick posters, pamphlets, brochures, and magazines was that of new frontiersmanship, individualism in the raw, silhouetted surveyors striding into Tanganyikan sunsets. . . . Well, this is not the total story. . . . Somebody had better point out that riding a bus in Borneo is just about as exciting as riding a bus in Middleburg, USA." A survey of 250 returned volunteers by the Peace Corps's research division determined that they "dislike being pictured as heroes, building schools with their bare hands while facing physical hardships in faraway lands. . . . The emphasis, the Volunteers contend, should be on the routine, the boredom, the humdrum fighting for maximum effectiveness."[92] In time, some returned volunteers would also be radicalized by their experiences and play leading roles as critics of the war in Vietnam.[93]

For the most part, however, the public and institutional ideology of the Peace Corps, grounded in a broad understanding of America's duty to modernize and thereby improve foreign societies, remained largely unchallenged. As a 1961 editorial in the *Economist* pointed out, "To vote against the Peace Corps Bill will look like voting against American youth and American idealism." Ira Mothner, senior editor of *Look*, was even more perceptive. The

Peace Corps, he explained, was a success "because we just couldn't bear for it not to be. The Peace Corps is our dream of ourselves, and we want the world to see us as we see the Volunteers—crew cuts and ponytails, soda fountain types, hardy and smart and noble, spreading the word to the heathen host."[94]

That appealing "dream of ourselves," moreover, was one with a deep ideological resonance throughout American history. While claiming to replace the legacy of European imperialism and associating America's own anticolonial revolution with the struggles of the "new states," public representations of the Peace Corps also reiterated apologies for imperial expansion and placed the agency's work in the context of the previous century's missionary efforts. As it promised to supply the necessary values and attitudes for "underdeveloped" regions to advance, the early Peace Corps also identified a "culture of poverty" that American social reformers had long condemned among "deviant" groups at home and abroad. As historian Eric Hobsbawm has explained, states attempting to define the "membership of groups, real or artificial communities," may often "invent traditions" that "establish continuity with a suitable historical past."[95] For the Kennedy administration and the nation's media, the Peace Corps served as a means to "reinvent" America's imperial history. Public discourse about the agency also raised questions about the limits to membership within the world's most "modern" nation.

Supporters of the Peace Corps placed its objectives in the context of a historical tradition of American benevolence overseas. Speaking in defense of the Peace Corps Act in the summer of 1961, Senator Jennings Randolph of West Virginia claimed that "it is appropriate that the Government of the United States take the lead in this field." At the end of the Spanish-American War, Randolph continued, the United States had "launched a modest experiment" in which many American soldiers remained in the Philippines, "going to the villages . . . living in the little one-room schoolhouses where they taught" and increasing the strength of "American-Philippine friendship."[96] In 1962, the Peace Corps informed Congress of its own proposal to send English teachers to the Philippines. The project, the agency's official presentation stated, was important for reasons beyond those of increasing the number of citizens speaking that nation's "language of culture, commerce and government." According to the Peace Corps's report, the "special relationship between the United States and the Philippines places an additional responsibility upon the U.S. to assist the Philippines towards rapid and effective development within a democratic framework. The Philippines is a showcase for American activity and assistance in the Far East."[97] Modernizing the Philippines and teaching English as the language of "culture," the Peace Corps suggested, only continued a long pattern of historical intervention that was entirely benign.

Other Peace Corps advocates compared the service of the volunteers to the spirit of dedication and sacrifice they identified in a past of Christian missionary activities. In lectures first delivered at the University of Pennsylvania in 1961, British historian Arnold J. Toynbee heralded the Peace Corps as "a new lay missionary army" and charged the volunteers with the task of "winning esteem and good will for America" in the same way that their resolute, nineteenth-century predecessors had.[98] Charles J. Wetzel, a Purdue University history professor, echoed that argument by explaining that the Peace Corps was part of a tradition in which "American servants of God have carried their message in ever widening circles, and with them they have taken the growing knowledge and technical skills of the American people."[99] Princeton University historians Richard Challener and Shaw Livermore Jr. also placed the Peace Corps in the context of an American commitment to voluntary and missionary service. The Peace Corps, they explained, reflected a long-standing belief that "we have a duty and obligation to enable others to enjoy the American way of life. . . . What gives basic momentum to the Peace Corps is the undeniable fact that, in the last instance, the underlying tradition of American foreign policy is idealistic."[100] According to many Peace Corps proponents, by sending citizens out to reform the "developing" world in America's image, the United States would act in accordance with the humanitarian, even spiritual mission that had always motivated U.S. policy.

In none of these lines of argument, moreover, did the subject of America's own imperial past rise to the surface of discourse. Attempts to relate the Peace Corps to the national past instead distanced the United States from its previous role as a colonial power and presented the new agency as evidence of a constant commitment to self-determination for all. As noted previously, the Peace Corps described the history of United States relations with the Philippines as "special," not colonial. The role of evangelical support in calling for the fulfillment of a divinely ordained, imperial duty to take possession of the Philippines and to "civilize" its inhabitants was similarly ignored. In a speech at Indiana's Hanover College, Peace Corps deputy director Warren Wiggins suggested that "cultural imperialism, the imposition of values, is as bad as the military kind. It is as insulting and self-defeating whether involving two people or two nations."[101] He did not, however, draw the connection that the "imposition of values" was a central goal of Peace Corps community development efforts. Claiming to be engaged in a unique enterprise, proponents of the Peace Corps distanced America from what they described as a specifically European colonial legacy. Where Europe had once pursued military conquest or sought to force alien values on indigenous peoples, the United States was identified as the historical agent of independent "nation building," the product of an anticolonial revolution unceasingly dedicated to the principle of government only by the consent of the governed. As Kennedy declared in a Fourth of July letter to Congress, the Peace Corps "exemplified the spirit of that revolution whose beginnings we celebrate today. . . . It was, as Jefferson perceived, a revolution unbounded by geography, race or culture. It was a movement for the political and spiritual freedom of man. Today, two centuries later and thousands of miles from its origin, the men and women of the Peace Corps are again reaffirming the universality of that revolution."[102] Where other nations had engaged in imperial intervention, American actions were characterized as fundamentally distinct. Modernization, Peace Corps advocates implied, was something altogether different than colonialism.

Official and popular sources sought to confirm the integrity of the nation's mission by reporting that the "underdeveloped" also recognized the singular virtues and superiority of American life. Sargent Shriver's account of his discussion with Ashadevi, an associate of Mahatma Gandhi who traveled for several days to meet him, creates a sense of desperation as the Indian woman pleads with the American man to rescue her materially and morally impoverished people: "Yours was the first revolution. . . . Do you think young Americans possess the spiritual values they must have to bring the spirit of that revolution to our country? There is a great valuelessness spreading around the world and in India too. . . . Your Peace Corps Volunteers must bring more than science and technology. They must touch the idealism of America and bring us that too. Can they do it?"[103] Shriver's response to her supplication, "Yes, based on faith," emphasizes the evangelistic, redemptive qualities of the exchange. Where other nations had sought to conquer foreign peoples by force, Americans would now respond to desperate calls for aid and even salvation. Drawing on the legacy of their own revolution, the volunteers would ferry their nation's principles abroad to modernize a world that sorely needed American help.

That sense of benevolent global expansion, moreover, was tightly linked to a much older conception that remaking the world in America's image would have a salutary effect at home. As William Appleman Williams and Walter LaFeber argued, America's late-nineteenth-century imperialism reflected a conviction that, in addition to serving strategic interests, expansion abroad would perpetuate the reinvigoration that Frederick Jackson Turner associated with the westward movement of the continental frontier.[104] Theodore Roosevelt and Henry Cabot Lodge, as Christopher Lasch reflected, were also "mindful of the connections between 'the strenuous life' and social conditions in the country as a whole." Imperialism, for Roosevelt and Lodge, was not only a means to enhance American military and economic power. It was also "a program of moral regeneration, by means of which the ruling class would acquire the courage and ruthlessness needed to govern unchallenged."[105]

As they framed the Peace Corps's purposes, Shriver and Kennedy also invoked Turner's vision of America's nineteenth-century westward expansion and his argument that the projection of power abroad could rejuvenate the nation. Echoing Turner's argument that "a return to primitive conditions along a continually advancing frontier line" and a "continuous touch with the simplicity of primitive society" provided for a "perennial rebirth" and revitalization of the "American character," the Kennedy administration recycled a much older cultural form and applied it to a new context.[106] At a March 1961 news conference, Kennedy explained that the Peace Corps volunteers would "live at the same level as the citizens of the country to which they are sent . . . doing the same work, eating the same food, speaking the same language."[107] Ostentatious living might have offended host nations, yet interaction with foreigners at their "level" also carried an important value of its own. Drawing a direct parallel between Turner's thesis and the declared theme of the Kennedy presidency, Shriver insisted that "the Peace Corps is truly a new frontier in the sense that it provides the challenge of self-reliance and independent action which the vanished frontier once provided on our own continent. Sharing in the progress of other countries helps us to rediscover ourselves at home."[108] Accelerating modernization and interacting with the "primitive" in conditions of "hardship" would provide the "virtue" of strength that men such as Roosevelt had sought. It would allow Americans to rally around a vision of national vitality and fortitude to meet the challenges presented by a dangerous Marxist ideology and the "reactionary nationalism" of "nonaligned" states. Understood as a means to help new nations overcome the legacy of imperialism, the Peace Corps also claimed to promote America's moral rehabilitation. World leadership during the height of the Cold War, moreover, seemed to demand nothing less.[109]

The idea that the Peace Corps would foster a resurgence of will and vigilance was constantly emphasized in descriptions of what the returned volunteers would contribute to their own society. After modernizing the "traditional" peoples of the world, the volunteers were to return and recharge a society in danger of becoming too complacent to respond to Cold War peril. In the celebratory prose of the Peace Corps's *Fifth Annual Report*, the returned volunteer represented "a new breed of American, different and special. . . . He is not someone who will slip, as one official put it, 'into the bog of affluent living." He is self-confident and committed. . . . He wants action; he wills himself to act. . . . Sophisticated, mature, toughened, confident and independent, the returned Volunteer refuses to be cast into a mold."[110] Modernizing the world abroad, the volunteers were to experience a rite of passage giving them a new perspective on America's own challenges. Freed from the concerns of their daily lives and in touch with the core intensity of the struggle for "development," they would bring new hope for the future of a republic faced with a dangerous, totalitarian adversary. Reinvigorated citizens, the returned volunteers would react "sharply to what they viewed as 'shortcomings' in American society—'commercialism,' 'racialism,' 'provincialism,' 'conformity,' and the immaturity of their own generation."[111] Many former volunteers eventually did have a decisive impact in the civil rights movement and as dissenters to the war in Vietnam. As presented by official sources and the nation's media, however, interacting with the "primitive" led to the revival of a society called to global leadership. If the imperialists of the 1890s recast Manifest Destiny in an "industrial frame," the "New Frontiersmen" of the 1960s "modernized" it to suit their perceptions of Cold War peril.

The relationship between development abroad and vitality at home also raised questions about the limits of American modernity. Benedict Anderson has suggested that nationalism can be understood as an "imagined political community" into which "others," if fully assimilated to the dominant culture and language, may possibly be invited.[112] Just as American Indians were labeled members of separate "domestic dependent nations" during the course of nineteenth-century westward expansion and the debate over the acquisition of the Philippines became deeply engaged in definitions of national citizenship, the ideology of the Peace Corps also reflected a sense that not all sectors of American society were fully integrated into national life. To fulfill their established mission, the Peace Corps volunteers, embodiments of the world's most "modern" nation, were to cross a "new frontier" and minister to societies and peoples that were deemed "undeveloped" in moral and structural terms. The Peace Corps, however, was also sent to aid the apathetic "primitive" and the passive "traditional" at home. Not all

Americans, it seemed, were part of a national community that government and media defined less by geography than by "modernity."[113]

The Peace Corps's assumptions about contrasting domestic populations become most clear in the organization's attempt to simulate overseas duty. Volunteers preparing for community development assignments, for example, were sent to assist ethnic and racial groups within the United States that, administrators believed, would provide an accurate replication of the challenges they faced overseas. As one training plan suggested, the volunteer should be assigned to "a real community differing from his own, e.g. Negro, Puerto Rican, Mexican American, or other ethnically distinct neighborhood." Spending ten hours a week, the trainee was to "learn and describe the community," "make at least three (disparate) friends," and, "if possible, to get underway a community development project."[114]

Given assignments on Indian reservations, in "slum neighborhoods," and at housing projects, volunteer trainees were sent out to test their skills in different parts of the United States. In each case, moreover, the volunteers were expected to encounter the same type of fatalism and paralysis they were charged with alleviating abroad. Through Columbia University's School of Social Work, trainees bound for South America served in New York City neighborhood organizations and with welfare agencies in order to prepare for community development assignments. The school's associate dean, Mitchell Ginsberg, explained that volunteers were charged with "stimulating and motivating individuals and groups to participate in programs of self-help and then helping them to organize and work together." Through their fieldwork with a "membership or clientele that was of low income and lower class and, if possible, Spanish speaking," trainees in neighborhood settlements and city offices participated in "home visiting" and frequently reported on the challenge of " 'how it felt to go into these tenements, to see the conditions which exist, to meet up with what seemed like overpowering apathy, to try to set up some sort of relationship and to try to sell ourselves and our objectives.' "[115]

At the Pima and Maricopa Indian Reservations on the Gila River outside Phoenix, volunteers went out to work alone or in pairs "in the expectation that the reservation experience would be of value when they would confront a different culture overseas." Like volunteers working abroad, trainees at home were reported as successfully empathizing with local predicaments and receiving sincere gratitude for the values and motivation that they brought. As the Peace Corps's project coordinator put it, "I had visualized hostilities on the reservation . . . but to my knowledge not one incident occurred. . . . The trainees made sincere friendships with the Pimas and the Maricopas. Such feelings were expressed in many ways—for example . . . an older Pima lady said grace before the breakfast meal and in her humble prayer she thanked the Creator for sending the wonderful Peace Corps volunteers, and it was said with genuine emotion." Just as they would be in dealing with the "underdeveloped" overseas, the volunteers were praised for their ability to "win the hearts and confidence of many of the Indian people." The "traditionals," in this case Native Americans, were appropriately grateful for the sacrifices made by the "modern" in their midst.[116]

At a public housing project outside the northern California town of Pittsburg, volunteer trainees were also lauded for producing essential changes in attitudes and worldviews. As they worked with the members of the Columbia–El Pueblo community, most of whom received public assistance, the volunteers attended committee meetings and engaged the residents in painting bedrooms, setting up playgrounds, building sandboxes, making a softball field, and constructing basketball backstops. According to the project director, one of the most significant results was that "residents, some of whom had been highly apathetic, began to recognize that they could help themselves and improve their conditions. . . . A feeling of their own importance emerged."[117] Because they suffered from the same cultural deficiencies as the "underdeveloped" hosts abroad, many populations within the United States could benefit from the Peace Corps's inspiring motivation.

As embodiments of the world's most modern nation, the Peace Corps volunteers were sent to aid those racial and ethnic populations that were not full-fledged members of the "imagined community" that theorists, official sources, and popular media envisioned. Like the "underdeveloped" overseas, those assisted at home were perceived as trapped within a "culture of poverty" characterized more by fatalism, lack of will, and a refusal to assimilate than by barriers of discrimination, lack of resources, or dearth of educational opportunity. According to one scholar, the "experiences of the volunteers in cross cultural work situations may contribute to ways of understanding and working with sub-cultural groups in the United States—poverty groups, the delinquent sub-cultures, etc."[118] Reiterating common expectations of the transformative power produced by contact between the socially advanced and those farther down the scale of progress, the Peace Corps's mission was defined in ways that clearly resonated with the efforts of the settlement house projects and "Americanization" programs that had gone before it.[119] Its rhetoric regarding the need to instill activism in the face of entrenched passivity would also emerge in the coming "War on Poverty," an enterprise led, once again, by Sargent Shriver. Returning volunteers, Shriver promised, would still find the "sense of adventure" and "sheer and irresistible intensity" that Peace Corps service provided if the United States committed itself to "building a Great Society."[120]

Institutionalized in the Peace Corps, the ideology of modernization mapped out a world in which American policymakers could accelerate the passage of societies through evolutionary stages at home and abroad. Revealing the historical depth of a cultural form that resonated with the ideals of America's frontier expansion, apologies for imperialism, and the rhetoric of domestic reform, the scientific discourse of modernization also proved applicable to the changing demands of a Cold War world. An ideology useful for the definition of strategic objectives, modernization allowed institutions such as the Peace Corps to affirm American superiority and credibility in a dangerous contest for the "hearts and minds" of the "emerging nations."

In fighting that battle, moreover, modernization was pursued through other institutions that often had little to do with peace. In a speech at the University of Kentucky in 1965, Lyndon Johnson linked America's global mission with a definition of the nation's moral purpose. As he argued: "Our struggle against colonial rule is still reshaping continents. Our achievements have lifted the hopes and ambitions of men who live everywhere. . . . And if the consequences of these forces sometimes cause us difficulty or create danger, then let us not be dismayed. For this is what America is all about; to show the way to the liberation of man from every form of tyranny over his mind, his body, and his spirit. We cannot, and we will not withdraw from this world. We are too rich, too powerful, and too important. But, most important, we are too concerned."[121] Well before the time of Johnson's speech, that mixture of hubris and "concern" had already led to dramatic increases in America's commitment to the Vietnam War. Although the motivations of the participants may have been quite distinct, at the ideological level the distance between "community development" pursued by the Peace Corps and "civic action" promoted by the United States Army was not a great one. Drawing from the same set of underlying principles, both practices proposed to alter the institutions of a malleable, "traditional" society and redirect its "development" in ways that would prove harmonious with America's Cold War struggle. In some cases modernization was conceived of as an instrument for the promotion of peace. In others, however, it became a weapon forged in war, and an especially forceful means for the United States to pursue the ends of "progress" it saw fit to define.

CHAPTER 5

Modernization at War

Counterinsurgency and the Strategic Hamlet Program in Vietnam

Observing the course of the Vietnam War in 1968, Harvard University political scientist and modernization theorist Samuel P. Huntington published an article in the journal *Foreign Affairs*. American military strategy, he determined, could be guided by an integrated model of social, economic, and political change. As he argued, "Societies are susceptible to revolution only at particular stages in their development. . . . The United States in Viet Nam may well have stumbled upon the answer to 'wars of national liberation.' The effective response . . . is . . . forced-draft urbanization and modernization which rapidly brings the country in question out of the phase in which a rural revolutionary movement can hope to generate sufficient strength to come to power."[1] The deployment of American combat troops and the continual intensification of the war, Huntington argued, would do more than inflict heavy losses on the Vietcong. The escalating violence would also engineer a fundamental transformation in the nature of Vietnamese society. Driving refugees into the government-controlled cities, it would make them aware of the material benefits to be found in a thriving, capitalist, metropolitan center and accelerate the development of a new set of modern values, loyalties, and ties between the South Vietnamese state and its citizens. As one historian has noted, where U.S. Air Force general Curtis LeMay argued that the United States should bomb the Vietnamese "into the Stone Age," Huntington had other ideas. America, he implied, could bomb them into the future.[2]

Huntington's argument reflects the degree to which the ideology of modernization linked the promotion of social and political development to the strategies of warfare. Approaching the Vietnam War as a highly visible "test case" of the U.S. ability to defeat Communist aggression in the "emerging world," many American policymakers and social scientists conceived of modernization as a most effective response. Just as American planners did in the Alliance for Progress and the community development programs of the Peace Corps, the architects of U.S. counterinsurgency policy in Vietnam sought to achieve what Talcott Parsons called a "rational engineering control." For those strategists attempting to "pacify" the countryside, build a strong South Vietnamese state, and defeat the National Liberation Front and its North Vietnamese allies, modernization promised victory in a war to determine the future of a "traditional" population. Committed to defeating a social revolution, American policymakers hoped to channel the rising aspirations of an imperiled Southeast Asian society toward liberal, capitalist forms before Communist insurgency could derail that supposedly natural process.

This chapter focuses on the Strategic Hamlet Program deployed in Vietnam during the Kennedy administration and explores several ways in which theories of modernization shaped American counterinsurgency policy. First, it investigates how social scientific ideas helped define and legitimate specific practices. Policymakers often appropriated theories of modernization as they planned programs designed to engineer dramatic changes in local worldviews and social life. As in the other cases this book explores, the relationship between theory and policy was not always direct. In some instances, social thinkers played a personal role in Kennedy administration decisions. In others, they remained outside policymaking circles and propagated ideas that resonated with underlying, broadly held expectations. Rather than an exclusive or determinative causal force, modernization functioned in ideological terms. In a specific historical context and institutional setting, theories of development crystallized widely shared cultural assumptions about America's global potential and suggested ways in which America's capability might be realized.

This chapter also illustrates the way the Strategic Hamlet Program projected a national identity for the United States as a credible world power ready to meet revolutionary challenges. As U.S. intervention in Vietnam deepened, officials invoked modernization to identify the deficiencies of a "passive," "traditional" peasantry and to explain how American action would remedy them. Village-level relocation and social engineering projects, as explained by administration spokesmen and the national media, were reflections of benevolent American power. According to their interpretations, the Strategic Hamlet Program demonstrated a commitment to help an embattled people fulfill their most pressing needs and dearest hopes. Nation building in Vietnam, official and public sources claimed, would inspire a primitive people and bring out the best of the United States in the process. It would also disprove claims that America was either unprepared or unwilling to fight the Communists in a "Third World" contest.

Finally, this interpretation suggests a strong continuity between the Strategic Hamlet Program and the history of imperial strategies based on "reconcentrating" and "developing" a potentially subversive population. American counterinsurgency policy in Vietnam, driven by visions of modernization, fit an older pattern in which "progress" and violence went hand in hand. Although its wartime context set it apart, it would also be a mistake to treat the Strategic Hamlet Program as an anomaly among Kennedy administration development initiatives. Like the Alliance for Progress and the Peace Corps, the Strategic Hamlet Program revised older ideologies of imperialism and Manifest Destiny to suit the demands of the Cold War. Like those other Kennedy programs, it also framed an American world role and appealing sense of self that strategists and social scientists continued to promote, even when confronted with growing evidence of policy failure.

Kennedy planners and the country's media fused claims of a perspectiveless, "rational" analysis of the Vietnam War with repeated descriptions of the nation's duty, values, and altruistic heritage. In one sense, they described the war as a scientific project. In another, it became a profoundly moral obligation. Characterizing Americans as the ideal cold warriors, proponents of intervention argued that the United States could meet the Marxist challenge because its leaders and citizens possessed "steady nerves," "the capacity for cold deliberate analysis," and a sense of detached, objective, "unemotional self-discipline and self-control."[3] At the same time, theorists, policymakers, and media also displayed, in Noam Chomsky's words, the mentality of the "colonial civil servant." "Persuaded of the benevolence of the mother country and the correctness of its vision of world order," they were certain that they understood "the true interests of the backward peoples whose welfare [they were] to administer."[4] In arguments that linked social analysis with America's own previous climb to enlightenment, rescuing South Vietnam became both an objective, scientific matter and an altruistic, national mission.

From early 1962 through the U.S.-backed coup that overturned Ngo Dinh Diem's regime in November 1963, the Strategic Hamlet Program was the centerpiece of the Kennedy administration's Vietnam policy. In an effort that drew on French colonial practices, South Vietnam's own social experiments, and British tactics in colonial Malaya, the United States endorsed, supplied, and advised Premier Diem's tactic of moving peasants from dispersed villages into more concentrated settlements. After "clearing" insurgents from a zone of South Vietnamese countryside, the South Vietnamese Army (ARVN) and its American advisers used a combination of persuasion and force to regroup the local population into "strategic hamlets," defended outposts that could be more easily subjected to military control and social engineering. By forcing peasants to construct homes and fortifications within a settlement protected by a perimeter of barbed wire, ditches, and bamboo stakes, the U.S. Agency for International Development and the U.S. Army's Military Assistance Command hoped to deny the Vietcong access to a population that could supply them with food, intelligence, and recruits. They also sought to create a new political culture by instilling the rural people with a sense of nationalist loyalty to Diem's South Vietnamese government. Committed to fighting communism through political and social modernization, the United States encouraged the formation of hamlet organizations, supported "self-help" plans, and called on South Vietnamese province chiefs to increase their contact with local settlements. Rural peasants, American policymakers hoped, would look beyond their isolated communities and develop an allegiance to Diem's regime instead of Ho Chi Minh's revolution.

Kennedy administration strategists expected that the provision of medical care, fertilizer, cooking oil, and livestock would give the "traditional" peasantry a "stake in the war," and they placed their so-called pacification effort in the context of a larger plan to modernize Diem's government from the bottom up and the top down. As the central state reached into provincial life to demonstrate its benevolent intentions, passive farmers were to be transformed into active, empowered citizens through voting in local elections, forming committees, and undertaking projects to meet community needs. After realizing their ability to improve their own lives and environment, villagers were expected to take up arms against the insurgency that repudiated their newfound, modern values and threatened the welfare that Diem's government had helped them achieve. Once that happened, policymakers believed, the revolution would lose momentum and begin to collapse. In addition to framing the war as a problem of development, the Strategic Hamlet Program also relied on a heightened level of social control. Subjected to constant surveillance, peasants were ordered to carry identification, report their movements and visitors, and request official permission to travel. The sphere of life within the physical and disciplinary boundaries of the hamlet, while cast in terms of freedom and self-determination, became ever more rigidly structured. The realm outside it, moreover, became a free-fire zone.

Investigating the Kennedy administration's perception of the Vietnam War and its promotion of the Strategic Hamlet Program requires at least a brief, retrospective look at the collapse of French colonial power and the historical pattern of American responses to it. President John F. Kennedy, in many ways, inherited a commitment put in place by his predecessors. As George Kahin's history of the war argues, America's involvement in Vietnam reflects a "continuing series of steps to apply external power in the effort to control the threat of nationalism."[5] Like Truman and Eisenhower before him, Kennedy pushed the United States deeper into an antirevolutionary struggle. Just as they did, moreover, he also considered the stakes in a global, Cold War context and understood the war as one that the United States could not afford to lose. A small Southeast Asian country thousands of miles across the Pacific, Vietnam eventually acquired immense, unparalleled significance for the United States. By the early 1960s, it became the point around which vast quantities of American energy, resources, and lives would revolve.

Since the late nineteenth century, France's harsh domination over its colonies in Indochina had aroused Vietnamese resentment and determined resistance against foreign imperialism. When he went to Versailles and the peace conference ending World War I, a young Ho Chi Minh failed to secure either an audience with President Woodrow Wilson or an American pledge to endorse the cause of Vietnamese independence. Even if a meeting between them had taken place, Robert Schulzinger notes, it was "doubtful that Wilson, who believed that national self-determination applied almost exclusively to Europeans, would have done much for the slightly-built twenty-nine-year-old Vietnamese."[6] In time, however, Ho and other revolutionary leaders found that the sufferings of the Second World War also provided Vietnam with a new measure of hope. Created in 1941 as the organizational structure for a long and bitter struggle against French colonialism, the Vietminh assembled a broad-based front among the disparate Vietnamese groups advocating independence. As they subordinated their Communist political objectives to a wider program promoting the immediate "survival of the nation and race," Ho and his associates built a strong nationalist coalition. Together they weathered a brutal Japanese occupation, endured popular hardship and a devastating wartime famine, and turned toward guerrilla warfare as a method of armed resistance against both the Japanese and the severely weakened French. When Japan's Asian empire crumbled under the Allied counterattack, the Vietnamese nationalists also prepared for a triumphant moment of their own. On August 19, 1945, close to a thousand Vietminh marched into Hanoi to the enthusiastic applause of a city filled with pro-independence demonstrators. When news of the event spread, similar scenes took place in the cities of Hue and Saigon. Finally, on September 2, 1945, from the center of Hanoi, Ho Chi Minh declared the establishment of the Democratic Republic of Vietnam. Borrowing Thomas Jefferson's famous words, he told a crowd of more than a half million supporters that his country was also committed to the principle that "all men are created equal, all men have a right to life, liberty and happiness." A nation "courageously opposed to French domination for more than eighty years," Vietnam would now "defend the right to freedom and independence."[7]

Ho's invocation of America's own founding document reflected his hope that the United States might throw its considerable weight behind Vietnam's cause. President Franklin Delano Roosevelt, strongly distrustful of France's postwar intentions, had made frequent statements opposing the return of imperial control in Indochina. As the war moved toward conclusion, he also proposed that France's Asian territories be turned over to the United Nations for an Allied trusteeship prior to their eventual independence. By early 1945, however, opposition from Britain and France, internal disagreements within the U.S. government, and a willingness to allow French forces back into the region to fight the Japanese helped destroy those plans. Concerns about the status of postwar Europe also raised serious questions and doubts among American policymakers. Influential advisers to Roosevelt, Lloyd Gardner explains, "put the case simply: the United States would need France in any conflict with the Soviet Union."[8] A hard-edged stance against French goals in Indochina, policymakers worried, would alienate an ally that the United States depended on in meeting potential Communist threats to a devastated, wartorn Europe. When Roosevelt died in April 1945, American policy regarding Indochina remained inconclusive and undefined.

Harry S. Truman, more firmly convinced of the need to keep France and its valuable colonial possessions from falling under hostile influence, led a government that revealed little of the earlier American ambivalence. Truman and his senior administration officials knew far less about Southeast Asia than Roosevelt did, and few had any reservations about allowing France to return to power in Indochina, especially if it would encourage the French to cooperate with American Cold War policy.[9] By 1947, U.S. policymakers also saw Ho Chi Minh's nationalist movement as a dangerous force. As vaguely worded compromises between France and Vietnamese nationalists collapsed and the Vietminh strength grew in both political and military terms, officials such as Secretary of State George Marshall took a dim view of the situation. Though they recognized his powerful nationalist appeal, Marshall and his colleagues remained wary of Ho Chi Minh's Communist Party affiliations, his periodic residency and study in Moscow during the 1920s and 1930s, and his possible long-term goals.[10] Refusing Ho's repeated petitions for American recognition and assistance, the United States retreated from the anticolonial principles of the Atlantic Charter and Roosevelt's wartime endorsement of self-determination for peoples under imperial control. Evaluated in terms of containment strategy, the sources and history of Vietnamese nationalism mattered far less than the apparent global balance of U.S. and Soviet power.

Though Stalin's support for Ho Chi Minh was only rhetorical until early 1950 and the Soviet Union gave Ho's government official recognition only after the United States had consistently denied it, the Truman administration perceived the Vietminh, its agrarian reform programs, and its war against French rule as evidence that the forces of monolithic communism would seek to expand wherever the West showed weakness. Determined to meet the Communist threat, the United States also attempted to preserve opportunities for markets and raw materials in a region considered important for the economic reconstruction of both Europe and Japan. Indochina's rubber and minerals, American advisers argued, would prove valuable in supplying French industry, helping the French economy recover, and blunting the attempt of France's own Communist Party to play upon the nation's postwar destitution. Tin and rubber exports from Malaya would also be important in relieving Britain's wartime debts. As historian Andrew Rotter argues, U.S. officials hoped that Southeast Asia would "become productive, exporting, as it had before the war, rice and raw materials, and importing from Japan and Western Europe any finished goods it needed."[11] A victory by Ho Chi Minh, many advisers feared, would prevent that outcome. Concerned with a combination of geopolitical and economic factors, the United States rejected the possibility of a revolutionary solution to the conflict and provided economic and military aid to prop up a fading empire. When the French proposed that Bao Dai, heir to the nineteenth-century Nguyen dynasty, be reinstalled as sovereign of a united Vietnamese state, the United States supported an agreement that would preserve complete French control over the country's external affairs and keep French armed forces in place. American officials also underestimated the determination of Ho Chi Minh and his comrades to settle for nothing less than full independence.[12]

Before long, American attempts to help France contain a social revolution failed as the Vietminh rapidly gained support throughout rural Vietnam and mounted a powerful military offensive. Although the French held the major cities and communication lines, their grasp on the rest of the nation continued to slip. According to James P. Harrison, by 1950 the revolutionaries "controlled over half of the countryside, and up to three-quarters of the south as well as over half of the northern delta. . . . At night and in the absence of government troops, or most of the time, many villages followed the Communist-led resistance forces, closely integrated with local activists in contrast to the more 'foreign' government sweeps by 'outside' troops."[13] Largely supplied with American-made arms that Mao Zedong's Communist army captured from Chiang Kai-shek's forces and sent to Vietnam, Ho's guerrillas settled in for a long, hard struggle. Light artillery, automatic weapons, mortars, and Chinese technical assistance helped the revolutionaries amplify their efforts. By early 1951, even the delivery of $50 million of U.S. military aid to France was not enough to turn the tide.[14]

The Truman and Eisenhower administrations, however, did not change course as the Korean War prevented any serious reassessment of U.S. policy and led to further American commitments in Vietnam. Coming hard on the heels of Mao's stunning victory in China, war in Korea confirmed impressions that the situation in Indochina was part of a larger strategy of Communist expansion throughout Asia. A failure to hold the line in Vietnam, U.S. planners agreed, would spell disaster. If the United States did not support the French effort in Vietnam while its own forces fought in Korea, a revolutionary triumph might embolden Communists elsewhere and place the entire region in jeopardy.[15] Such thinking accelerated plans for aid that were already under way, and by 1954 the United States was paying 78 percent of the French war bill, almost certainly a far higher percentage of external support than the Vietminh received.[16] The inflexible logic of containment pushed only in the direction of further engagement.

American aid, moreover, made little difference in the overall course of the conflict. When French general Henri Navarre attempted to lure the Vietminh into a decisive, set-piece battle at the northern village of Dienbienphu, France suffered a disastrous defeat. Navarre dropped some thirteen thousand paratroopers into the village and expected that their position, in the center of a wide valley near the border with Laos, would prove an ideal point from which to destroy "human waves" of attacking Vietminh soldiers. Guerrilla forces and Vietnamese peasants under Vo Nguyen Giap had other plans. They transported artillery, ammunition, and supplies by animal cart, bicycle, and foot over three hundred miles of rough terrain and dug a huge network of tunnels surrounding the isolated French outpost. Porters dragged heavy weapons up the peaks and ridges overlooking the garrison, fired down on French fortifications, and placed their enemy under siege. After seven weeks of intense fighting, the revolutionaries finally forced the exhausted survivors to surrender. Some American officials, including Secretary of State John Foster Dulles, publicly called for military action to rescue the French. A few figures, such as chairman of the Joint Chiefs of Staff Admiral Arthur Radford, even considered the possibility of using nuclear weapons against the Vietminh. Such proposals, however, were rejected by U.S. Army Chief of Staff General Matthew Ridgeway, influential members of the U.S. Congress, and important allies such as Britain, Australia, and New Zealand. With confidence in the French dwindling and long-term objectives for an expanded intervention undefined, the risks of direct engagement aroused little enthusiasm.[17]

The Vietminh victory pressed the defeated French and their frustrated American supporters toward the negotiated settlement worked out in the Geneva Accords of 1954. Interested in keeping their frontiers secure, China and the Soviet Union backed the accords. Unwilling to run the risk of escalating the conflict and starting another costly and prolonged Korean-type engagement with China, the United States, though not a formal party to the negotiations, pledged it would not violate them. With provisions for the withdrawal of all foreign military forces and the temporary partition of Vietnam into two military zones at the seventeenth parallel, the accords also scheduled national elections to reunify the country in 1956 and established an international commission made up of representatives from Canada, India, and Poland to oversee compliance. Confident that their superior organizational structure and Ho Chi Minh's prestige would give them the edge in the coming electoral contest, the Vietminh leaders patiently accepted an agreement that did not fully recognize the extent of their military victories and battlefield strength. Within two years, they expected, the shift from a military contest to a political one would ensure their control over the nation as a whole.[18]

The national elections, however, were never held, and the military struggle did not end. Acting with a confidence inspired by the U.S. effort to control communism in Greece, the campaign against the Hukbalahap rebellion in the Philippines, CIA success in overthrowing the Arbenz government in Guatemala, and Britain's ability to combat an insurgency in Malaya, American strategic planners ignored the accords and took steps to make the seventeenth parallel a permanent boundary. The Geneva settlement, Eisenhower and his advisers feared, could very well lead to a Vietnam united under Ho Chi Minh's leadership. Rather than accept the negotiated solution, the United States rejected the prohibition on foreign military forces and began a new initiative to improve its position in Southeast Asia. Because sending combat troops might lead to a reciprocal action by China, the Eisenhower administration turned toward a plan of political, social, and military assistance designed to construct an independent South Vietnam that could serve as a barrier to further revolutionary success in the region.[19] The administration also sent CIA operative Edward Lansdale from the Philippines to Vietnam, directed a clandestine program of sabotage against Hanoi, and established the Southeast Asia Treaty Organization (SEATO) as a defensive alliance offering South Vietnam its protection.

Committed to creating a new South Vietnamese state, policymakers searched for a man to govern it. Ngo Dinh Diem, prime minister in the government that the French had established under Bao Dai, appeared to Eisenhower administration officials as the most suitable anti-Communist candidate. Diem also enjoyed the active support of the American Friends of Vietnam, an influential lobby that included New York archbishop Cardinal Francis Spellman, Montana senator Mike Mansfield, Supreme Court justice William O. Douglas, and Massachusetts senator John F. Kennedy.[20] A Catholic leader who had demanded greater autonomy from France, traveled through Europe, lived in a seminary in Lakewood, New Jersey, and described an independent Vietnam based on an American model, Diem caught Lansdale's attention in particular. Influenced by his own experience in the Philippines, the American came to see Diem as a potential Ramon Magsaysay for Vietnam, "a man of integrity with a sense of responsibility for his country who might with the proper advice become a hero to his people."[21]

From 1954 on, the Eisenhower administration supported Ngo Dinh Diem in an effort to consolidate anti-Communist control over the South and to carve out a separate country within a single nation. American aid and advice, however, did little to address popular grievances or derail the revolution. The Central Intelligence Agency helped Diem to eliminate the armed religious sects that rivaled his authority in urban areas. Edward Lansdale also assisted Diem's effort to manipulate a referendum deposing emperor Bao Dai and placing all state power entirely in his hands. Michigan State University, under contract to the U.S. government and Diem's regime, trained public administrators and police forces. As a cover for the CIA, Michigan State also facilitated the paramilitary recruitment of mountain tribespeople and sent agents across the border to the North.[22] Eventually paying two-thirds of the government's expenses, the Eisenhower administration funneled approximately $200 million in economic aid each year into South Vietnam. But it never produced the economic growth or attracted the levels of private investment it hoped for.

Diem and his American supporters also alienated much of South Vietnam's population. In 1954, one-quarter of 1 percent of the rural population owned approximately 40 percent of rice lands in the South, but conservative land reforms did little to address that disparity or compete with the revolution's practice of redistributing landlord holdings. The Commodity Import Plan proved equally ineffective in putting the South Vietnamese regime on more popular ground. American dollars and import credits typically funded consumer purchases by upper- and middle-class urbanites. They had scant results elsewhere and failed to stimulate domestic industry or consistent economic progress.[23] The United States also stood by Ngo Dinh Diem as he put a system of ruthless repression in place. During the 1950s, the South Vietnamese leader created a powerful secret police, killed tens of thousands of Vietminh sympathizers, and imprisoned and tortured hundreds of thousands more. Challenged by a broad-based revolution, Diem's government became a corrupt, intolerant, and rigid dictatorship committed to little beyond its own survival. Even as Diem moved to crush all dissent and amplified his own rigid, personal control, the United States continued to uphold him as the democratic, progressive leader of "Free Vietnam." Most tellingly, American policymakers failed to acknowledge the degree to which many of those living in the South identified themselves not with Diem's artificial state but with a larger, historically and culturally defined Vietnamese nation. Alienated by Diem's violence and brutality, many of South Vietnam's most influential political, religious, and social leaders found themselves aligned together against his government and the American power that shored it up.[24]

Diem never possessed more than a tenuous hold on the region he governed, and by the late 1950s the revolutionaries turned toward more violent means to oppose him. Directing its southern cadres to focus on building political infrastructure, the Hanoi-led Communist Party (Lao Dong) had previously attempted to keep armed resistance to South Vietnam's regime at a low level so that the United States would not intervene before the promised reunification elections took place. As it became clear that those elections would not be held at all and Diem's repression took a heavy toll, Communist Party members and former Vietminh in the South called for a change in strategy. The time had come, southern revolutionaries told their northern leaders, for a more aggressive response to Diem's punishing campaign against them. Persuaded by those appeals, the Lao Dong approved a new strategy of "revolutionary violence" and "insurrection" in early 1959. Over the next several months, southerners mounted armed counterattacks across many different provinces, captured weapons from government troops, and pushed forward with their plans to redistribute power and wealth at the local level. Southern radicals also combined with intellectuals, laborers, students, and members of dissenting religious bodies to form a more activist, broadly defined, anti-Diem alliance. Officially founded in the South in December 1960, this rapidly growing National Liberation Front (NLF), labeled the "Vietcong" by Diem and his American allies, dedicated itself not only to political organizing but also to the forceful overthrow of Diem's government. Organizing guerrilla units, the NLF executed or intimidated local government representatives, mounted an effective propaganda campaign, and gradually took control of the countryside in which the vast majority of South Vietnam's population lived.[25]

As the Kennedy administration began, therefore, the Vietnam War had reached a critical phase. Between 1955 and 1961, the United States channeled more than $1 billion in economic and military aid to South Vietnam, and the country ranked fifth among all recipients of U.S. foreign assistance. By the time Kennedy took office, more than fifteen hundred Americans were also stationed in the capital of Saigon, working in public administration and serving in the Military Assistance and Advisory Group (MAAG), which trained Diem's armed forces.[26] Kennedy advisers soon decided, moreover, that the level of American assistance was insufficient. On his return from a visit to Vietnam in January 1961, Edward Lansdale, now working in the Pentagon, told the new administration that the revolution was rapidly gaining ground. As he related in a memo that Walt Rostow sent to the president: "It was a shock to me to look over maps of the estimated situation with U.S. and Vietnamese intelligence personnel [and learn that] thousands of disciplined and trained Communist graduates of 'proletarian military science' had been able to infiltrate the most productive area of South Vietnam and gain control of nearly all of it except for narrow corridors protected by military actions."[27] In March 1961, a CIA National Intelligence Estimate confirmed Lansdale's alarming report. Diem's authority was under constant pressure, "over 2,600 civilians, mostly government officials and sympathizers, were assassinated or kidnapped by the Viet Cong in 1960," and the out-look for the future remained grim. "Despite growing Vietnamese Army aggressiveness and substantial casualties inflicted by the army," the CIA warned, "the Viet Cong guerrillas continue to retain the initiative in the field."[28] A few months later, author and Kennedy friend Theodore White also delivered a bleak assessment. In a letter to the president from Saigon, he despaired that "the situation gets steadily worse almost week by week. . . . Guerrillas now control almost all the Southern delta—so much so that I could find no American who was willing to drive me outside Saigon in his car even by day without military convoy. . . . What perplexes the hell out of me is that the Commies, on their side, seem to be able to find people willing to die for their cause."[29] As committed revolutionaries moved forward, time was running out for Diem's regime and its American supporters.

The situation appeared all the more grave in light of the Kennedy administration's worries about America's international credibility. In addition to conceiving of Vietnam as a Southeast Asian "domino," American strategists argued that the country's fate would have a tremendous psychological impact across all the "underdeveloped" regions. A loss in Vietnam, Lansdale insisted, would eliminate the "toughest local force on our side" and "be a major blow to U.S. prestige and influence, not only in Asia but throughout the world, since the world believes that Vietnam has remained free only through U.S. help. Such a victory would tell leaders of other governments that it doesn't pay to be a friend of the U.S. "[30] Lyndon Johnson was even more adamant about the stakes in Southeast Asia. After visiting Vietnam in early 1961, the vice president told Kennedy that the region's leaders had started to view United States intentions with "doubt and concern." If America did not back the anti-Communist governments with "strength and determination," he argued, "the island outposts—Philippines, Japan, Taiwan—have no security and the Pacific becomes a Red Sea." Painting an all-or-nothing scenario for the president, Johnson insisted that security in Southeast Asia would depend on the world's "knowledge and faith in United States power." "We must decide," he insisted, "whether to help these countries to the best of our ability or throw in the towel in the area and pull back our defenses to San Francisco and a 'Fortress America' concept. . . . We would say to the world in this case that we don't live up to our treaties and don't stand by our friends."[31] Like other officials, Lansdale and Johnson believed that America's public image and identity were inseparable from its Cold War strategy.

A series of recent international setbacks, moreover, made Vietnam's significance loom even larger. In the wake of the humiliating Bay of Pigs failure,

Walt Rostow advised Secretary of Defense Robert McNamara and Secretary of State Dean Rusk that a "clean cut success in Vietnam" would counter any perception that the United States was less than committed to containment or less than capable of pursuing it worldwide.[32] When the Pathet Lao guerrillas challenged the fragile government in Laos and the United States settled for an agreement neutralizing that country through a coalition including Communist forces, the need to draw the line in Vietnam seemed even more crucial. To make matters worse, at the summit meeting in Vienna in June 1961, Khrushchev threatened to sign a separate peace treaty with East Germany. Such a move, American officials believed, would jeopardize the Western position in Berlin and deal a further blow to U.S. prestige around the world. The cumulative damage at home, many expected, would also be severe. Kennedy had campaigned against Eisenhower's foreign policy record and narrowly won election against Richard Nixon by claiming that the "New Look" was actually closer to "Look the Other Way" or even "No Look at All."[33] A more engaged, committed approach than "massive retaliation," Kennedy had promised, would make for a safer world. If Vietnam went the way of China or Cuba, however, Kennedy himself would fall victim to charges of failing to stem the Communist tide. Because they considered every setback a danger to credibility and evaluated international conflicts less on their own terms than in the crucial fulcrum of American and Soviet power, Kennedy and his advisers soon turned to Vietnam as a vital, high-profile test of American commitment.

Determined to hold the line, Kennedy searched for effective ways to prop up South Vietnam's regime from his first days in the White House.[34] Only one week after his inauguration, the president approved a plan to offer Diem $41 million in support for a 20,000-man increase in South Vietnam's army, and the United States proposed to train and equip a 32,000-man civil guard at a cost of $12.7 million. In May 1961, after the administration's Vietnam task force warned that "the number of Viet Cong hard-core Communists has increased from 4400 in early 1960 to an estimated 12,000 today," the Kennedy strategists ratcheted up their efforts again. Plans to enhance military effectiveness, an administration task force insisted, would not suffice. The United States would also have to promote "political and economic conditions which will create a solid and widespread support" for Diem's government.[35] That same month, Kennedy ordered an increase in aerial surveillance, deployed a special forces training group, and sent additional funding for public works projects.[36]

The pace of the war, however, continued to accelerate. In September 1961, the administration received reports that the NLF threatened to take control of the entire Mekong Delta, and the CIA estimated that the trained insurgent forces had now grown to sixteen thousand. Mounting three attacks with units of more than one thousand men, the guerrillas also demonstrated their new vitality by briefly taking control of a province capital located only fifty-five miles from Saigon itself.[37] While still predominantly active in rural areas, the revolutionaries were starting to expand a covert, urban infrastructure as well. They were also revealing that, contrary to the views of many American officials, the revolution was hardly a simple case of northern aggression. Although supplies, advice, and training from Ho's government certainly made a difference, the NLF clearly enjoyed a high degree of local support.

Confronted with that evidence of growing revolutionary strength, Kennedy and his advisers spent the fall of 1961 searching for a more comprehensive strategy. Unwilling to move toward the negotiated settlement they feared would damage American credibility and amplify the Communist threat to other Southeast Asian states, the president and several of his leading aides also remained wary of making the public commitment to Diem's unstable regime that U.S. combat troops would represent. Though the Joint Chiefs of Staff suggested that a limited troop deployment might put the ARVN on a more aggressive footing, demonstrate U.S. resolve, and prevent the need for further escalation, other advisers were more skeptical, and Diem himself offered only indifferent responses. Admiral Harry Felt, commander in chief of the Pacific Fleet, worried about the possible consequences of a limited war. Once the United States became publicly committed, he wondered, under what circumstances would it be able to pull out?[38] General Maxwell Taylor, Kennedy's personal military adviser, and Walt Rostow visited Vietnam in October 1961 and recommended that Kennedy send eight thousand regular U.S. ground troops and a five-thousand-man combat engineering unit. Robert McNamara argued for a troop commitment as well. The opposition of advisers such as Dean Rusk, George Ball, Chester Bowles, Averell Harriman, and John Kenneth Galbraith, however, confirmed the president's own reservations.[39] Kennedy told his National Security Council that the United States would not be able to count on help from its major European allies. Involved in their own colonial struggles, Britain and France would not be willing to contribute to an anti-Communist force in Vietnam. Sending American infantry to prop up Diem's repressive government, the president also worried, might expose his administration to criticism from more liberal members of the Democratic Party and provoke a military response on the part of the Chinese and the Soviets. While maintaining the freedom to deploy U.S.

combat troops at a later time, in late 1961 Kennedy looked for other ways to fight the revolution in Vietnam.[40]

The Kennedy administration did not give up on military measures. The deployment of helicopter companies manned by U.S. servicemen, an increase in funding for Diem's army, and the delivery of napalm, white phosphorous, and chemical defoliants all reflected a continued search for military success. As Marilyn Young's history of the war notes, eight hundred U.S. military advisers and personnel worked in Vietnam when Kennedy first took office. Within a year, eleven thousand were stationed there.[41] Having decided not to engage American combat forces directly, however, Kennedy and his advisers turned toward an alternative strategy to defeat the NLF. Military power, they determined, could be coordinated with programs designed to strike at the revolution's political and social roots. If Diem's regime could be made the focus of popular aspirations, Kennedy planners expected that nation building and political development might stem the tide. With a new emphasis on the countryside and the peasantry, Kennedy, his advisers, and the American foreign aid mission began to shift away from conventional military tactics and toward a comprehensive counterinsurgency program that integrated military action with a strategy of social engineering. By the end of 1961, the administration would become committed to defeating the Vietcong through modernization.

A guerrilla war, Kennedy and his advisers believed, could be controlled by manipulating the nature of the development process. America's power, they insisted, could direct the course of social and political change. According to Douglas Blaufarb, a former CIA station chief in Laos, Kennedy used his first National Security Council meeting to request that Robert McNamara increase American counterguerrilla resources and training. The president immersed himself in U.S. Army manuals, the writings of Che Guevara and Mao Zedong, and analyses of guerrilla warfare in Cuba, Colombia, Venezuela, Algeria, and Vietnam. Kennedy also authorized the Green Berets as an anti-guerrilla force and ordered Richard Bissell, the deputy director of the CIA, to study counterinsurgency theory and report on ways the United States might apply it. To coordinate planning between the armed forces, the U.S. Information Agency (USIA), the Agency for International Development (AID), and the CIA, the president approved the formation of a high-level, inter-agency, counterinsurgency committee. In what was perhaps the clearest indicator of the subject's importance to him, Kennedy appointed his brother Robert as his personal representative.[42]

The president also called for a "national level school" to educate senior

U.S. officials, an organization that would teach courses and design programs to "improve the U.S. capability for guiding underdeveloped countries through the modernization barrier."[43] Kennedy, national security adviser McGeorge Bundy, Walt Rostow, and Maxwell Taylor solicited proposals for an official "Modernization Institute" from the State and Defense departments before finally deciding that social scientific theory and counterinsurgency doctrine could be most effectively disseminated through a series of five-week seminars titled "Current Problems in the Underdeveloped Areas."[44] The course was taught at the State Department's Foreign Service Institute and included Rostow, Lucian Pye, and Max Millikan as expert instructors. Edward Lansdale, veteran of the U.S. effort to defeat the Hukbalahap rebellion in the Philippines, also shared his experience in putting modernization into practice. With eight to ten classes made up of forty to seventy middle- and senior-level AID, CIA, USIA, and State Department officers each year, the seminar focused on "problems of underdevelopment," "the Communist effort to preempt the West," and counterinsurgency strategies designed to meet revolutionary challenges. The goal, planners agreed, was to develop a new, activist approach to the management of social change. As Dean Rusk declared at the program's inauguration, "We must become guardians of the development process rather than custodians of the *status quo*. We must be *pro*-modernization as well as *anti*-communist."[45]

Modernization theory profoundly influenced the Kennedy administration's understanding of counterinsurgency. American policymakers, political scientist D. Michael Shafer has argued, "put academic specialists to work marrying the most up-to-date theories of Third World development to a government doctrine for coping with its consequences."[46] Sent to address the graduating class of the "Counter Guerrilla Course" at Fort Bragg, North Carolina, Walt Rostow made the connections between military strategy, counterinsurgency, and modernization explicit. In a speech reviewed and approved as an official policy statement by Kennedy himself, he argued that the Communists promoted guerrilla warfare as part of their attempt to "exploit the inherent instabilities of the underdeveloped world." To meet the danger involved, one had to realize that, "like all revolutions, the revolution of modernization is disturbing. Individual men are torn between the old and familiar way of life and the attractions of a modern way of life. The power of the old social groups—notably the landlord who usually dominates traditional society—is reduced. Power moves to those who can command the tools of modern technology. . . . Men and women in the villages and the cities, feeling that the old ways of life are shaken and that new possibilities are open to them, express old resentments and new hopes." Communists, Rostow emphasized, attempted to exploit this "grand arena of revolutionary change" and sought to capitalize on "the resentments built up in many of these areas against colonial rule." By promoting their own developmental model of "national liberation," they tried to "associate themselves effectively with the desire of the emerging nations for independence, for status on the world scene, for material progress."[47]

Responses to this type of Communist warfare, Rostow insisted, would have to harness the very same modernization process that insurgents sought to exploit. Because the guerrilla forces were "scavengers" of the transition from "traditional" to "modern" forms, attempts to contain them needed to accelerate social progress. The Communists, he explained, "know that their time to seize power in the underdeveloped areas is very limited. They know that, as momentum takes hold in an underdeveloped area—and the fundamental social problems inherited from the traditional society are solved—their chances to seize power decline."[48] By promoting modernization, the United States could slam shut the narrow window of opportunity on which aggressors depended. By speeding up and managing the course of change, America could drive countries such as Vietnam into a higher historical stage and destroy a revolution's power.

The containment of communism and the construction of "truly independent nations," Rostow concluded, would also allow the United States to pursue its own historical and benevolent international destiny. Modernizing the "emerging" world would "permit American society to continue to develop along the old humane lines which go back to our birth as a nation—which reach deeper than that—back to the Mediterranean roots of Western life." Calling guerrilla warfare "an intimate affair, fought not merely with weapons but fought in the minds of the men who live in the villages and in the hills; fought by the spirit and policy of those who run the local government," Rostow linked counterinsurgency with the transmission of what he identified as distinctly advanced, particularly Western values. Victory in a guerrilla war, he claimed, demanded a plan to provide more than material resources; it also required transforming the indigenous culture itself.[49]

In his own formulation of the link between battlefield tactics and social engineering, Edward Lansdale reached similar conclusions. As he explained to U.S. Army officers, the Hukbalahap rebels were initially successful because they were "running a revolution" while the Philippine government attempted to fight them as "formal enemy armed forces." Once Magsaysay's army conducted extensive social operations, gave farmers material assistance, gained their trust, and started to "construct a true political base for their fight," however, victory was certain.[50] With an appeal to the same basic theory of community development used in the Peace Corps, Lansdale also told an audience of professional soldiers that successful counterinsurgency programs had to begin at the village level. As an isolated indigenous community became involved in the construction of wells, schools, or latrines, he explained, it underwent a dramatic and deeply transformative shift in its view of the world. Once peasants recognized their mutual investment of labor and learned to appreciate the assistance they received from the state, they would find their community "becoming linked up closely to the nation, a real part of something bigger. As it does so, the political life of the community grows also, demanding more meaning and answers to the question: 'what is worth a man's life to defend?' As the community resolves these factors at the grass-roots level, as the national government becomes responsive itself, as the bond between the people and the soldiers grows stronger, the Communist guerrillas find themselves forced out of existence as their cause is exposed for the paltry thing that it is."[51] Shaking the peasantry out of its apathetic and traditional fatalism, modernizers claimed, would destroy a revolution that exploited people held back by their own cultural limits.

The arguments of men such as Rostow and Lansdale stand out even more strikingly in the official statement titled "U.S. Overseas Internal Defense Policy," a directive that became the basis of American counterinsurgency programs from August 1962 through 1968.[52] Arguing that "social patterns and institutions in most underdeveloped nations are extremely malleable," the document explained that "purposefully or otherwise societies are gearing themselves to higher levels of economic and social activity. The necessary substructures inevitably cut into traditions and habits fostered by rural isolation. . . . The revolution of modernization can disturb, uproot, and daze a traditional society. While the institutions required for modernization are in the process of being created, this revolution contributes to arousing pressures, anxieties, and hopes which seem to justify violent action."[53] Especially dangerous in "loosely constructed countries" where "an apathetic rural population is a vulnerable target for communist political activity," the problem of revolutionary insurgency demanded that the battle "be joined in the villages which normally represent the critical social and political organizational level." Expanded communications, public health programs, housing construction, and agricultural aid, political analysts agreed, could all help engineer the required transformations. Because success depended on meeting the "aspirations of the under-privileged for a better life and greater participation in the life of the society," strategists arrived at a single, central conclusion. As the policy statement phrased it, without a trace of irony, "The *ultimate and decisive target is the people.* Society itself is at war and the resources, motives and targets of the struggle are found almost wholly within the local population."[54]

Kennedy administration planning also built on earlier South Vietnamese practices. Starting in 1959, Diem and Ngo Dinh Nhu, his brother and principal adviser, had experimented with the imperial French practice of creating "secure zones" through the relocation of peasant communities. By moving farmers into unsettled regions, they hoped to strengthen their network of personal patronage and authoritarian political control over a population they distrusted and from which they remained distant. In a program that forced peasants to leave behind their homes, gardens, fields, and ancestral lands, the South Vietnamese government created twenty-two "prosperity and density centers" or "agrovilles" by late 1960. Located along strategic routes connecting larger towns and housing approximately four hundred families, the agrovilles were built through the corvée labor of the peasants themselves. Land was divided into plots on which families were expected to build new homes and raise poultry, farm animals, and fruit trees. Settlements also typically included a school, church, and communal fishpond or irrigation canal. During the day, peasants worked on rice fields up to three miles away. At night, government administrators ordered them to remain in the agroville and claimed that a local self-defense force, often made up of village inhabitants, would protect them from the revolutionaries.[55]

The agroville program was unsuccessful. As an analysis prepared for AID by Michigan State University concluded, it also placed heavy burdens on South Vietnam's rural population. Corrupt administrators often denied peasants the supplies that the government promised them, and villagers bitterly resented being driven from their homes and forced to pay rent on the small agroville parcels. Peasants also suffered greatly in other ways. At one agroville, several unattended children drowned in a canal while adults from the settlement were away doing mandated construction work. In another location, peasant women were raped and assaulted by men wearing the national army uniform when their husbands were sent out on forced labor details. Despite a campaign mounted with films, loudspeakers, and lectures, peasants also rejected the government's attempts to indoctrinate them politically. Rather than associating improved welfare with the benevolence of Diem's South Vietnamese government, many alienated families instead came to align themselves with the guerrillas who frequently entered agrovilles at will, burned the sites, and attacked or executed local administrators.[56]

Despite the apparent failures of the scheme, however, the United States made such resettlement programs an integral part of its support for the Diem government. Concerned with the overall stability of the regime, in June 1961 the Kennedy administration sent Stanford Research Institute economist and development theorist Eugene Staley to Saigon as head of a joint U.S.–South Vietnamese mission charged with drafting a national financial plan. Though initially expected to limit their recommendations to the level of U.S. economic assistance and the measures South Vietnam could take to increase its defense budget, the analysts took on a much broader set of issues. In addition to proposing increased funding for medical assistance, civil service training, agricultural reform, and expanded industry, the Staley group also related development to counterinsurgency. Describing the Vietcong as an enemy "supplied, reinforced, and centrally directed by the international Communist apparatus operating through Hanoi," the team's final report argued that the "primary problem is the restoration of internal security." An effective solution, the authors explained, would require a program of "stepped up economic and social action, especially in rural areas, closely integrated with military action." Diem's plans to reorganize "scattered rural populations into more readily defensible communities so designed and assisted as also to offer improved opportunities for livelihood," moreover, seemed to fit the bill. According to Staley and his colleagues, the South Vietnamese government had produced "one of the more promising counter-guerrilla methods tried up to this time." To fight the revolution by promoting local development, the authors recommended that the United States provide $3.5 million for the construction of one hundred additional agrovilles over the next eighteen months.[57]

The American response to the Staley team's recommendations was highly favorable. Secretary of State Dean Rusk advised President Kennedy that the joint mission had produced "a good economic program on which to strengthen Vietnamese security" and emphasized his belief that the measures would "strengthen the Government, especially in its relations with the rural population," and bring the Vietnamese peasantry "more securely within the nation."[58] In January 1962, the Kennedy administration made the group's recommendations the basis of an eleven-point plan to improve health care, raise agricultural productivity, promote industrial growth, and enhance overall peasant welfare. To support the measure, the United States also pledged a substantial increase over the previous year's $136 million in military and development aid.[59]

Peasant resettlement and village-level modernization programs, therefore, were included early on as integral parts of American counterinsurgency strategy in Vietnam. A social scientist with a long record of experience working in both government and academic institutions, Staley himself believed that the "underdeveloped areas" presented the United States with a "decisive test." The issue, he told a Stanford University audience, had profound strategic as well as moral significance: "Either the benefits of modern civilization in the form of better living conditions and greater human dignity will also become widely available in the non-Western world, so that they are no longer almost exclusively enjoyed by the peoples of the West where they originated, or these benefits will be lost even to us in the West."[60] As he wrote on another occasion, because the Western nations were the primary source for both material advance and democratic values, they had an obligation to "pull societies out of the mire of ancient customs [and] onto the road of modern economic development." Programs of "community development," moreover, could promote that process by sending trained workers to "stimulate the villagers to want and seek better things—a clean well, a school, improved crop practices, a road."[61] Once the peasants were shaken from their ancient, static ways of life by transformative values, Staley argued, they could be motivated to improve their environment and seek their own advancement.

Much like University of Michigan political scientist and Peace Corps consultant Samuel Hayes, Eugene Staley had initially hoped that the bulk of U.S. development aid worldwide might be channeled through international organizations such as the United Nations. In late 1960, he had even proposed that the incoming Kennedy administration take development assistance "out of the Cold War" by inviting the Soviets to join in the creation and funding of a UN institution for that purpose. Like other theorists and Kennedy strategic planners, however, Staley did not question the fundamental assumption that Vietnam was a clear case of external Communist aggression demanding direct and decisive U.S. action. Staley also described Diem's tactic as one that could effectively diminish the appeal of a Communist insurgency by creating peasant loyalties toward the nation-state. Almost certainly unaware of the degree to which Diem's government had implemented the agroville program in exploitative and abusive ways, Staley conceived of the strategy as a progressive response to a dangerous and violent threat. "There is a hot war going on in South Vietnam. . . . It's a bloody, ruthless, no holds barred war conducted by skillful people," he told a journalist in 1961. Improving village communications by providing radios and building roads to connect settlements, he argued, would provide "a way for the views of the populace to reach the government" and give the people information about Diem's programs. In the case of Vietnam, he explained, "You've got to do something on the economic-social side to improve the spirit of the people and show that things will move ahead under the present government." By linking international security with the provision of homes, schools, stores, and community centers, Staley cast the agrovilles as part of a comprehensive, modernizing effort. Like other theorists and government advisers, he also integrated altruistic, economic advance and the creation of a new set of peasant values with a more expansive, more powerful South Vietnamese state.[62]

Between late 1961 and early 1962, the Diem government and the United States made rural population resettlement the foundation of their counterinsurgency program. William E. Colby, at that point the CIA station chief in Saigon, helped push efforts in that direction. For several months the CIA and U.S. Special Forces units had experimented with village self-defense and material assistance programs among the "Montagnards," the indigenous, nonethnic Vietnamese peoples living in highland areas. Colby encouraged Diem and Nhu to step up their own strategic, village-level efforts and also advised them to meet with Robert G. K. Thompson, head of the British Advisory Mission to Vietnam and a veteran of the successful attempt to control the "Malayan Emergency."[63] Attracted to Thompson's ideas, Diem and Nhu became increasingly interested in combining military operations with a nationwide program of "strategic hamlets." Drawing on his experience fighting the Chinese insurgents in Malaya for the British Colonial Service, Thompson argued that a guerrilla movement became powerful less because of its military strength than its ability to develop a sympathetic, highly motivated network of intelligence, supply, and manpower in the agrarian countryside. To defeat the Vietcong, he maintained, Diem's government would have to attack the revolutionary infrastructure itself.[64]

That effort, Thompson argued, should be made through three overlapping stages. The first of these, he wrote in his memoirs, involved "clearing" a target region adjacent to an already secure area and "saturat[ing] it with joint military and police forces. This will force the insurgent units either to disperse within the area or possibly to withdraw to neighbouring areas still under their control or disputed." Thompson cautioned, however, that police and military operations could not simply "sweep" through a region, depart, and allow insurgents to return. They also had to promote a second, "holding" phase designed to "restore government authority in the area and to establish a firm security framework."[65] It was here, he explained, that strategic hamlets had proved so effective in the Malayan case. The pivotal requirement for a strategic hamlet, he told Diem, was to isolate the local peasantry from the insurgent forces: "It is most important that province chiefs and the responsible military commanders should fully understand the concept which lies behind successful anti-communist guerrilla operations, i.e. the physical and political separation of the guerrillas from the population. One must get all the 'little fishes' out of the 'water' and keep them out; then they will die." The relocation of peasants into more easily defended hamlets of roughly a thousand persons, Thompson insisted, was essential to deny insurgents their necessary resources. The settlements also had to be protected by military forces while under construction. Once the perimeter had been fortified with moats, fencing, and stakes, the regular army then needed to draft, arm, and train a hamlet militia. Military forces would also monitor, interrogate, and discipline the population to ensure "the elimination within the hamlet of the insurgent underground organization."[66]

After resettling the peasantry and defending it from the guerrillas, the government could then move on to the third stage, "winning" the rural population. School construction, new canals, road repairs, and the provision of fertilizer, seeds, and livestock would all "give the impression not only that the government is operating for the benefit of the people but that it is carrying out programmes of a permanent nature and therefore intends to stay in the area." This psychological impact, Thompson believed, gave fatalistic peasants a "stake in stability and hope for the future." It stimulated "necessary positive action to prevent insurgent reinfiltration" and encouraged local people "to provide the intelligence necessary to eradicate any insurgent cells which remain." After the peasantry had demonstrated its allegiance to the government, the state could then begin "more ambitious self-help projects" and gradually remove restrictions on the population's movement.[67]

When he formally presented his plan to Ngo Dinh Diem in November 1961, Thompson argued that it would provide the key to winning the war. Because the goal was to "win loyalties rather than kill insurgents," Thompson advised Diem to concentrate his initial efforts in the delta region south of Saigon, a still contested area in which there was a large rural population but a lesser degree of NLF strength. His approach, Thompson maintained, could eventually provide the basis for a nationwide effort. In time, it would "lead by stages to a reorganization of the government machinery for directing and coordinating all action against the communists and to the production of an overall strategic operational plan for the country as a whole."[68]

Thompson's method did not meet with universal approval. Some U.S. military officers, in particular, were troubled by the preference for "clear and hold" operations over more conventional "search and destroy" tactics. Since the 1950s, the U.S. Military Assistance and Advisory Group had trained the South Vietnamese army to fight a conventional war. Even when the Kennedy White House embraced counterinsurgency and development doctrines, many officers still argued that they should fight in Vietnam with the same kind of tactics the United States had used in World War II and Korea. General Lyman Lemnitzer, chairman of the Joint Chiefs of Staff, had a particularly visceral reaction to Thompson's approach and wrote to Kennedy's adviser Maxwell Taylor urging him to prevent the scheme from being incorporated into administration planning. As Lemnitzer and other officers insisted, the situation was too dangerous to try a long-term approach based on strategic hamlets. The war, they claimed, would be won only by concentrating firepower, strengthening the ARVN, and killing Vietcong faster than they could be replaced. Attrition, not village-level counterinsurgency, military critics asserted, would ultimately ensure victory.[69]

Although influential U.S. military leaders held fast to the more conventional tactics they favored and continued to use them, they did not succeed in squelching what soon became the Strategic Hamlet Program. Thompson's plan, already applied in the defense of Britain's empire, fit perfectly with the Kennedy administration's own vision of the challenge in Vietnam. In late 1961, the CIA had warned that although the NLF organization looked "to Hanoi for political and military guidance and various forms of support," they were still "largely a self-supporting operation in respect to recruitment and supplies." The source of their strength, moreover, derived from their manipulation of the vulnerable rural peasantry. "The Viet Cong," a CIA intelligence estimate argued, "live upon locally produced food which they either grow themselves or levy upon villages. They meet most of their currency needs by taxing areas under their control, by robbery, or by blackmail. . . . Local inhabitants in many areas provide the Viet Cong with food, refuge and operational support, in some cases voluntarily and in others as the result of intimidation or coercion."[70] Because the NLF was a movement that depended on the agrarian population to remain effective, an attempt to separate the peasants from the guerrillas might break a key link in the insurgency's chain of support. A proposal such as Thompson's, therefore, seemed to make sense in strategic terms.

Thompson's imperial British strategy also conformed with America's own historical experience in the Philippines. At the start of Kennedy's term in office, Rostow had advised Dean Rusk that "guerrilla counter-measures—like Magsaysay's—have depended for their success on a mixture of attractive political and economic programs in the underdeveloped areas and a ruthless projection to the peasantry that the central government intends to be the wave of the future."[71] The successful campaign of agrarian resettlement and civic action against the Hukbalahap rebellion during the early 1950s, Rostow explained, would suggest ways to win in Vietnam.[72] Although advocates of modernization never acknowledged it directly, Thompson's recommendations resonated even more strongly with a much older American program. According to historian Stuart Miller, U.S. Army officers fighting a Filipino revolt against American colonial rule in 1901 and 1902 had embarked on a "ruthless projection" of their own: "The entire population was herded into concentration camps, which were bordered by . . . 'dead lines.' Everything outside the camps was systematically destroyed—humans, crops, food stores, domestic animals, houses, and boats."[73] Though not explicitly advocating that kind of wholesale, comprehensive destruction, the Kennedy administration adopted and promoted a strikingly similar combination of resettlement and violence. Once an area had been "cleared" and a strategic hamlet established, all those resisting government surveillance and population control were no longer considered mere peasants or farmers. They became instead suspected insurgents and targets for massive firepower.

Thompson's "holding" and "winning" stages also made sense to American advisers already convinced of the potential to promote modernization and social engineering as effective counterinsurgency weapons. When he conducted fieldwork in Malaya during 1952 and 1953, Lucian Pye, the U.S. government's hired expert on the subject, interviewed sixty "Surrendered Enemy Personnel" with the cooperation of the Malayan Federation Police Force. The Communist insurgents, he concluded, did not gain recruits because of the appeal of Marxist doctrine or even the redistribution of particular material goods. According to Pye, Malayan Chinese instead joined the insurgency because it met their need to find a "stable element in their otherwise highly unstable societies." The Western impact reflected in the rise of cities, the growth of a new market economy, changes in agriculture, and the emergence of industry had unsettled an older, "traditional" pattern of

Asian existence and, at the same time, stimulated powerful new desires. During a transitional process in which "large numbers of people are losing their identity with their traditional ways of life and are seeking restlessly to realize a modern way," the Malayan Communist Party provided a force to which a disoriented people could "hitch their ambitions." Hierarchy, organization, the potential for personal advancement up the ranks, and the rules of revolutionary discipline, Pye claimed, led the recruits to believe that "in the structure of the party they can find a closer relationship between effort and reward than anything they have known in either the static old society or the unstable, unpredictable new one."[74] The rural insurgents, he determined, did not join the movement because of a sense of injustice, nationalism, or ethnic solidarity. They joined it because they wanted to be modern.

Walt Rostow's analysis of peasant motivation in revolutionary, "underdeveloped" Vietnam echoed Pye's view of Malaya. During his mission to Saigon with Maxwell Taylor in October 1961, Rostow also conducted interviews with captured guerrillas in the hope of determining their reasons for aligning themselves with the Communist cause. Like Pye, he found "young men in a developing region who had been caught up for the first time—and found various degrees of satisfaction and disappointment—in a modern organizational structure reaching beyond family, hamlet and village."[75] The dislocated and rootless peasants who became guerrillas or sympathizers, Rostow argued, had little exposure to the ideas of Marx, Lenin, or even Ho Chi Minh. They did not espouse a historical, cultural vision of a united Vietnamese nation, desire a redistribution of local wealth and power, or even seek to end the abuses of Diem's government. They simply wanted to be part of a larger, modern institution, and they pinned their hopes on the structure they found in the Vietcong.

Despite the problems of small sample sizes and the obvious limitations to objectivity involved in assessing political beliefs through interviews conducted in jails with state-selected prisoners, the "evidence" gained by Pye and Rostow confirmed the worldview through which Thompson's plan was appropriated and amplified. Since a restless, "transitional" peasantry joined revolutionary organizations to gain a modern sense of achievement and advance, the key to defeating the Communists would be to supply appealing government institutions to replace those of the insurgency. That task, moreover, would require extending the power of the state down to the local level to provide the peasantry with a chance to participate in the functioning of government and to derive a sense of belonging from it. As Pye argued, the problem in Malaya was that the colonial state was simply not expansive enough. "Indeed," he wrote, "over 70 per cent of the respondents indicated that they perceived the colonial administration as existing completely apart from the Chinese community in Malaya. The government operated in distant and limited spheres, and they could not always comprehend how its acts might impinge on their daily lives. . . . The possibility of a central government effectively and consistently concerning itself with the well-being and activities of the great masses of the population was apparently a completely foreign idea to them."[76] If the government could make itself a daily presence in the lives of the villagers, become the central focus of their aspirations, and involve the peasantry directly in the process of governance, Pye suggested, the insurgency would lose its appeal as the route toward modernity. The problem, as the Kennedy administration's Vietnam task force put it 1961, was to "bring the rural people of Vietnam into the body politic."[77]

Thinking of counterinsurgency in these terms, the Kennedy administration and its team of social scientists converted Diem's experiments and Robert Thompson's model into a strategy for nation building of the most profound kind. Determined to extend the state's reach, the Kennedy administration also proposed to create a distinctly South Vietnamese nationalism from the bottom up by instilling a dislocated people with a new political culture. As Lucian Pye explained in a paper he presented to AID's advisory committee, all "developing" governments faced the fundamental crises of "legitimacy," "penetration," and "participation." They needed to secure control over the population and gain its support by actively involving it in the political process.[78] The Strategic Hamlet Program, as the Kennedy administration came to understand it, could provide the structure required to capture popular allegiance and win the war. "Traditional" peasants, American officials and advisers expected, could be made "modern" citizens.

In Vietnam, moreover, many planners believed that appropriate instruments for that process were readily available. Since the 1950s, ARVN troops had been assigned roles in "civic action" projects, and, in 1959 alone, four thousand South Vietnamese soldiers reportedly built 152 bridges and 274 kilometers of forest highway. Trained and supplied by the United States, such forces were expected to help serve as agents in the modernization process. By demonstrating new, activist ideals and a "modern" organization and hierarchy to a malleable, impressionable peasantry, they would help stimulate transformations at the local level. Contact with modern military forces, experts believed, would stimulate self-defense efforts as well as an identification with the larger national government structure beyond the boundaries of peasant lives. Research efforts by Edward Shils, Daniel Lerner, and other social scientists during the late 1950s and early 1960s singled out countries such as Turkey as successful cases of rapid, lasting "military modernization." The Strategic Hamlet Program, Kennedy officials believed, could generate a similar impact and defeat a revolution in Vietnam.[79]

State Department intelligence chief Roger Hilsman, himself a West Point graduate, World War II Office of Strategic Services veteran, and a Yale-trained political scientist, shared the conceptual framework elaborated by scholars such as Shils, Lerner, Pye, and Rostow. Sent to Vietnam in January 1962, he also found the British plan for warfare based on social engineering particularly appealing. In addition to meeting with Robert Thompson in Saigon, Hilsman witnessed a series of failed conventional military operations that convinced him of the need for a method to defeat the insurgency by destroying its relationship to the rural population. Dismayed to find that South Vietnamese bombing and infantry strikes killed villagers, eroded popular support, and drove away the NLF before the revolutionaries could be captured, Hilsman became more certain than ever that a successful strategy would have to couple military operations with social and political progress.[80]

At Kennedy's direction, in February 1962 Hilsman set about defining the hamlet program as the basis of the administration's "Strategic Concept for Vietnam." Strategic hamlets, he argued, could be integrated into a more comprehensive, nation-building approach. Like Thompson, Hilsman emphasized that "the struggle for South Vietnam, in sum, is essentially a battle for the control of the village." Victory would be achieved only by "cutting the Viet Cong off from their local sources of strength." To clarify the method of regrouping villagers into "one compact easily defended area," Hilsman also detailed a model settlement. "Each strategic village," he explained, "will be protected by a ditch and a fence of barbed wire. It will include one or more observation towers, guard posts, and a defense post for central storage of arms. . . . The area immediately around the village will be cleared for fields of fire and the area approaching the clearing, including the ditch, will be strewn with booby-traps (spikes, pits, explosives etc.) and other personal obstacles." In addition to such physical barriers, "field telephones and an alarm system," as well as "a Self-Defense Corps unit of 75 to 150 men . . . armed with carbines, 45 caliber grease guns and shotguns," made Hilsman's proposed strategic hamlet seem a formidable outpost indeed. The settlement's watchtowers, moreover, would survey and discipline life inside as well as outside the hamlet. In addition to repelling attack, the self-defense patrols, supplemented by regular government forces, were charged with "enforcing curfews, checking identity cards, and ferreting out hard-core Communists."[81]

The South Vietnamese government, Hilsman also maintained, would have to win the "hearts and minds" of the peasantry by improving popular welfare. Including medics and teachers on proposed "civic action" teams would demonstrate the state's genuine concern for the livelihood of the people. In Hilsman's terms, however, strategic hamlets could do far more than separate the guerrillas from the farmers and present the Diem regime in a good light. They could also ignite a powerful, nationalistic sense of affinity between a formerly apathetic rural population and the South Vietnamese government. The "civic action team," he pointed out, was the "most important element in eliminating the Viet Cong" because it was responsible for building the "essential socio-political base." Because the insurgency was "a political and not a military problem," the formation of a new set of ties between Diem's government and the rural population became a "first principle." Public administration workers, he expected, "will set up village government and tie it into the district and national levels assuring the flow of information on village needs and problems upward and the flow of government services downward." Enlisting peasants in the Self-Defense Corps and enlarging Diem's organized youth movement of three hundred thousand members, Hilsman expected, would also increase bonds between the village and the state.[82]

Though not using the same terminology as Pye's social scientific assessment of peasant motivations, Hilsman clearly shared the same body of underlying cultural assumptions. As villagers in the throes of modernization came to an awareness that the government intended to improve their quality of life, they were expected to gain a sense of empowerment by taking part in a local political process modeled on Western, democratic forms. As the patronage of the state came down to meet their needs, the peasants would willingly accept the obligations and responsibilities of their new citizenship and actively defend the benefits it provided. "Traditional" obligations of filial piety in the formerly isolated, largely autonomous village would be replaced by a "modern" loyalty to the specifically South Vietnamese nation. Once that transformation was made, moreover, strategists such as Hilsman believed that the Vietcong wouldn't stand a chance.[83]

Systematic implementation of the Strategic Hamlet Program got off to a rocky start in March 1962 with "Operation Sunrise," an attempt to implement the plan in Binh Duong, a province north of Saigon that was largely controlled by the NLF. Although Thompson had urged that the Strategic Hamlet Program start in a relatively secure area and then slowly spread outward to prevent the reestablishment of insurgent forces, the choice of

Binh Duong reflected the preference of the United States for a site that would provide a dramatic victory and Diem's goal to secure a politically important region close to the capital.[84] As ARVN forces swept through the area to drive the NLF guerrillas out, the United States Operations Mission (USOM), the branch of AID at work in Vietnam, provided $300,000 (about $21 per family) to compensate resettled peasants for property losses and equip civic action teams with medicine, identification cards, fertilizer, and farming equipment. Eager to make its own unique contribution, the U.S. Information Service also distributed a specially printed pamphlet entitled *Toward the Good Life*. After the military sweep was complete, the resettlement effort got under way on March 22, 1962, in Ben-Cat district, a heavily infiltrated area surrounded by rubber plantations and forests. Seventy families agreed to move; 140 others were resettled at gunpoint. All were forced to build new homes as well as trenches and walls to protect the fledgling strategic hamlet. ARVN soldiers were also careful to burn old dwellings to prevent farmers and agricultural wage laborers from returning to them. The results were unimpressive. In May 1962, a government-controlled Saigon newspaper admitted that, after six weeks of operations, only 2,769 (7 percent) of the district's 38,000 inhabitants had been permanently moved by force or of their own will. In June, the NLF also demonstrated that it had not been rejected by the rural population when guerrillas successfully ambushed an eleven-vehicle ARVN convoy with the help of villagers who sabotaged roads and prevented government reinforcements from arriving.[85]

Such an inauspicious beginning, one might expect, would have caused even the Strategic Hamlet Program's strongest backers to wonder about its prospects for success. But, in a pattern that would be endlessly repeated, the strategic hamlet concept itself, and the set of deeper, ideological assumptions on which it was based, were accepted as sound and went unchallenged. The problem, U.S. planners insisted, was largely one of coordination and administration. If the program was implemented in the correct order of steps, in the proper location, with the right personnel and the necessary funding, most believed it was simply bound to work. An ideology firmly linked to an overwhelming sense of American confidence in the nation's ability to engineer sweeping, progressive change, modernization prevented planners and strategists from recognizing the evidence challenging its validity. In a memorandum to senior State Department official Averell Harriman in April 1962, Roger Hilsman ignored the less than encouraging results of Operation Sunrise and instead painted a confident picture. Reporting that Diem had strengthened his "Department of Civic Action," created a special

"Interministerial Committee for Strategic Hamlets," and approved a "Pacification Plan" to use the strategic hamlet concept in the Mekong Delta, he brazenly predicted that the strategy would be successfully applied "throughout most of the country" to protect villagers and destroy the insurgency.[86]

In mid-1962, the United States also put in place a network of institutional structures to control and support the program's national implementation. Under the influence of Rufus Phillips III, a former CIA operative and member of Lansdale's covert team in the Philippines, the USOM connected its larger nation-building efforts with rural counterinsurgency by creating the Office for Rural Affairs and establishing a "Rehabilitation Committee" in each South Vietnamese province. Made up of the U.S. military adviser for the region, a USOM provincial representative, and the South Vietnamese government's province chief, each committee was charged with implementing the Strategic Hamlet Program in its own area. After the South Vietnamese province chief estimated the amount of personnel, funding, and building materials needed for the region, his report was sent to Saigon for review by both the Diem government and a U.S. committee made up of working-level representatives from all the American agencies involved in the hamlet program. Following approval of the plan and its budget, a check was drawn and sent to the South Vietnamese province chief. Actual expenditures, however, continued to require the approval of the two American members of each provincial rehabilitation committee. South Vietnamese province chiefs, with the consent of their American military and aid advisers, then met with their subordinate district chiefs and directed them to recruit villagers for service as hamlet construction cadres, local officials, and militia members. The South Vietnamese government built sites for the training of these local recruits, and graduates were sent out in teams led by an administrator from the provincial civic action office. Charged with gathering information regarding the population targeted for resettlement, these groups also planned social and economic programs, organized peasants into work details, and explained the need for them to move into the new strategic hamlet.[87]

To support these operations, AID provided a tremendous amount of funding. During the fiscal year 1963, the State Department's task force on Southeast Asia proposed $87.6 million for hamlet programs that would emphasize "direct allocation of materials to the countryside" and praised AID's shift in emphasis toward rural pacification activities. As one status report put it, "In contrast to prior year project programs, which were managed through the central government with trickle down benefits, the new program emphasizes direct injection of economic, social and security benefits into the rural sector by means of decentralized machinery." With a recommendation that 93 percent of the year's funding increase be dedicated to counterinsurgency support and materials, the report firmly endorsed "hamlet, village and district programs directly altering rural life."[88] During the fiscal year ending in June 1964, AID provided $82 million in building materials, medical kits, school equipment, livestock, pesticides, and food in conjunction with the Strategic Hamlet Program in addition to $215 million for military equipment, services, and supplies.[89] The idea of "directly altering rural life" became embedded in both institutional programming and financial allocation. American resources, many policymakers expected, would certainly transform a malleable, traditional world.

Though the specifics of implementation varied across different regions, the architecture of hamlet construction and civic action programs generally reflected the combination of security measures and civic action that Hilsman had prescribed. South Vietnamese government "Rural Reconstruction" teams of ten to twenty men typically arrived to make a census of the local population and often produced a photographic map for each hamlet that noted families with NLF relationships, land ownership, and the location of houses. The teams broke villagers into work groups, assigned labor schedules, and required peasants to construct the fortifications for the new hamlet. Officials moved houses in outlying areas into the perimeter or destroyed them and gave relocated families small plots of land on which to erect new homes. In addition to laying a fence of barbed wire around the settlement, villagers often dug a moat, built defensive walls, and placed bamboo spikes around the border. Officials also organized a hamlet militia or self-defense corps numbering from five to twelve men by recruiting volunteers or drafting conscripts if necessary. If the government sent the "self-defense force" to a local capital for training, villagers might also receive American arms and equipment.[90]

The government also complemented external defenses with the creation of internal ones and subjected hamlet residents to aggressive surveillance and relentless, personal control. In many areas, peasants were issued identification certificates, and the inhabitants of each house were photographed. Copies of the photos were sometimes pinned inside the house and kept at the local government's administrative center. During the day farmers went out to work on neighboring fields, but the government also established evening curfews, and those violating them risked being shot on sight. If they arrived in the hamlet from other regions, peasants were required to report themselves to the village administrative center to receive official certificates of residence. If they wanted to leave the hamlet, they needed to notify local officials, detail their plans, and receive permission for travel. Visitors staying overnight also had to be registered with the local government or police forces.[91] Becoming "modern" citizens of South Vietnam, ironically, entailed a loss of personal freedom and liberty. Membership in the polity demanded that peasants accept the rigid prohibitions and security apparatus of a mature, "rational" order. In James Scott's words, such disciplinary tactics facilitated an "effort to create and sharply distinguish state spaces from nonstate spaces." Once reconcentrated in a planned settlement, the previously existing community could be disrupted and then rebuilt "from above and outside." Those willfully remaining beyond the realm of official visibility, direction, and control, moreover, became outlaws, threats to be destroyed.[92]

Assessing the way Vietnam's rural population responded to these programs presents a difficult task. Not many historical accounts provide much more than an overview of the hamlet program or treat its daily operations in any detail. A number of U.S. government-supported studies do cover these issues. They also reveal, however, that American observers often interpreted results from a perspective highly sympathetic to the modernizing mission. If the program experienced difficulties, they surmised, the problems were at the level of implementation or administration, not conception. According to a Rand Corporation study of the hamlets created out of the larger village of Duc Lap in Long An Province, the Strategic Hamlet Program could be very disruptive. As that report noted, "The whole pattern of the village was to undergo a drastic change. People were relocated from their homes in the surrounding areas to the newly created hamlets of Duc Hanh A and B. Prior to the Strategic Hamlet Program there were only four or five houses in each of these hamlets; after the program was completed Duc Hanh A and B would each have over 200 houses. . . . A great deal of relocation of the village population into the strategic hamlets had to take place." Some villagers, moreover, did not recognize the advantages that the change would bring, and "recalcitrant" individuals "had to be moved either forcibly or through threats which certainly did not improve the government's image in their eyes." The government, the report suggested, had failed to convey the substantial benefits of the larger organization and institutional structure it created. That failure also exposed a stubborn peasant to grave danger from South Vietnamese forces as well as the NLF. As one government-supported militia commander put it, "We warned them of the insecure conditions outside the hamlet at night and that we could not guarantee their safety if they stayed outside. If we were fired on from outside then we would have to shoot mortars out."[93] As the interior of the hamlet became a type of prison camp, the exterior became a no-man's-land. Resisting modernization appeared more than just short sighted. It also became life-threatening.

Rand Corporation analysts did relate that the construction of strategic hamlets sometimes burdened peasants with serious economic and financial hardships. Government officials forced peasants to build walls and moats, to pay for the barbed wire and concrete used to erect fortifications, and to give up valuable rice paddy land. In one hamlet near Saigon, farmers worked on compulsory projects from mid-December through mid-March and received only a five-day break around the New Year in early February. Confronted with a reduction in the time given to their crops and often required to forfeit bamboo supplies for hamlet defenses, many villagers fell into serious debt. Government officials also commonly stole the relocation subsidies to which peasants were legally entitled. Social scientists John Donnell of Dartmouth and Gerald Hickey of Yale recounted those problems in a survey they conducted for Rand. In one of the hamlets they visited, the two found that a "district chief claimed to have paid 1,000 piastres (about $14) to each resettled family and to have made free labor available to it for the re-assembling of its house, but the farmers themselves denied having received any such payments."[94] As compensation was delayed, denied, or embezzled and peasants living on the margins of subsistence suffered, observers blamed the South Vietnamese government for failing to complete the reforms necessary to catalyze the transformation toward modernity. Without a clear projection of the material and psychological benefits to be derived from an increase in political participation and identification with the nation-state, the peasantry would not embrace citizenship or reject the Vietcong.

Despite the clear abuses, the backers of the Strategic Hamlet Program continued to believe that civic action and the organization of a new political culture could provide the institutional framework and activist values to win the allegiance of a dislocated population. As Donnell and Hickey explained, "A certain amount of discontent is unavoidable in the developmental stage of such a project. This discontent, however, need not pose a serious political problem for the government so long as the regrouping of people and the construction of strategic hamlets are organized efficiently, and provided the Vietnamese government follows through on its assurances that it will re-establish and expand regular administrative services and economic reconstruction projects in these rural areas."[95] The organization of local, democratic elections and the delivery of supplies to meet the "felt needs" of hamlet inhabitants, many believed, simply had to turn the tide of the war. The "central idea of the Strategic Hamlet Program," AID's Rufus Phillips maintained, "is that through the institution of their own self-government, the people will be given a political stake in their own hamlets, and ultimately in the national government, worth defending."[96] Modernization was inevitable. The protests of the peasants, in this view, were merely temporary reactions to a pattern of change that all South Vietnamese would eventually recognize as benevolent and desirable.

The Strategic Hamlet Program, its advocates insisted, would win loyalties by creating local democracies among a previously static, politically isolated, and generally ignorant population. After a visit to Vietnam in early 1963, even a team representing the Joint Chiefs of Staff got on board: "Historically the central government in Vietnam has not reached down and made itself felt to the peasant. Likewise, the peasant has not truly identified himself, his activities, or his future with his government, nor has he thought in terms of national political issues, as we know them." The institution of democratic elections and government-supported self-help projects, however, appeared to be changing that. "Following the election of a hamlet chief and hamlet council," the survey team explained, "the new officials, themselves, decide on projects for the improvement of the well-being and living conditions of the people. It is through this 'rice-roots' program that the framework for a democratic political process is being developed. It is the intention of the government to extend this process from the hamlets and villages up through the districts and provinces, whose officials are now appointed by the central government."[97] Driven ahead with American advice and funding, nation building of the most sweeping type, born and raised to its highest level in the industrial democracies of the West, would now be introduced in the jungles and paddies of Southeast Asia. Because it could transform what one U.S. Army colonel referred to as the indigenous "ossification of the mind,"[98] the United States expected to modernize a paralyzed, culturally deficient people, hamlet by hamlet, up through the government hierarchy itself.

Field reports on hamlet elections and self-help programs continued to find problems. Not surprisingly, however, they also placed the blame at the foot of the Vietnamese administering the program. In one province, the CIA noted, South Vietnamese authorities reported the election of a hamlet administrative committee and submitted a list of the new officeholders. "Investigation revealed," however, "that the elected officials were unaware that an election had taken place, that they were supposed to serve on the committee, or what their functions should be."[99] Written shortly after the fall of the

Diem regime, an early 1964 survey conducted by the U.S. Information Service also made the promise of democratic revolution appear much less tenable. Buddhists claimed that Catholic officials manipulated ballot distribution, one winning village chief candidate was forced to give up his office because the Vietnamese district officer argued that he was unfit for the position, and, most important, "considerably less than half of the eligible voters" participated in the election.[100] The South Vietnamese government, these reports suggested, was not committed to or effective enough in putting the democratic framework into place. U.S. government assessments of hamlet "self-help" projects also charged South Vietnamese officials with a failure to promote the communal decision making necessary to generate empowering, cooperative, empathetic action. As one former USOM official recalled, "The projects were supposed to be the idea of the hamlet people, selected by them from different projects discussed in an open meeting of citizens." Plans were often drafted, however, only after "repeated explanation of the program by pacification cadres." "Self-help" projects were, in these cases, sometimes "'rigged' by various technical service chiefs who wanted their own programs featured." In one area, forty of sixty initial projects included requests for meeting halls, but "field checks indicated that over-eager information cadres had influenced those preparing the applications" to request "facilities where they could conduct their rallies."[101]

In light of the extensive controls placed on hamlet residents and the pervasive surveillance of their daily lives, it seems very clear that whatever "democratic" decisions were arrived at came only from within the spectrum of views and behaviors tolerated and even mandated by the United States and the Diem regime. U.S. policies, however, ignored the contradiction between the promotion of freedom and the construction of forced labor camps. American aid officials also continued to describe "civic action" in strategic hamlets as part of a community development program in which "the people in the existing or newly created villages have a sense of the full participation in the modernization process."[102] With plans under way for sixty-two hundred self-help projects in 1964, the USOM expected to make grants to approximately five thousand hamlets in 1965 and imported valuable cement, metal sheeting, pumps, and machinery not available locally. By the middle of the decade, the USOM also started a plan to train Vietnamese teachers for service in thirteen thousand hamlet classrooms.[103] Building schools and instilling new political values through education, many American officials believed, would create a new cultural perspective. By giving peasants supplies to build the schools, markets, pig pens, chicken coops, irrigation canals, and wells that they had supposedly voted for and volunteered to construct, American officials hoped to produce what Hilsman called the "enormous political gain" of "having a choice" and the "development of community spirit."[104]

That "political gain," strategists emphasized, would also fulfill a different need. It would enable the United States to refute the NLF's portrayal of America as an imperial power, a nation much like those that had attempted to dominate Vietnam in the past. Charles T. R. Bohannan, another Lansdale associate and CIA veteran, notified the U.S. embassy that his hired Filipino field operatives had encountered "very thorough acceptance . . . of the Viet Cong propaganda line that the Americans have taken the place of the French as a colonial power." They had also discovered that peasants believed "the presence of Americans at district and hamlet level tends to confirm the truth of the Viet Cong charge." The remedy, Bohannan argued, was a relatively simple one. An enlarged propaganda effort, he claimed, could "explain to the people the actions and motives of the Americans in-country." An increased use of Asians in the provinces, especially Filipinos, would also help. They could show to the Vietnamese, "as one brownskin to another, what the real purpose of American assistance is."[105]

Although directly influenced by British imperial policy in Malaya, Kennedy administration strategists thought of their altruistic, nation-building effort as anything but colonial. Certain that the Filipino "brownskins" would convey America's genuine ideals, modernizers expected to succeed where the French had failed. In their view, indigenous nationalism, like indigenous people, was highly malleable. Once it became clear to the South Vietnamese that their government could provide the resources and inspiration for them to make concrete advances, strategists were convinced that social engineering would succeed. And who better to use in creating that "demonstration effect" than the Filipinos, themselves considered the remodeled products of enlightened and benevolent American tutelage? In the eyes of the modernizer, victory was only a matter of time.

Public presentations made before audiences in the United States reflected an ideological construction very similar to the ones produced in private, policymaking settings. The U.S. government and the nation's media repeatedly characterized the Strategic Hamlet Program as an effort to assist a threatened people in its desperate attempt to modernize in America's image. While journalists such as David Halberstam and Neil Sheehan detailed the continuing brutality of Diem's regime, U.S. policymakers emphasized the strategic hamlets as evidence that America was planting the seeds of democracy and popular government. When the *New York Times* printed Halberstam's report that the Strategic Hamlet Program was failing to stop Vietcong gains, Robert McNamara reassured Kennedy that the journalist was sorely mistaken. "Hard analysis," he explained, showed that hamlet construction continued to advance and "give individuals an identity as citizens of a community." Even in "hard-core areas," the United States was successfully handling problems of development that were "never solved by either the Japanese or the French."[106] Secretary of State Dean Rusk shared similar interpretations with the public. As he told an audience of New York City businessmen in April 1963, complaints that "South Vietnam is not a full constitutional democracy and that our aid has been subject to waste and mismanagement" should not serve as "alibis for inaction." Diem's government, he emphasized, had been "responsible for its own affairs for less than a decade" and had "little experience in direct participation in political affairs." But the United States was making headway. Bolstered by evidence of the "thousands of elected hamlet councils, and their forthcoming village council elections," Rusk argued that South Vietnam showed "steady movement toward a constitutional system resting on popular consent." As he declared that more than 7 million Vietnamese seeking socioeconomic advance lived in more than five thousand hamlets "governed by secret ballot," Rusk also legitimated the growing U.S. role in the war as a requirement of national mission. The United States, in his terms, was not cooperating with a repressive regime, forcibly moving peasants off their ancestral lands, demanding their labor, or controlling the intimate details of their lives. It was instead providing the guidance necessary for South Vietnam to become more like America and helping that country "take an honored place among modern nations."[107]

David Bell, the administrator of AID, echoed Rusk's arguments and went on to craft a public presentation of America's modernizing power that made victory in Vietnam seem an inevitable, historically determined outcome. Reporting that American aid had provided "the barbed wire, the weapons, and the radios," he emphasized the Strategic Hamlet Program's success in getting the local villagers to contribute "the manpower, the organization, the energy, and, above all, the will to defend themselves." As Bell told a Nevada convention, one might have expected the isolated peasantry to "remain passive while the government troops and the guerrillas fought over the rice fields." But the results, he maintained, were quite different as the villagers placed their hopes in the "program of achieving a better life" and eagerly demonstrated their newfound resolve by taking up arms against the NLF. Recounting his visit to "two young Americans" working among the South

Vietnamese farmers, Bell proclaimed his confidence that U.S. efforts were providing the villagers with "an increasing stake in the progress and independence of the country" and "pushing the Viet Cong back." "Two years ago," he explained, South Vietnam was "ripe for plucking by the communists." Now, however, it was "on the way to becoming a securely free nation, with early prospects for achieving economic independence." Though the struggle would be a tough one, modernization under American auspices would surely prevail. The United States, after all, had started South Vietnam down the natural, transitional path.[108]

Though many U.S. military officers continued to view the hamlets with disdain, some of them took up the cause and described the program as evidence of America's transformative power. Army Chief of Staff General Earle Wheeler told the nation's news services that the United States had learned to fight an "elusive enemy" by providing "opportunities for political and economic growth." In conjunction with Ngo Dinh Diem, America had ensured that the "government is beginning to reach the people and the people are beginning to reach the government." By expanding democratic processes through hamlet elections and self-help projects, the "United States advisory effort" was enabling peasants to meet the "expectations for a better life" that the West aroused. The once fatalistic Vietnamese, moreover, were now rejecting the revolution. Inspired by Americans and their values, they had started to fight the insurgency "every day all over the country." The strategic hamlets, according to Wheeler, were neither detention centers nor sites for discipline and surveillance. They were part of a far-reaching program that brought the fruits of modernity to a people who were "beginning to appreciate more every day that they have something to fight for."[109]

The statements made by American officials and military leaders provide examples of how modernization, as an ideology, functioned in different ways. In a narrow, instrumental, and deliberate sense, modernization was used to present only one side of a more complex picture. When Rusk, Bell, and Wheeler selectively omitted the brutal facts of forced relocation, mandated labor, and constant surveillance, they were acting in the spirit of government policy. As early as Operation Sunrise, the Kennedy administration's Special Group for Counterinsurgency had warned that "the uprooting of families from their homes and resettlement in strategic hamlets ... could give the U.S. a black eye." To avoid creating the wrong image, the advisers suggested, "groups of Americans should not be present during the resettlement movements."[110] In their public statements, Kennedy administration officials followed suit. They gave America credit for modernizing the Vietnamese and used those claims to distance the United States from questions about the realities of specific practices. At this level, modernization was an instrument, a framework used to project a particular image and obscure another. In a broader and more powerful sense, however, the U.S. officials who invoked modernization articulated popular cultural assumptions that they and many other Americans shared about their nation's potential. From a position of authority, they expressed a formulation that crystallized a more general, broadly held understanding in a powerful way. Confident that the United States could transform the "developing" world, they professed their faith.

Popular media interpretations also presented the hamlet program as clear evidence of America's benevolent, modernizing intentions and capabilities in Southeast Asia. In a report on Operation Sunrise, *Newsweek* did acknowledge that many of the "bewildered farm families" ordered to "pack up their belongings" had to be forced into the new settlement. But the magazine also explained that the 866 new residents of Ben Tuong hamlet were provided with "new homes, new land, free education, and medical care" in addition to protection from the Vietcong. Citing a U.S. officer's opinion, the report concluded that the program was "our first aggressive action against the guerrillas that makes any sense."[111] *U.S. News and World Report* was even more effusive in describing the program as a "combination of military, economic, social and—in some ways—political action to meet the challenge of Communism." The relocated peasants, an article maintained, were "encouraged to volunteer for work in their spare time" and would be "paid for their labor." The magazine also emphasized the South Vietnamese government's plan to provide comprehensive social services and readily accepted official descriptions of the program. With essential U.S. backing and guidance, the hamlets built behind barbed wire and bamboo spikes would become centers for a type of cultural incubation. They would "produce a sense of civic awareness among the peasants" and serve as the "first systematic effort to defeat the guerrillas and drive them out of South Vietnam."[112]

A few years later, *Time* echoed these sentiments by invoking the coastal village of Hoaimy as evidence soundly disproving arguments that "the West really has nothing much to offer these poor and frightened peasants, that the Viet Cong alone know how to reach the villagers of Viet Nam." Hoaimy, pronounced "why me," the magazine explained, was a timeless, static settlement of sixteen thousand that, "for centuries," had asked "nothing of the world beyond the mountains and the sea except that it provide a market for the village's rice crop." The NLF guerrillas, however, had invaded the region and replaced Diem's light-handed rule with high taxes, the doctrines of class warfare, and requirements for guerrilla service. When government forces finally repelled the Communists, "Vietnamese and U.S. medics went in with the troops to treat sick civilians," and the government handed out "cloth, cooking oil, medicines and tools." Then, the magazine reported, a miraculous thing happened: "Suddenly, and, as far as anyone can tell, on their own initiative, 10,000 villagers—all except the sick, the aged and the very young children—turned out for 27 straight days and dug a ten-mile ditch around the elongated village." After constructing a formidable barrier that was ten feet deep and twenty feet wide, the peasants reinforced their moat with a four-foot-high wall. As *Time* correspondent John Shaw marveled, there was "something mysterious and mystical about the great wall at Hoaimy. The spectacle of 10,000 villagers building it voluntarily and without payment, the phenomenon of their will to resist so suddenly and spectacularly revealed, gives both sides much to think about. . . . The spirit of Hoaimy matters. In this may lie a partial answer to how to compete with the Viet Cong—perhaps even how to defeat them."[113] In *Time*'s portrayal, under the auspices of American advice and through the provision of American resources, the corvée labor became "voluntary" and the rigid controls imposed under the hamlet program vanished. All that remained was the newly created will that contact with modernity had inspired. While the NLF may indeed have placed repressive burdens on the population, the emphasis on the way government action, planned and guided by the United States, could instill rural, fatalistic Asians with a "mysterious" resistance reflected a firmly held set of cultural convictions. America and the West, such accounts argued, could engineer the dramatic changes in social life and personal values necessary to mobilize an isolated, traditional peasantry against the forces of international communism.

The most extravagant praise for resettlement and modernization through American assistance came from an active government-media partnership. Impressed by a report that Edward Lansdale wrote about a determined band of Catholic villagers on the far southern tip of Vietnam, Kennedy himself suggested to national security adviser McGeorge Bundy that Lansdale's "story of the counter-guerrilla case study would be an excellent article for [a] magazine like the *Saturday Evening Post*." Though the memo could not be published under the CIA operative's signature, Kennedy commented, it might be passed along to another writer for expansion and submission. As the president told Bundy, "You should make sure that this type of material has good distribution."[114] The *Post* was happy to cooperate with the White House by printing "The Report the President Wanted Published," authored by "an American Air Force officer" who remained unidentified "for professional reasons." Father Nguyen Loc Hoa, a former officer in Chiang Kaishek's army, the magazine explained, led a group of exiles from Communist China. Recounting the way they built the village of Binh Hung, planted rice, and armed themselves with "staves and knives," in addition to American carbines, ammunition, and artillery, the *Post* turned the group into a symbol of the way Western values and U.S. aid gave Asians the fortitude to fight off totalitarianism. Descriptions of the settlement's training center, "our little Fort Bragg," and a militia cheerfully flashing the same "Boy Scout salute" as middle-class American adolescents portrayed a people given the strength to resist Marxist oppression by America's own ideals. Before long, "The Village That Refused to Die" also became a television film, and *Reader's Digest* joined the *Saturday Evening Post* in publicizing the story of a people who, having "tasted slavery and found it bitter," now used American help to go about "enlarging the area of freedom in the world."[115] Though not an official "strategic hamlet," Father Hoa's settlement became a cultural touchstone and the framework through which many Americans perceived a U.S. program to support a struggling, childlike peasantry. If motivated by Western ideals and backed by American resources, such representations argued, the Vietnamese would surely recognize all that genuine modernity had to offer and fight against the Communists who threatened to lead them astray.

As in the case of the Peace Corps volunteers, images of Americans working with Vietnam's besieged villagers were also used to represent a benevolent United States possessing the vitality, toughness, and resolve to meet Cold War challenges. In an article titled "Internal War," Roger Hilsman argued that the United States "must be prepared to become deeply involved" in the arduous battle against the Communists. By "broadening the will and capacity of friendly governments to augment social and political reform programs as a basis for modernization," Hilsman emphasized, Americans fighting totalitarian aggression continued a much older tradition of self-sacrifice. As he recounted the story of the massacre of Company C of the Ninth Infantry in the early-twentieth-century Philippine "counterguerrilla campaign," the State Department intelligence chief described how men lined up at the "cook shack" were charged by 450 ruthless guerrillas and heroically fought back with a baseball bat and a meat cleaver. Although only twenty-four of the company's men escaped death, the Americans eventually defeated the savage insurgency not through force of arms but by using their values to inspire the wayward, indigenous population. Recruiting teams of "native Filipinos—men wise to jungle ways," the Americans placed each group under the direction of "a trained American officer—a bold and determined leader."[116] With an emphasis on the sacrifices and influence of dedicated Americans fighting to control their colonial possession, Hilsman reframed the tale of imperial gallantry to fit the campaign of Cold War counterinsurgency.

Applied directly to the Vietnamese case, those themes were continually repeated in official discourse. Vice President Hubert Humphrey, through his description of the work done by AID employees in "New Life" hamlets, settlements that differed only in name from those of the Diem era, recounted the selfless heroics of a "shirtsleeves war." In language quite similar to that used by Kennedy to describe the Peace Corps volunteers, Humphrey maintained that ordinary U.S. citizens were bringing "home to the farmers and the fishermen of Vietnam the understanding that Americans are fighting for more than just military victories, that we are also fighting 'the other war'—the war against poverty, ignorance, and disease" and helping to "save and build a nation." Humphrey also recounted stories of AID men captured, ambushed, and killed by the NLF. Quoting one injured province representative, he crafted an image of saintlike devotion: "No money could pay me, no medals they could ever pin on me could ever match the satisfaction I got from the thanks of the Vietnamese people. They didn't have to say a word. I could see the appreciation in their eyes." Though many individual AID workers willingly risked their lives and may have cared for the people they sought to assist, Humphrey represented them in ways that characterized the United States as a whole. "Americans," he argued, "have always responded to the needs of others—a characteristic that has made us a great people, a great Nation. And, despite the dangers and hardships that go along with helping the people of Vietnam, American civilians are in there with sleeves rolled up, doing battle just as surely as our military people are. It's an unbeatable combination."[117] AID's work, in such terms, represented nothing less than the essence of national character. Self-sacrificing and humanitarian, the United States would lead victims of Communist aggression through a developmental process that, once started, would prove irrepressible.

In a publication titled "Quiet Warriors," the State Department also argued that the American civilians stationed in Vietnam were "diplomats, doctors, school teachers, police instructors, engineers, farmers, information specialists, jacks of many trades and skills." Though diverse in profession, all were representatives of the world's most modern country and had gone to Vietnam "to build the things—the social links and services and the common institutions—without which no people can have and be a nation."[118] As

Lyndon Johnson himself put it, American civilians were working in Vietnam in a "spirit of patriotic self-sacrifice" to win the war "not with bombs and bullets, but with all the wondrous weapons of peace in the 20th century."[119] By allowing Johnson to draw that false dichotomy between warfare and social engineering, modernization facilitated the projection of an altruistic image that rationalized and legitimated the violence it involved. The practices used by police and military forces to "destroy" the "insurgent cell" within hamlets, of course, went unmentioned. Although a devastating war was fought inside as well as outside the hamlet fortifications, American actions were continually presented in terms of sacrifice, assistance, and moral, ethical duty.

The Agency for International Development also incorporated decidedly missionary rhetoric into its effort to recruit workers for Vietnam. In a letter addressed to the Advertising Council, the same agency that handled public relations for the Peace Corps, AID's director of information staff drafted what he thought would make the perfect recruiting pitch. Americans, he explained, were "working shoulder to shoulder with the Vietnamese" to "distribute emergency supplies," "advise local government officials," and "fight pain and hunger and need." Their work, moreover, reflected a moral calling to which all citizens could aspire. As he phrased it, "The hours are long and the work is hard and may be dangerous but a thousand highly skilled Americans are carrying on day and night in Vietnam. If you are a doer, a mover, a leader, if you are a college graduate with experience in community development or local government . . . you may be needed for one of the most important jobs in the world today. . . . The rewards are as high as the jobs are tough."[120] Some public sources went further by making the ideological resonance between the early Peace Corps and AID's work in Southeast Asia explicit. As one urban newspaper put it, the civilians at work in Vietnam included "doctors, engineers, propagandists, farmers and technicians. . . . Few of them live in the comfort of Saigon. They constitute a kind of heavy-duty Peace Corps, with the stakes high and bullets whizzing around them. They do good works and try to explain to peasants what a government is, and why they should bear it allegiance."[121] Though Sargent Shriver tried to limit comparisons between his agency and the war's "pacification" efforts, in 1964 AID also attempted to recruit former Peace Corps volunteers with "Rural and or Community Development background and experience" for its "Vietnam Rural Affairs Program."[122]

Like the creators of the Alliance for Progress, proponents of the Strategic Hamlet Program also described America's past as a source of lessons for a modernizing people to follow. As early as the end of the Eisenhower administration, Diem's land resettlement programs and agrovilles were likened to America's experience in conquering its own western territories. Wyoming senator Gale W. McGee, a former history professor, argued that moving peasants into sparsely inhabited regions allowed a farmer to "claim his own acreage" and "seek his own economic independence" with a "new lease on life." Diem's programs, in McGee's analogy, followed the example America had set long ago: "This is not unlike what happened in our own land resettlement history here in the United States, when if a man could not find economic independence in our own more congested regions of the East, the Government gave him a new start in life in the public land territories of the West. This parallel ought to excite Americans because of our own historic experience. It ought also to give us some measure of pride that our example has provided the inspiration for this experiment in Vietnam." Moving people into unoccupied regions, he argued, would also provide "intelligence, defense, and security systems" against the guerrillas.[123] A century later and half a world away, the stockades and Indian fighting of America's Great Plains were now envisioned on the banks of the Mekong Delta. Roger Hilsman argued that the South Vietnamese should also search for lessons of development in the history of twentieth-century America. Just as Franklin D. Roosevelt had once been "Dr. New Deal" as well as "Dr. Win the War," Hilsman insisted that Diem's government could also combine "military action and a social new deal" in a program that would tie the "isolated villages" into the "governmental structure."[124] America's past, in those arguments, was a model for Vietnam's future. Presented that way, understanding the situation in Vietnam did not demand a thorough knowledge of that country's history or culture. It merely required a familiarity with America's own heroic narrative.

John O'Donnell, a former AID province representative, echoed McGee and Hilsman by picking out yet another point for emulation. South Vietnam, he claimed, needed to infuse the Strategic Hamlet Program with statements of the "aims and ideals of the government" that "could provide something to which all citizens could rally and for whose preservation they would willingly risk their lives. We have such a statement in our Declaration of Independence and Constitution strengthened and reaffirmed by the words of Patrick Henry, Thomas Jefferson, Abraham Lincoln, and others." In trying to mobilize the population through the hamlets, the South Vietnamese were on the right track, a track America had traveled in its own development. "The designers of the U.S. Constitution and government,"

O'Donnell explained, "were well aware of the necessity to create an atmosphere in which struggle (between haves and have nots, management and unions, black and white, etc.) could take place with a minimum of violence. . . . The Vietnamese government attempted to implement this concept when it included provisions for free elections of local officials, formation of social and economic action groups within the hamlets, and majority selection of self-help projects in the Strategic Hamlet Program."[125] Transforming Ngo Dinh Diem into a devoted follower of Thomas Jefferson was no mean feat, but the ideology of modernization allowed for just that kind of construction.

The power and appeal of modernization also proved a durable barrier to systematic dissent against the Strategic Hamlet Program. Convinced of the truth claims embedded in an ideology so tightly linked to America's own identity and world role, most critics of the program spoke from well within the boundaries of the modernization paradigm itself. For official contemporaries and most later analysts as well, the problems cited were largely those of administration and implementation, not the fundamental assumptions or core concepts involved. Time after time, critics faulted the execution of the Strategic Hamlet Program but tempered their statements with a reverence for its objectives and theoretical underpinning. As the Kennedy administration attempted to account for the program's growing failures, that pattern of analysis prevented a more searching, productive critique.

For a brief period, it appeared that the strategic hamlets were in fact changing the course of the war. In July 1962, the CIA's Saigon station chief reported that Diem and his brother Nhu understood the importance of the program and the need to blend security and civic action to give the peasants a "stake in support of [the] GVN [South Vietnamese government] and [the] defeat of [the] enemy." Confident that the program was "definitely moving forward," the agent argued that it "has [a] fair chance of being sold to people and as [a] specific tactic in preventing [the] spread [of] Viet Cong influence."[126] Other reports from the summer of 1962 also argued that the program was turning back the NLF. After he visited Phu Yen Province, U.S. ambassador Frederick Nolting told Washington that the South Vietnamese had completed sixty-three of a projected eighty-four hamlets in the area. More than a thousand villagers, he related, had also fled Vietcong control and entered a hamlet to ask for government protection. Most important, Nolting added, was the fact that local peasants in several regions had started to provide the South Vietnamese government and U.S. advisers with information regarding the whereabouts of Vietcong forces. Encouraged that the "turning point in [the] Malayan Emergency was defined when increasing numbers of the population began volunteering more and better intelligence against Communist terrorists," the ambassador claimed that the "opening up of rural areas and [the] provision [of] tangible benefits" to the peasantry were "winning back [the] population."[127]

As recent studies and memoirs of the Vietnamese revolution point out, however, the NLF moved quickly and successfully to counter the Strategic Hamlet Program. When peasants became alienated by their resettlement and chafed under the forced labor requirements and pervasive restrictions, NLF guerrillas played on their resentment by telling them that when the revolution triumphed, they could return home. The NLF also responded to the Strategic Hamlet Program by escalating the intensity of its recruiting and military operations. Communist Party leaders in Hanoi advised southerners to target the strategic hamlets using direct, armed assault if possible and techniques of political and psychological infiltration where necessary. Women and elderly peasants, northern officials suggested, could be particularly useful operatives for work within hamlet boundaries because government authorities would be less likely to suspect them. According to William Duiker's account, "above all, southern leaders were advised to be patient and to be prepared to attack and destroy the hamlets time and time again until government control had been eliminated."[128] Truong Nhu Tang, a founder of the NLF and former minister of justice in its Provisional Revolutionary Government, explains that secret actions within Diem's administration may have also assisted the persistent revolutionaries. Pham Ngoc Thao, a member of the Vietminh resistance and friend of Tang's, worked his way into Ngo Dinh Diem's confidence during the 1950s. Thao so impressed Diem that the prime minister sent his trusted adviser to Malaya to study British attempts to control the insurgency there. When the United States and South Vietnam deployed the Strategic Hamlet Program in 1962, Thao was also appointed the military officer in charge of the operation. As Tang suggests, his associate may have tried to undermine and overextend the program from within. "It is certainly a fact," Tang points out, "that under his supervision the strategic hamlets created even more hostility among the peasants than had the Agrovilles before them."[129] In the countryside of Vietnam, and possibly in the center of Saigon, the NLF effectively met the program's challenge.

Over the next several months, official U.S. assessments took note of the NLF gains and cast a shadow over earlier, more optimistic assessments. The guerrillas, officials acknowledged, were able to infiltrate the newly established settlements, often using local assistance. Yet, even in the face of mounting evidence that the Strategic Hamlet Program was failing to produce the sweeping changes desired, American strategists steadfastly defended its fundamental objectives and assumptions. Although they pointed out real problems of administration or execution, they never doubted the idea that the United States was capable of generating a new, distinctly South Vietnamese nationalism and loyalty. In a letter to the State Department in October 1962, Ambassador Nolting admitted that the arming of self-defense units had proceeded too slowly. Hamlet militias, he wrote, often relied on "a small arsenal consisting of shotguns and old French weapons" that left them vulnerable to organized NLF assaults. Nolting also acknowledged that "the poorest inhabitants are bearing the brunt of unpaid work on the strategic hamlet defenses" and commented that "misbehavior" by the ARVN and civil guard among the peasants remained a serious issue. Those disconcerting signs aside, however, he went on to argue, incredibly, that the ill-fated Operation Sunrise was a major success. Relocating the peasantry, he claimed, had been both "wise and necessary." Rural people had been brought "back under [South Vietnamese Government] control, the logistic support they provided the VC was reduced, and they were offered a better and more secure life." Determined to press on, Nolting also explained that he did not believe "that a serious problem arises from any impression that we are replacing the French in their colonial rule."[130]

Other reports from late 1962 were more forthright in pointing out problems, but even these generally centered on matters of implementation instead of underlying assumptions. As Robert H. Johnson, a staff member on the State Department Policy Planning Council, told his boss, Walt Rostow, in Central Vietnam the Strategic Hamlet Program was "mostly pure facade" owing to inadequate defenses, squabbles between Nhu and his brother Can, and the "customary defects of Vietnamese administration." In a more penetrating comment, Johnson did suggest that hamlet elections would have little meaning "as long as the councils were fundamentally the instrument of the central Government for the imposition of certain programs in the countryside." Like other analysts, however, he, too, implied that once abuses in implementation were corrected, democracy could be put in place, communications between people and government could be opened, and progress could be made.[131] General Maxwell Taylor also told Robert McNamara that, although the program was started too quickly and the hamlets still had inadequate defenses, "there would seem to be no reason for modifying the views . . . regarding the long-term virtues of the program. It is only now commencing to mature."[132] In November, Nolting again told his superiors that "we *are* making progress." As the ambassador put it, U.S. officials in Vietnam were learning to "whistle while we work." "As the security situation improves," he argued, "we should expect an accelerated and cumulative effect from the economic and civic action measures."[133]

By 1963, even the more critical reports were blunted by an overwhelming faith that, in time, the counterinsurgency strategy would work its magic. In March, Robert Thompson observed that the Strategic Hamlet Program had "gone much better in [the] last six months than he had ever expected," and U.S. admiral Harry Felt sent the good news on to Washington.[134] General Paul Harkins, head of the U.S. Military Assistance Command for Vietnam, also reported that "improvement is a daily fact." "Thanks to the combined efforts of the RVN [Republic of Vietnam] and the U.S.," Harkins declared, "the success of the counterinsurgency is attainable and we are confident of the outcome."[135] In October 1963, Secretary of Defense Robert McNamara and General Maxwell Taylor did sound an unusual note of caution. Although the "economic and civic action element of the program" had been "carried forward on the U.S. side with considerable effectiveness," they noted that it "lagged behind the physical completion of the hamlets." "Without this element, coupled with effective defensive measures," they warned, "what are called 'strategic hamlets' may be only nominally under GVN control." The two insisted, however, that they "found unanimous agreement that the strategic hamlet program is sound in concept" and argued that the presence of Americans was having a transformative influence on the countryside. "The stiffening and exemplary effect of U.S. behaviour and attitudes," they explained, "has had an impact which is not confined to the war effort, but which extends deeply into the whole Vietnamese way of doing things."[136] Although the hamlet program may have had only a tenuous grasp, the ideology of modernization held firm.

In the end, the Kennedy administration soured on Ngo Dinh Diem, not its ambitions for social engineering. Diem and his brother Nhu, frustrated by American efforts to take more of the war's management away from them, angrily declared that South Vietnam's sovereignty and independence were threatened by an excessive U.S. presence. Such complaints, tarnishing the image of a fledgling nation fighting external Communist aggression in harmonious partnership with the United States, won Diem few points in Washington. Diem's regime also became a liability for the Kennedy administration when its long history of political repression was suddenly thrust into the media spotlight. Always intolerant of dissent, Diem was particularly sensitive to criticism of South Vietnam's privileged Catholic minority, and in the spring of 1963, he unleashed his troops on the Buddhists who defied him by displaying their banners when only the national flag was permitted. After South Vietnamese soldiers opened fire on a crowd in Hue and killed nine people, thousands of Buddhists marched in response. But rather than seek a rapprochement, Diem simply branded them Communist-inspired agitators and tried to cut off all debate by arresting his religious opponents and their vocal supporters. When an elderly Buddhist monk publicly immolated himself in protest, shocking photos of Thich Quang Duc's burning body exposed the degree of popular revulsion for Diem, a man so often presented by the United States as a heroic, enlightened leader. Over the summer, continued violence and arrests only did further damage.

As protests escalated and news accounts revealed evidence of Diem's dictatorial repression, the Kennedy administration first tried to solve the problem with discrete, partial measures. Henry Cabot Lodge, a Republican who could insulate the White House from right-wing attacks, was sent to replace Frederick Nolting, an ambassador thought by many to have become too friendly and tolerant with Diem. The United States also demanded the removal of Diem's brother and sister-in-law from the government. Leaders of the anti-Buddhist crusade, Ngo Dinh Nhu and Madame Nhu had become symbols of the regime's worst abuses. Once shed of them and their influence, some U.S. policymakers hoped, Diem's government would turn toward necessary reforms. By late August, however, the situation reached a point that many Kennedy officials could no longer accept. When rumors spread that Nhu had started a clandestine effort to negotiate with Hanoi, the administration began an extensive debate on whether or not it should continue to back Diem's regime at all. While some advisers suggested that a delay in economic or military funding might force Diem to moderate his attacks on the Buddhists and rededicate himself to fighting the NLF, other policymakers determined that only a coup and a change of power could set things right. In early October, when the United States cut off aid for Nhu's Special Forces troops, opponents of the government within South Vietnam's army decided that their time had come. As the American commitment to Diem wavered, the plotters met with CIA officers in Saigon to discuss ways of replacing or possibly assassinating him. Expecting that the United States would back them once they were in power, the generals captured Diem and Nhu and murdered the two brothers in an armored personnel carrier on November 2. They also declared a new government under their authority, gained U.S. approval, and pledged themselves to an enhanced war effort.[137]

In the tumultuous weeks following Diem's assassination, the extent to which the hamlet program had failed as a counterinsurgency measure became clear. As a survey of Long An Province reported, the NLF had greatly strengthened its hold in the region. In one settlement after another, U.S. Information Service teams reported utter disaster. According to one typical account: "Both the hamlet gate and barbed wires are 100 percent destroyed by the enemies. The barbed wires and the iron stakes are cut down, there is not even a spare piece. . . . The hamlet hall was burnt down by the VC. . . . All the members of the service of administration, the hamlet council and all the hamlet armed forces cannot carry on any more work because there is no security and their morale is rather confused, being afraid of the enemies. The system of defense is completely destroyed." In another hamlet, a U.S. Information Service group reported, "[The] administrative committee and Council are disintegrated, peace-seeking, pro-communist. Popular organizations also are disintegrated and already cease activities." In other cases, survey teams concluded that all the hamlet's young men had gone off to join the Vietcong or discovered that the peasants were unwilling to speak to them at all.[138]

Even in the midst of these developments, however, attempts to account for the apparent failure were firmly centered within the framework of the modernization model. If the hamlet program did not achieve expected results, U.S. officials maintained, the problem was entirely due to Vietnamese mismanagement, not America's conceptual approach. As one field report that Ambassador Henry Cabot Lodge sent on to Washington noted, the guerrillas had successfully gained popular acceptance, entered, and started living in many of the strategic hamlets. In accounting for that result, however, the report placed the blame directly at the feet of the previous South Vietnamese government. Instead of following the proposed plan of slow expansion from one secure sector to another, the "strategic hamlets were terribly overextended by Nhu in order to extend Nhu's control over the country as fast as possible, regardless of the fact that many of the hamlets were worthless."[139]

A report by Earl Young, the USOM province representative in Long An, came to the same conclusion. The Vietcong, he notified Lodge, had achieved "a day-by-day elimination" of the strategic hamlets, and "of the 219 hamlets containing armed defenders (hamlet militia) in September, 50 remained armed today. The remainder have turned in their arms or deserted." In Young's terms, however, the problem had nothing to do with the assumption that elections and community development would make the peasantry willing to fight in defense of an externally imposed, repressive social order that radically altered the patterns of their lives. "The reason for this unhappy situation," Young argued, "is the failure of the government of Vietnam to support and protect the hamlets." Because ARVN troops refused to conduct night operations and could not defend scattered settlements and their district headquarters at the same time, the "will and desire of the people to resist dropped." The Strategic Hamlet Program, Young concluded, "can be made workable and very effective against the Viet Cong," but additional troops would be required, and South Vietnamese corruption would have to be curtailed.[140]

"Pacification by proxy," as the *Pentagon Papers* revealed, certainly did present serious obstacles. Diem and Nhu did not implement the Strategic Hamlet Program by slowly moving like an "oil spot" from one secure region to another, as Thompson and Hilsman directed. They also had goals of their own. In Diem's eyes, the hamlet program was part of a larger effort to make the United States "committed to South Vietnam (and to his own administration) without surrendering his independence." Diem and Nhu also sought to preclude the rise of political rivals by using the program and its resources as a direct means to control local politics and province-level structures of authority. By placing loyal servants of their regime in power as province and district chiefs, they hoped to deny opponents any chance at using U.S. resources or establishing a popular base.[141] American civic action supplies lagged behind rapid hamlet construction, defenses were often inadequate, and local officials frequently failed to compensate relocated peasants and embezzled the funds they were supposed to distribute.

Focusing only on these administrative factors, however, official analyses of the Strategic Hamlet Program did not challenge the ideas at its core. Despite the failure of the Diem period, few explored the possibility that constant surveillance, rigid controls, and participation in the South Vietnamese state may not have been desired by the indigenous peasantry at all. The expectation that rural values and ways of life could be easily molded to suit anti-Communist objectives also endured as the war escalated. Although the U.S. security establishment abandoned the term "strategic hamlet" following the assassinations of Diem and Nhu, the American counterinsurgency approaches that followed simply reheated the old program's fundamental principles. In December 1963, Dean Rusk optimistically told Lyndon Johnson that South Vietnam's new military regime could "correct defects in the implementation" of the program, and National Security Council staff member Michael Forrestal advised the president that it would be "rather easy" for the United States to "set up a new program for the villages . . . since it would draw heavily from the old Strategic Hamlet Program."[142] The "New Life" hamlets instituted at the end of that year were different only on the surface. The Vietnamese leaders pledged phased implementation starting in secure areas, promised to cooperate with the United States in training hamlet militias to patrol more actively, and accepted the idea of using locally based civic action teams instead of centrally administered ones.[143] But the fundamental assumptions that security controls, participation in an expanded state structure, and the provision of social services would create a modern, nationalistic bond to the South Vietnamese government remained largely unquestioned at the close of the Kennedy era.

Basically unchallenged, the tenets of modernization also flowed through American counterinsurgency thinking until much later in the decade. In 1964, when Ambassador Henry Cabot Lodge detailed a hamlet-level program that would "saturate the minds of the people with some socially conscious and attractive ideology," he revealed a continuing faith in modernization's relevance for counterinsurgency. Like Roger Hilsman, Lodge was convinced that a census, identification cards, a curfew, and the use of a "fine tooth comb" in each hamlet to "apprehend the terrorists" would provide security. "At the first quiet moment," teachers, agricultural experts, and local elections would begin to generate progressive, anti-Communist development and eventual American success. Robert Komer, Lyndon Johnson's assistant for "pacification" planning in South Vietnam, also integrated modernization into his program of Civilian Operations and Revolutionary Development Support (CORDS). Initiated in late 1966 and expanded through 1967, CORDS, like the strategic hamlet and New Life efforts before it, combined warfare and security measures with civic action and welfare plans designed to produce a new political culture among the rural population.[144] Like other strategists before him, Komer also displayed overwhelming confidence in his concept and told the nation's press that, although Vietnamese administrative problems remained, "we begin '68 in a better position than we have ever been in before."[145] Unfamiliar with Vietnam's culture, most American policymakers never understood the revolution against which they fought. The abstract, universal assumptions of modernization, moreover, appeared to make that understanding unnecessary. As Marilyn Young argues, U.S. officials had no doubt that they "could give a people as rooted in history as the Vietnamese a ready-made set of 'beliefs' for which they would be willing to die."[146]

That basic assumption also went unchallenged in public interpretations. Like many other popular sources, *Time* dropped its early enthusiasm for

Diem and emphasized his "unwillingness to delegate authority, the ineffi-
ciency of his administration," and "the low morale of his officer corps." "The
charge most often made," the magazine reported, was that "Diem is alienated from the 14 million people of South Vietnam."[147] As valid as such points
may have been, however, their constant repetition only contributed to a
public interpretation of the war that placed the blame for failure on the
Vietnamese alone, not the popular belief that American resources and ideals
could catalyze a wave of dramatic nation building throughout Southeast
Asia. As the Buddhist crisis mounted in the summer and fall of 1963, the
brutality with which Diem and Nhu repressed dissent only confirmed that
conviction. When he quoted an American field officer in 1963, Stanley Karnow wrote what many believed: "There's a basic difference between ourselves and Vietnamese officialdom." The United States, Karnow and others
suggested, had the method and the means to defeat the NLF and build a new
South Vietnam. The short-sighted Vietnamese, however, had simply failed
to grasp "the political aspect of this war."[148]

A few dissenters in the early and mid-1960s reached beyond identifying
the genuine shortcomings of the Diem regime and edged toward challenging
the ideology of modernization itself. On the more progressive wing of the
Democratic Party, members of Congress such as Montana senator Mike
Mansfield voiced their growing doubts regarding the Strategic Hamlet Program. As Mansfield and several colleagues argued after visiting South Vietnam, the hamlet concept was "based on the assumptions that the Vietcong
are sustained by the rural populace primarily out of fear, and in part, because the peasants are not aware of the superior social, economic, and
political advantages which are offered by support of the Government and
participation in its processes. *Assuming the accuracy of the assumptions* successful military action within the dimensions of the present effort is conceiv-
able. . . . But even to give an initial military victory meaning will require a
massive job of social engineering."[149] Though willing to accept the underlying argument at the present, Mansfield and his colleagues at least made the
rarely discussed assumptions explicit and, unlike most commentators, argued that they remained unverified.

The work of reporters such as David Halberstam also raised serious questions regarding the ability of America to win the Vietnam War through
modernization. Although Halberstam placed most of the blame for the
failure of the Strategic Hamlet Program on the shoulders of Diem and Nhu
and reiterated the vision of a passive, "traditional" society, he did raise the
possibility that such a program would not have succeeded under any admin-

istration. In his 1964 account titled *The Making of a Quagmire*, Halberstam explained that "the war shuttled back and forth for the peasants: they endured the Government troops during the day, the Vietcong at night." When the rural population lost its ancestral lands, homes, crops, and families to the unrelenting violence, the arrival of government forces did not arouse aspirations for a better life through American aid or a desire for participation in Diem's national state. It produced only fear, anguish, resentment, and a deep longing to end the terror that invaded their lives: " 'The war,' a young Vietnamese said to me bitterly . . . 'only lasts a lifetime.' "[150]

In the first half of the 1960s, however, even these somewhat indirect expressions of dissent were comparatively rare. Tightly connected to a strong cultural sense of identity and mission, the modernization of Southeast Asia appeared to fulfill the nation's duty to assist a people striving to advance along the same historical course that the United States had once traveled. Because "traditional" peoples were shaken out of their apathetic stasis only by the arrival of more advanced ideals and technology from external sources, indigenous nationalism could never be genuine or authentic. The NLF, in this understanding, was an organization wholly motivated by the forces of international communism. The Vietnamese peasantry, in this worldview, was not drawn to the revolution out of an allegiance to the larger historical and cultural concept of a united, independent Vietnam or even because of the appeal presented by a promised redistribution of power and wealth in the agrarian social structure. Peasants joined the NLF simply because they wanted to be like Westerners; they wanted the social values, political institutions, and economic organizations that would make them modern. The war, in this sense, was viewed through a framework in which there was very little middle ground. Confronted with a developmental model antithetical to their vision of a liberal, capitalist world order, American policymakers understood their duty as one of helping South Vietnam advance through the volatile period in which social revolution might prevent destined progress.

Not all Americans imagined themselves as altruistic, nation-building missionaries, and U.S. strategy in Vietnam encompassed far more than social engineering and counterinsurgency tactics. The violence deployed through the Strategic Hamlet Program during the Kennedy administration was also raised to a new level by the deployment of U.S. combat troops in 1965 and the relentless bombing of the Vietnamese countryside. But, throughout much of the 1960s, the sense of national mission projected by an ideology of modernization retained its powerful appeal. Resonating with older images of Manifest Destiny, the vision of America's superior society and its transformative potential preserved claims to imperial authority in an age of decolonization. Measures such as the Strategic Hamlet Program drew on the legacy of America's own experience in the Philippines as well as the British attempt to maintain empire in Malaya. They were also quite similar in form to older British practices in South Africa, Spanish tactics in Cuba, and French efforts at village resettlement and reconcentration in Egypt and Algeria. Presented in an "objective," social scientific framework, however, the striking parallels between the U.S. role in Vietnam, America's own imperial past, and the history of colonialism in Indochina disappeared. The world's most "modern" nation, many believed, was fulfilling its historical obligation by fighting for liberal democracy in Vietnam. In later years, the Rolling Thunder bombing campaign, resistance to the draft, a massacre at My Lai, and the invasion of Cambodia would finally make the claim of modernizing Vietnam a focus for contentious national debate. The spiraling death toll among both Americans and Vietnamese would also provoke serious and painful reassessments. In the early 1960s, however, the ultimate costs of that course remained unclear.

As an ideology, modernization functioned in powerful ways during the early 1960s. Responding to a perceived Communist threat in the midst of a collapsing European colonial order, social scientists and Kennedy administration policymakers conceived of it as a means to promote a liberal world in which the development of "emerging" nations would protect the security of the United States. In addition to charting a course for the continued expansion of American power, modernizers also identified America as an altruistic, anticolonial nation prepared to meet revolutionary challenges around the world. Modernization was not simply a rhetorical strategy invoked to legitimate government actions. The high degree of continuity between private, policymaking materials and public interpretation reveals that it was also a conceptual framework. Modernization shaped specific practices and articulated widely shared beliefs about the nature of the United States, its ethical duty, and its ability to direct global change. Embedded in social scientific discourse, foreign policy institutions, and forms of cultural representation, it promised to accelerate the "progress" of a world requiring America's resources and enlightened tutelage.

Social scientific theories of modernization were not determinative or exclusive forces. Neither they nor the cultural assumptions they reflected and reinforced were the sole causes of Kennedy-period policy. The Alliance for Progress was created in the context of previous success with the Marshall Plan, decades of Latin American appeals for aid, the Cuban revolution, and a U.S. disaster at the Bay of Pigs. Community development was only one of many Peace Corps programs, and its implementation stemmed from practical concerns about the high numbers of liberal arts graduates in the volunteer pool in addition to larger ambitions for social engineering. In Vietnam, the Strategic Hamlet Program also had multiple sources, including Ngo Dinh Diem's own population resettlement experiments, British plans deployed in Malaya, and the Kennedy administration's search for a way to win the war that, while keeping the option open, did not yet involve the deployment of U.S. combat troops. In each case, however, thinking about modernization shaped institutional understandings of the development process, explained the strategic significance of decolonization, and suggested specific ways in which American policy might direct and accelerate global change. As diverse as the Alliance for Progress, the Peace Corps, and the Strategic Hamlet Program might appear, all of them proposed to transform "traditional" societies and cultures through material assistance and the demonstration of rational organizations and social structures.

In promoting modernization, Kennedy policymakers also approached societies as integrated systems. Economic growth and political reform, planners argued, were to be pursued in tandem with desired changes in the indigenous worldview. Peace Corps volunteers working on community development projects were expected to provide the democratic values and structures that would inspire "passive" peasants to undertake self-help projects and improve their quality of life. Strategic hamlets were designed to win the "hearts and minds" of rural farmers by transforming them into activist citizens and creating a new sense of loyalty to the South Vietnamese regime. Even the Alliance for Progress sought to link economic growth and democratic government with the "emotional" and supposedly inchoate forces of Latin American nationalism. In each case, policymakers, much like modernization theorists, agreed that "underdevelopment" was more than a purely structural problem. It was also a "state of mind," a condition in which cultural failings were as decisive as political or economic ones.

Each program was also firmly linked to American perceptions of Cold War danger. Policymakers and their social scientific advisers envisioned a world in which the aspirations aroused by Western ideas, technology, and markets detached "traditional" societies from the older family and religious bonds that once provided a measure of social cohesion. They also understood the transition toward modernity as a crisis, a moment of profound opportunity and serious risk. Because societies in the midst of transition lacked the type of integrative values that theorists identified with the equilibrium of stable, Western democracies, policymakers considered them extremely vulnerable to communism and its seductive claims of social reform, political order, and economic growth. To meet that threat and push fragile societies through the critical period, each Kennedy program proposed a material and moral blueprint designed to facilitate a liberal, capitalist "take-off" before revolution or insurgency could disrupt that "natural" process. The Alliance for Progress was intended to do more than alleviate poverty and repression. It was also designed to confront Soviet ideology and the deviant Cuban example with a vision of economic advance and social change based on an American model. Peace Corps community development programs were expected to transform malleable, passive poor into active citizens committed to liberal advance. Symbols of the nation's altruism, toughness, and empathy, Peace Corps volunteers "living at the level of their hosts" were also invoked to demonstrate that America could meet the Communist threat on any plain of battle. In Vietnam, the United States responded to the National Liberation Front in similar ways. Convinced that the enemy derived its appeal from a projection of hierarchy and order, Kennedy strategists tried to combine security measures with the construction of an extensive South Vietnamese state in which peasants might find a sense of purpose, commitment, and belonging. Economic growth, community development, and counterinsurgency were all shaped by expectations that liberal modernization could preclude Communist revolution.

Modernization also simplified an analytical process in unfortunate ways. Because modernizers typically evaluated foreign, "undeveloped" societies almost entirely in terms of their relative position on a unitary, abstract scale of progress, they frequently paid little attention to specific historical conditions or distinct cultural features. Convinced that the "traditional" world was plastic and malleable, policymakers also overestimated their ability to redirect and channel nationalist forces. In places such as Vietnam, that problem would eventually lead to crisis. Bolstered by a confident vision of American power, modernization also enjoyed such popularity that few dissented against its assumptions and predictions, even when clear evidence pointed in other directions.

The theory and practice of modernization, moreover, had much in common with older patterns of American nationalist thought and ideology. Although the quantitative indexes, structural-functional diagrams, and ardent scientism were relatively new, the celebration of an American historical trajectory and its redemptive potential certainly were not. In a 1966 book, historian Frederick Merk argued that, while the nation's characteristic benevolence persisted, "Manifest Destiny, in the twentieth century, vanished. Not only did it die; it stayed dead through two world wars."[1] In similar terms, many historians of U.S. foreign relations have described American imperialism as a brief aberration, rashly pursued and quickly disavowed.[2] Attempts to put modernization into practice, I believe, cast such claims into question and open challenging avenues of inquiry concerning the Cold War period. What elements of older thinking about Manifest Destiny and an imperial calling were interred at the end of the nineteenth century? What elements might have survived and reappeared in different forms? If defined narrowly as the idea that the United States enjoyed providential sanction for westward expansion across its own continent, or as the practice of taking formal, territorial possession of foreign lands, then perhaps Manifest Destiny and American imperialism did pass away. But there are good reasons to believe that rumors of their demise have been greatly exaggerated. As scholars such as Anders Stephanson have suggested, Manifest Destiny may also be considered in a broader sense, as a conviction that "the nation had been allowed to see the light and was bound to show the way for the historically retrograde," and the reflection of "a particular (and particularly powerful) nationalism constituting itself not only as prophetic but also universal."[3] Imperialism, in a similar sense, may also be interpreted on a cultural plane, as a practice that defined the deficiencies of a foreign people and outlined the reforms and progress that tutelage by an advanced society might produce. Evaluated along those lines, modernization clearly resonated with older conceptions of national identity and potential.

The task for the historian, then, is to explore the ways in which a larger ideology was reformulated in a changing historical context. Modernization, during the Cold War, was not identical to Manifest Destiny in the nineteenth century or imperialism at the turn of the twentieth. Sanction by Providence, or the hand of God, was replaced by appeals to objective social science, and the rational power of man. Citations to Max Weber's *Protestant Ethic and the Spirit of Capitalism* and treatises based on production data and indexed "modernity scales" defended claims that, previously, might have been cast in the millenarian language of evangelical Christianity. Rather than considering themselves an instrument of divine order to be worked out in the world, modernizers sought to identify the universal course of history itself and then, with supreme self-confidence, attempted to accelerate it. The kind of expansion anticipated, moreover, shifted as well. Where their predecessors had described a landed, territorial mission for the propagation of democracy, modernizers would speak of a transference of values and institutions that depended on a "demonstration effect," not formal conquest. Explicit arguments about biological and racial factors, moreover, were also jettisoned in favor of those stressing America's relative cultural advance and moral mission. As Reginald Horsman argues, much early-nineteenth-century racial thought described supposed inferiors in terms of immutable biology— they were peoples capable of only limited reform and doomed to extinction in competition with vital, energetic Anglo-Saxons.[4] Turning toward culture and stressing the essential malleability of the "traditionals," American modernizers, like the more optimistic advocates of Indian assimilation and over-seas imperialism, carved out another kind of redemptive mission for them-selves.[5] The foreign would not fade away, but, under American influence, their deficient cultures would.

Such variations are important to note if one is to avoid an ahistorical, blanket description. Understandings of America's world role and potential were not unchanging or static. Nevertheless, it is clear that modernization was not an entirely new creation. Although theorists spoke of a pivotal breakthrough grounded in rigorous, empirical analysis and policymakers cast their programs as unprecedented efforts, their definitions of a linear, historical road to progress and attempts to drive the inferior along it had much in common with earlier nationalist visions. America, in the eyes of the modernizer, stood at the apex of a universal, historical course. It was a society that had advanced more successfully and more rapidly than those continuing to struggle in its wake. A progressive force in the world, the United States would also fulfill a moral mission by sharing its resources and values with those who lacked them. Though invoking science instead of Providence, modernizers also defined and projected a destiny for America and the nations to which it would minister. In the ideological contest of the Cold War, moreover, many strategists believed that success demanded noth-ing less.

Proposing to replace European colonialism with a new, enlightened form of international assistance, the ideology of modernization also reconstructed America's imperial past. In statements that ignored the U.S. role in defending many of Latin America's repressive dictatorships as well as the history of repeated U.S. intervention in the region, the Alliance for Progress promised to take America's anticolonial revolution south of the nation's borders for the benefit of societies hoping to apply its solutions to their own problems. As they sent Peace Corps volunteers to teach English in the Philippines, U.S. officials spoke of continuing a humanitarian, "special relationship" with that country and made no reference to the colonial one. Through a policy of population resettlement and concentration in Vietnam, American policy-makers also claimed to build a new, independent nation even as they re-peated a violent tactic that, in different forms, was previously applied to shore up the empire by the British in Malaya and the United States in the Philippines. Modernization, social scientists and policymakers argued, would replace colonial control with plans to facilitate national indepen-dence. But the programs based on it often defined the failings of the "under-developed" and the need for American intervention in ways that strongly paralleled imperial discourse and practice. In the early 1960s, moreover, that tension aroused little protest. In an age of formal decolonization, modernization promised a progressive future in which all people, except those bent on subversion, would surely benefit.

The framework of modernization also resonated with a history of American liberalism and contemporary assumptions about "cultures of poverty" within the United States. When he described the Alliance for Progress as a means to ease Latin America off the "international dole," Walt Rostow equated foreign aid with welfare assistance. Other advocates of the alliance described a "New Deal" for Latin America. Peace Corps community development workers trained for their overseas assignments by assisting the supposedly "underdeveloped" and "apathetic" populations of New York City tenement houses and Arizona Indian reservations. Lyndon Johnson envisioned the building of a Tennessee Valley Authority on the Mekong Delta and, after meeting with South Vietnamese officials in Honolulu, told reporters that it was "unprecedented" for a U.S. president to "sit down and discuss the nuts and bolts of reform just like a social worker in Chicago." Green Beret civic action teams returning from Vietnam were sent to assist the black and Indian populations settled around Fort Bragg as well as the poor residents of a South Carolina "hamlet." Liberal reformers, as these examples suggest, often perceived modernization abroad and public assistance at home in quite similar ways.[6] In both contexts, poverty was considered a basically "foreign" affliction. As historian Michael Katz observes, "Most of the writing about poor people, even by sympathetic observers, tells us that they are different, truly strangers in our midst. Poor people think, feel, and act in ways unlike middle-class Americans. Their poverty is to some degree a matter of personal responsibility, and its alleviation requires personal transformation."[7]

In the 1960s, liberal reformers found "traditionals" within America's borders and outlined solutions resembling the ones they deployed abroad. Persons trapped by apathy could be redeemed by "maximum feasible participation." "Community development" could empower inner-city residents to seek out federal government agencies for necessary resources. Because they longed for order, structure, and a sense of belonging, the poor could be mobilized by a new awareness of what the national government might help them achieve. With an emphasis on personal values and morality over politics or power relations, the early years of the Great Society shared strong similarities with Kennedy-era modernization programs. In a society repeatedly defined by its "modernity" as much as its geography, such evidence also suggests that not all Americans were considered full or genuine members of the nation's "imagined community."[8]

By the close of the 1960s, events at home as well as abroad raised serious questions about the modernization model. As the war in Vietnam ground on, many Americans realized that neither strategic hamlets nor extensive bombing could engineer the sweeping transformations that social scientists and policymakers hoped for. When American cities burned in urban riots and a more radical civil rights movement pushed beyond desegregation and equal rights toward demands for socioeconomic equality and calls for redistribution, the "traditionals" at home also seemed far from passive or apolitical. Dissenters increasingly challenged more than the details of administration, funding, or implementation. They also attacked the core, foundational assumptions of an ideology promising that reform could be achieved without a fundamental reordering of power or resources. As a New Left and a New Right emerged, the consensus and "vital center" of Cold War liberalism shattered. Though its assumptions continue to animate discussions of development and definitions of America's world role, modernization no longer possesses the same degree of unquestioned acclaim it once enjoyed.

During the early 1960s, however, American social scientists, Kennedy administration policymakers, and the nation's media perceived a world in which transformative social engineering was both entirely possible and urgently necessary. Certain that they were meant to play a pivotal role at a historically crucial moment, modernizers saw little conflict between American self-interest and what they considered an internationalist mission. Confident in their vision of liberal, linear advance, they had few doubts that their scientifically determined and rationally promoted plans would dramatically improve the world. Who, besides the Communists, after all, could possibly dissent from development or reject the promise of progress? Modernization, in both theory and practice, told Americans who they were and what a projection of their nation's vital lessons and valuable resources could achieve. As an ideology of destined progress, benevolent mission, and historical triumph, it resonated strongly with a heroic narrative of the American past. A vision of power expressed at the height of the Cold War, it also proposed to chart, define, and accelerate the world's future.

Abbreviations Used in Notes

AIDC   Agency for International Development, Center for Development
                Information and Evaluation, Rosslyn, Va.
FRUS   State Department, *Foreign Relations of the United States*
HIA   Hoover Institution Archives, Stanford University, Stanford, Calif.
JFKL   John F. Kennedy Library, Boston, Mass.
LBJL   Lyndon B. Johnson Library, Austin, Tex.
NSF   National Security Files
PCL   Peace Corps Library, Washington, D.C.
POF   President's Office Files
Public Papers Public Papers of the President

Chapter One

1. Rostow, "Countering Guerrilla Attack," 464, 468, 471.
2. LaFeber, *American Age*, 563.
3. *FRUS, 1950*, 1:237–38; Sherry, *In the Shadow of War*, 128.
4. Beschloss, *Crisis Years*, 60–61.
5. See, for example, the argument Rostow made as chairman of the State Department Policy Planning Council in his *View from the Seventh Floor*, 85.
6. Important works by the authors mentioned include Rostow, *Stages of Economic Growth*; Pye, *Politics, Personality, and Nation Building*; Lerner, *Passing of Traditional Society*; Almond and Coleman, *Politics of Developing Areas*.
7. Black, *Dynamics of Modernization*, 7.
8. For a similar formulation of these central points, see Alexander, "Modern, Anti, Post, and Neo," 168.
9. Gusfield, "Tradition and Modernity," 354.
10. For key works in the critical historiography, see Tipps, "Modernization Theory"; Nisbet, *Social Change and History*. In an attempt to refine the modernization model, Samuel P. Huntington also pointed out some of its flaws in "Political Development and Political Decay."
11. Gunder Frank, *Latin America*, provides a striking case of the dependency critique. See also Cockcroft, Johnson, and Gunder Frank, *Dependence and Underdevelopment*. World systems theorist Immanuel Wallerstein wrote an epitaph

with his "Modernization," 132–37. P. T. Bauer led the conservative counterattack in *Dissent on Development*. For an attempt to revive a chastened modernization theory, see Alexander's reflections on a "neo-modern" approach in "Modern, Anti, Post, and Neo." The most dramatic recycling of the modernization theme, however, appears in Fukuyama, *End of History and the Last Man*. Sutton, "Development Ideology," and Binder, "Natural History of Development Theory," provide useful overviews of the concept's career.

12. This very issue is now starting to generate substantial interest among historians of science as well as scholars concerned with American foreign relations. See, for example, the collection of essays by Michael A. Bernstein, Stephen P. Waring, Ellen Herman, Deborah Welch Larson, Daniel Lee Kleinman, and Mark Solovey, "The Cold War and Expert Knowledge," *Radical History Review* 63 (Fall 1995).

13. Ross, *Origins of American Social Science*, xxi, xvii.

14. May, *Homeward Bound*. On this theme also see Whitfield, *Culture of the Cold War*; Fried, *Nightmare in Red*.

15. See Needell, " 'Truth Is Our Weapon.' "

16. Geiger, *Research and Relevant Knowledge*, 165; Diamond, *Compromised Campus*, 65. See also Rosenzweig, *Research Universities*, 111.

17. The phrase, of course, is from Halberstam, *Best and the Brightest*.

18. Carey, *Peace Corps*, viii–ix. See also Redmon, *Come As You Are*; Lowther and Lucas, *Keeping Kennedy's Promise*.

19. Arthur M. Schlesinger Jr. also claims that the alliance "came to an end with Kennedy's death." See his "Myth and Reality," 71, in addition to his earlier arguments in *Thousand Days*. For similar views, see Perloff, *Alliance for Progress*; May, *Problems and Prospects*; and Rogers, *Twilight Struggle*. More aggressive in pointing out the program's limitations, Levinson and de Onís still argued that "the democratic ideal of the Alliance is the true heading for this hemisphere's peace and development." See *Alliance That Lost Its Way*, long the standard work on the subject.

20. Nolting, *From Trust to Tragedy*, 39–40, 59; Hilsman, *To Move a Nation*, 442, 512.

21. See Amin, *Peace Corps in Cameroon*, and Rice, *Bold Experiment*. Cobbs Hoffman, *All You Need Is Love*, sets forth a more nuanced interpretation by emphasizing the way in which Americans understood self-interest and altruism as mutually reinforcing.

22. See Walker, "Mixing the Sweet with the Sour"; Tulchin, "United States and Latin America"; Rabe, "Controlling Revolutions"; Wiarda, "Misreading Latin America—Again."

23. Herring, *America's Longest War*; Schulzinger, *Time for War*; Kahin, *Intervention*.

24. Windmiller, *Peace Corps and Pax Americana*, vi, 39, 48.

25. Dosal, "Accelerating Dependent Development"; LaFeber, "Alliances in Retrospect"; Hanson, *Dollar Diplomacy Modern Style*. LaFeber, *Inevitable Revolutions*, 145–95, echoes this theme but also provides a powerful account of the way security itself was often defined in economic and material terms.

26. For a general, introductory history based on an economic framework, see Hearden, *Tragedy of Vietnam*. Chomsky, *Rethinking Camelot*, provides a sharp cri-

tique of Kennedy administration Vietnam policy situated in the context of a larger capitalist system.

27. Hunt, "Long Crisis in U.S. Diplomatic History," 118–19. On this point, also see Hunt, *Ideology and U.S. Foreign Policy*, 2–8. Works by these authors include Kennan, *American Diplomacy*; Morgenthau, *In Defense of the National Interest*; and Gaddis, *Strategies of Containment*.

28. Stephanson, "Ideology and Neorealist Mirrors," 285. Stephanson, *Kennan and the Art of Foreign Policy*, provides an insightful treatment that makes Kennan himself seem less the "realist" than one influenced by conceptual frameworks of his own.

29. Kolko, *Confronting the Third World*, 12, 123. Focusing on the class interests of America's diplomatic elite and the connections between business and government, Kolko made a similar argument in *Roots of American Foreign Policy*.

30. Ninkovich, "Interests and Discourse in Diplomatic History," 136. Ninkovich has recently attempted to address that issue through an analysis of a "belief system" that, from the Wilson through the Johnson administrations, shaped U.S. policies designed to maintain America's international credibility and image. See his *Modernity and Power*. "Corporatist" interpretations have devoted attention to the definition of interests by focusing on institutional settings. Tracing the rise of an alliance between the state and the nation's corporate powers in the 1920s, they have connected it to the promotion of private enterprise, technical assistance, and economic growth as means to secure a global capitalist order. For an overview, see Hogan, "Corporatism."

31. Foner, *Free Soil, Free Labor, Free Men*, 4.

32. Rosenberg, *Spreading the American Dream*, 7. After Rosenberg's work, Packenham, *Liberal America and the Third World*, and Shafer, *Deadly Paradigms*, come closest to the type of ideological analysis I have undertaken. Packenham is more intent on falsifying the specific cognitive framework he identifies, however, than fully exploring the way ideology was related to much older, imperial understandings. Concerning themselves primarily with the connections between theory and strategy, moreover, neither author fully investigates the degree to which ideologies of development were also integrally related to a powerful conception of national identity and mission articulated in public as well as private contexts.

33. Mannheim identified the difference between the two meanings of ideology outlined here by distinguishing a "particular conception" from a "total" one. In the first case, "ideas and representations" are "regarded as more or less conscious disguises of the real nature of a situation." In the second, however, Mannheim referred to a "more inclusive" conception of "the ideology of an age or of a concrete historico-social group, e.g. of a class, when we are concerned with the characteristics and composition of the total structure of the mind of this epoch or of this group." See *Ideology and Utopia*, 49–53.

34. Geertz, "Ideology as a Cultural System," 232, 220.

35. Biersack, "Local Knowledge, Local History," 80.

36. Walters, "Signs of the Times," 553.

37. Williams, *Tragedy of American Diplomacy*; LaFeber, *New Empire*. On the critical reception to their work and its impact, see Perkins, "Tragedy of American Diplo-

macy." Williams also developed an argument stressing the ideological impact of a Turnerian vision in "Frontier Thesis and American Foreign Policy."

38. Williams, *Tragedy of American Diplomacy*, 46–47.

39. Foucault, *Discipline and Punish*, 27, 98, 160. White, "Value of Narrativity in the Representation of Reality," also provides a perceptive analysis of the way the writing of history is related to the construction of power and authority.

40. Among cultural anthropologists concerned with the way development theory has defined the profile of the modern and constrained the potential formulation of policy alternatives, these themes have received a great deal of attention. See, for example, Ferguson, *Anti-politics Machine*; Escobar, *Encountering Development*; Wood, "Politics of Development Policy Labeling"; Dahl and Hjort, "Development as Message and Meaning." On Foucault and the pervasive sense of institutional power, see Young, *White Mythologies*, 5.

41. Said, *Orientalism*, 12, 7. Stoler, "Rethinking Colonial Categories," places a similar analysis in an imperial frame by explaining how issues of health, education, and socialization all involved a careful construction of boundaries between the identity of the colonizer and that of the colonized. Campbell, *Writing Security*, has also analyzed the way the "foreign" defines the "domestic" to provide a challenging reconceptualization of the Cold War. As he argues, through the identification of external threats in both private and public contexts, policymakers have repeatedly "written and rewritten" America's "security" needs and national identity. Gramer, "On Poststructuralisms, Revisionisms and Cold Wars," reviews that work and other recent applications of poststructural theory to the study of foreign relations.

42. Memorandum, Rostow to Theodore Sorenson, March 16, 1961, NSF, box 325, "Rostow, Foreign Aid, 3/16/61–3/18/61," JFKL.

43. On this theme, see Said, *Culture and Imperialism*, xvii, 8–9.

44. See Memmi, *Colonizer and the Colonized*; Galeano, *Open Veins of Latin America*; Rodney, *How Europe Underdeveloped Africa*; Prakash, "Writing Post-Orientalist Histories"; Appadurai, *Modernity at Large*.

45. See, for example, Zimmerman, "Beyond Double Consciousness."

46. Williams, *Empire as a Way of Life*.

Chapter Two

1. Bundy, "Battlefields of Power," 3, 9, 15.

2. Rostow, *Stages of Economic Growth*, 167.

3. Katznelson, "Subtle Politics of Developing Emergency," 236–37.

4. Herman, *Romance of American Psychology*, 9.

5. Kunz, *Butter and Guns*, 12. See also Cohen, *America in the Age of Soviet Power*, 4–7.

6. Hogan, *Marshall Plan*, 19.

7. Kunz, *Butter and Guns*, 35.

8. Ibid., 48–49, 52.

9. Quoted in Leffler, *Preponderance of Power*, 267.

10. Ibid.

11. Escobar, *Encountering Development*, 36.

12. Leffler, *Preponderance of Power*, 291.

13. *FRUS, 1950*, 1:240. For background on this period, see Sherry, *In the Shadow of War*, 128–29; Leffler, *Specter of Communism*, 56–96.

14. Gaddis, *We Now Know*, 154.

15. Cohen, *America in the Age of Soviet Power*, 116–17.

16. LaFeber, *America, Russia, and the Cold War*, 176.

17. Merrill, *Bread and the Ballot*, 137–38.

18. Ibid., 140; Cobbs Hoffman, *All You Need Is Love*, 106.

19. Kennedy campaign speech, November 2, 1960, as printed in Sorenson, *"Let the Word Go Forth,"* 119. See also Giglio, *Presidency of John F. Kennedy*, 14, 17.

20. Paterson, "Introduction," 9–11.

21. Sorenson, *"Let the Word Go Forth,"* 12.

22. For general background on these conflicts, see the essays in Paterson, *Kennedy's Quest for Victory*, and Kunz, *Diplomacy of the Crucial Decade*.

23. Alexander, *Twenty Lectures*, 18–19.

24. Shils, *Present State of American Sociology*, 3–4, 6.

25. Ibid., 54–55.

26. Alexander, *Twenty Lectures*, 22–28; Buxton, *Talcott Parsons*, 21–24, 30–31; Savage, *Theories of Talcott Parsons*, 200–207.

27. Rocher, *Talcott Parsons and American Sociology*, 20.

28. The general theoretical argument is found in Parsons and Shils, *Towards a General Theory of Action*, and Parsons, *Social System*. For an overview of these ideas, also see Alexander, *Twenty Lectures*, 37–51. For Parsons's analysis of Germany, first written in 1942, see "Democracy and Social Structure in Pre-Nazi Germany."

29. Savage, *Theories of Talcott Parsons*, 204.

30. Bierstedt, *American Sociological Theory*, 421–24.

31. Savage, *Theories of Talcott Parsons*, 205–7.

32. Rocher, *Talcott Parsons and American Sociology*, 22. As another commentator put it, this assumption led readers to assume that, in development, "all good things go together." See Packenham, *Liberal America and the Third World*, 20.

33. Savage, *Theories of Talcott Parsons*, 208–16. While his evolutionary view is implicit in much of his earlier work, Parsons made it most clear in *Structure and Process in Modern Societies*; "Evolutionary Universals in Society"; and *Societies*.

34. Mills, *Sociological Imagination*, 35–36.

35. Bierstedt, *American Sociological Theory*, 441. For examples of the criticism directed at Parsons and his intellectual allies, see Smith, *Concept of Social Change*, and Lauer, "Scientific Legitimation of Fallacy." For an overview of critical responses and a partial defense, see Turner, "Parsons and His Critics."

36. Levy, *Family Revolution in Modern China*, 6, 274–79, 281, 352–65.

37. Parsons, foreword to Levy, *Family Revolution in Modern China*, ix.

38. For examples, see Shils, "On the Comparative Study of the New States"; Eisenstadt, *Protestant Ethic and Modernization*; Inkeles, "Modernization of Man."

39. Lerner, *Passing of Traditional Society*, esp. 45–48.

40. Ibid., 69, 411.

41. For material on the early SSRC, see Fisher, *Fundamental Development of the Social Sciences*.

42. Kahin, Pauker, and Pye, "Comparative Politics of Non-Western Countries." In keeping with these views, the committee confined its initial program to the study of selected, specific political groups in both Western and non-Western areas and secured eighteen fellowships for that more limited purpose from the Ford Foundation. Social Science Research Council, *Annual Report, 1956–1957*, 19–20.

43. Almond, "Seminar on Comparative Politics," 46–47.

44. Ibid. (emphasis in original).

45. The titles of the studies commissioned by the committee reflect this new emphasis. In addition to hiring sociologist S. N. Eisenstadt "to make a comparative analysis of historical political systems," the group requested memorandums on "Intellectuals and Political Development," "Political Modernization in Japan," and "Nationalism and Political Development." Social Science Research Council, *Annual Report, 1957–1958*, 19.

46. Gendzier, *Managing Political Change*, 87–96.

47. Pye, "Political Modernization and Research on the Process of Political Socialization," 26.

48. Almond and Coleman, *Politics of Developing Areas*, 3–4.

49. See, for example, Deutsch, "Social Mobilization and Political Development"; Spengler, "Economic Development," 387–416; Ward, *Studying Politics Abroad*.

50. Pye, *Politics, Personality, and Nation Building*, xiii–xiv, 286.

51. Hirschman, "Rise and Decline of Development Economics," 374.

52. See, for example, the description of the "dual economy" that Lewis presented in his landmark article "Economic Development with Unlimited Supplies of Labour."

53. These arguments are often associated with the economists R. F. Harrod and Evsey Domar. See Meier, "Formative Period," 15–16.

54. Escobar, *Encountering Development*, 69–70.

55. Little, *Economic Development*, 20.

56. For an overview, see Love, "Raúl Prebisch."

57. Rosenstein-Rodan, "International Aid for Underdeveloped Countries"; Rosenstein-Rodan, "Natura Facit Saltum"; Little, *Economic Development*, 38–39.

58. Myrdal, *Development and Underdevelopment*, 68, as cited in Little, *Economic Development*, 58.

59. Rostow, *Stages of Economic Growth*, ix.

60. Ibid., 4–7, 17–27.

61. Schwartz, "Review of *The Stages of Growth*," 6. For a later and much less laudatory response, see Gerschenkron, *Economic Backwardness*, 355–61.

62. Hoover, *Vital Need for Greater Financial Support*, 2; Leslie, *Cold War and American Science*, 4.

63. Leslie, *Cold War and American Science*, 6–7.

64. Geiger, *Research and Relevant Knowledge*, 30.

65. Leslie, *Cold War and American Science*, 8.

66. Katz, *Foreign Intelligence*; Winks, *Cloak and Gown*, 70–71, 87, 90–91.

67. Waring, "Cold Calculus," 30–32.

68. Herman, *Romance of American Psychology*, 17–47.

69. Buxton, *Talcott Parsons*, 117.

70. On the debate, see Larsen, *Milestones and Millstones*, 8–9.

71. Parsons, "Social Science," 107, as cited in Herman, *Romance of American Psychology*, 128.

72. Buxton, *Talcott Parsons*, 128.

73. Kleinman and Solovey, "Hot Science/Cold War," 121. See also Solovey, "Politics of Intellectual Identity," 40–49.

74. Hollinger, "Free Enterprise and Free Inquiry," 900.

75. For similar cases in the history of science, see Porter, *Trust in Numbers*.

76. Black, *Dynamics of Modernization*, 10–26, 67–68, 90–96.

77. Lerner, *Passing of Traditional Society*, 438–46.

78. Inkeles and Smith, *Becoming Modern*, 5, 6–8, 18–35. Though not published until 1974, the massive study was designed and initiated by Inkeles at Harvard's Center for International Affairs in the mid-1960s.

79. Ibid., 7, 12–14, 34–98, 290.

80. *FRUS, 1950*, 1:288.

81. Diamond, *Compromised Campus*, 50–110; Geiger, *Research and Relevant Knowledge*, 50–52.

82. Buxton, *Talcott Parsons*, 168–69, 175. By 1975, that total grew to $340 million. See Rosenzweig, *Research Universities*, 111.

83. Geiger, *Research and Relevant Knowledge*, 165.

84. Needell, " 'Truth Is Our Weapon,' " 417; Killian, *Education of a College President*, 65–67.

85. Rostow, "Development," 240–41.

86. Ibid., 241.

87. Geiger, *Research and Relevant Knowledge*, 69.

88. Millikan and Blackmer, *Emerging Nations*, v, ix–x.

89. Rostow, "Development," 241.

90. Millikan and Rostow, "Notes on Foreign Economic Policy," Memorandum to Allen Dulles, May 21, 1954, as printed in Simpson, *Universities and Empire*, 41, 42, 44.

91. Millikan and Rostow, *Proposal*, 3–4, 8, 70–71, 131.

92. Rostow, Oral History Interview by Richard Neustadt, April 11, 1964, transcript, JFKL; Rostow, *Eisenhower, Kennedy, and Foreign Aid*, xiii, 36–44.

93. Merrill, *Bread and the Ballot*, 155.

94. Millikan to Kennedy, February 6, 1959, Millikan Papers, box 1, "Correspondence, 1959–1961," JFKL.

95. Memorandum, Millikan on "Foreign Aid Program," NSF, box 324, "Staff Memoranda, W. W. Rostow, Foreign Aid, 1/1/61–1/10/61," JFKL.

96. Kennedy, "Special Message to the Congress on Foreign Aid," *Public Papers*, 1:203, 205–6.

97. Schlesinger, *Thousand Days*, 586–94. For examples of their thinking on these issues, see Mason, *Promoting Economic Development*; Galbraith, "Positive Approach to Economic Aid."

98. Rostow, *Diffusion of Power*, 125.

99. Pye, interview by author, October 19, 1994, Cambridge, Mass. According to Pye, this group was initially established to assist with the formation of AID but continued to meet for some time through the Johnson administration as a forum for the identification of foreign assistance problems and the suggestion of new development concepts. General biographical information for many of these individuals is available in Lichtenstein, *Political Profiles*.

100. On scientific claims to objectivity, see Nagel, *View from Nowhere*.

101. Quoted in Decter, "Kennedyism," 20, as cited in Paterson, "Introduction," 15.

102. Ng, "Knowledge for Empire," 124–29; Asad, *Anthropology and the Colonial Encounter*.

103. Cmiel, "Destiny and Amnesia," 355.

104. Stocking, *Victorian Anthropology*, 3–6.

105. Mitchell, *Colonising Egypt*, 6.

106. See, for example, Wallerstein, *Unthinking Social Science*.

107. Smith, *Wealth of Nations*, bk. 1:12.

108. Weber, *Protestant Ethic*, 13 (emphasis in original).

109. Ibid., 181–82.

110. Tönnies, *Community and Society*.

111. Smith, *Theory of Moral Sentiments*, pt. 4, chap. 1, para. 8, as cited in Hont and Ignatieff, "Needs and Justice in the Wealth of Nations," 10.

112. Said, *Orientalism*, 3.

113. Rostow, *Stages of Economic Growth*, 17; Parsons, *Structure and Process*, 138–39; Eisenstadt, *Modernization*, 55–58.

114. Spencer, *First Principles*, sec. 134, as cited in Leaf, *Man, Mind, and Science*, 76–77.

115. Bock, "Theories of Progress and Evolution," 24.

116. Stocking, *Race, Culture, and Evolution*, 114, 131. On this theme, see also Pratt, *Imperial Eyes*.

117. Parsons, *Structure and Process*, 163; Rostow, *Stages of Economic Growth*, 36.

118. Tipps, "Modernization Theory," 207.

119. Nisbet, *Social Change and History*, 205.

120. Chambers, *Political Parties in a New Nation*, 13.

121. Lipset, *First New Nation*, 2, 11, 130.

122. Lauer, "Scientific Legitimation of Fallacy," 885.

123. See, for example, Asad, *Anthropology and the Colonial Encounter*. Rosaldo, *Culture and Truth*, 68–87, also contains reflections on this issue in the case of American imperialism in the Philippines.

124. Dirks, introduction to *Colonialism and Culture*, 3, 11.

125. Rostow, *Stages of Economic Growth*, 27.

126. Wood, "Future of Modernization," 41.

127. Mazrui, "From Social Darwinism to Current Theories of Modernization," 76.

128. Rostow, *Stages of Economic Growth*, 26–27.

129. Pye, *Politics, Personality, and Nation Building*, 300.

130. See Hollinger, "How Wide the Circle?," on a related theme.

Chapter Three

Parts of this chapter first appeared as an article titled "Ideology, Social Science, and Destiny: Modernization and the Kennedy-Era Alliance for Progress," in *Diplomatic History* 22 (Spring 1998): 199–229.

1. Memorandum, Rostow to Kennedy, March 2, 1961, POF, box 64a, "Rostow, 3/61–5/61," JFKL.

2. "Charter of Punta del Este Establishing an Alliance for Progress within the Framework of Operation Pan America," as printed in House of Representatives, *Regional and Other Documents*, 101–3.

3. See Walker, "Mixing the Sweet with the Sour"; Tulchin, "United States and Latin America"; and Rabe, "Controlling Revolutions," on strategic fears and their impact on the alliance's formation and fate. LaFeber, "Alliances in Retrospect," and Dosal, "Accelerating Dependent Development," stress the economic forces at work. Kunz, *Butter and Guns*, and Smith, *America's Mission*, include chapters placing the alliance in the context of previous development experience. On Latin American initiatives, see Levinson and de Onís, *Alliance That Lost Its Way*.

4. Rabe, *Eisenhower and Latin America*, 8–9.

5. Skidmore and Smith, *Modern Latin America*, 60–61; LaFeber, "Alliances in Retrospect," 342–43.

6. Skidmore and Smith, *Modern Latin America*, 340–41; Rabe, *Eisenhower and Latin America*, 74–75. For background on Prebisch's theoretical stance, see Love, "Raúl Prebisch."

7. As quoted in Smith, *Last Years of the Monroe Doctrine*, 59.

8. Skidmore and Smith, *Modern Latin America*, 334–37; Smith, *Last Years of the Monroe Doctrine*, 41–62.

9. Escobar, *Encountering Development*, 29.

10. Smith, *Last Years of the Monroe Doctrine*, 66; Levinson and de Onís, *Alliance That Lost Its Way*, 37.

11. Kennan, *Memoirs*, 476, as cited in Smith, *Last Years of the Monroe Doctrine*, 68. On Kennan's view of Latin America, the Communist threat, and the need to consider "coercive measures," see Stephanson, *Kennan and the Art of Foreign Policy*, 162–65.

12. Rabe, *Eisenhower and Latin America*, 75; Kunz, *Butter and Guns*, 122.

13. Levinson and de Onís, *Alliance That Lost Its Way*, 38–42; Kunz, *Butter and Guns*, 122; Rabe, *Eisenhower and Latin America*, 86–87. For histories of the Guatemalan coup, see Gleijeses, *Shattered Hope*; Immerman, *CIA in Guatemala*; Schlesinger and Kinzer, *Bitter Fruit*.

14. Rabe, *Eisenhower and Latin America*, 3–4, 97; Paterson, *Contesting Castro*, 135–36; 244–45.

15. Rabe, *Eisenhower and Latin America*, 107–29; Levinson and de Onís, *Alliance That Lost Its Way*, 44–48.

16. Schoultz, *Beneath the United States*, 353. For the text of the Act of Bogotá, see House of Representatives, *Regional and Other Documents*, 92–97.

17. Task Force Report, January 4, 1961, Moscoso Papers, box 9, "Report of the Task Force on Immediate Latin American Problems, Winter, 1960," JFKL.

18. Ibid.

19. Gordon, "Alliance at Birth," 74.

20. Kunz, *Butter and Guns*, 55.

21. Gordon, "Alliance at Birth," 74–75.

22. Memorandum, Schlesinger to Kennedy, March 10, 1961, Schlesinger Papers, box WH-14, "Latin America, Report 3/10/61," JFKL.

23. Memorandum, Lincoln Gordon to Richard Goodwin, March 6, 1961, NSF, box 290, "Alliance for Progress, 1/61–12/61," JFKL.

24. Kennedy, *Public Papers*, 1:172.

25. For background on the failed invasion and its significance, see Paterson, "Fixation with Cuba"; Giglio, *Presidency of John F. Kennedy*, 48–63; Lyman B. Kirkpatrick, "Inspector General's Survey of the Cuban Operation," February 16, 1962, obtained from the Central Intelligence Agency through the Freedom of Information Act by the National Security Archive, Washington, D.C.

26. Memorandum, Rostow to Richard Goodwin, June 20, 1961, NSF, box 290, "Alliance for Progress, 1/61–12/61," JFKL.

27. Memorandum, Schlesinger to Arturo Morales Carrión, July 19, 1961, Schlesinger Papers, box W-1, "Alliance for Progress, General Memoranda," JFKL.

28. House of Representatives, *Regional and Other Documents*, 101–3.

29. Ibid., 106–7.

30. De Oliveira Campos, *Reflections on Latin American Development*, 132–34.

31. Hirschman, "Dissenter's Confession," 90–91.

32. Statement of Teodoro Moscoso before the Senate Appropriations Committee, May 17, 1963, Moscoso Papers, box 11, "Senate Appropriations Committee, 5/17/63," JFKL.

33. Task Force Report, not dated, Millikan Papers, box 1, "Task Force Recommendations, 1960" JFKL.

34. Rosenstein-Rodan, "International Aid for Underdeveloped Countries," 107. See also Rosenstein-Rodan's draft in NSF, box 324, "Staff Memoranda, Walt W. Rostow, Foreign Aid, 1/61," JFKL.

35. Rosenstein-Rodan, "International Aid for Underdeveloped Countries," 108.

36. Ibid., 113–15.

37. Memorandum, Hollis Chenery, "Policy Guidance for Foreign Assistance," 1963, AID Historical Collection, AIDC. For a quantitative treatment, see Chenery, "Foreign Assistance and Economic Development."

38. Rostow, *View from the Seventh Floor*, 7, 106. See also Rostow, *Two Major Communist Offensives*; Rostow, *Great Transition*.

39. Rostow, speech at Dartmouth College, February 29, 1960, Rostow Papers (not indexed), LBJL.

40. Berle to Latin American Task Force Members, January 10, 1961, Moscoso Papers, box 4, "Correspondence, 12/60–4/61," JFKL.

41. Gardner, *New Directions in U.S. Foreign Economic Policy*, 14–18

42. Morse and Hickenlooper, *Report of the Second Punta del Este Conference*. For the text of the resolutions and vote results, see House of Representatives, *Regional and Other Documents*, 115–22.

43. Rusk, "Alliance in the Context of World Affairs," 103.

44. Telegram, Department of State to U.S. Delegation at Punta del Este, January 30, 1962, NSF, box 244, "Secretary of State, Punta del Este, 1/62, General, 4/61–1/62," JFKL.

45. Memorandum, "A Doctrine to Preserve the Independence of the Latin American Revolution," not dated, Vice-President's Security File, box 4, "National Security Council—1961, 2 of 2," LBJL.

46. Memorandum, State Department, "The Inter-American System and Cuba," NSF, box 244, "Secretary of State, Punta del Este 1/62, General, 4/61–1/62," JFKL.

47. Report, U.S. Information Agency, "The Economic and Political Climate of Opinion in Latin America and Attitudes toward the Alliance for Progress," June 1963, POF, box 91, "USIA Alianza Opinion Survey," JFKL.

48. Speech, Muñoz Marín to the AFL-CIO National Conference on Community Services, May 3, 1962, Moscoso Papers, box 10, "Speech Materials, 5/62–6/62," JFKL.

49. Memorandum, Morales Carrión to McGeorge Bundy, NSF, box 290, "Alliance for Progress, 4/62–6/62," JFKL.

50. Memorandum, Kennedy to Bundy, April 23, 1962, POF, box 62a, "Bundy, McGeorge, 1962," JFKL.

51. Upton to Kennedy, March 16, 1962, POF, box 95, "Alliance for Progress," JFKL.

52. Memorandum, Rostow to Kennedy, March 2, 1961, POF, box 64a, "Rostow, 3/61–5/61," JFKL.

53. "Secretary Rusk's News Conference of February 6," 298.

54. Kennedy, *Public Papers*, 2:217.

55. Rostow, "Economic Development," speech to the American Chamber of Commerce, Mexico City, August 19, 1963, Moscoso Papers, box 11, "Speech Materials, 6/63–9/63," JFKL.

56. Mann, "Experience of the United States in Economic Development," 772–75.

57. Gordon, *New Deal for Latin America*, 105–8.

58. Ibid., 109.

59. Kennedy and Hamilton cited in Kennedy, *Public Papers*, 2:818–20.

60. Rusk, "America's Destiny in the Building of a World Community," 898–99.

61. Moscoso, "Social Change and the Alliance for Progress," speech, April 18, 1962, Moscoso Papers, box 10, "School of Advanced International Studies, Johns Hopkins University, Lectures on Alliance for Progress," JFKL.

62. Martin, speech to the University of Southern California World Affairs Institute, December 4, 1962, Moscoso Papers, box 10, "Speech Materials, 11/62–12/62," JFKL.

63. Robinson, "Now the U.S. Is Exporting Union Ideas to Latin America," 86, 88–89.

64. Moscoso, speech to the American Council of Voluntary Associations for Foreign Service, November 26, 1962, Moscoso Papers, box 10, "American Council of Voluntary Associations for Foreign Service," JFKL.

65. Agency for International Development, "Putting PEP in AID," 7.
66. "Is the Alliance for Progress Progressing?" 380.
67. Szulc, "Selling a Revolution in Latin America," 10; "Evangelist for Progress," 54–55.
68. Memorandum, W. B. Dale and D. C. Fulton, "Do the States Have a Role to Play in Foreign Aid?," January, 1961, Eugene Staley Papers, box 23, "Development: Misc. Material," HIA; Dale and Fulton, "On Statesmanship," 52.
69. Memorandum, Goodwin to Kennedy, February 2, 1961, POF, box 63, "Goodwin, R.," JFKL.
70. Alliance for Progress Information Team, Weekly Newsletter, December 23, 1963, Moscoso Papers, box 3, "Partners of the Alliance," JFKL.
71. Rostow, "American Strategy on the World Scene," 628.
72. House of Representatives, *Foreign Assistance Act of 1962*, 468.
73. "Progreso, Sí," 29; "Help on the Way," 46; "Alliance Progresses," 44.
74. "Fresh Breeze from South," 46; "Yanquis Open a New World Series against the Reds," 40.
75. Gross, "Has the Alliance for Progress a Chance?" 80; "How Much Progress in the Alliance for Progress?" 42–44; "Quasi Stagnation," 44; "For 'Alianza' a Warning," 4.
76. Organization of American States, "The Alliance for Progress: Its First Year, 1961–1962," NSF, box 290, JFKL.
77. Organization of American States, "The Alliance for Progress: Its Second Year, 1962–1963," Moscoso Papers, box 3, JFKL.
78. Memorandum, Moscoso to Kennedy, April 27, 1962, NSF, box 291, "Alliance for Progress Reports, 3/62–4/62," JFKL.
79. Memorandum, Moscoso to Kennedy, October 2, 1963, NSF, box 291, "Alliance for Progress Reports, 8/63–10/63," JFKL.
80. Memorandum, unknown author to Kennedy, undated, POF, box 95, "Alliance for Progress," JFKL.
81. "Troubled Alliance," 22.
82. Memorandum, Haddad to Kennedy, March 9, 1962, POF, box 95, "Alliance for Progress," JFKL.
83. Memorandum, Moscoso to Kennedy, May 18, 1962, NSF, box 291, "Alliance for Progress Reports, 5/62–7/62," JFKL.
84. Bureau of the Budget, "Survey of the Alliance for Progress Program in Brazil, Argentina, Chile, and Bolivia," NSF, box 290, "Alliance for Progress, 7/1962," JFKL.
85. Memorandum, Haddad to Kennedy, March 9, 1962, POF, box 95, "Alliance for Progress," JFKL.
86. Memorandum, Moscoso to Kennedy, May 18, 1962, NSF, box 291, "Alliance for Progress Reports, 5/62–7/62," JFKL.
87. Bureau of the Budget, "Survey of the Alliance for Progress Program in Brazil, Argentina, Chile, and Bolivia," NSF, box 290, "Alliance for Progress, 7/1962," JFKL.
88. Memorandum, Goodwin to Kennedy, September 10, 1963, POF, box 63, "Goodwin, R.," JFKL.
89. Levinson and de Onís, *Alliance That Lost Its Way*, 71–73.

90. Memorandum, Schlesinger to Ralph Dungan, Schlesinger Papers, box WH 2, "Alliance for Progress, 9/28/62–10/18/62," JFKL.

91. David Rockefeller, "Development in Latin America: The Role of the United States," speech to the Economic Club of Chicago, April 23, 1963, Moscoso Papers, box 11, "Speech Materials, 54/63–5/63," JFKL.

92. "A Progress Report on the Alliance," 10.

93. "Troubles and Remedies," 26.

94. Gruening, "Why the Alianza May Fail," 11.

95. "Alianza, Sí, Progreso No," 33.

96. Bowles memorandum "Setting the Pace in the Alliance for Progress in Colombia," August 7, 1962, POF, box 28, "Chester Bowles," JFKL.

97. "Alliance for Progress: The Big Need Is Deeds," 50.

98. "Where the Reds May Take Over Next in Latin America," 50.

99. Chester Bowles memorandum "Setting the Pace for the Alliance for Progress in Colombia," August 7, 1962, POF, box 28, "Chester Bowles," JKFL.

100. Attorney General's Assistant Jim Symington memorandum to Arthur M. Schlesinger Jr., March 15, 1963, *FRUS, 1961–1963*, 12:134.

101. "For 'Alianza' a Warning," 4.

102. Lindblom, "New Look at Latin America," 81–86.

103. "Back to the Drawing Board," 334–35.

104. "Mexico: No Aid for the Competent," 9.

105. Morgenthau, "Political Theory of Foreign Aid," 302.

106. Hirschman, "Second Thoughts on the 'Alliance for Progress,'" 21.

Chapter Four

1. Minutes of meeting, Bradley Patterson, December 6, 1961, Bush Papers, box 2, "Director's Staff Meeting Records, 10/2/61–1/8/62," JFKL.

2. Peace Corps, *Peace Corps Fact Book*, 3.

3. "The 'Peace Corps' Starts," 26.

4. May, "Passing the Torch," 294.

5. Cobbs Hoffman, *All You Need Is Love*, 179–80.

6. Amin, *Peace Corps in Cameroon*, 177.

7. Cobbs Hoffman, *All You Need Is Love*, 4.

8. See, for example, Fischer, *Making Them Like Us*; Schwarz, *What You Can Do for Your Country*.

9. Reuss, "Point Four Youth Corps"; Amin, *Peace Corps in Cameroon*, 18.

10. For a description of these early initiatives, see Rice, *Bold Experiment*, 10–11; May, "Passing the Torch," 285. See also Congress, Senate, Senator Humphrey of Minnesota speaking for the Establishment of Peace Corps, 86th Cong., 2d sess., *Congressional Record* (June 15, 1960), vol. 106, pt. 10:12634–38.

11. Debate, Technical Appropriations Bill, House of Representatives, June 28, 1952, as reprinted in Sorenson, *"Let the Word Go Forth,"* 330.

12. Senate speech, July 2, 1957, as reprinted in Sorenson, *"Let the Word Go Forth,"* 331.

13. Quoted in Redmon, *Come As You Are*, 4.
14. Campaign speech, November 2, 1960, as reprinted in Sorenson, *"Let the Word Go Forth,"* 119–21.
15. Needell, " 'Truth Is Our Weapon,' " 412.
16. Kennedy to Rostow, November 16, 1960, Millikan Papers, box 1, "Correspondence, 1959–1961," JFKL.
17. Hayes to George Sullivan, Hayes Papers, box 2, "International Peace Corps, Correspondence, S–Z," JFKL.
18. Max F. Millikan, "International Youth Service," January 9, 1961, Bush Papers, box 1, "Beginnings and Background," JFKL.
19. Albertson, Birky, and Rice, "Preliminary Report: A Youth Corps for Service Abroad," February 1961, Hayes Papers, box 2, "Colorado State University, 1960–1961," JFKL.
20. Rostow, *Stages of Economic Growth*, 142–43.
21. Samuel P. Hayes, "International Youth Service: The Promise and the Problems," January 1961, White House Central Files, box 670, "PC 5, PC Prog, 1/24/61–3/7/61," JFKL.
22. Albertson et al., "Final Report: The Peace Corps, May, 1962," Peace Corps Agency Microfilm, roll 6, JFKL.
23. Amin, *Peace Corps in Cameroon*, 25–27; Cobbs Hoffman, *All You Need Is Love*, 41–44; May, "Passing the Torch," 286–87.
24. Shriver, Draft Report on the Peace Corps, February 20, 1961, POF, box 85, "Shriver Report," JFKL.
25. Kennedy, *Public Papers*, 1:134–35.
26. Amin, *Peace Corps in Cameroon*, 29–30.
27. Ibid., 35–42.
28. Memorandum, "Survey of Peace Corps Activities since the Beginning of the Administration," Bush Papers, box 4, "Organization Folder: 6 of 6," JFKL. Redmon, *Come As You Are*, and Carey, *Peace Corps*, both provide detailed though hagiographic narratives regarding early planning and selection.
29. Memorandum, Peace Corps Division of Training, September 1, 1962, White House Aides Files—Moyers, box 41, "Middle Level Manpower Conference," LBJL. A list of terms for one unit on the "Theory of Political and Economic Development" included the following list under the heading of "terminology": "Capitalism, Socialism, Communism, Underdevelopment and Development, Stages of Economic Growth, Relation between Economic and Political Development, Characteristics of political and economic institutions and behavior in underdeveloped countries." See Gerald Bush, handwritten notes on Peace Corps Training Program, Bush Papers, box 3, "Organization File ," JFKL. On the requirement for anti-Communist training, see Amin, *Peace Corps in Cameroon*, 39.
30. Castagno, "Political Science, the Developing Areas, and the Peace Corps," 1963, photocopied, PCL.
31. Stone, "The Role of Interdisciplinary, Intercultural Studies in Peace Corps Training Programs," 1963, photocopied, PCL.

32. Memorandum, Peace Corps Division of Training, September 1, 1962, White House Aides Files—Moyers, box 41, "Middle Level Manpower Conference," LBJL.

33. Rice, *Twenty Years of the Peace Corps*, 24.

34. Ashabranner, *Moment in History*, 142–45; Memorandum, Gail Switzer to R. E. Nolan, March 5, 1965, "Peace Corps—History, 1961–1966 (Shriver), Folder #1," PCL.

35. Ashabranner, *Moment in History*, 145.

36. Ibid., 161; Peace Corps, "Liberal Arts Students and the Peace Corps," PCL.

37. Kennedy, *Public Papers*, 2:12.

38. Peace Corps, *Second Annual Report*, 39.

39. Cobbs Hoffman, *All You Need Is Love*, 133.

40. Rice, *Twenty Years of the Peace Corps*, 24; Peace Corps, *Who's Working Where*, 11.

41. Bradley Patterson, Meeting Minutes, November 29, 1961, Bush Papers, box 2, "Director's Staff Meeting Records, 10/2/61–1/8/62," JFKL.

42. Poston, "Community Development: An Instrument of Foreign Aid," 1963, photocopied, PCL.

43. Lodge, *Case for the Generalist*, 4, 6.

44. Mankiewicz, "The Peace Corps: A Revolutionary Force," 1964, photocopied, PCL (emphasis in original).

45. Ashabranner, *Moment in History*, 166–67; Cobbs Hoffman, *All You Need Is Love*, 67–68.

46. Jones, "Peace Corps Volunteer in the Field," 64–65.

47. Cobbs Hoffman, *All You Need Is Love*, 203–4.

48. Memorandum, "Community Development Training: Jack Donoghue and Jeremy Taylor, Escondido Peace Corps Training Center," not dated, "Peace Corps Community Development," PCL.

49. Jones, "Peace Corps Volunteer in the Field," 66–67.

50. James P. Moody, Memorandum "Community Development and the Peace Corps," August 21, 1964, "Peace Corps—Community Development," PCL.

51. Lodge, *Case for the Generalist*, 8–9.

52. Report on community development in Colombia, Bush Papers, box 4, "Peace Corps News," JFKL.

53. Peace Corps, "Colombia: *Acción Comunal*," 8–9.

54. Lodge, *Case for the Generalist*, 8–9.

55. Moody, Memorandum "Community Development and the Peace Corps," August 21, 1964, "Peace Corps—Community Development," PCL.

56. Ashabranner, *Moment in History*, 163–64.

57. Peace Corps, *What Can I Do in the Peace Corps?*, 21.

58. Memorandum "Community Development—P.C.—Training," not dated, "Peace Corps—Community Development," PCL.

59. Ashabranner, *Moment in History*, 161.

60. Amin, *Peace Corps in Cameroon*, 136.

61. Fischer, *Making Them Like Us*, 144.

62. Ashabranner, *Moment in History*, 162.

63. Memorandum, Kennedy to Rusk, POF, box 85, "Peace Corps, 1/61–6/61," JFKL.

64. Shriver to Kennedy, not dated, POF, box 85, "Peace Corps, 1/61–6/61," JFKL. On Shriver's effort to keep the agency free from CIA influence and to send volunteers only where requested, see Dean, "Masculinity as Ideology," 60–61.

65. Kennedy, *Public Papers*, 1:391–92; 3:556.

66. Peace Corps, *First Annual Report*, 69; Peace Corps, "Tubman Sees Object Lesson in Peace Corps," 5.

67. Brochure, "What You Can Do for Your Country," 1961, "Peace Corps—History, 1961–1966 (Shriver), Folder #1," PCL; Brochure, "The Peace Corps Generalist: Practitioner of an Uncertain Science," not dated, "Peace Corps—BA Generalists," PCL.

68. Davis, "Peace Corps Volunteer an American Image," 165; Shriver, *Point of the Lance*, 55.

69. Kennedy, *Public Papers*, 1:554 (emphasis added); Shriver, *Point of the Lance*, 9.

70. Lederer and Burdick, *Ugly American*, 284; Rice, *Bold Experiment*, 29.

71. Lederer and Burdick, *Ugly American*, 181.

72. The fit between the fictional portrayal by Lederer and Burdick and the Peace Corps's understanding of its real-world mission was so close that the agency actually put the two novelists to work evaluating its programs. Lederer visited the Philippines to survey early Peace Corps projects and traveled to Hilo, Hawaii, to show prospective volunteers how to fight communism in Asia. See Dean, "Masculinity as Ideology," 58–59; Donovan, "Peace Corps to Hire State Dept.'s Foremost Critics?," 2.

73. Whyte, *Organization Man*; Goodman, *Growing Up Absurd*; Riesman, with Glazier and Denney, *Lonely Crowd*, 18; Galbraith, *Affluent Society*, 140, 159.

74. Cobbs Hoffman, *All You Need Is Love*, 22–38.

75. Kennedy, *Public Papers*, 1:134–35.

76. Shriver, "Ambassadors of Goodwill," 302.

77. Leyden, "British Scientist Salutes Tanganyika Project," 2.

78. See "Peace Corps History, 1961–1966 (Shriver), Folder #2," PCL, for the ceremony program and song lyrics.

79. "Report on the Peace Corps," 10–11; "Corpsmen in Ghana," 20–21.

80. Lederer and Burdick, *Ugly American*, 235.

81. Memorandum, Schlesinger to Kennedy, February 15, 1962, POF, box 65a, "Schlesinger, January–March, 1962," JFKL.

82. Shriver, "Five Years with the Peace Corps," 26.

83. Tilman, *Peace Corps*, 15.

84. Peace Corps, "I Learned More in Ten Months," 4.

85. Senate, *Nomination of R. Sargent Shriver, Jr.*, 50.

86. May, *Homeward Bound*, 10. Whitfield, *Culture of the Cold War*, also describes the way in which McCarthyism broke down barriers between the public and private realms to politicize American culture during the 1950s and 1960s. As Boyer points out in *By the Bomb's Early Light*, these anxieties were also sharpened by resurgent fears of nuclear war.

87. Shriver, Commencement Address, University of Notre Dame, June 4, 1961, NSF, box 284, "Peace Corps, General, 1961," JFKL.

88. Press Statement, Sargent Shriver, November 18, 1961, Bush Papers, box 6, "Weekly Report to the President," JFKL.

89. Draft memorandum, not dated, White House Aides Files—Moyers, box 18, "Congressional Presentation—1961," LBJL. For an analysis of that argument's gendered components, see Dean, "Masculinity as Ideology."

90. White House Aides Files—Moyers, box 40, "Endorsements," LBJL; Braestrup, "Peace Corpsman No. 1—A Progress Report," 64; Trussell, "Peace Corps Rise Is Voted by House," 1; Memorandum, "A Pleasant View from Capitol Hill," POF, box 85, "Peace Corps, 1–3/62," JFKL; Memorandum, Bill Haddad to Pierre Salinger, November 20, 1962, White House Central Subject Files, box 670, "Peace Corps Program," JFKL; Memorandum, Edwin Bayley to Richard Maguire, August 4, 1961, Bayley Papers, box 1, "August 1961 Responses to July 27 Meeting on Information Activities," JFKL.

91. Elizabeth C. Barnes to Thomas E. Morgan, August 16, 1961, "Peace Corps History, 1961–1961 (Beginnings)," PCL; Sevareid, "Writer Says Time Is Ripe," 2; Karney, "Peace Corps a Farce," 2; Belshaw, "Experts, Not Youths Needed," 68, 70.

92. Peace Corps, "Volunteer Image," 4; Barnett, "Volunteers Resent 'Hero' Role," 2, 24.

93. For one case of radical dissent, see Cowan, Making of an Un-American.

94. "Peace Corps in Training," 334; Mothner, "Peace Corps," 40.

95. Hobsbawm, "Introduction," 1, 9.

96. Congress, Senate, 87th Cong., 1st sess., Congressional Record (June 1, 1961), vol. 107, pt. 7:9302.

97. Peace Corps, "Presentation of FY 1962 Program to United States Congress," June 1, 1961, Bush Papers, box 5, "Policy File, 1 of 3," JFKL.

98. Toynbee, "America's New Lay Army," 10–11, 15.

99. Wetzel, "Peace Corps in Our Past," 2.

100. Challener and Livermore, "Challener, Livermore Recount Corps History," 3.

101. Wiggins, "A Question of Values," speech at Hanover College, Indiana, April 4, 1966, Bush Papers, box 5, "A Question of Values," JFKL.

102. Kennedy, Public Papers, 3:555.

103. Shriver, Point of the Lance, 16.

104. Williams, "Frontier Thesis and American Foreign Policy"; LaFeber, New Empire. Horsman, Race and Manifest Destiny, 298–303, traces this theme as well. As Horsman points out, advocates of American territorial expansion held that, because other peoples remained incapable of forming democratic governments, the growth of American commerce would provide for both the triumph of Christian civilization and the creation of a stable international order.

105. Lasch, World of Nations, 82–85. Slotkin, Gunfighter Nation, 490, describes Kennedy's image in terms that resonate with the treatment Lasch gives Roosevelt. As Slotkin puts it, Kennedy also "projected a vision of the President as a heroic

figure tested and qualified for power by deeds in battle and prepared to take a militant stance toward the nation's concerns."

106. Turner, "Significance of the Frontier," 199–200.

107. Kennedy, *Public Papers*, 1:136.

108. Shriver, "Two Years of the Peace Corps," 706–7.

109. Rosenthal, *Character Factory*, 6, illustrates an interesting parallel. In an early-twentieth-century Britain troubled with the fading empire, many expected that "Scout training, rightly understood and liberally applied, could bring about the regeneration of the nation."

110. Peace Corps, *Fifth Annual Report*, 70.

111. Peace Corps, *Third Annual Report*, 87.

112. Anderson, *Imagined Communities*, 6, 145.

113. American Indians have historically been viewed as "primitive contemporaries," groups that have failed to move up the developmental scale along with the rest of the nation. As Rogin points out in *Fathers and Children*, "The evolution of societies from savagery to civilization was identical to the evolution of individual men. The Indian was the elder brother, but he remained in the 'childhood' of the human race" (6).

114. Memorandum, "Outline of Proposed Community Development Training for Peace Corps," American Institutes for Research, May 13, 1966, "CD—Peace Corps Training," PCL.

115. Peace Corps, "Peace Corps Trainees Work, Study in New York Slums," 1, 3; Ginsberg, "Short-Term Training in Urban Community Development," paper presented at conference "The Peace Corps and the Behavioral Sciences," March 4–5, 1963, photocopied, PCL.

116. Peace Corps, "Journey to a Reservation," 1, 7.

117. Jacobs, "Peace Corps Trainees Do Field Work," 41–42.

118. Zalba, "The Peace Corps," 125, 135.

119. Katz, *In the Shadow of the Poorhouse*, 76, illustrates the historical depth of these parallels. As he notes, theorists of nineteenth-century "Scientific Charity" believed that visitation of the poor by their social superiors provided "a real friend, whose education, experience, and influence, whose general knowledge of life" would greatly assist those lacking "the tact or the opportunity to extract the maximum good from their slender resources."

120. Shriver, speech at the University of Michigan, October 9, 1964, Bush Papers, box 5, "Shriver Speeches," JFKL.

121. Johnson, *Public Papers*, 1:212.

Chapter Five

1. Huntington, "Bases of Accomodation," 652.

2. For the LeMay statement and a brief treatment of Huntington's views, see Drinnon, *Facing West*, 370–73. Chomsky, *American Power and the New Mandarins*, 20 n. 5, also cites Huntington's argument.

3. Hilsman, speech to the Conference on Cold War Education, Tampa, Fla., June 14, 1963, Thomson Papers, box 9, "Speeches—R. Hilsman," JFKL.

4. Chomsky, *American Power and the New Mandarins*, 41.

5. Kahin, *Intervention*, 33.

6. Schulzinger, *Time for War*, 9.

7. Cited in Harrison, *Endless War*, 96.

8. Gardner, *Approaching Vietnam*, 14.

9. Schulzinger, *Time for War*, 22.

10. Ibid., 30.

11. Rotter, *Path to Vietnam*, 6.

12. In addition to the interpretations of this period by Kahin and Rotter, see Young, *Vietnam Wars*; Herring, *America's Longest War*.

13. Harrison, *Endless War*, 116.

14. Schulzinger, *Time for War*, 52; Harrison, *Endless War*, 116–17.

15. Smith, *International History of the Vietnam War*, 1:40; Schulzinger, *Time For War*, 47.

16. Harrison, *Endless War*, 117.

17. For treatments of Dienbienphu and its impact, see Fall, *Hell in a Very Small Place*; Harrison, *Endless War*, 123–25; Schulzinger, *Time for War*, 58–68.

18. Kahin, *Intervention*, 61; Schulzinger, *Time for War*, 76–77. For the details of the Geneva Accords, see Randle, *Geneva 1954*.

19. Herring, *America's Longest War*, 44–46; Young, *Vietnam Wars*, 37–59.

20. Schulzinger, *Time for War*, 78.

21. FitzGerald, *Fire in the Lake*, 98.

22. Young, *Vietnam Wars*, 53; Schulzinger, *Time for War*, 89–90. In the country from 1954 through 1962, Michigan State's involvement in the effort to build a "modern" South Vietnamese nation is an interesting chapter in itself. Accounts by members of the Michigan State University mission include Fishel, "Problems of Democratic Growth in Free Vietnam," and Scigliano and Fox, *Technical Assistance in Vietnam*. See also Ernst, *Forging a Fateful Alliance*.

23. Wiegersma, *Vietnam*, 180–82; Harrison, *Endless War*, 183–85, 210–11,

24. Kahin, *Intervention*, 95–103; Wiegersma, *Vietnam*, 203; Harrison, *Endless War*, 216. Halberstam, *Making of a Quagmire*, also provides a thorough treatment of the Diem regime's corruption and systematic repression.

25. For accounts of the founding of the NLF, its southern roots, and its relationship to Hanoi, see Kahin, *Intervention*, 112–21; Harrison, *Endless War*, 175–78, 225–30. For the impact of the NLF's formation on local revolutionary efforts, see Race, *War Comes to Long An*, 105–30.

26. Herring, *America's Longest War*, 56–57.

27. Memorandum, Lansdale to Secretary of Defense, Deputy Secretary of Defense, and others, January 17, 1961, Lansdale Papers, box 42, "Memoranda, 1950–1961," HIA. For Rostow's recollection of passing Lansdale's analysis on to Kennedy, see Rostow, Oral History Interview by Richard Neustadt, April 11, 1964, transcript, 44–45, JFKL.

28. Central Intelligence Agency, National Intelligence Estimate No. 50–61, March 28, 1961, Vice-President's Security File, box 10, "27 April-Viet Nam, Col. Burris EOB (I)," LBJL.

29. As cited in Olson and Roberts, *Where the Domino Fell*, 87.

30. Memorandum, Lansdale to Secretary of Defense, Deputy Secretary of Defense, and others, January 17, 1961, Lansdale Papers, box 42, "Memoranda, 1950–1961," HIA.

31. Memorandum, Johnson to Kennedy, May 23, 1961, Vice-Presidential Security File, box 1, "Vice-President's Visit to Southeast Asia, May 9–24, 1961 (I)," LBJL.

32. Buzzanco, *Masters of War*, 87–88; Gardner, *Pay Any Price*, 44.

33. Gardner, *Pay Any Price*, 26–27, 45–47.

34. Kahin, *Intervention*, 126.

35. Presidential Task Force, "A Program to Prevent Communist Domination of South Vietnam," *FRUS, 1961–1963*, 1:93, 99.

36. For a detailed chronology of early Kennedy administration decisions, see Senate, *Pentagon Papers (Gravel edition)*, 2:5–17.

37. Kahin, *Intervention*, 133.

38. Buzzanco, *Masters of War*, 96–99.

39. Kahin, *Intervention*, 136–37.

40. Minutes of NSC Meeting, November 15, 1961, Vice-Presidential Security File, box ·4 "National Security Council (II)," LBJL.

41. Young, *Vietnam Wars*, 82.

42. Blaufarb, *Counterinsurgency Era*, 52–56, 67–68. The other members of the executive branch counterinsurgency committee were Kennedy's personal military adviser, General Maxwell Taylor, Deputy Secretary of Defense Roswell Gilpatric, Joint Chiefs of Staff chair General Lyman Lemnitzer, CIA director John McCone, national security adviser McGeorge Bundy, AID director Fowler Hamilton, and USIA head Edward R. Murrow. For the National Security Action Memorandum establishing the team, see Senate, *Pentagon Papers (Gravel edition)*, 2:660–61. For the Joint Chiefs of Staff report on the implementation of training programs, see Memorandum, Lemnitzer to McGeorge Bundy, July 21, 1962, NSF, box 319, "Special Group (Ci) Military Organization and Accomplishments, July, 1962," JFKL.

43. McGeorge Bundy, National Security Action Memorandum 131, March 13, 1962, Senate, *Pentagon Papers (Gravel edition)*, 2:667–69.

44. Memorandum, Taylor to the Special Group for Counterinsurgency, NSF, box 319, JFKL; Memorandum, Special Group for Counterinsurgency to Kennedy, NSF, box 319, "Special Group (Ci), 1/61–6/62," JFKL.

45. Blaufarb, *Counterinsurgency Era*, 71–73; State Department, "FSI Begins Seminars on Problems of Development and Internal Defense," 42 (emphasis in original).

46. Shafer, *Deadly Paradigms*, 21.

47. Rostow, "Countering Guerrilla Attack," 464–66. Regarding Kennedy's approval of the speech text as an official statement of administration policy, see Blaufarb, *Counterinsurgency Era*, 57.

48. Rostow, "Countering Guerrilla Attack," 464–66.

49. Ibid., 466–68.

50. Report of Seminar on Counter-Guerrilla Operations in the Philippines, U.S. Army Special Warfare Center, June 15, 1961, NSF, box 326, "Rostow, Guerrilla and Unconventional Warfare, June 14–30, 1961," JFKL.

51. Lansdale, speech to the Special Warfare School, Fort Bragg, N.C., August 30, 1962, Lansdale Papers, box 45, HIA.

52. Shafer, *Deadly Paradigms*, 112–13.

53. Memorandum, Inter-Departmental Seminar on Counterinsurgency, August, 1962, NSF, box 338, "NSAM 182, Counterinsurgency," JFKL.

54. Ibid. (emphasis in original).

55. BDM Corporation, "A Study of Strategic Lessons Learned in Vietnam," 1980, vol. 5, BDM Study, 5-14–5-16, LBJL; Senate, *Pentagon Papers (Gravel edition)*, 2:133–34; Zasloff, *Rural Resettlement in Vietnam*, 16–17, 24–25.

56. Zasloff, *Rural Resettlement in Vietnam*, 13–32.

57. Memorandum, Viet Nam–United States Special Financial Groups to Ngo Dinh Diem and John F. Kennedy, July 1961, Staley Papers, box 23, "Historian, Dept. of State Re: Vietnam Mission, 1961," HIA. The document is also available at the Johnson Library, Vice-Presidential Security File, box 10, "27 April-Viet Nam Col. Burris EOB (II)."

58. Memorandum, Rusk to Kennedy, July 28, 1961, Staley Papers, box 23, "Historian, Dept. of State, RE: Vietnam Mission, 1961," HIA.

59. Frankel, "U.S. Giving Saigon New Economic Aid in Fight on Reds."

60. Staley, "American Interests and the Underdeveloped Areas of the World," speech delivered at Stanford University, November 9, 1954, Staley Papers, box 3, "Staley Speeches, Articles 1946–60," HIA.

61. Staley, "The Revolution of Rising Expectations," unpublished paper, ca. 1957, Staley Papers, box 3, "Staley Speeches, Articles, 1946–1960," HIA. For similar formulations of this idea, see Staley, *Future of Underdeveloped Countries*.

62. Madison, "S.R.I. Aide Offers Plan to Beat South Viet Nam Reds." For Staley's UN proposal, see his "Taking Economic and Social Development of New Countries Out of the Cold War," Staley Papers, box 3, HIA.

63. Gibbons, *U.S. Government and the Vietnam War*, 104.

64. Senate, *Pentagon Papers (Gravel edition)*, 2:139–40.

65. Thompson, *Defeating Communist Insurgency*, 111–12.

66. Ibid., 123–24.

67. Ibid., 112–13.

68. Senate, *Pentagon Papers (Gravel edition)*, 2:140.

69. Ibid., 2:140–41; Buzzanco, *Masters of War*, 119–20; Gibbons, *U.S. Government and the Vietnam War*, 105–6.

70. Central Intelligence Agency, Special National Intelligence Estimate Number 53-2-61, October 5, 1961, National Intelligence Estimates, box 7, "53, South Vietnam," LBJL.

71. Memorandum, Rostow to Rusk, January 6, 1961, POF, box 64a, "Rostow, 11/61–2/61," JFKL (emphasis added).

72. As Nick Cullather has pointed out, advisers such as Rostow did not recognize the degree to which Magsaysay himself successfully used such programs to "manage"

the United States as well as the insurgency. See Cullather, *Illusions of Influence*, 102–3.

73. Miller, *"Benevolent Assimilation,"* 208–9. As Miller notes, the Spanish, in Cuba, and the English, in the Boer War, used similar tactics to fight colonial wars.

74. Pye, *Guerrilla Communism in Malaya*, 3, 7.

75. Rostow, *Diffusion of Power*, 273–74.

76. Pye, *Guerrilla Communism in Malaya*, 201–2.

77. Memorandum, Sterling Cottrell to National Security Council, May 9, 1961, NSF, box 330, "NSAM 52, Vietnam," JFKL.

78. Pye, "Political Development and Foreign Aid," November 1963, Bell Papers, box 23, "AID's Advisory Committee on Economic Development (Mason Committee), 1963–1964," JFKL.

79. Smith, *International History of the Vietnam War*, 1:183–84. For theoretical literature on "military modernization," see Shils, "Military in the Political Development of the New States"; Lerner and Robinson, "Swords and Ploughshares." For a U.S. government view, see unidentified author, "The Role of the Military in Underdeveloped Areas," prepared for the Secretary of State's Policy Planning Meeting, January 29, 1963, Thompson Papers, box 6, "Department of State, Policy Planning Council, 1/63," JFKL.

80. Rust, *Kennedy in Vietnam*, 67–68. A memorandum sent from White House staff member William H. Brubeck to national security adviser McGeorge Bundy also notes a visit by Thompson to Washington in early 1962 and refers to plans for Kennedy to meet with him in the spring of 1963. See NSF, box 197, "Vietnam, 3/1–3/19/63," JFKL.

81. Hilsman, "A Strategic Concept for South Vietnam," February 2, 1962, Hilsman Papers, box 3, Vietnam, "Strategic Concept," JFKL.

82. Ibid.

83. Some officials found Hilsman's view of the world and America's ability to manipulate it so appealing that they could hardly contain themselves. After reading the "Strategic Concept," Edward R. Murrow of the U.S. Information Agency called Hilsman and told him that "by God, [it was] the first time in many months . . . that he had read prose that is not only intelligible but has a small cutting edge. . . . Reading the first three pages was like having a long mint julep at the end of a hot day." Hilsman, Memo to File, April 25, 1962, Hilsman Papers, box 3, "Vietnam, A Strategic Concept for South Vietnam, 2/2/62," JFKL.

84. Senate, *Pentagon Papers (Gravel edition)*, 2:129.

85. Fall, *Two Viet-Nams*, 376–79; Memorandum, Sterling Cottrell to Special Group (Ci), March 22, 1962, NSF, box 319, "Special Group (Ci), 1/61–6/62," JFKL.

86. Memorandum, Hilsman to Harriman, April 3, 1962, Hilsman Papers, box 3, "Vietnam, A Strategic Concept for South Vietnam," 2/2/62, JFKL.

87. Tanham, *War without Guns*, 24–27; O'Donnell, "Strategic Hamlet Program in Kien Hoa Province," 711–18; Agency for International Development, *Administrative History 1963–1969*, vol. I, pt. 1:391–92, LBJL. As AID administrative histories note, the emphasis on provincial counterinsurgency produced an institutional conflict between AID personnel preferring to limit their efforts to the more

technical problems of economic assistance and those praising more comprehensive social engineering. In the early 1960s, however, the counterinsurgency emphasis enjoyed the administration's overwhelming political and financial backing. See Indochina Terminal Report, Vietnam, July 12, 1976, AIDC.

88. State Department Task Force, Status Report on Southeast Asia, August 8, 1962, Vice-Presidential Security File, box 1, "Vice President's Visit to Southeast Asia (II)," LBJL.

89. Agency for International Development, "United States Assistance to Vietnam," August 1964, Lansdale Papers, box 27, "U.S. Aid to Vietnam—Misc.," HIA.

90. Nighswonger, *Rural Pacification in Vietnam*, 99–100; Donnell and Hickey, *Vietnamese "Strategic Hamlets."*

91. Memorandum, author unknown, Rural Reconstruction Efforts, Operational Guidelines, 1964, Lansdale Papers, box 23, "Vietnam Conflict, 1961–1965, Pacification. Binh Dinh Province. Operational Guidelines, Administrative Cell," HIA; Memorandum, National Security Council, Delta Counterinsurgency Plan, January 1962, Hilsman Papers, box 3, "Vietnam, 1/62–2/62," JFKL.

92. Scott, *Seeing Like a State*, 188–89, 191.

93. Pearce, *Evolution of a Vietnamese Village*, 40–41.

94. Donnell and Hickey, *Vietnamese "Strategic Hamlets,"* 11–15.

95. Ibid., 16.

96. Phillips, Report on Counterinsurgency in Vietnam, August 31, 1962, Lansdale Papers, box 49, "Vietnam, General, 1961–1963 (2)," HIA.

97. Report of Visit by Joint Chiefs of Staff Team to South Vietnam, January 1963, NSF, box 197, "Vietnam, General, 1/10–1/30/63," JFKL.

98. Huppert, "Bullets Alone Won't Win," 39.

99. Central Intelligence Agency, anonymous field report, November 29, 1962, NSF, box 197, "Vietnam, General, 11/26–11/30/62," JFKL.

100. U.S. Information Service, Village Elections in Kien Giang Province, April 1964, Fall Papers, box 29, "Vietnam—South—Politics and Government," JFKL.

101. Nighswonger, *Rural Pacification in Vietnam*, 168.

102. Agency for International Development, "The Role of the Agency for International Development in Counterinsurgency," 326.

103. Agency for International Development, "Country Assistance Program—Vietnam, Part III, December, 1964," AID Historical Collection, AIDC.

104. Hilsman, Memorandum to Record, December 1962, Hilsman Papers, box 3, "Hilsman Trip, 12/62–1/63," JFKL.

105. Memorandum, Bohannan to John M. Dunn, January 13, 1964, Lansdale Papers, box 42, "Memoranda 1962–1964," HIA.

106. Memorandum, McNamara to Kennedy, September 21, 1963, NSF, box 204, "Halberstam Article, 9/63," JFKL.

107. Rusk, "Stake in Vietnam."

108. Bell, speech to National Rural Electric Cooperative Association, January 14, 1963, Moscoso Papers, box 10, "Speech Materials 1/63," JFKL.

109. Wheeler, Press Statement, February 4, 1963, Hilsman Papers, box 3, "Vietnam, 3/1–8/21/63," JFKL.

110. Thomas Davis, Special Group (Ci) Meeting Minutes, April 3, 1962, NSF, box 319, "Special Group (Ci) Meetings, 1961–63," JFKL.

111. "South Vietnam: New Strategy."

112. Martin, "Latest Report from the Front in Vietnam."

113. "South Viet Nam: Miracle at Hoaimy."

114. Memorandum, Kennedy to Bundy, February 6, 1961, NSF, box 328, "NSAM 9," JFKL.

115. Drinnon, *Facing West*, 380–82; Lansdale, "Report the President Wanted Published," 31, 69–70; Schanche, "Father Hoa's Little War," 74–79; Chapelle, "Fighting Priest of South Vietnam," 200.

116. Hilsman, "Internal War," 455–56.

117. Humphrey, "American Civilians Who Are Fighting the Shirtsleeves War," 2–3, 6–7.

118. State Department, "Quiet Warriors: Supporting Social Revolution in Viet-Nam," 1966, USIA Agency Records, microfilm reel 40, LBJL.

119. Johnson, *Public Papers*, 1:526.

120. Michael W. Moynihan to Allan Wilson, April 27, 1966, Advertising Council Files, box 1, "AID (Program for Civilian Help in Vietnam)," LBJL.

121. "The Quiet Struggle in Viet Nam: U.S. Civilian Employees Working to Show Peasants the Functions and Fruits of Democracy," included in AID compilation on "Nation Building in Vietnam," reprinted from *St. Louis Post Dispatch*, April 24, 1966, USIA Agency Records, microfilm reel 40, LBJL.

122. David Bell to Shriver, April 20, 1964, NSF, box 42, "Peace Corps," LBJL; memorandum, McGeorge Bundy to Shriver, May 13, 1964, NSF, box 42, "Peace Corps," LBJL.

123. *Congressional Record*, Senate, 86th Cong., 2d. sess., February 9, 1960, vol. 106, pt. 2:2331.

124. Hilsman, speech to the American Hospital Association, September 18, 1962, Hilsman Papers, box 3, "Vietnam, 2/1–8/21/63," JFKL.

125. O'Donnell, "Strategic Hamlet Program in Kien Hoa Province," 738–39.

126. Senate, *Pentagon Papers (Gravel edition)*, 2:685–86.

127. Nolting, Ambassador's Weekly Status Report, July 12, 1962, NSF, box 196, Countries "Vietnam, General, 7/11–7/19/62," JFKL.

128. Duiker, *Sacred War*, 153; Olson and Roberts, *Where the Domino Fell*, 97–98.

129. Truong, *Viet Cong Memoir*, 46–47.

130. Nolting to Sterling Cottrell, October 15, 1962, *FRUS, 1961–1963*, 2:699–701.

131. Memorandum, Johnson to Rostow, October 16, 1962, *FRUS, 1961–1963*, 2:703–6.

132. Memorandum, Taylor to McNamara, November 17, 1962, *FRUS, 1961–1963*, 2:736–38.

133. Nolting to Harriman, November 19, 1962, *FRUS, 1961–1963*, 2:738–41 (emphasis in original).

134. Memorandum, Felt to Joint Chiefs of Staff, March 26, 1963, NSF, box 197 "Vietnam, 3/20–3/29/63," JFKL.

135. Memorandum, Felt to Joint Chiefs of Staff, March 9, 1963, NSF, box 197, "Vietnam, 3/1–3/19/63," JFKL.

136. Report, McNamara and Taylor to Kennedy, October 2, 1963, NSF, Vietnam Country File, Addendum, "Hilsman, Roger (Vietnam-Diem) (1963)," LBJL.

137. Young, *Vietnam Wars*, 93–102; Schulzinger, *Time for War*, 119–23.

138. U.S. Information Service, Long An Province Survey, January 1964, Lansdale Papers, box 23, "Pacification and Land Reform/General, 1964–1969," HIA.

139. Memorandum, Lodge to Rusk, December 11, 1963, NSF, Vietnam Country File, box 1, "Vietnam Cables, Vol. I, 11/63–12/63 (2 of 2)," LBJL.

140. Telegram, Lodge to Rusk, December 7, 1962, NSF, Vietnam Country File, box 1, "Vietnam Cables, Vol. I, 11/63–12/63 (2 of 2)," LBJL.

141. Senate, *Pentagon Papers (Gravel edition)*, 2:128–31.

142. Memorandum, Rusk to Johnson, December 1963, NSF, box 1 "Vietnam Cables, Vol. I (2 of 2) 11/63–12/63," LBJL; memorandum, Forrestal to Johnson, December 11, 1963, NSF, box 1 "Vietnam Cables, Vol. I (2 of 2) 11/63–12/63," LBJL.

143. Lens, "Only Hope," 23–24, lists these points.

144. Young, *Vietnam Wars*, 144–45; 212–13. As Young points out, moreover, CORDS operations were bolstered by the brutal violence and terrorism of the American-led Phoenix program, an effort to identify and "neutralize" NLF cadres and supporters.

145. Cited in FitzGerald, *Fire in the Lake*, 486.

146. Young, *Vietnam Wars*, 145.

147. "South Viet Nam: What the People Say."

148. Karnow, "Edge of Chaos," 34. This emphasis also persists in many historical accounts. See, for example, Smith, *International History of the Vietnam War*, 2:168.

149. Senate, *Vietnam and Southeast Asia*, 7 (emphasis in original).

150. Halberstam, *Making of a Quagmire*, 50.

Conclusion

1. Merk, *Manifest Destiny and Mission*, 266. For an earlier, contrasting perspective, see Weinberg, *Manifest Destiny*, first published in 1935.

2. See, for example, the interesting argument made in Schwabe, "Global Role of the United States."

3. Stephanson, *Manifest Destiny*, xii, xiii.

4. Horsman, *Race and Manifest Destiny*.

5. On the continuity between Western and imperial history, see Williams, "United States Indian Policy and the Debate over Philippine Annexation."

6. For Rostow's language, see memorandum, Rostow to Kennedy, March 2, 1961, POF, box 64a, "Rostow, 3/61–5/61," JKFL. Johnson's "social worker" comment appeared in a *Time* article titled "The War." For the Green Beret story, see the *Time* article "Nation-Mending at Home." On Johnson's fascination with a Tennessee Valley Authority on the Mekong, see Gardner, *Pay Any Price*.

7. Katz, *Undeserving Poor*, 7.

8. On the concept, see Anderson, *Imagined Communities*.

BIBLIOGRAPHY

Archival and Manuscript Collections

Agency for International Development, Center for Development Information and
    Evaluation, Rosslyn, Virginia
    AID Historical Collection, 1961–69
Hoover Institution Archives, Stanford, California
    Charles T. R. Bohannan Papers
    Edward Lansdale Papers
    Eugene Staley Papers
John F. Kennedy Library, Boston, Massachusetts
    Edwin Bayley Papers
    Carmine Bellino Papers
    David Bell Papers
    Gerald Bush Papers
    Bernard Fall Papers
    Fowler Hamilton Papers
    Roger Hilsman Papers
    William Josephson Papers
    Samuel P. Hayes Papers
    John F. Kennedy Papers
        National Security Files
            Departments and Agencies
            National Security Action Memoranda
            Country File—Vietnam
            Meetings and Memoranda
            Staff File of Carl Kaysen
        Pre-Presidential Papers
        1960 Task Force Report on Foreign Affairs
        President's Office Files
            Special Correspondence
            Legislative Files
            Staff Memoranda
            Departments and Agencies
            Subjects—Alliance for Progress

White House Central Subject File
   Peace Corps
Robert F. Kennedy Papers
   Attorney General's Correspondence
Frank Mankiewicz Papers
Max Millikan Papers
Teodoro Moscoso Papers
Arthur M. Schlesinger Jr. Papers
James Thomson Papers
Oral History Collection
Lyndon B. Johnson Library, Austin, Texas
   Brent Ashabranner Papers
   William P. Bundy Papers
   Lyndon B. Johnson Papers
      Vice-Presidential Security File
      National Security Files
         National Security Action Memoranda
         National Intelligence Estimates
         Declassified and Sanitized Documents from Unprocessed Files
         Agency File—AID and Alliance for Progress
         Country File—Vietnam
         Name Files
      Records from Government Agencies
         United States Information Agency
      Task Force Reports
      Special Files
         Administrative Histories—AID
      White House Central Files
         Office Files of White House Aides
   Oral History Collection
U.S. Peace Corps Library, Washington, D.C.
   Historical Collection, 1961–63
   Files on Community Development Programs and Training
   Files on Advertising, Recruiting

Published Primary and Secondary Sources

Agency for International Development. "Putting PEP in AID." *Area Digest* 2 (Fall 1963): 7.
———. "The Role of the Agency for International Development in Counterinsurgency." In *Insurgency and Counterinsurgency: An Anthology*, edited by Richard M. Leighton and Ralph Sanders, 325, 29. Washington, D.C.: Industrial College of the Armed Forces, 1962.
Alba, Victor. *Alliance without Allies: The Mythology of Progress in Latin America.* New York: Praeger, 1965.

Alexander, Jeffrey C. "Modern, Anti, Post, and Neo: How Social Theories Have Tried to Understand the 'New Problems of Our Time.'" *Zeitschrift für Soziologie* 23 (June 1994): 165–97.

———. *Twenty Lectures: Sociological Theory since World War II.* New York: Columbia University Press, 1987.

"Alianza, Sí, Progreso, No." *Time*, March 16, 1962, 33.

"Alliance for Progress: The Big Need Is Deeds." *Newsweek*, August 27, 1962, 50.

"Alliance Progresses." *Newsweek*, August 21, 1961, 44.

Almond, Gabriel. "The Seminar on Comparative Politics." *Social Science Research Council Items* 10 (December 1956): 45–48.

Almond, Gabriel, and James S. Coleman, eds. *The Politics of Developing Areas.* Princeton: Princeton University Press, 1960.

Amin, Julius A. *The Peace Corps in Cameroon.* Kent, Ohio: Kent State University Press, 1992.

Anderson, Benedict. *Imagined Communities: Reflections on the Origin and Spread of Nationalism.* London: Verso, 1983.

Appadurai, Arjun. *Modernity at Large: Cultural Dimensions of Globalization.* Minneapolis: University of Minnesota Press, 1996.

Appleby, Joyce. "Modernization Theory and the Formation of Modern Social Theories in England and America." *Comparative Studies in Society and History* 20 (April 1978): 259–85.

Apter, David E. *Ghana in Transition.* 2d rev. ed. Princeton: Princeton University Press, 1972.

———. *Rethinking Development: Modernization, Dependency, and Postmodern Politics.* Newbury Park, Calif.: Sage, 1987.

———. *Some Conceptual Approaches to the Study of Modernization.* Englewood Cliffs, N.J.: Prentice-Hall, 1968.

Arndt, H. W. *Economic Development: The History of an Idea.* Chicago: University of Chicago Press, 1987.

Asad, Talal, ed. *Anthropology and the Colonial Encounter.* Atlantic Highlands, N.J.: Humanities Press, 1973.

Ashabranner, Brent. *A Moment in History: The First Ten Years of the Peace Corps.* Garden City, N.Y.: Doubleday, 1971.

"Back to the Drawing Board." *National Review*, October 22, 1963, 334–35.

Ball, Terence. "The Politics of Social Science in Postwar America." In *Recasting America: Culture and Politics in the Age of the Cold War*, edited by Lary May, 76–92. Chicago: University of Chicago Press, 1989.

Banuri, Tariq. "Development and the Politics of Knowledge: A Critical Interpretation of the Social Role of Modernization Theories in the Development of the Third World." In *Dominating Knowledge: Development, Culture, and Resistance*, edited by Stephen A. Marglin and Frédérique Apffel Marglin, 29–72. Oxford: Clarendon Press, 1990.

Baritz, Loren. *Backfire: A History of How American Culture Led Us into Vietnam and Made Us Fight the Way We Did.* New York: Morrow, 1985.

Barnes, Barry. "On Authority and Its Relationship to Power." In *Power, Action, and*

Belief: A New Sociology of Science?, edited by John Law, 180–95. London: Routledge and Kegan Paul, 1986.

Barnet, Richard J. *Roots of War: The Men and Institutions behind U.S. Foreign Policy.* New York: Atheneum, 1972.

Barnett, David. "Volunteers Resent 'Hero' Role—Researcher." *Peace Corps Volunteer,* July 1963, 2.

Bauer, P. T. *Dissent on Development: Studies and Debates in Development Economics.* Cambridge: Harvard University Press, 1972.

Belshaw, Michael. "Experts, Not Youths Needed." *Foreign Policy Bulletin,* January 15, 1961, 68, 70.

Bendix, Reinhard. *Nation-Building and Citizenship: Studies of Our Changing Social Order.* Berkeley: University of California Press, 1977.

Benjamin, Jules R. "The Framework of U.S. Relations with Latin America in the Twentieth Century: An Interpretive Essay." *Diplomatic History* 11 (Spring 1987): 91–112.

Bernstein, Michael A. "American Economics and the National Security State, 1941–1953." *Radical History Review* 63 (Fall 1995): 8–26.

Beschloss, Michael. *The Crisis Years: Kennedy and Khrushchev, 1960–1963.* New York: HarperCollins, 1991.

Biersack, Aletta. "Local Knowledge, Local History: Geertz and Beyond." In *The New Cultural History,* edited by Lynn Hunt, 72–96. Berkeley: University of California Press, 1989.

Bierstedt, Robert. *American Sociological Theory: A Critical History.* New York: Academic Press, 1981.

Binder, Leonard. "The Natural History of Development Theory." *Comparative Studies in Society and History* 28 (January 1986): 3–33.

Black, C. E. *The Dynamics of Modernization: A Study in Comparative History.* New York: Harper and Row, 1966.

Blaufarb, Douglas S. *The Counterinsurgency Era: U.S. Doctrine and Performance, 1950 to the Present.* New York: Free Press, 1977.

Bock, Kenneth E. "Theories of Progress and Evolution." In *Sociology and History: Theory and Research,* edited by Werner J. Cahnman and Alvin Boskoff, 21–41. New York: Free Press, 1964.

Bodenheimer, Susanne J. "The Ideology of Developmentalism: American Political Science Paradigm Surrogate for Latin American Studies." *Berkeley Journal of Sociology* 15 (1970): 95–137.

Boyer, Paul. *By the Bomb's Early Light: American Thought and Culture at the Dawn of the Atomic Age.* New York: Pantheon, 1985.

Braestrup, Peter. "Peace Corpsman No. 1—A Progress Report." *New York Times Magazine,* December 17, 1961, 64.

Brown, Richard D. "Modernization and the Modern Personality in Early America, 1600–1865: A Sketch of a Synthesis." *Journal of Inter-Disciplinary History* 2 (Winter 1972): 201–28.

Bundy, McGeorge. "The Battlefields of Power and the Searchlights of the Academy."

In *The Dimensions of Diplomacy*, edited by E. A. J. Johnson, 1–15. Baltimore: Johns Hopkins University Press, 1964.

Butler, Dorothy. "50 Peacecorpsmen Doing Well in Ghana." *Washington Post*, December 18, 1961, A22.

Buxton, William. *Talcott Parsons and the Capitalist Nation-State: Political Sociology as a Strategic Vocation*. Toronto: University of Toronto Press, 1985.

Buzzanco, Robert. *Masters of War: Military Dissent and Politics in the Vietnam Era*. Cambridge: Cambridge University Press, 1996.

Campbell, David. *Writing Security: United States Foreign Policy and the Politics of Identity*. Minneapolis: University of Minnesota Press, 1992.

Carey, Robert G. *The Peace Corps*. New York: Praeger, 1970.

Challener, Richard D., and Shaw Livermore Jr. "Challener, Livermore Recount Corps History." *Daily Princetonian*, January 19, 1962, 3.

Chambers, William Nisbet. *Political Parties in a New Nation: The American Experience, 1776–1809*. New York: Oxford University Press, 1963.

Chapelle, Dickey. "The Fighting Priest of South Vietnam." *Reader's Digest*, July 1963, 194–200.

Chenery, Hollis. "Foreign Assistance and Economic Development." *American Economic Review* 56 (September 1966): 679–729.

Chomsky, Noam. *American Power and the New Mandarins*. New York: Random House, 1969.

———. *Rethinking Camelot: JFK, the Vietnam War, and U.S. Political Culture*. Boston: South End Press, 1993.

Clifford, James. "On Orientalism." In *The Predicament of Culture: Twentieth-Century Ethnography, Literature, and Art*, edited by James Clifford, 255–76. Cambridge: Harvard University Press, 1988.

Cmiel, Kenneth. "Destiny and Amnesia: The Vision of Modernity in Robert Wiebe's The Search for Order." *Reviews in American History* 21 (June 1993): 352–68.

Cobbs, Elizabeth A. "Decolonization, the Cold War, and the Foreign Policy of the Peace Corps." *Diplomatic History* 20 (Winter 1996): 79–105.

Cobbs Hoffman, Elizabeth. *All You Need Is Love: The Peace Corps and the Spirit of the 1960s*. Cambridge: Harvard University Press, 1998.

Cockcroft, James D., Dale L. Johnson, and André Gunder Frank. *Dependence and Underdevelopment: Latin America's Political Economy*. Garden City, N.Y.: Doubleday, 1972.

Cohen, Warren I. *America in the Age of Soviet Power, 1945–1991*. Cambridge: Cambridge University Press, 1993.

The Congressional Record. Washington: U.S. Government Printing Office.

"Corpsmen in Ghana." *Time*, November 17, 1961, 20–21.

Cowan, Paul. *The Making of an Un-American: A Dialogue with Experience*. New York: Viking, 1967.

Cullather, Nick. *Illusions of Influence: The Political Economy of United States–Philippines Relations, 1942–1960*. Stanford: Stanford University Press, 1994.

Dahl, Gudrun, and Anders Hjort. "Development as Message and Meaning." *Ethnos* 49, no. 3 (1984): 165–85.

Dale, W. B., and D. C. Fulton. "On Statesmanship." *Saturday Review*, November 4, 1961, 52.

Davis, Watson. "Peace Corps Volunteer an American Image." *Science Newsletter*, March 16, 1963, 165.

Dean, Robert D. "Masculinity as Ideology: John F. Kennedy and the Domestic Politics of Foreign Policy." *Diplomatic History* 22 (Winter 1998): 29–62.

Decter, Midge. "Kennedyism." *Commentary* 49 (January 1970): 19–27.

de Oliveira Campos, Roberto. *Reflections on Latin American Development*. Austin: University of Texas Press, 1967.

Deutsch, Karl. *Nationalism and Social Communication*. Cambridge: Harvard University Press, 1953.

——. "Social Mobilization and Political Development." *American Political Science Review* 55 (September 1961): 493–514.

Diamond, Sigmund. *Compromised Campus: The Collaboration of Universities with the Intelligence Community, 1945–1955*. New York: Oxford University Press, 1992.

Dirks, Nicholas. Introduction to *Colonialism and Culture*, edited by Nicholas Dirks, 1–25. Ann Arbor: University of Michigan Press, 1992.

Donnell, John C., and Gerald C. Hickey. *The Vietnamese "Strategic Hamlets": A Preliminary Report*. Santa Monica: Rand Corporation, 1962. Memorandum RM-3208-ARPA.

Donovan, R. J. "Peace Corps to Hire State Dept.'s Foremost Critics?" *New York Herald Tribune*, April 28, 1962, 2.

Dosal, Paul J. "Accelerating Dependent Development and Revolution: Nicaragua and the Alliance for Progress." *Inter-American Economic Affairs* 38 (Spring 1985): 75–96.

Dow, Maynard Weston. *Nation Building in Southeast Asia*. Boulder, Colo.: Pruett Press, 1965.

Dreier, John C. *The Alliance for Progress: Problems and Perspectives*. Baltimore: Johns Hopkins University Press, 1962.

Drinnon, Richard. *Facing West: The Metaphysics of Indian-Hating and Empire-Building*. Minneapolis: University of Minnesota Press, 1980.

Duiker, William J. *The Communist Road to Power in Vietnam*. Boulder, Colo.: Westview Press, 1981.

——. *Sacred War: Nationalism and Revolution in a Divided Vietnam*. New York: McGraw-Hill, 1995.

Eisenstadt, S. N. *Modernization: Protest and Change*. Englewood Cliffs, N.J.: Prentice-Hall, 1966.

——. "Social Change, Differentiation, and Evolution." *American Sociological Review* 29 (June 1964): 375–86.

——. "Studies of Modernization and Sociological Theory." *History and Theory* 13, no. 3 (1974): 225–52.

——, ed. *The Protestant Ethic and Modernization: A Comparative View*. New York: Basic Books, 1968.

Ernst, John. *Forging a Fateful Alliance: Michigan State University and the Vietnam War*. East Lansing: Michigan State University Press, 1998.

Escobar, Arturo. "Discourse and Power in Development: Michel Foucault and the Relevance of His Work to the Third World." *Alternatives* 10 (Winter 1984–85): 377–400.

———. *Encountering Development: The Making and Unmaking of the Third World.* Princeton: Princeton University Press, 1995.

———. "Power and Visibility: Development and the Invention and Management of the Third World." *Cultural Anthropology* 3, no. 4 (1988): 428–43.

———. *The Professionalization and Institutionalization of "Development" in Colombia in the Early Post–World War II Period.* Berkeley: Stanford-Berkeley Joint Studies Center for Latin American Studies, 1988.

"Evangelist for Progress." *Newsweek,* February 19, 1962, 54–55.

Fall, Bernard. *Hell in a Very Small Place: The Siege of Dien Bien Phu.* Philadelphia: Lippincott, 1966.

———. *The Two Viet-Nams: A Political and Military Analysis.* New York: Praeger, 1963.

Ferguson, James. *The Anti-politics Machine: "Development," Depoliticization, and Bureaucratic Power in Lesotho.* Cambridge: Cambridge University Press, 1990.

Fischer, Fritz. *Making Them Like Us: Peace Corps Volunteers in the 1960s.* Washginton, D.C.: Smithsonian Institution Press, 1998.

Fishel, Wesley R. "Problems of Democratic Growth in Free Vietnam." In *Problems of Freedom: South Vietnam since Independence,* edited by Wesley R. Fishel, 9–28. New York: Free Press, 1961.

Fisher, Donald. *Fundamental Development of the Social Sciences: Rockefeller Philanthropy and the United States Social Science Research Council.* Ann Arbor: University of Michigan Press, 1993.

FitzGerald, Frances. *Fire in the Lake: The Vietnamese and the Americans in Vietnam.* New York: Vintage, 1972.

Foner, Eric. *Free Soil, Free Labor, Free Men: The Ideology of the Republican Party before the Civil War.* London: Oxford University Press, 1970.

"For 'Alianza' a Warning." *Life,* March 16, 1962, 4.

Foucault, Michel. *Discipline and Punish: The Birth of the Prison.* New York: Vintage, 1979.

———. *The History of Sexuality.* Vol. 1, *An Introduction.* New York: Vintage, 1978.

———. *The Order of Things: An Archaeology of the Human Sciences.* New York: Vintage, 1973.

Frank, André Gunder. *Latin America: Underdevelopment or Revolution, Essays on the Development of Underdevelopment and the Immediate Enemy.* New York: Monthly Review Press, 1969.

Frankel, Max. "U.S. Giving Saigon New Economic Aid in Fight on Reds." *New York Times,* January 5, 1962, 1–2.

"Fresh Breeze from the South." *Life,* August 25, 1961, 46.

Fried, Richard M. *Nightmare in Red: The McCarthy-Era in Perspective.* New York: Oxford University Press, 1990.

Fukuyama, Francis. *The End of History and the Last Man.* New York: Free Press, 1992.

Gaddis, John Lewis. *Strategies of Containment: A Critical Appraisal of Postwar American National Security Policy.* Oxford: Oxford University Press, 1982.

———. *We Now Know: Rethinking Cold War History*. Oxford: Oxford University Press, 1997.

Galbraith, John Kenneth. *The Affluent Society*. Boston: Houghton Mifflin, 1958.

———. "A Positive Approach to Economic Aid." *Foreign Affairs* 39 (April 1961): 444–57.

Galeano, Eduardo. *Open Veins of Latin America*. New York: Monthly Review Press, 1973.

Galula, David. *Counter-Insurgency Warfare: Theory and Practice*. New York: Praeger, 1964.

Gardner, Lloyd C. *Approaching Vietnam: From World War II through Dienbienphu*. New York: Norton, 1988.

———. *Pay Any Price: Lyndon Johnson and the Wars for Vietnam*. Chicago: Ivan R. Dee, 1995.

Gardner, Richard. *New Directions in U.S. Foreign Economic Policy*. New York: Foreign Policy Association, 1959.

Geertz, Clifford. "Ideology as a Cultural System." In *The Interpretation of Cultures*, 193–233. New York: Basic Books, 1973.

Geiger, Roger L. *Research and Relevant Knowledge: American Research Universities since World War II*. New York: Oxford University Press, 1993.

Gendzier, Irene L. *Managing Political Change: Social Scientists and the Third World*. Boulder, Colo.: Westview Press, 1985.

———. "Play It Again Sam: The Practice and Apology of Development." In *Universities and Empire: Money and Politics in the Social Sciences during the Cold War*, edited by Christopher Simpson, 57–95. New York: Free Press, 1998.

Gerschenkron, Alexander. *Economic Backwardness in Historical Perspective*. Cambridge: Harvard University Press, 1966.

Gibbons, William Conrad. *The U.S. Government and the Vietnam War: Executive and Legislative Roles and Relationships, Part II, 1961–1964*. Princeton: Princeton University Press, 1986.

Gibson, James William. *The Perfect War: Technowar in Vietnam*. Boston: Atlantic Monthly Press, 1986.

Giddens, Anthony. "Classical Social Theory and the Origins of Modern Sociology." *American Journal of Sociology* 81 (January 1976): 703–29.

Giglio, James N. *The Presidency of John F. Kennedy*. Lawrence: University Press of Kansas, 1991.

Gilderhus, Mark T. "An Emerging Synthesis? U.S.–Latin American Relations since the Second World War." In *America in the World: The Historiography of American Foreign Relations since 1941*, edited by Michael J. Hogan, 424–61. Cambridge: Cambridge University Press, 1995.

Gleijeses, Piero. *Shattered Hope: The Guatemalan Revolution and the United States, 1944–1954*. Princeton: Princeton University Press, 1991.

Goldstein, Judith, and Robert Keohane, eds. *Ideas and Foreign Policy: Beliefs, Institutions, and Political Change*. Ithaca, N.Y.: Cornell University Press, 1993.

Goodman, Paul. *Growing Up Absurd: Problems of Youth in the Organized System*. New York: Random House, 1956.

Gordon, Lincoln. "The Alliance at Birth: Hopes and Fears." In *The Alliance for*

Progress: A Retrospective, edited by L. Ronald Scheman, 73–79. New York: Praeger, 1988.

———. *A New Deal for Latin America: The Alliance for Progress.* Cambridge: Harvard University Press, 1963.

Gramer, Regina U. "On Poststructuralisms, Revisionisms, and Cold Wars." *Diplomatic History* 19 (Summer 1995): 515–24.

Gross, Leonard. "Has the Alliance for Progress a Chance?" *Look*, August 28, 1962, 80.

Gruening, Ernest. "Why the Alianza May Fail." *New Republic*, March 30, 1963, 11.

Gusfield, Joseph R. "Tradition and Modernity: Misplaced Polarities in the Study of Social Change." *American Journal of Sociology* 72 (January 1967): 351–62.

Halberstam, David. *The Best and the Brightest.* New York: Random House, 1972.

———. *The Making of a Quagmire: America and Vietnam during the Kennedy Era.* Rev. ed. New York: Alfred A. Knopf, 1988.

Hammer, Elizabeth. *A Death in November: America in Vietnam, 1963.* New York: Oxford University Press, 1987.

Hanson, Simon G. *Dollar Diplomacy Modern Style: Chapters in the Failure of the Alliance for Progress.* Washington: Inter-American Affairs Press, 1970.

Harrison, James P. *The Endless War: Vietnam's Struggle for Independence.* New York: Columbia University Press, 1989.

Hartz, Louis. *The Liberal Tradition in America: An Interpretation of American Political Thought since the Revolution.* New York: Harcourt, Brace and World, 1954.

Hearden, Patrick J. *The Tragedy of Vietnam.* New York: HarperCollins, 1991.

Hein, Laura E. "Free Floating Anxieties on the Pacific: Japan and the West Revisited." *Diplomatic History* 20 (Summer 1996): 411–37.

"Help on the Way." *Time*, September 22, 1961, 46.

Herman, Ellen. *The Romance of American Psychology: Political Culture in the Age of Experts.* Berkeley: University of California Press, 1995.

Herring, George C. *America's Longest War: The United States and Vietnam, 1950–1975.* 2d ed. New York: Alfred A. Knopf, 1986.

Hill, Polly. *Development Economics on Trial: The Anthropological Case for the Prosecution.* Cambridge: Cambridge University Press, 1986.

Hilsman, Roger. "Internal War: The New Communist Tactic." In *Modern Guerrilla Warfare: Fighting Communist Guerrilla Movements, 1941–1961*, edited by Franklin Mark Osanka, 452–63. New York: Free Press, 1962.

———. *To Move a Nation: The Politics of Foreign Policy in the Administration of John F. Kennedy.* Garden City, N.Y.: Doubleday, 1967.

Hirschman, Albert O. "A Dissenter's Confession: *The Strategy of Economic Development* Revisited." In *Pioneers in Development*, edited by Gerald M. Meier and Dudley Seers, 87–111. New York: Oxford University Press, 1984.

———. *Essays in Trespassing: Economics to Politics and Beyond.* Cambridge: Cambridge University Press, 1981.

———. "The Rise and Decline of Development Economics." In *The Theory and Practice of Economic Development: Essays in Honor of Sir W. Arthur Lewis*, edited by Mark Gersovitz, Carlos F. Diaz-Alejandro, Gustav Ranis, and Mark R. Rosenzweig, 372–90. London: Allen and Unwin, 1982.

——. "The Search for Paradigms as a Hindrance to Understanding." In *Interpretive Social Science: A Second Look*, edited by Paul Rabinow and William M. Sullivan, 177–94. Berkeley: University of California Press, 1987.

——. "Second Thoughts on the Alliance for Progress." *Reporter*, May 25, 1961, 20–23.

Hobsbawm, Eric. "Introduction: Inventing Traditions." In *The Invention of Tradition*, edited by Eric Hobsbawm and Terence Ranger. Cambridge: Cambridge University Press, 1983.

Hogan, Michael J. "Corporatism." In *Explaining the History of American Foreign Relations*, edited by Michael J. Hogan and Thomas G. Paterson, 226–36. Cambridge: Cambridge University Press, 1991.

——. *The Marshall Plan: America, Britain, and the Reconstruction of Western Europe, 1947–1952*. Cambridge: Cambridge University Press, 1987.

Holbik, Karel. *The United States, the Soviet Union, and the Third World*. Hamburg: Uerlag Weltarchiv, 1968.

Hollinger, David A. "Free Enterprise and Free Inquiry: The Emergence of Laissez-Faire Communitarianism in the Ideology of Science in the United States." *New Literary History* 21 (Autumn 1990): 897–919.

——. "How Wide the Circle of the 'We'?" *American Historical Review* 98 (April 1993): 317–37.

Hont, Istvan, and Michael Ignatieff. "Needs and Justice in the Wealth of Nations: An Introductory Essay." In *The Shaping of Political Economy in the Scottish Enlightenment*, edited by Istvan Hont and Michael Ignatieff, 1–44. Cambridge: Cambridge University Press, 1983.

Hoover, Herbert. *The Vital Need for Greater Financial Support of Pure Science Research*. New York: National Research Council, 1925.

Horesh, Edward. "Labelling and the Language of International Development." *Development and Change* 16 (July 1985): 503–14.

Horsman, Reginald. *Race and Manifest Destiny: The Origins of American Racial Anglo-Saxonism*. Cambridge: Harvard University Press, 1981.

House of Representatives. U.S. Congress. Committee on Foreign Affairs. *Foreign Assistance Act of 1962*. 87th Cong., 2d sess. Washington, D.C.: U.S. Government Printing Office, 1962.

——. *Regional and Other Documents Concerning United States Relations with Latin America*. Washington, D.C.: U.S. Government Printing Office, 1966.

"How Much Progress in the Alliance for Progress?" *U.S. News and World Report*, October 20, 1962, 42–44.

Humphrey, Hubert. "American Civilians Who Are Fighting the Shirtsleeves War in Vietnam." *Civil Service Journal*, June 1966, 2–3, 6–9.

Hunt, Michael H. *Ideology and U.S. Foreign Policy*. New Haven: Yale University Press, 1987.

——. "The Long Crisis in U.S. Diplomatic History: Coming to Closure." *Diplomatic History* 16 (Winter 1992): 115–40.

——. *Lyndon Johnson's War: America's Cold War Crusade in Vietnam, 1945–1968*. New York: Hill and Wang, 1996.

Huntington, Samuel P. "The Bases of Accommodation." *Foreign Affairs* 64 (July 1968): 642–56.

——. "The Change to Change: Modernization, Development, and Politics." *Comparative Politics* 3 (April 1971): 283–322.

——. "Political Development and Political Decay." *World Politics* 17 (April 1965): 386–430.

Huppert, G. Harry. "Bullets Alone Won't Win." *Infantry*, August 1964, 38–42.

Immerman, Richard H. *The CIA in Guatemala: The Foreign Policy of Intervention.* Austin: University of Texas Press, 1982.

Inkeles, Alex. "The Modernization of Man." In *Modernization: The Dynamics of Growth*, edited by Myron Weiner, 138–50. New York: Basic Books, 1966.

Inkeles, Alex, and David H. Smith. *Becoming Modern: Individual Change in Six Developing Countries.* Cambridge: Harvard University Press, 1974.

Iriye, Akira. "Culture." *Journal of American History* 77 (June 1990): 99–107.

——. "Culture and Power: International Relations as Intercultural Relations." *Diplomatic History* 3 (Spring 1979): 115–28.

"Is the Alliance for Progress Progressing?" *Christian Century*, March 28, 1962, 380.

Jacobs, Frankie W. "Peace Corps Trainees Do Field Work at California Housing Project." *Journal of Housing* 1, no. 1 (1965): 41–42.

Johnson, John J., ed. *The Role of the Military in Underdeveloped Countries.* Princeton: Princeton University Press, 1962.

Johnson, Lyndon B. *Public Papers of the Presidents of the United States: Lyndon B. Johnson, 1963–1969.* Washington, D.C.: U.S. Government Printing Office, 1965–69.

Jones, Kirby. "The Peace Corps Volunteer in the Field: Community Development." *Annals of the American Academy of Political and Social Science* 365 (May 1966): 63–71.

Kahin, George McT. *Intervention: How America Became Involved in Vietnam.* New York: Alfred A. Knopf, 1986.

Kahin, George McT., Guy J. Pauker, and Lucian W. Pye. "Comparative Politics of Non-Western Countries." *American Political Science Review* 49 (December 1955): 1022–41.

Kaplan, Amy. "Domesticating Foreign Policy." *Diplomatic History* 18 (Winter 1994): 97–106.

——. " 'Left Alone with America': The Absence of Empire in the Study of American Culture." In *Cultures of United States Imperialism*, edited by Amy Kaplan and Donald Pease, 3–21. Durham, N.C.: Duke Univeristy Press, 1993.

Karney, Rex. "Peace Corps a Farce, Says Editor of Illinois Newspaper." *Peace Corps Volunteer*, February 1962, 2.

Karnow, Stanley. "The Edge of Chaos." *Saturday Evening Post*, September 28, 1963, 27–36.

Katz, Barry M. *Foreign Intelligence: Research and Analysis in the Office of Strategic Services, 1942–1945.* Cambridge: Harvard University Press, 1989.

Katz, Michael B. *In the Shadow of the Poorhouse: A Social History of Welfare in America.* New York: Basic Books, 1986.

——. *The Undeserving Poor: From the War on Poverty to the War on Welfare.* New York: Pantheon, 1989.

Katznelson, Ira. "The Subtle Politics of Developing Emergency: Political Science as Liberal Guardianship." In *The Cold War and the University: Toward an Intellectual History of the Postwar Years,* edited by Andre Schiffrin, 233–58. New York: New Press, 1997.

Keller, Evelyn Fox. "The Paradox of Scientific Subjectivity." *Annals of Scholarship* 9, nos. 1–2 (1992): 135–53.

Kennan, George F. *American Diplomacy, 1900–1950.* Chicago: University of Chicago Press, 1951.

——. *Memoirs: 1925–1950.* Boston: Little, Brown, 1967.

Kennedy, John F. *Public Papers of the Presidents of the United States: John F. Kennedy, 1961–1963.* Washington, D.C.: U.S. Government Printing Office, 1962–64.

Kiernan, V. G. *Imperialism and Its Contradictions.* New York: Routledge, 1995.

Killian, James R., Jr. *The Education of a College President.* Cambridge: MIT Press, 1985.

Kleinman, Daniel Lee. *Politics on the Endless Frontier: Postwar Research Policy in the United States.* Durham, N.C.: Duke University Press, 1995.

Kleinman, Daniel Lee, and Mark Solovey. "Hot Science/Cold War: The National Science Foundation after World War II." *Radical History Review* 63 (Fall 1995): 110–39.

Kolko, Gabriel. *Anatomy of a War: Vietnam, the United States, and the Modern Historical Experience.* New York: Pantheon, 1985.

——. *Confronting the Third World: United States Foreign Policy, 1945–1980.* New York: Pantheon, 1988.

——. *The Roots of American Foreign Policy: An Analysis of Power and Purpose.* Boston: Beacon Press, 1969.

Kuhn, Thomas. *The Structure of Scientific Revolutions.* 2d ed. Chicago: University of Chicago Press, 1970.

Kunz, Diane. *Butter and Guns: America's Cold War Economic Diplomacy.* New York: Free Press, 1997.

——. "The Power of Money: The Historiography of American Economic Diplomacy." In *America in the World: The Historiography of American Foreign Relations since 1941,* edited by Michael J. Hogan, 536–61. Cambridge: Cambridge University Press, 1995.

——, ed. *The Diplomacy of the Crucial Decade: American Foreign Policy during the 1960s.* New York: Columbia University Press, 1964.

LaFeber, Walter. "The Alliances in Retrospect." In *Bordering on Trouble: Resources and Politics in Latin America,* edited by Andrew Maguire and Janet Welsh Brown, 337–88. Bethesda, Md.: Adler and Adler, 1986.

——. *America, Russia, and the Cold War, 1945–1990.* 6th ed. New York: McGraw-Hill, 1991.

——. *The American Age: U.S. Foreign Policy at Home and Abroad.* 2d ed. New York: Norton, 1994.

———. *Inevitable Revolutions: The United States in Central America*. New York: Norton, 1984.

———. *The New Empire: An Interpretation of American Expansion, 1860–1898*. Ithaca, N.Y.: Cornell University Press, 1963.

Landis, Mark. *Joseph McCarthy: The Politics of Chaos*. London: Associated University Press, 1987.

Lansdale, Edward G. "The Report the President Wanted Published." *Saturday Evening Post*, May 20, 1961, 31, 69–70.

Larsen, Otto N. *Milestones and Millstones: Social Science at the National Science Foundation, 1945–1991*. New Brunswick, N.J.: Transaction Publishers, 1992.

Lasch, Christopher. *The World of Nations: Reflections on American History, Politics, and Culture*. New York: Alfred A. Knopf, 1973.

Lauer, Robert H. "The Scientific Legitimation of Fallacy: Neutralizing Social Change Theory." *American Sociological Review* 36 (October 1971): 881–89.

Leaf, Murray J. *Man, Mind, and Science: A History of Anthropology*. New York: Columbia University Press, 1979.

Lederer, William J., and Eugene Burdick. *The Ugly American*. New York: Norton, 1958.

Leffler, Melvyn P. "The American Conception of National Security and the Beginnings of the Cold War, 1945–1948." *American Historical Review* 89 (April 1984): 346–81.

———. *A Preponderance of Power: National Security, the Truman Administration, and the Cold War*. Stanford: Stanford University Press, 1992.

———. *The Specter of Communism: The United States and the Origins of the Cold War, 1917–1953*. New York: Hill and Wang, 1994.

Lens, Sidney. "The Only Hope." *Progressive* 28 (November 1964): 22–27.

Lerner, Daniel. *The Passing of Traditional Society: Modernizing the Middle East*. New York: Free Press, 1958.

Lerner, Daniel, and Richard D. Robinson. "Swords and Ploughshares: The Turkish Army as a Modernizing Force." In *The Military and Modernization*, edited by Henry Bienen, 117–48. Chicago: Aldine-Atherton, 1971.

Leslie, Stuart W. *The Cold War and American Science: The Military-Industrial-Academic Complex at MIT and Stanford*. New York: Columbia University Press, 1993.

Levinson, Jerome, and Juan de Onís. *The Alliance That Lost Its Way*. Chicago: Quadrangle Books, 1970.

Levy, Marion J., Jr. "Armed Force Organizations." In *The Military and Modernization*, edited by Henry Bienen, 41–78. Chicago: Aldine-Atherton, 1971.

———. *The Family Revolution in Modern China*. Cambridge: Harvard University Press, 1949.

Lewis, Bernard. *The Emergence of Modern Turkey*. 2d ed. London: Oxford University Press, 1961.

Lewis, W. Arthur. "Economic Development with Unlimited Supplies of Labour." *Manchester School* 22 (May 1954): 139–91.

Lewontin, R. C. "The Cold War and the Transformation of the Academy." In *The Cold War and the University: Toward an Intellectual History of the Postwar Years*, edited by Andre Schiffrin, 1–34. New York: Free Press, 1997.

Leyden, John. "British Scientist Salutes Tanganyika Project." *Peace Corps Volunteer*, November 1962, 2.

Leys, Colin. "Conflict and Convergence in Development Theory." In *Imperialism and After: Continuities and Discontinuities*, edited by Wolfgang J. Mommsen and Jurgen Osterhammel, 315–24. London: Allen and Unwin, 1986.

Lichtenstein, Nelson, ed. *Political Profiles: The Kennedy Years*. New York: Facts on File, 1976.

Lindblom, Charles E. "A New Look at Latin America." *Atlantic*, October 1962, 81–86.

Lipset, Seymour Martin. *The First New Nation: The United States in Historical and Comparative Perspective*. New York: Basic Books, 1963.

Lipsitz, George. *Class and Culture in Cold War America: "A Rainbow at Midnight."* New York: Praeger, 1981.

Little, Ian M. D. *Economic Development: Theory, Policy, and International Relations*. New York: Basic Books, 1982.

Lodge, George C. *The Case for the Generalist in Rural Development*. Washington, D.C.: Peace Corps Office of Public Affairs, 1969.

Love, Joseph L. "Raúl Prebisch and the Origins of the Doctrine of Unequal Exchange." *Latin American Research Review* 15, no. 3 (1980): 45–72.

Lowther, Kevin, and C. Payne Lucas. *Keeping Kennedy's Promise: The Peace Corps— Unmet Hope of the New Frontier*. Boulder, Colo.: Westview Press, 1978.

Lumsdaine, David Halloran. *Moral Vision and Its Politics: The Foreign Aid Regime, 1949–1989*. Princeton: Princeton University Press, 1993.

Lynd, Robert S. *Knowledge for What?: The Place of Social Science in American Culture*. Princeton: Princeton University Press, 1939.

Mackenthun, Gesa. "State of the Art: Adding Empire to the Study of American Culture." *Journal of American Studies* 30 (August 1996): 263–69.

Madison, Mary. "S.R.I. Aide Offers Plan to Beat Viet Nam Reds." *Daily Palo Alto Times*, August 7, 1961, 3.

Mann, Thomas. "The Experience of the United States in Economic Development: Its Relevance for Latin America." *Department of State Bulletin* 47 (November 19, 1962): 772–75.

Mannheim, Karl. *Ideology and Utopia*. New York: Harcourt, Brace and World, 1968.

Martin, Robert P. "Latest Report from the Front in Vietnam." *U.S. News and World Report*, April 9, 1962, 60–62.

Mason, Edward S. *Promoting Economic Development: The United States and South Asia*. Claremont, Calif.: Claremont College, 1955.

May, Elaine Tyler. *Homeward Bound: American Families in the Cold War Era*. New York: Basic Books, 1988.

——. "Ideology and Foreign Policy: Culture and Gender in Diplomatic History." *Diplomatic History* 18 (Winter 1994): 71–78.

May, Ernest R. *American Imperialism: A Speculative Essay*. New York: Atheneum, 1968.

May, Gary. "Passing the Torch and Lighting Fires: The Peace Corps." In *Kennedy's Quest for Victory: American Foreign Policy, 1961–1963*, edited by Thomas G. Paterson, 284–316. New York: Oxford University Press, 1989.

May, Herbert K. *Problems and Prospects of the Alliance for Progress*. New York: Praeger, 1968.

Mazrui, Ali A. "From Social Darwinism to Current Theories of Modernization: A Tradition in Analysis." *World Politics* 21 (October 1968): 69–83.

Megill, Allan. "Introduction: Four Senses of Objectivity." *Annals of Scholarship* 8, nos. 3–4 (1991): 301–20.

Meier, Gerald M. "The Formative Period." In *Pioneers in Development*, edited by Gerald M. Meier and Dudley Seers, 1–26. New York: Oxford University Press, 1984.

Memmi, Albert. *The Colonizer and the Colonized*. London: Earthscan, 1990.

Merk, Frederick. *Manifest Destiny and Mission in American History: A Reinterpretation*. New York: Vintage, 1966.

Merrill, Dennis. *Bread and the Ballot: The United States and India's Economic Development, 1947–1963*. Chapel Hill: University of North Carolina Press, 1990.

———. "The United States and the Rise of the Third World." In *American Foreign Relations Reconsidered, 1890–1993*, edited by Gordon Martel, 166–86. London: Routledge, 1994.

"Mexico: No Aid for the Competent." *New Republic*, November 2, 1963, 9.

Miller, Stuart Creighton. *"Benevolent Assimilation": The American Conquest of the Philippines, 1899–1903*. New Haven: Yale University Press, 1982.

Millikan, Max F., and W. W. Rostow. "Notes on Foreign Economic Policy." In *Universities and Empire: Money and Politics in the Social Sciences during the Cold War*, edited by Chistopher Simpson, 39–55. New York: Free Press, 1998.

———. *A Proposal: Key to an Effective Foreign Policy*. New York: Harper and Brothers, 1957.

Millikan, Max F., and Donald L. M. Blackmer, eds. *The Emerging Nations: Their Growth and United States Policy*. Boston: Little, Brown, 1961.

Mills, C. Wright. *The Sociological Imagination*. New York: Oxford University Press, 1959.

Mitchell, Timothy. *Colonising Egypt*. Berkeley: University of California Press, 1991.

Montgomery, David. "Prosperity under the Shadow of the Bomb." In *The Cold War and the University: Toward an Intellectual History of the Postwar Years*, edited by Andre Schiffrin, xi–xxxvii. New York: Free Press, 1997.

Morgenthau, Hans J. *In Defense of the National Interest: A Critical Examination of American Foreign Policy*. New York: Alfred A. Knopf, 1951.

———. "A Political Theory of Foreign Aid." *American Political Science Review* 56 (June 1962): 301–9.

Morse, Wayne, and Bourke B. Hickenlooper. *Report of the Second Punta del Este Conference, January 22–31, 1962*. Washington, D.C.: U.S. Government Printing Office, 1962.

Mothner, Ira. "The Peace Corps: Revolutions without Blood." *Look*, June 14, 1966, 40.

Myrdal, Gunnar. *Development and Underdevelopment*. Cairo: National Bank of Egypt, 1956.

Nagel, Thomas. *The View from Nowhere*. New York: Oxford University Press, 1986.

Najita, Tetsuo. "Presidential Address: Personal Reflections on Modernity and Modernization." *Journal of Asian Studies* 52 (November 1993): 845–53.

"Nation-Mending at Home." *Time*, June 21, 1970, 21.

Needell, Allan A. " 'Truth Is Our Weapon': Project TROY, Political Warfare, and Government-Academic Relations in the National-Security State." *Diplomatic History* 17 (Summer 1993): 399–420.

Nehemkis, Peter. *Latin America: Myth and Reality*. New York: Alfred A. Knopf, 1964.

Nelkin, Dorothy. *The University and Military Research: Moral Politics at M.I.T.* Ithaca, N.Y.: Cornell University Press, 1972.

Ng, Franklin. "Knowledge for Empire: Academics and Universities in the Service of Imperialism." In *On Cultural Ground: Essays in International History*, edited by Robert David Johnson, 123–46. Chicago: Imprint, 1994.

Nighswonger, William A. *Rural Pacification in Vietnam*. New York: Praeger, 1966.

Ninkovich, Frank. "Culture, Power, and Civilization: The Place of Culture in the Study of International Relations." In *On Cultural Ground: Essays in International History*, edited by Robert David Johnson, 1–22. Chicago: Imprint, 1994.

———. "Interests and Discourse in Diplomatic History." *Diplomatic History* 13 (Spring 1989): 135–61.

———. *Modernity and Power: A History of the Domino Theory in the Twentieth Century*. Chicago: University of Chicago Press, 1994.

Nisbet, Robert A. "Ethnocentrism and the Comparative Method." In *Essays on Modernization of Underdeveloped Societies*, edited by A. R. Desai, 1:95–114. Bombay: Thacker, 1971.

———. *Social Change and History: Aspects of the Western Theory of Development*. New York: Oxford University Press, 1969.

Nolting, Frederick. *From Trust to Tragedy: The Political Memoirs of Frederick Nolting, Kennedy's Ambassador to Diem's Vietnam*. New York: Praeger, 1988.

Nye, John V. C. "An Interview with W. W. Rostow." *Newsletter of the Cliometric Society* 9 (July 1994): 3–8, 26–32.

Nystrom, J. Warren, and Nathan A. Haverstock. *The Alliance for Progress: Key to Latin America's Development*. Princeton: D. Van Nostrand Co., 1966.

O'Connell, James. "The Concept of Modernization." *South Atlantic Quarterly* 64 (Autumn 1965): 549–64.

O'Donnell, John B. "The Strategic Hamlet Program in Kien Hoa Province, South Vietnam: A Case Study of Counter-Insurgency." In *Southeast Asian Tribes, Minorities, and Nations*, edited by Peter Kunstadter, 2:703–44. Princeton: Princeton University Press, 1967.

Olson, James S., and Randy Roberts. *Where the Domino Fell: America and Vietnam, 1945 to 1990*. New York: St. Martin's Press, 1991.

Omvedt, Gail. "Modernization Theories: The Ideology of Empire." In *Essays on Modernization of Underdeveloped Societies*, edited by A. R. Desai, 1:119–38. Bombay: Thacker, 1971.

Packenham, Robert A. *Liberal America and the Third World: Political Development Ideas in Foreign Aid and Social Science*. Princeton: Princeton University Press, 1973.

Parsons, Talcott. "Democracy and Social Structure in Pre-Nazi Germany." In *Essays in Sociological Theory*, edited by Talcott Parsons, 104–23. New York: Free Press, 1964.

———. "Evolutionary Universals in Society." *American Sociological Review* 29 (June 1964): 339–57.

———. "Social Science: A Basic National Resource." In *The Nationalization of the Social Sciences*, edited by Samuel Z. Klausner and Victor M. Lidz, 41–112. Philadelphia: University of Pennsylvania Press, 1986.

———. *The Social System*. New York: Free Press, 1951.

———. *Societies: Evolutionary and Comparative Perspectives*. Englewood Cliffs, N.J.: Prentice-Hall, 1966.

———. *Structure and Process in Modern Societies*. New York: Free Press, 1960.

Parsons, Talcott, and Edward Shils. *Towards a General Theory of Action*. Cambridge: Harvard University Press, 1951.

Paterson, Thomas G. "Bearing the Burden: A Critical Look at JFK's Foreign Policy." *Virginia Quarterly Review* 54 (Spring 1978): 196–201.

———. *Contesting Castro: The United States and the Triumph of the Cuban Revolution*. New York: Oxford University Press, 1994.

———. "Fixation with Cuba: The Bay of Pigs, Missile Crisis, and Covert War against Castro." In *Kennedy's Quest for Victory: American Foreign Policy, 1961–1963*, edited by Thomas G. Paterson, 123–55. New York: Oxford University Press, 1989.

———. "Introduction: John F. Kennedy's Quest for Victory and Global Crisis." In *Kennedy's Quest for Victory: American Foreign Policy, 1961–1963*, edited by Thomas G. Paterson, 3–23. New York: Oxford University Press, 1989.

———, ed. *Kennedy's Quest for Victory: American Foreign Policy, 1961–1963*. New York: Oxford University Press, 1989.

Paterson, Thomas G., and Stephen G. Rabe, eds. *Imperial Surge: The United States Abroad: The 1890s–Early 1900s*. Lexington, Mass.: Heath, 1992.

Peace Corps. *Annual Reports*. Washington, D.C.: U.S. Government Printing Office, 1962–66.

———. "Colombia: Acción Comunal." *Peace Corps Volunteer*, November 1962, 8–9.

———. "I Learned More in Ten Months with Volunteer Than I Have Learned in Thirty Years, Co-Worker." *Peace Corps Volunteer*, April 1963, 4.

———. "Journey to a Reservation." *Peace Corps News*, March 1962, 1, 7.

———. *The Peace Corps Fact Book*. Washington, D.C.: U.S. Government Printing Office, 1961.

———. *The Peace Corps Reader*. Washington, D.C.: U.S. Government Printing Office, 1967.

———. "Peace Corps Trainees Work, Study in New York Slums." *Peace Corps Volunteer*, November 1962, 1, 3.

———. "Tubman Sees Object Lesson in Peace Corps." *Peace Corps Volunteer*, May 1963, 5.

———. "The Volunteer Image." *Peace Corps Volunteer*, February 1963, 4.

———. *What Can I Do in the Peace Corps?* Washington, D.C.: U.S. Government Printing Office, n.d.

——. *Who's Working Where: A Catalogue of Peace Corps Volunteer Skills.* Washington, D.C.: U.S. Government Printing Office, 1964.

"Peace Corps in Training." *Economist*, July 22, 1961, 334.

"The Peace Corps Starts." *New York Times*, March 2, 1961, 26.

Pearce, R. Michael. *Evolution of a Vietnamese Village—Part II: The Past, August 1945 to April 1964.* Santa Monica: Rand Corporation, 1966. Memorandum RM-4692-ARPA.

Perkins, Bradford. "The Tragedy of American Diplomacy: Twenty-five Years After." *Reviews in American History* 12 (March 1984): 1–18.

Perloff, Harvey S. *Alliance for Progress: A Social Invention in the Making.* Baltimore: Johns Hopkins University Press, 1969.

Popkin, Samuel L. *The Rational Peasant: The Political Economy of Rural Society in Vietnam.* Berkeley: University of California Press, 1979.

Porter, Theodore M. *Trust in Numbers: The Pursuit of Objectivity in Science and Public Life.* Princeton: Princeton University Press, 1995.

Poster, Mark. "Foucault and History." *Social Research* 49 (Spring 1982): 116–42.

Potter, David M. *People of Plenty: Economic Abundance and the American Character.* Chicago: University of Chicago Press, 1954.

Prakash, Gyan. "Writing Post-Orientalist Histories of the Third World." In *Colonialism and Culture*, edited by Nicholas B. Dirks, 353–88. Ann Arbor: University of Michigan Press, 1992.

Pratt, Mary Louise. *Imperial Eyes: Travel Writing and Transculturation.* London: Routledge, 1992.

Price, Don K. *The Scientific Estate.* Cambridge: Harvard University Press, 1965.

"Progreso, Sí." *Time*, March 24, 1961, 29.

"A Progress Report on the Alliance." *Morgan Guaranty Survey*, February 1963, 10.

Pursell, Carroll. "Science Agencies in World War II: The OSRD and Its Challengers." In *The Sciences in the American Context: New Perspectives*, edited by Nathan Reingold, 359–78. Washington: Smithsonian Institution Press, 1979.

Pye, Lucian W. "Armies in the Process of Political Modernization." In *The Role of the Military in Underdeveloped Countries*, edited by John J. Johnson, 69–89. Princeton: Princeton University Press, 1962.

——. *Guerrilla Communism in Malaya: Its Social and Political Meaning.* Princeton: Princeton University Press, 1956.

——. "Political Modernization and Research on the Process of Political Socialization." *Social Science Research Council Items* 13 (September 1959): 25–28.

——. *Politics, Personality, and Nation Building: Burma's Search for Identity.* New Haven: Yale University Press, 1962.

——, ed. *Communications and Political Development.* Princeton: Princeton University Press, 1963.

"Quasi Stagnation." *Newsweek*, October 15, 1962, 44.

Rabe, Stephen G. "Controlling Revolutions: Latin America, the Alliance for Progress, and Cold War Anti-Communism." In *Kennedy's Quest for Victory: American Foreign Policy, 1961–1963*, edited by Thomas G. Paterson, 105–22. New York: Oxford University Press, 1989.

——. *Eisenhower and Latin America: The Foreign Policy of Anticommunism*. Chapel Hill: University of North Carolina Press, 1988.

Rabinow, Paul, ed. *The Foucault Reader*. New York: Pantheon, 1984.

Race, Jeffrey. *War Comes to Long An: Revolutionary Conflict in a Vietnamese Province*. Berkeley: University of California Press, 1972.

Rafael, Vicente L. "White Love: Surveillance and Nationalist Resistance in the U.S. Colonization of the Philippines." In *Cultures of United States Imperialism*, edited by Amy Kaplan and Donald Pease, 185–218. Durham, N.C.: Duke University Press, 1993.

Randle, Robert F. *Geneva 1954: The Settlement of the Indochinese War*. Princeton: Princeton University Press, 1969.

Redmon, Coates. *Come As You Are: The Peace Corps Story*. San Diego: Harcourt Brace Jovanovich, 1986.

"Report on the Peace Corps." *Time*, December 29, 1961, 10–11.

Reuss, Henry S. "A Point Four Youth Corps." *Commonweal*, May 5, 1960, 146–48.

Rice, Gerard T. *The Bold Experiment: JFK's Peace Corps*. Notre Dame, Ind.: University of Notre Dame Press, 1985.

——. *Twenty Years of the Peace Corps*. Washington, D.C.: U.S. Government Printing Office, 1982.

Ridinger, Robert B. Marks. *The Peace Corps: An Annotated Biliography*. Boston: G. K. Hall and Co., 1989.

Riesman, David, with Nathan Glazier and Reuel Denney. *The Lonely Crowd: A Study of the Changing American Character*. Abridged ed. New Haven: Yale University Press, 1961.

Ritzer, George. *Modern Sociological Theory*. 4th ed. New York: McGraw-Hill, 1996.

Robinson, Archie W. "Now the U.S. Is Exporting Union Ideas to Latin America." *U.S. News and World Report*, May 20, 1963, 86, 88–89.

Rocher, Guy. *Talcott Parsons and American Sociology*. New York: Barnes and Noble, 1975.

Rodney, Walter. *How Europe Underdeveloped Africa*. Washington, D.C.: Howard University Press, 1982.

Rogers, William D. *The Twilight Struggle: The Alliance for Progress and the Politics of Development in Latin America*. New York: Random House, 1967.

Rogin, Michael. *Fathers and Children: Andrew Jackson and the Subjugation of the American Indian*. New York: Alfred A. Knopf, 1985.

Rosaldo, Renato. *Culture and Truth: The Remaking of Social Analysis*. Boston: Beacon Press, 1989.

Rosenberg, Emily S. "Presidential Address: Revisiting Dollar Diplomacy, Narratives of Money and Manliness." *Diplomatic History* 22 (Winter 1998): 155–76.

——. *Spreading the American Dream: American Economic and Cultural Expansion, 1890–1945*. New York: Hill and Wang, 1982.

Rosenstein-Rodan, P. N. "International Aid for Underdeveloped Countries." *Review of Economics and Statistics* 43 (May 1961): 107–38.

——. "Natura Facit Saltum: Analysis of the Disequilibrium Growth Process." In

Pioneers in Development, edited by Gerald M. Meier and Dudley Seers, 207–21. New York: Oxford University Press, 1984.

Rosenthal, Michael. *The Character Factory: Baden-Powell and the Origins of the Boy Scout Movement*. New York: Pantheon, 1984.

Rosenzweig, Robert M. *The Research Universities and Their Patrons*. Berkeley: University of California Press, 1982.

Ross, Dorothy. "Grand Narrative in American Historical Writing: From Romance to Uncertainty." *American Historical Review* 100 (June 1995): 651–77.

———. "Historical Consciousness in Nineteenth-Century America." *American Historical Review* 89 (October 1984): 909–28.

———. "Modernism Reconsidered." In *Modernist Impulses in the Human Sciences, 1870–1930*, edited by Dorothy Ross, 1–25. Baltimore: Johns Hopkins University Press, 1994.

———. "Modernist Social Science in the Land of the New/Old." In *Modernist Impulses in the Human Sciences*, edited by Dorothy Ross, 171–89. Baltimore: Johns Hopkins University Press, 1994.

———. *The Origins of American Social Science*. Cambridge: Cambridge University Press, 1991.

Rostow, W. W. "American Strategy on the World Scene." *Department of State Bulletin* 46 (April 16, 1962): 628.

———. "Countering Guerrilla Attack." In *Modern Guerrilla Warfare: Fighting Communist Guerrilla Movements, 1941–1961*, edited by Franklin Mark Osanka, 464–71. New York: Free Press, 1962.

———. "Development: The Political Economy of the Marshallian Long Period." In *Pioneers in Development*, edited by Gerald M. Meier and Dudley Seers, 229–61. New York: Oxford University Press, 1984.

———. *The Diffusion of Power: An Essay in Recent History*. New York: Macmillan, 1972.

———. *Eisenhower, Kennedy, and Foreign Aid*. Austin: University of Texas Press, 1985.

———. *The Great Transition: Tasks of the First and Second Post-War Generations*. Cambridge, England: Leeds University Press, 1967.

———. *The Stages of Economic Growth: A Non-Communist Manifesto*. Cambridge: Cambridge University Press, 1960.

———. *Theorists of Economic Growth from David Hume to the Present*. New York: Oxford University Press, 1990.

———. *The Two Major Communist Offensives*. Washington, D.C.: U.S. Government Printing Office, 1964.

———. *View from the Seventh Floor*. New York: Harper and Row, 1964.

Rotter, Andrew J. *The Path to Vietnam: Origins of the American Commitment to Southeast Asia*. Ithaca, N.Y.: Cornell University Press, 1987.

Rusk, Dean. "The Alliance in the Context of World Affairs." In *The Alliance for Progress: Problems and Perspectives*, edited by Jim Dreier, 102–17. Baltimore: Johns Hopkins University Press, 1962.

———. "America's Destiny in the Building of a World Community." *Department of State Bulletin* 46 (December 10, 1962): 898–99.

——. *As I Saw It*. New York: Norton, 1990.

——. "Secretary Rusk's News Conference of February 6." *Department of State Bulletin* 44 (February 27, 1961): 298.

——. "The Stake in Vietnam." *Department of State Bulletin* 48 (May 13, 1963): 729–30.

Rust, William J. *Kennedy in Vietnam*. New York: Charles Scribner's Sons, 1985.

Sahlins, Marshall. *Islands of History*. Chicago: University of Chicago Press, 1985.

Said, Edward. *Culture and Imperialism*. New York: Alfred A. Knopf, 1993.

——. *Orientalism*. New York: Vintage, 1979.

Sapolsky, Harvey M. "Academic Science and the Military: The Years since the Second World War." In *The Sciences in the American Context: New Perspectives*, edited by Nathan Reingold, 379–99. Washington: Smithsonian Institution Press, 1979.

Savage, Stephen P. *The Theories of Talcott Parsons: The Social Relations of Action*. London: Macmillan, 1981.

Schanche, Don. "Father Hoa's Little War." *Saturday Evening Post*, February 17, 1962, 74–79.

Schlesinger, Arthur M., Jr. "Myth and Reality." In *The Alliance for Progress: A Retrospective*, edited by L. Ronald Scheman, 67–72. New York: Praeger, 1988.

——. *The Politics of Hope*. Boston: Houghton Mifflin, 1963.

——. *A Thousand Days: John F. Kennedy in the White House*. Boston: Houghton Mifflin, 1965.

——. *The Vital Center: The Politics of Freedom*. Boston: Houghton Mifflin, 1949.

Schlesinger, Stephen C., and Stephen Kinzer. *Bitter Fruit: The Untold Story of the American Coup in Guatemala*. Garden City, N.Y.: Doubleday, 1982.

Schoultz, Lars. *Beneath the United States: A History of U.S. Policy toward Latin America*. Cambridge: Harvard University Press, 1998.

Schrecker, Ellen W. *No Ivory Tower: McCarthyism and the Universities*. New York: Oxford University Press, 1986.

Schulzinger, Robert D. *A Time for War: The United States and Vietnam, 1941–1975*. New York: Oxford University Press, 1997.

Schwabe, Klaus. "The Global Role of the United States and Its Imperial Consequences, 1898–1973." In *Imperialism and After: Continuities and Discontinuities*, edited by Wolfgang J. Mommsen and Jurgen Osterhammel, 13–33. London: Allen and Unwin, 1986.

Schwartz, Harry. "Review of *The Stages of Growth*." *New York Times Book Review*, May 6, 1960, 6.

Schwarz, Karen. *What You Can Do for Your Country: An Oral History of the Peace Corps*. New York: Morrow, 1991.

Scigliano, Robert, and Guy H. Fox. *Technical Assistance in Vietnam: The Michigan State University Experience*. New York: Praeger, 1965.

Scott, James C. *Seeing Like a State: How Certain Schemes to Improve the Human Condition Have Failed*. New Haven: Yale University Press, 1998.

Seers, Dudley. "The Birth, Life, and Death of Development Economics." *Development and Change* 10 (October 1979): 707–19.

Senate. U.S. Congress. Committee on Foreign Relations. *Nomination of R. Sargent*

Shriver, Jr. to Be Director of the Peace Corps. 87th Cong., 1st sess. Washington, D.C.: U.S. Government Printing Office, 1961.

——. *Vietnam and Southeast Asia: Report of Senators Mike Mansfield, J. Caleb Boggs, Claiborne Pell, Benjamin A. Smith.* 88th Cong., 1st sess. Washington, D.C.: U.S. Government Printing Office, 1963.

Senate. U.S. Congress. Subcommittee on Public Buildings and Grounds. *The Pentagon Papers, Senator Gravel Edition. The Defense Department History of United States Decisionmaking on Vietnam.* 4 vols. Boston: Beacon, 1971.

Sevareid, Eric. "Writer Says Time Is Right to Evaluate Peace Corps." *Peace Corps Volunteer,* February 1963, 2.

Shafer, D. Michael. *Deadly Paradigms: The Failure of U.S. Counterinsurgency Policy.* Princeton: Princeton University Press, 1988.

Sherry, Michael S. *In the Shadow of War: The United States since the 1930s.* New Haven: Yale University Press, 1995.

Shils, Edward. Introduction to *Criteria for Scientific Development: Public Policy and National Goals: A Selection of Articles from Minerva,* edited by Edward Shils, v–xiv. Cambridge: MIT Press, 1968.

——. "The Military in the Political Development of the New States." In *The Role of the Military in Underdeveloped Countries,* edited by John J. Johnson, 7–67. Princeton: Princeton University Press, 1962.

——. "On the Comparative Study of the New States." In *Old Societies and New States: The Quest for Modernity in Africa and Asia,* edited by Clifford Geertz, 1–26. New York: Free Press, 1963.

——. *The Present State of American Sociology.* Glencoe, Ill.: Free Press, 1948.

Shriver, R. Sargent, Jr. "Ambassadors of Goodwill: The Peace Corps." *National Geographic* 126 (September 1964): 298–313.

——. "Five Years with the Peace Corps." In *The Peace Corps Reader,* edited by the Peace Corps, 18–26. Washington, D.C.: U.S. Government Printing Office, 1967.

——. *Point of the Lance.* New York: Harper and Row, 1964.

——. "Two Years of the Peace Corps." *Foreign Affairs* 41 (July 1963): 694–707.

Simpson, Christopher. "Universities, Empire, and the Production of Knowledge: An Introduction." In *Universities and Empire: Money and Politics in the Social Sciences during the Cold War,* edited by Christopher Simpson, xi–xxxiv. New York: Free Press, 1998.

——, ed. *Universities and Empire: Money and Politics in the Social Sciences during the Cold War.* New York: Free Press, 1998.

Skidmore, Thomas E., and Peter H. Smith. *Modern Latin America.* New York: Oxford University Press, 1984.

Slotkin, Richard. *Gunfighter Nation: The Myth of the Frontier in Twentieth-Century America.* New York: Atheneum, 1992.

Smith, Adam. *The Theory of Moral Sentiments.* London: Oxford University Press, 1976.

——. *The Wealth of Nations.* New York: Modern Library, 1937.

Smith, Anthony D. *The Concept of Social Change: A Critique of the Functionalist Theory of Social Change.* London: Routledge and Kegan Paul, 1973.

Smith, Gaddis. *The Last Years of the Monroe Doctrine, 1945–1993*. New York: Hill and Wang, 1994.

Smith, R. B. *An International History of the Vietnam War*. Vol. 1, *Revolution versus Containment, 1955–61*. London: Macmillan, 1983.

———. *An International History of the Vietnam War*. Vol. 2, *The Kennedy Strategy*. New York: St. Martin's Press, 1985.

Smith, Tony. *America's Mission: The United States and the Worldwide Struggle for Democracy in the Twentieth Century*. Princeton: Princeton University Press, 1994.

Social Science Research Council. *Annual Report, 1956–1957*. New York: SSRC, 1957.

———. *Annual Report, 1957–1958*. New York: SSRC, 1958.

Solovey, Mark. "The Politics of Intellectual Identity and American Social Science, 1945–1970." Ph.D. diss., University of Wisconsin, Madison, 1996.

Sorenson, Theodore, ed. *"Let the World Go Forth": The Statements, Speeches, and Writings of John F. Kennedy, 1947–1963*. New York: Dell, 1988.

"South Vietnam: New Strategy." *Newsweek*, April, 9, 1962, 46.

"South Viet Nam: Miracle at Hoaimy." *Time*, May 1, 1964, 26.

"South Viet Nam: What the People Say." *Time*, February 2, 1962, 26.

Spencer, Herbert. *First Principles*. New York: H. M. Caldwell, 1900.

Spengler, J. J. "Economic Development: Political Preconditions and Political Consequences." *Journal of Politics* 22 (August 1960): 387–416.

Sprinker, Michael, ed. *Edward Said: A Critical Reader*. Oxford: Basil Blackwell, 1992.

Staley, Eugene. *The Future of Underdeveloped Countries: Political Implications of Economic Development*. New York: Harper and Bros. for the Council on Foreign Relations, 1954.

State Department. *Foreign Relations of the United States*. Washington, D.C.: U.S. Government Printing Office.

———. "FSI Begins Seminars on Problems of Development and Internal Defense." *Department of State Bulletin* 47 (July 2, 1962): 41–42.

Stephanson, Anders. "Considerations on Culture and Theory." *Diplomatic History* 18 (Winter 1994): 107–120.

———. "Ideology and Neorealist Mirrors." *Diplomatic History* 17 (Spring 1993): 285–95.

———. *Kennan and the Art of Foreign Policy*. Cambridge: Harvard University Press, 1989.

———. *Manifest Destiny: American Expansion and the Empire of Right*. New York: Hill and Wang, 1995.

Stocking, George W., Jr. *Race, Culture, and Evolution: Essays in the History of Anthropology*. New York: Free Press, 1968.

———. *Victorian Anthropology*. New York: Free Press, 1987.

Stoler, Ann Laura. "Rethinking Colonial Categories: European Communities and the Boundaries of Rule." In *Colonialism and Culture*, edited by Nicholas B. Dirks, 319–52. Ann Arbor: University of Michigan Press, 1992.

Sutton, Francis X. "Development Ideology: Its Emergence and Decline." *Daedalus* 118 (Winter 1989): 35–58.

Szulc, Tad. "Selling a Revolution in Latin America." *New York Times Magazine*, December 17, 1961, 10.

Tanham, George K. *War without Guns: American Civilians in Rural Vietnam*. New York: Praeger, 1966.

Thompson, Robert G. K. *Defeating Communist Insurgency: Experiences from Malaya and Vietnam*. London: Chatto and Windus, 1966.

Tilman, Seth. *The Peace Corps: From Enthusiasm to Disciplined Idealism*. Washington, D.C.: Peace Corps Office of Public Affairs, 1969.

Tipps, Dean C. "Modernization Theory and the Comparative Study of Societies: A Critical Perspective." *Comparative Studies in Society and History* 15 (March 1973): 199–226.

Toews, John E. "Intellectual History after the Linguistic Turn: The Autonomy of Meaning and the Irreducibility of Experience." *American Historical Review* 92 (October 1987): 879–907.

Tönnies, Ferdinand. *Community and Society (Gemeinschaft und Gesellschaft)*. Translated by Charles P. Loomis. East Lansing: Michigan State University Press, 1957.

Toye, John. *Dilemmas of Development: Reflections on the Counter-Revolution in Development Theory and Policy*. Oxford: Basil Blackwell, 1987.

Toynbee, Arnold J. "America's New Lay Army." In *The Peace Corps Reader*, edited by the Peace Corps, 10–17. Washington, D.C.: U.S. Government Printing Office, 1967.

"Troubled Alliance." *Time*, October 10, 1962, 22.

"Troubles and Remedies." *Time*, May 3, 1963, 26.

Truong Nhu Tang. *A Viet Cong Memoir*. New York: Vintage, 1985.

Trussell, C. P. "Peace Corps Rise Is Voted by House." *New York Times*, April 4, 1962, 1.

Tulchin, Joseph S. "The United States and Latin America in the 1960s." *Journal of Interamerican Studies and World Affairs* 30 (Spring 1988): 1–36.

Turner, Bryan S. "Parsons and His Critics: On the Ubiquity of Functionalism." In *Talcott Parsons on Economy and Society*, edited by Robert J. Holton and Bryan S. Turner, 181–206. London: Routledge and Kegan Paul, 1986.

Turner, Frederick Jackson. "The Significance of the Frontier in American History." In *Annual Report for 1893*, edited by the American Historical Association, 199–227. Washington, D.C.: American Historical Association, 1894.

Walker, William O., III. "Mixing the Sweet with the Sour: Kennedy, Johnson, and Latin America." In *The Diplomacy of the Crucial Decade: American Foreign Relations during the 1960s*, edited by Diane B. Kunz, 42–79. New York: Columbia University Press, 1994.

Wallerstein, Immanuel. "Modernization: Requiescat in Pace." In *The Capitalist World Economy*, 132–37. Cambridge: Cambridge University Press, 1979.

———. *Unthinking Social Science: The Limits of Nineteenth-Century Paradigms*. Cambridge, Mass.: Polity Press, 1991.

Walterhouse, Harry F. *A Time to Build, Military Civic Action: Medium for Economic Development and Social Reform*. Columbia: University of South Carolina Press, 1964.

Walters, Ronald G. "Signs of the Times: Clifford Geertz and the Historians." *Social Research* 47 (Autumn 1980): 537–56.

"The War." *Time*, February 18, 1966, 19–21.

Ward, Robert, ed. *Studying Politics Abroad: Field Research in the Developing Areas.* Boston: Little, Brown, 1964.

Waring, Stephen P. "Cold Calculus: The Cold War and Operations Research." *Radical History Review* 63 (Fall 1995): 28–51.

Weber, Max. *The Protestant Ethic and the Spirit of Capitalism.* London: Routledge, 1992.

Weinberg, Albert K. *Manifest Destiny: A Study of Nationalist Expansion in American History.* Chicago: Quadrangle Books, 1963.

Weiner, Myron, ed. *Modernization: The Dynamics of Growth.* New York: Basic Books, 1966.

Wetzel, Charles J. "The Peace Corps in Our Past." *Annals of the American Academy of Political and Social Science* 365 (May 1966): 1–11.

"Where the Reds May Take Over Next in Latin America." *U.S. News and World Report*, March 18, 1963, 50.

Whitaker, C. S., Jr. "A Dysrhythmic Process of Political Change." *World Politics* 19 (January 1967): 190–217.

White, Hayden. "The Value of Narrativity in the Representation of Reality." In *The Content of the Form: Narrative Discourse and Historical Representation*, 1–25. Baltimore: Johns Hopkins University Press, 1987.

Whitfield, Stephen J. *The Culture of the Cold War.* Baltimore: Johns Hopkins University Press, 1991.

Whyte, William H., Jr. *The Organization Man.* New York: Simon and Schuster, 1956.

Wiarda, Howard J. *The Democratic Revolution in Latin America: History, Politics, and U.S. Policy.* New York: Holmes and Meier, 1990.

——. "Misreading Latin America—Again," *Foreign Policy* 65 (Winter 1986–87): 135–53.

Wiegersma, Nancy. *Vietnam: Peasant Land, Peasant Revolution.* New York: St. Martin's Press, 1988.

Williams, Walter L. "United States Indian Policy and the Debate over Philippine Annexation: Implications for the Origins of American Imperialism." *Journal of American History* 66 (March 1980): 810–31.

Williams, William Appleman. *Empire as a Way of Life: An Essay on the Causes and Character of America's Present Predicament along with a Few Thoughts about an Alternative.* New York: Oxford University Press, 1980.

——. "The Frontier Thesis and American Foreign Policy." *Pacific Historical Review* 24, no. 4 (1955): 379–95.

——. *The Tragedy of American Diplomacy.* Cleveland: World Publishing Co., 1959.

Windmiller, Marshall. *The Peace Corps and Pax Americana.* Washington, D.C.: Public Affairs Press, 1970.

Winks, Robin W. *Cloak and Gown: Scholars in the Secret War, 1939–1961.* New York: Morrow, 1987.

Wolfe, Patrick. "History and Imperialism: A Century of Theory, from Marx to Postcolonialism." *American Historical Review* 102 (April 1997): 388–420.

Wood, Geof. "The Politics of Development Policy Labeling." *Development and Change* 16 (July 1985): 347–73.

Wood, Robert C. "The Future of Modernization." In *Modernization: The Dynamics of Growth*, edited by Myron Weiner, 40–52. New York: Basic Books, 1966.

"Yanquis Open a New World Series against the Reds." *Life*, August 18, 1961, 40.

Young, Marilyn. *The Vietnam Wars, 1945–1990*. New York: HarperCollins, 1991.

Young, Robert. *White Mythologies: Writing History and the West*. London: Routledge, 1990.

Zalba, Serapio R. "The Peace Corps—Its Historical Antecedents and Its Meaning for Social Work." *Duquesne Review* (Fall 1966): 125–37.

Zasloff, Joseph J. *Rural Resettlement in Vietnam: An Agroville in Development*. Washington, D.C.: U.S. Department of State, 1962.

Zimmerman, Jonathan. "Beyond Double Consciousness: Black Peace Corps Volunteers in Africa, 1961–1971." *Journal of American History* 82 (December 1995): 999–1028.

INDEX

Castro, Fidel: rise to power, 28, 76, 139–40; assassination attempts on, 82

Center for International Studies (MIT), 54–55; John F. Kennedy and, 56–57

Central Intelligence Agency (CIA), 39; and Russian Research Center, 53; in Bay of Pigs, 81; aid to Diem, 160, 173; in counterinsurgency planning, 166, 167; on NLF, 175; on Strategic Hamlet Program, 186; influence in Peace Corps, 232 (n. 64)

Challener, Richard, 143

Change, global, modernization in, 2, 4, 15

Change, historical, sociological analyses of, 36

Change, social: global, 3; modernization model of, 4, 23, 52; integrated process of, 37, 39, 41, 59, 63; holistic process of, 44; under Alliance for Progress, 84, 107; in Latin America, 95–96, 211

Chambers, William Nisbet, 64

Chapultepec meeting (1945), 73, 74

Chase Manhattan Bank, 103–4

Chenery, Hollis, 86

Chiang Kai-shek, 158

Chicago School of Sociology, 31

Chijnaya, Peru, 130

China: Communist revolution in, 2; five year plan, 27; as traditional society, 35; influence in Latin America, 78; "loss" of, 139; in Geneva Accords, 159

Chomsky, Noam, 11, 153, 218 (n. 26)

Church, Frank, 76

CIA. See Central Intelligence Agency

Civilian Conservation Corps, 94

Civilian Operations and Revolutionary Development Support (CORDS), 204, 241 (n. 144)

Civilization, Western: superiority of, 14, 65, 66; social values of, 16; rationalization in, 33, 36; John F. Kennedy on, 135

Civil rights movement, 215; Peace Corps volunteers in, 111, 146

Class, middle: Latin American, 80, 81; of developing nations, 120

Class, sociological study of, 31

Class interests, in Latin America, 11, 105

Cobbs Hoffman, Elizabeth, 111, 218 (n. 21)

Colby, William E., 173

Cold War: U.S. ideology during, ix; U.S. identity in, 5, 18, 23, 67, 163; scholarly inquiry in, 6–7; U.S. strategy in, 12; modernization theory during, 13, 23–30, 55, 58, 61, 212, 215; view of power in, 15; role of social scientists in, 21–23, 49; development process during, 22, 149; influence on John F. Kennedy, 28–29; emerging nation theory in, 64; in Latin America, 71, 77, 87; Alliance for Progress's role in, 91; Peace Corps' role in, 112, 133, 137; Vietnam policy in, 155; France in, 157; perception of danger in, 210; Manifest Destiny during, 211; liberalism of, 215. See also Containment; Counterinsurgency

Coleman, James, 3; The Politics of Developing Areas, 120

Colombia: under Alliance for Progress, 83–84, 105; rural electrification for, 94; Peace Corps in, 110, 128

Colonialism: collapse of, 26; in historical process, 41; modernization theorists on, 65; Latin American, 72, 98; French, 114, 154, 155–59; British, 207, 209, 213; European, 213. See also Imperialism

Colorado State University Research Foundation, 115, 116, 117

Columbia University: war contracts of, 46; School of Social Work, 147

Commodity Import Plan (South Vietnam), 161

Communication, mass, 35; in modern-

Guerrillas: Pathet Lao, 29, 164; Vietnamese, 156. *See also* National Liberation Front
Guevara, Che, 99
Guinea, Peace Corps in, 133

Haddad, Bill, 101, 102
Halberstam, David, 188; *The Making of
a Quagmire*, 205–6
Hamilton, Fowler, 94, 236 (n. 42)
Hanson, Simon G., 11
Harriman, Averell, 165, 181
Harrod, R. F., 222 (n. 53)
Hart, Thomas C., 48
Hartz, Louis, 45
Harvard University: sociological studies
at, 31; Department of Social Rela-
tions, 32; war contracts of, 46; and
Russian Research Center, 53
Hayes, Samuel P., 115, 116–17, 172
Hearden, Patrick, 11
Herman, Ellen, 22
Herring, George, 11
Hickey, Gerald, 185
Hilsman, Roger, 10, 196, 204; Vietnam
mission of, 179–80, 183, 188; "Internal
War," 193–94; world view of, 238
(n. 83)
Hirschman, Albert O., 41, 83–84; on
Alliance for Progress, 107
History, as modality of power, 15
History, American: market in, 93; in
Strategic Hamlet Program, 195–97.
See also Manifest Destiny
Hoaimy, South Vietnam, 191–92
Hobsbawm, Eric, 142
Ho Chi Minh: peasants' allegiance to,
154; rise to power of, 155–56; Stalin's
support of, 157; American policy-
makers on, 158; Eisenhower adminis-
tration on, 160
Hogan, Michael J., 25
Holborn, Fred, 56
Hollinger, David, 50
Honduras, aid to, 101

Hoover, Herbert, 46
Horsman, Reginald, 212, 233 (n. 104)
Hukbalahap rebellion (Philippines),
159–60, 176, 238 (n. 72)
Human agency, in social structure, 31
Human empathy, in modernization
theory, 51, 52, 95, 135
Humphrey, Hubert, 76; on Peace
Corps, 113, 141; on strategic hamlets,
194
Hunt, Michael H., 12
Huntington, Samuel P., 151–52, 217
(n. 10), 234 (n. 2)

Idealism: U.S., 9, 109; in foreign policy,
143. *See also* Altruism
Identity: construction of, 8, 15–16; ethnic, 31.
Identity, national: Latin American, 71;
in colonialism, 220 (n. 41)
Identity, national, U.S.: in Cold War,
5, 18, 23, 67, 163; older constructions
of, 6; ideological influences on, 8;
cultural understandings of, 12, 13;
modernization in, 14, 108, 191, 212; in
evaluation of foreign societies, 64; in
Strategic Hamlet Program, 152–53;
and ideology of development, 219
(n. 32); and national security, 220
(n. 41)
Ideology: as guide to action, ix; modernization as, 5–6, 13, 17, 107, 190,
209; and identity, 8; and economic
interests, 12; as cultural system, 13
Imperialism: influence on modernization theory, 6, 19, 23, 59, 68; U.S.
rejection of, 112; cultural, 143, 212;
French, 155
Imperialism, European, 142; erosion
of, 22, 27, 59; and U.S. imperialism,
213
Imperialism, U.S., 14, 16–17, 241 (n. 5);
reconstruction under modernization, 19; Peace Corps' role in, 142,
143–45; regenerative effect of, 144–45;

apologies for, 149; in Vietnam, 188; as aberration, 211, 212; in the Philippines, 224 (n. 123). *See also* Manifest Destiny

India, aid to, 30

Indian reservations, Peace Corps volunteers at, 147–48

Individualism, in modern social organization, 45

Indochina: French in, 156; colonialism in, 207

Indonesia, U.S. intervention in, 3

Industrialization: Chinese, 35; British, 60; Latin American, 72

Infrastructure: in economic change, 43; aid for, 113

Inkeles, Alex, 129; wartime contributions of, 47; *Becoming Modern*, 52–53, 223 (n. 78)

Institution building, 86

Institutions, pluralist, 22

Institutions, social: comparative study of, 35; political processes in, 39; of advanced nations, 97

Insurgencies, effect of modernization on, 7

Insurgency, Malayan, 176–78, 198, 207; Chinese in, 173

Inter-American Development Bank, 70

"Interministerial Committee for Strategic Hamlets," 182

"International Aid for Underdeveloped Countries" (Rosenstein-Rodan), 84–86

International Bank for Reconstruction and Development, 24

International Cooperation Administration (ICA), 27

International Monetary Fund (IMF), 24, 70

Investment, foreign: in Latin America, 11, 99, 100, 103–4; in modernization theory, 55; under Alliance for Progress, 103

Iran: U.S. intervention in, 3; Eisen-

hower administration's aid to, 26; Peace Corps in, 110

Iraq, U.S. intervention in, 26

James, William, 110

Jiménez, Marcos Pérez. See Pérez Jiménez, Marcos

Johnson, Lyndon: Alliance for Progress under, 9; on colonialism, 149; on civilians in Vietnam, 195; strategic hamlets under, 203–4, 241 (n. 6)

Jones, Kirby, 126

Josephson, William, 118

Justice, social: U.S., 93; for Latin America, 103, 104, 107

Kahin, George McT., 11, 38, 155

Katanga province, Congo, 30

Katz, Michael, 214, 234 (n. 119)

Katznelson, Ira, 22

Kennan, George F., 12, 219 (n. 28); on Latin America, 74–75, 225 (n. 11)

Kennedy, John F.: Latin American task force of, 7, 58, 69, 78; influence of Cold War on, 28–29; presidential campaign of, 28, 114, 164; inaugural address of, 29; on decolonization, 56; and Center for International Studies, 56–57; on development process, 57; on Senate Foreign Relations Committee, 76; on Alliance for Progress, 81; rhetoric of, 113; campaign for Peace Corps, 113–14; on imperialism, 114; criticism of Eisenhower's policies by, 114, 164; on Peace Corps, 123, 133, 144, 145; on western tradition, 135; assassination of, 138, 218 (n. 19); Vietnam strategy of, 155, 166–67; in American Friends of Vietnam, 160; on troops in Vietnam, 165–66; counterinsurgency policy of, 167, 236 (n. 47); use of media, 192; image of, 233 (n. 105)

Kennedy, Joseph, Sr., 117

Kennedy, Robert, 166

Western scholarship on, 15, 61–62; development in, 26, 36, 37; community development in, 123

Military Assistance and Advisory Group (MAAG, Saigon), 162, 175

Military strategy. See Strategy, military

Miller, Stuart, 176

Millikan, Max, 54, 55; *A Proposal: Key to an Effective Foreign Policy*, 56; in Kennedy administration, 57; and Peace Corps, 115–16; and Modernization Institute, 167

Mills, C. Wright, 18, 34

Mitchell, Timothy, 60

Mobility, social, 95

Modernity: in Burma, 41; computer analysis of, 52–53; mimicry of, 66; for Latin America, 91; United States as model for, 111–12, 121, 133, 195–96, 212

Modernization: Rostow on, 2, 3, 45; definition of, 4; political relevance of, 5; as ideology, 5–6, 13, 17, 107, 190, 209; effect on insurgencies, 7; counterinsurgency based, 10, 108, 152, 153, 169, 176, 204; political power of, 12–13; as tool of capitalism, 12, 45; as perceptual framework, 13, 15; as Manifest Destiny, 14; in American national identity, 14, 108, 191, 212; in global change, 15; in postcolonialism, 16; responses to, 17; under Great Society, 18, 214–15; Enlightenment models of, 23; under Marshall Plan, 24–25; under Truman, 25; as universal process, 46; holistic process of, 50–51; in expansion of political power, 59; evolution as model for, 62–63; under Alliance for Progress, 82, 83, 107; in Latin America, 89; and wars of liberation, 151; ARVN's role in, 178; military, 179; cultural assumptions of, 191; dissent against, 205–6; flaws in model, 217 (n. 10). See also Modernization theory

Modernization Institute, 167

Modernization theory: in containment policy, 3–4, 55, 166–69, 188; scholarship on, 4; in social change, 4, 23, 52; cultural meaning of, 5; in social sciences, 5–6, 17, 22, 209; influence of imperialism on, 6, 19, 23, 59, 68; under Kennedy administration, 7, 17, 209; during Cold War, 13, 23–30, 55, 58, 61, 212, 215; scientism of, 16, 46–59, 149, 211; as conceptual framework, 19, 209; political context of, 22; rise of, 22, 23; strategic significance of, 23, 67; in social analysis, 30; in European scholarship, 30–31; Parsons's role in, 32–33; urbanization in, 36, 51; comparative analysis in, 37; conceptual unity of, 40; in national security state, 50; sociological variables in, 51; social psychology in, 52; foreign investment in, 55; poverty in, 55; empirical basis for, 58, 67, 70, 213; missionary vision of, 60, 67; rhetoric of, 68; in Alliance for Progress, 70, 79, 108; in Peace Corps, 117, 121, 125, 128, 149; in military strategy, 151–52; in Vietnam War, 152, 190, 200, 205; revival of, 218 (n. 11)

Monks, Buddhist, 201

Montagnards (Vietnam), 173

Moody, James, 127

Moore, Barkley, 139

Morales Carrión, Arturo, 78, 82, 90

Morgan Guaranty Survey, on Latin America, 104

Morgenthau, Hans, 12, 107

Morison, Robert S., 115

Morse, Wayne, 76

Moscoso, Teodoro, 78, 84, 96–97; on colonialism, 98; on Alliance for Progress's problems, 100, 102

Moyers, Bill, 119, 140

Multilateralism, 24

Muñoz Marín, Luis, 90

Murrow, Edward R., 236 (n. 42), 238 (n. 83)

Mutual assured destruction, 28
Mutual Security Program (1957), 27
My Lai massacre, 207
Myrdal, Gunnar, 44

Napalm, 164, 165–66
Nasser, Gamal Abdel, 26, 30
National Defense Education Act (1958), 7, 54
National identity. *See* Identity, national
Nationalism: and U.S. imperialism, 17, 211; U.S. policymakers on, 27, 29; in historical process, 41; in developing countries, 66; Latin American, 76, 210; Vietnamese, 157; South Vietnamese, 178, 199, 204
National Liberation Front (NLF, South Vietnam), 29, 152; founding of, 162, 235 (n. 25); growth of, 164; control of Mekong Delta, 165; Kennedy administration strategy for, 166, 175–76, 211; Hanoi's support for, 171, 175, 235 (n. 24); peasants' support of, 177, 181, 183, 185; in hamlet strategy, 179, 180, 197–98; media coverage of, 191–92; infiltration of Diem regime, 198; recruitment by, 198; in Long An, 202; popular acceptance of, 202; modernizers' view of, 206
National Research Council (NRC), 46
National Review, 106–7
National Science Foundation (NSF), 48
National security. *See* Security, national
National Security Council: on Latin America, 88; in Vietnam War, 165
National Socialism, 33
Nation building: political scientists on, 39; U.S. sponsored, 67, 144; role of Peace Corps in, 118, 128; social engineering for, 124; through Strategic Hamlet Program, 153, 186; in South Vietnam, 166; by USOM, 182; in Southeast Asia, 205, 206
Nations, developing: foreign aid to, 1, 2; Soviet aid to, 2, 27–28; transitional stages of, 4; capitalism for, 22; American policymakers on, 22–23; economy of, 23, 41–44; modernization theory for, 23, 30, 36; Eisenhower administration's aid to, 26; non-aligned, 26–27, 145; central planning for, 44; in Cold War theory, 64; interactions with advanced nations by, 65; absorptive capacity of, 85; lack of middle class in, 120; perceptual framework for, 124; Peace Corps's mission to, 133; private enterprise in, 141. *See also* Societies, traditional
Navarre, Henri, 158
Nehru, Jawaharlal, 26
Neuberger, Richard, 113
New Deal, 17, 93–94; Tennessee Valley Authority of, 25, 94, 241 (n. 6)
The New Empire (LaFeber), 14
New Frontier: as benevolent society, 91; progress under, 108
New Left, 215; rise of, 18
New Life hamlets, 204
Newsweek magazine: on Alliance for Progress, 99, 105; on Operation Sunrise, 191
New York Times: on the Peace Corps, 110; on Strategic Hamlet Program, 189
Ngo Dinh Diem, 3, 29, 197; use of foreign aid, 18; Eisenhower administration support for, 160–62; repression by, 161–62, 165, 200; relocation of peasants, 170–73, 196, 203, 205, 209; assassination of, 201, 203; media coverage of, 204–5. *See also* Diem regime
Ngo Dinh Nhu, 173, 197, 200; relocation of peasants, 170–71, 202, 203, 205; assassination of, 201, 203; negotiations with Hanoi, 201
Nguyen Loc Hoa, 193
Nhu, Madame, 201
Nicaragua, rural electrification for, 94
Ninkovich, Frank, 12

Peasants, Vietnamese: resettlement of, 10, 180–88; U.S. policymakers on, 154; surveillance of, 154–55, 183–84; relocation under Diem of, 170–74; appeal of NLF to, 177; modernization strategy for, 178; motivations of, 180; under Strategic Hamlet Program, 180, 184–88, 198; compensation for, 181; media on, 191–93; modernizers' view of, 206. See also Strategic Hamlet Program

Pentagon Papers, 203

Pérez Jiménez, Marcos, 76

Personality: as pattern variable, 33; mobile, 36, 51; modern, 52

Peru, community development in, 129–30

Philippines: U.S. intervention in, 3, 176, 207; Peace Corps in, 110, 121, 142, 213, 232 (n. 72); modernization of, 142–43; U.S. acquisition of, 146; Hukbalahap rebellion in, 159–60; counterinsurgency in, 168–69, 193–94; American imperialism in, 224 (n. 123)

Phillips, Rufus, III, 182, 186

Phoenix program (Vietnam), 241 (n. 144)

Pluralism, containment of, 64

Policy, foreign: influence of Marxism on, ix; social science in, ix; scientific theory in, 6; economic influences on, 8; role of American culture in, 12, 204; idealism of, 143

Policymakers, American: Cold War strategies of, 12, 22–23; on non-aligned countries, 27; on Latin America, 74; on Cuba, 88; civil servant mentality of, 153; on Vietnamese peasants, 154; on Ho Chi Minh, 158; cultural assumptions of, 204

Policymakers, Kennedy: on decolonization, 23; development policies of, 57; on Latin America, 79, 89–90; use of academics by, 167; on social

engineering, 215. See also Kennedy administration

Policy Planning Council (State Department), 58

Political science. See Science, political

Politics, comparative, 38, 39, 222 (n. 45)

The Politics of Developing Areas (Almond and Coleman), 120

Politics, Personality, and Nation Building, 41

Population, growth of in social order, 33

Postcolonialism, 16

Poston, Richard W., 124

Poverty: culture of, 18, 142, 148, 214; effect of international trade on, 42; in modernization theory, 55; Latin American, 69, 73, 91, 126, 210; Panamanian, 124; U.S., 214

Power, Western: older representations of, 15; and knowledge, 65; construction of, 220 (n. 39)

Power transfer, timing of, 50

Prebisch, Raúl, 73, 75, 225 (n. 6)

Princeton University Press, 40

Processes, political: in social institutions, 4, 39; universal functions of, 40

Production: economic relations of, 32; barriers to, 43

Project TROY (MIT), 54

A Proposal: Key to an Effective Foreign Policy (Rostow and Millikan), 56

Protestant Ethic and the Spirit of Capitalism (Weber), 61, 212

Psychology, social, in modernization theory, 52

Pye, Lucian: modernization theories of, 3; counterinsurgency theory of, 7; on Comparative Politics Committee, 38, 39–40; Politics, Personality, and Nation Building, 41; in Center for International Studies, 54; on AID advisory committee, 58, 224 (n. 99); on transitional peoples, 67; and Modernization Institute, 167; in

to, 67; of Latin America, 71, 79, 89; agriculture in, 116. *See also* Transition

Society, traditional; Vietnam as, 152, 180, 205

Society, U.S.: cultural assumptions of, 8; humanitarian ideals of, 9; shortcomings in, 146; traditional populations in, 146–49; apathy in, 148, 149, 214; altruism in, 153, 195, 206, 209

Society, Vietnamese: transformations in, 151; fatalism in, 190, 192

Sociology: modernization theory for, 30–31; Chicago School of, 31

Somoza family (Nicaragua), 76

Southeast Asia: development issues in, 56; Truman's policy on, 156, 158; markets of, 157; State Department task force on, 182–83; nation building in, 205; modernization of, 206

Southeast Asia Treaty Organization (SEATO), 160

South Vietnam: U.S. aid to, 26; Commodity Import Plan of, 161; land reforms for, 161; military advisers in, 162, 166, 175; strategic importance of, 163–64; public works projects in, 164; U.S. troops in, 165–66, 206, 210; nation building in, 166; "clear and hold" operations in, 175; war of attrition in, 175; nationalism for, 178, 199, 204; socio-political base for, 180; province chiefs of, 182; political culture of, 185, 188; Filipinos in, 187; American civilians in, 194–95; U.S. as model for, 195–97; sovereignty of, 200; Catholic minority of, 200–201. *See also* Diem regime; Peasants, Vietnamese; Strategic Hamlet Program; Vietnam

South Vietnamese Army (ARVN), 154, 163; increase in, 164; civic action projects of, 178, 180, 200; in Operation Sunrise, 181; abuses by, 199

Soviet Union: collapse of, ix; aid to emerging nations, 2, 27–28, 86–87; five year plan of, 24; influence in Latin America, 78; growth of economy, 87; symbolism of, 139; in Geneva Accords, 159

Special Group for Counterinsurgency (Kennedy administration), 190

Spellman, Cardinal Francis, 160

Spencer, Herbert, 62–63

Sputnik, 7, 54, 139

The Stages of Economic Growth (Rostow), 44–45, 50, 79, 116, 120

Staley, Eugene, 8; as Vietnam advisor, 58; *The Future of Underdeveloped Countries*, 120; resettlement report of, 171–73

Stalin, Josef, 24

Standards, living: Latin American, 72; U.S., 136

Stanford Research Institute, 171

States, U.S.: partnerships in Latin America, 97

Stephanson, Anders, 12, 212, 219 (n. 28)

Stocking, George, 60, 63

Stone, James H., 120–21

"Strategic Concept for Vietnam," 179

Strategic Hamlet Program (South Vietnam), ix; scientific theory in, 6; U.S. national identity in, 152–53; nation building through, 153, 186; as social engineering, 154, 179; Agency for International Development in, 154, 182–83, 194; stages of, 173–74, 176; Malayan model for, 173–76, 179, 209; psychological impact of, 174; goals of, 178–79, 186, 210; as strategy against NLF, 179, 180, 197–98; implementation of, 180–82; problems with, 181, 184; corruption in, 185, 186–87; self government under, 186; self help in, 187, 190, 197; media on, 188–89, 191–93; officials' defense of, 189–90, 197–200, 202–4; use of American history in, 195–97; dissent against, 197, 199–200; failures of, 197, 199, 202;

developmental model, 92–94, 107; anticolonialism of, 98, 142, 209, 213; bureaucracy of, 102–3; humanitarian mission of, 108, 213, 215; as model for modernity, 111–12, 121, 133, 195–96, 212; living standards in, 136; as benevolent society, 139, 153, 188, 193; moral regeneration of, 145; traditional societies in, 146–49, 214; urban riots in, 215. *See also* Expansion, U.S.; Imperialism, U.S.; Manifest Destiny

United States Army: Special Warfare Center, 1; civic action of, 149, 214; Green Berets, 214, 241 (n. 6)

United States Information Agency (USIA), 89, 90; in counterinsurgency planning, 166, 167

United States Information Service, 181, 187, 202

United States Operations Mission (USOM), 181; nation building by, 182; grants to hamlets, 187

United States State Department: Policy Planning Council, 58, 217 (n. 5); Cuban policy of, 88; task force on Southeast Asia, 182–83; "Quiet Warriors," 194

Upton, T. Graydon, 90

Urbanization, in modernization theory, 36, 51

U.S. News and World Report: on Alliance for Progress, 105; on Strategic Hamlet Program, 191

"U.S. Overseas Internal Defense Policy," 169–70

Vaughn, Jack Hood, 129

Versailles Treaty, 33

Vietcong. *See* National Liberation Front

Vietminh: Communist support for, 157; at Dienbienphu, 159; southern sympathizers of, 161

Vietnam: Communist movement in, 1, 154, 155–56; counterinsurgency planning for, 10, 108, 166, 167, 183,

203; pacification strategy for, 152, 182; French in, 154, 155–59; in Cold War policy, 155; during World War II, 155–56; partition of, 159; elections in, 159, 197; cultural unity of, 161; aerial surveillance of, 164; U.S. combat troops in, 165–66, 206, 210; as underdeveloped country, 177; U.S. imperialism in, 188; decolonization in, 207. *See also* South Vietnam

"Vietnam Rural Affairs Program," 195

Vietnam War: Peace Corps volunteers' criticism of, 141, 146; modernization theory in, 152, 190, 200, 205; media on, 153; Rostow on, 162; American credibility in, 165; chemical warfare in, 166; disillusionment with, 215. *See also* National Liberation Front; Strategic Hamlet Program

"The Village That Refused to Die," 192–93

Voice of America, 54

Volunteers, Peace Corps, 109; humanitarian efforts of, 110–11, 137; in civil rights movement, 111, 146; altruism of, 112, 134; as agents of modernization, 116–19, 128, 140; partnership with hosts, 118; training of, 119–21, 127, 131, 147, 214; assignments of, 121–22; community development by, 122, 123–24, 126–28, 169, 209, 210; liberal arts graduates among, 122–23, 127, 132; as models, 126; nation building by, 128; as cultural catalysts, 128, 134; quantitative techniques of, 130; frustrations of, 131; media coverage of, 134–35, 141–42; fitness of, 138; monuments to, 139; criticism of Peace Corps by, 141; criticism of Vietnam war by, 141; sacrifice by, 141, 143, 145; John F. Kennedy on, 145; returning, 149; in AID, 195. *See also* Peace Corps

Walker, William, 10

Wallerstein, Immanuel, 217 (n. 11)